Convergence of Productivity

Convergence of Productivity

Cross-National Studies and Historical Evidence

Edited by
WILLIAM J. BAUMOL
RICHARD R. NELSON
EDWARD N. WOLFF

Oxford University Press

Oxford New York Toronto
Delhi Bombay Calcutta Madras Karachi
Kuala Lumpur Singapore Hong Kong Tokyo
Nairobi Dar es Salaam Cape Town
Melbourne Auckland Madrid

and associated companies in
Berlin Ibadan

Library of Congress Cataloging-in-Publication Data
Convergence of productivity : cross-national studies and historical evidence /
edited by William J. Baumol, Richard R. Nelson, and Edward N. Wolff.
p. cm. Includes bibliographical references and index.
ISBN 0-19-508389-X. — ISBN 0-19-508390-3 (pbk.)
1. Industrial productivity—History—20th century—Congresses.
2. Income—History—20th century—Congresses.
3. Technological innovations—Economic aspects—History—20th century—Congresses.
4. Economic history—1945– —Congresses.
5. Comparative economics—Congresses.
I. Baumol, William J.
II. Nelson, Richard R.
III. Wolff, Edward N.
HC79.I52C66 1994 338'.06—dc20 93-11494

9 8 7 6 5 4 3 2 1

Printed in the United States of America
on acid-free paper

To
Hilda, Katherine, and Jane
For their patience and understanding.

Preface

This book is a compendium of papers presented at New York University in the spring of 1992 at a conference on the convergence hypothesis. The hypothesis asserts that at least since World War II, and perhaps for a considerable period before that, the group of industrial countries was growing increasingly homogeneous in terms of levels of productivity, technology, and per-capita income. In addition, there was a general catch-up toward the leader, with the gradual erosion of the gap between the leader economy, the United States throughout most of the pertinent period, and those of the countries lagging most closely behind it. The conference was intended to review the evidence for and against the hypothesis, to discuss methods for testing the hypothesis, to investigate the position of the less developed countries in the observed scenario, and to offer explanatory material on the observed developments.

The importance of the subject seems clear: It offers a vantage point from which one can systematically approach a discussion of recent trends in the world economy and the plausible possibilities for its future. More particularly, it deals directly with the course of economic equality or inequality among nations. Tautologically, to the extent that convergence takes place in reality, the disparity among wealthy and impoverished nations must decline, which obviously has major implications for the well-being and good relations of the countries of the world. It is, consequently, understandable why, when new data and other pertinent evidence recently became available, the subject should have elicited considerable interest among economists and others.

The organizers of the conference were extremely fortunate in being able to arrange for the participation of several of the most distinguished contributors to the pertinent literature, most notably Moses Abramovitz—who besides being a founder of this field of investigation has consistently provided wisdom and balanced judgment on the subject—and Angus Maddison—whose efforts in gathering, cleansing, and analyzing the pertinent data made progress in the arena possible. In addition, the organizers were able to gather talented contributors to the field from younger generations, whose work, as reported here, is a clear indication of their ability.

We believe that the conference did succeed in providing new evidence on and new insights into the central subject. This book is their concrete manifestation.

The efforts of several persons were critical to the efficiency and pleasantness with which the conference was run. For this we are most heavily indebted to Ms. Cindy Heilberger, executive director of the C. V. Starr Center for Applied Economics at New York University, who took full charge of all the arrangements and carried them out in a manner that can elicit only admiration and gratitude. In this work she was assisted capably and with dedication by Ms. Janeece Roderick, secretary of the Starr Center.

Before the conference whose presentations are reported here, a smaller preparatory meeting took place at Columbia University. That meeting was designed to review and discuss preliminary drafts of each of the papers, seeking to sharpen their analyses and improve their presentations. We would like to thank the School of International and Public Affairs at Columbia for hosting this workshop.

We also would like to acknowledge gratefully the generous financial support provided by the Alfred P. Sloan Foundation, the C. V. Starr Center for Applied Economics at New York University, and the Columbia University Consortium on Competition and Cooperation. Finally, we are also greatly indebted to the commentary and discussion provided at the conference by four eminent scholars in this field: Martin N. Baily of the University of Maryland, Jagdish Bhagwati of Columbia University, J. Bradford De Long of Harvard University, and Jeffrey Williamson of Harvard University.

New York   W.J.B.
June 1993   R.R.N.
                                                                          E.N.W.

Contents

Contributors

Moses Abramovitz
Stanford University

Alice H. Amsden
New School of Social Research

William J. Baumol
Princeton University and New York University

Magnus Blomström
Stockholm School of Economics and National Bureau of Economic Research

David Dollar
World Bank

Takashi Hikino
Harvard Business School

Gregory K. Ingram
World Bank

William Lazonick
Barnard College and Harvard Institute for International Development

Frank R. Lichtenberg
Columbia Business School and National Bureau of Economic Research

Robert E. Lipsey
Queens College, Graduate Center (CUNY), and National Bureau of Economic Research

Angus Maddison
University of Groningen

Richard R. Nelson
Columbia University

Edward N. Wolff
New York University

Gavin Wright
Stanford University

Mario Zejan
Stockholm School of Economics

I

General Patterns of
Convergence

1

Introduction: The Convergence of Productivity, Its Significance, and Its Varied Connotations

WILLIAM J. BAUMOL
RICHARD R. NELSON
EDWARD N. WOLFF

This collection of essays reviews the current state of knowledge of the convergence hypothesis, which asserts that at least a fairly restricted set of countries, the members of the "convergence club," are undergoing a process that brings their levels of productivity and living standards increasingly close to one another. The book summarizes the available empirical information and contributes a considerable amount of new evidence. It examines the patterns exhibited by individual industries in particular countries as well as the behavior of the aggregate economies of those countries and their manufacturing sectors. It reports evidence, old and new, on the influences underlying the degree of convergence that appears in fact to have occurred. It studies the role that convergence has played and promises to play in the future of the newly industrialized countries and the less developed countries. There are separate investigations of performance in earlier periods, notably that of the United States, and analytic comparisons with the record after World War II. The chapters are about equally divided in focusing on two different convergence concepts to which we will refer, respectively, as *homogenization* and *catch-up*. The first refers to a state of affairs in which most of the countries in some specified group constantly grow closer to one another in terms of per-capita incomes and other pertinent variables. The second concept refers to the case in which laggard countries narrow the distance separating them from the leading economy. More will be said shortly about the distinction between the two orientations.

It is impossible to provide a unified set of conclusions that can claim to represent the results of all of the studies reported here, because the information and analyses they offer constitute too rich and too heterogeneous a body of materials for that to be feasible. The general tenor of the conclusions is that convergence has indeed been a reality but that its domain in regard to time period and geographic coverage has been fairly restricted. So far convergence has accomplished relatively little for the less developed countries, though it may have yielded some useful insights for the guidance of those nations' future development policies. The patterns of convergence by industrial sector have been even more convoluted than the patterns displayed by the aggregate economies that convergence has encompassed. And although there is reason to believe that we have considerably better evidence than was available only a few years ago on the influences that promote convergence, as the cliché asserts, much more research on the subject clearly remains to be done.

There seems recently to have been an upsurge in interest in the subject of convergence, primarily and presumably because of its profound implications for the welfare of nations and for the design of policy. This interest among economists has also undoubtedly been stimulated by the availability of rich datasets contributed by Maddison, Summers and Heston, and others that permit empirical studies far more probing than had been possible before. Still, we must not forget that the idea of convergence, the basic hypotheses about the influences that underlie it, and the early empirical evidence go back a considerable length of time. The idea was contributed by the giants of our discipline, including Kuznets (1973), Gerschenkron (1952), and Abramovitz. We will not attempt here to recount the history of the early literature, but we must note that the work described in this volume represents a continuation of earlier lines of investigation and further construction built on a foundation of profound earlier ideas.

Why Convergence Matters

The reasons for studying the convergence hypothesis may appear to be obvious. It has substantial implications for the welfare of nations and for the prospects for reduction and even the near elimination of poverty in the international community. After all, by its very definition, convergence is tantamount to diminution in the degree of economic inequality among countries. If inequality is a matter of substantial concern, the same, tautologically, must be true about the presence or absence of convergence. However, there are some subtle sides to the matter.

Absolute Versus Relative Poverty

First, the subject brings our attention back to the old distinction between relative and absolute poverty and their comparative significance. If virtually all that matters for the economic welfare of the individual person is his or her own real income and its rate of growth, however measured, then convergence becomes a secondary issue. A world in which per-capita income was everywhere growing, say, at a steady 3 percent per annum, might then be considered a very satisfactory state of affairs, even though it condemned every economy to remain in its relative position for the foreseeable future.

Under a social welfare function that values *absolute* incomes alone, convergence matters only to the extent that it facilitates (or impedes) the absolute growth process. It certainly is plausible that convergence does have at least some such influence, and there is some empirical evidence indicating that this role may well be substantial.

Nonetheless, *relative* wealth and poverty surely do matter. It is little comfort to a modern slum family to learn that its absolute standards of consumption exceed any poverty line that might reasonably have been selected only a few decades ago. The family or the country that finds itself far behind its contemporary counterparts surely feels its poverty to be manifest, unambiguous, and debilitating, whether or not it qualifies as poverty on any absolute standard or one based exclusively on its own rate of growth. If so, convergence must be an indispensable component of any remedy for impoverishment.[1]

When we turn next to a discussion of the various meanings that have been assigned to the term *convergence,* we note that there is one interpretation of the concept—as a catch-up toward the leader—that must, by definition, entail reductions in both the absolute and the relative levels of poverty. If all or most of the poorest countries succeed in moving closer to a leader whose living standard is climbing, then there must be not only an erosion of the gap between them but, in addition, a rise in the real per-capita income of the laggard.

Thus, convergence, in one or another of its senses, is surely a key matter for our evaluation of the world economy's well-being. A world of convergence is in a felicitous state, with poverty eroding and international disparities declining. If not offset by detrimental developments of other sorts, it is a desirable condition and a state of affairs in which one of the most intractable of economic problems, inequality among countries in the distribution of income, is improving.

Self-Undermining Properties of Convergence Processes

There are two reservations, however, that are worth noting. First, convergence may well be a process whose logic condemns it to be a victim of its own success. That is, as one comes closer to attaining international equality, the disparities—the "advantages of (moderate) backwardness"—that may constitute the engine of the process will unavoidably grow less substantial, and as a result, still more convergence may become increasingly difficult to achieve. If, for example, as many observers suspect, the transfer of technology from the leaders to the laggards is a principal cause of convergence, then once all countries in the convergence club have acquired similar stocks of production techniques and technological knowledge, further convergence may be difficult to achieve. This may help explain the slowdown in the convergence process that has apparently occurred since the mid-1970s and, very likely, even the absolute slowdown in productivity growth throughout the OECD countries since the mid-1970s. Note also that the more successful and the more rapid the initial stages of the convergence process have been, the more powerful such a self-terminating propensity of the convergence process is likely to be.

Convergence as Trauma for the Leaders

A second reservation about the virtues of convergence harks back to the psychology of *relative* performance. For convergence to occur, it is unavoidable—indeed, it is true tautologically—that the leaders in productivity or per-capita income must grow more slowly than the laggards do. Otherwise it would be impossible for the laggards to approach the level of accomplishment of the leaders. But the necessarily slower growth of the leading countries invariably seems to produce a feeling of malaise in those nations. Time and again such countries begin to doubt their capabilities, and predictions of decline and loss of leadership accompany, with predictable regularity, any spate of rapid convergence. Such forebodings sometimes prove to have been justified. It is also possible that a nation's loss of confidence in its own future serves as something of a self-fulfilling prophecy. In any event, it remains true that a successful convergence process must condemn the initial leaders to the role of runners-up in terms of growth rate in the variables whose absolute levels are being assimilated, and this is sure to constitute a traumatic experience for those leaders.

Indeed, as Moses Abramovitz pointed out in a letter,

> Convergence is more than a psychological trauma for the leaders who are being overtaken. As followers approach the average productivity of the leaders, their productivity in some particular industries comes to equal or exceed that of the leaders. . . . In the leading countries (still leading in an average sense), the advance of the followers throws particular industries and whole regions into depression. Serious and painful problems of adjustment and structural change must then be faced.

We can perhaps conclude that convergence is apt to be an enormous boon for most of those who participate, except for those at the top of the heap whose advantages are thereby eroded. Convergence is also no virtue to those at the bottom, who usually seem to be left behind, though they are by no means the only nations that have been excluded from the process.

Studying Convergence for Its Own Sake

Academic investigators, of course, have other reasons to study our subject. Policy implications and similar considerations are not needed as an excuse to study a phenomenon such as convergence. As Veblen reminded us, we academics pursue such topics out of "idle curiosity." For us, it is sufficient to acquire, through an analysis of the mechanism of convergence, an enhanced understanding of the forces underlying economic growth and the patterns it exhibits in the world economy. There can be little doubt that the convergence literature has indeed contributed knowledge of this sort, and for us that should be reason enough for continued study of the field.

Alternative Concepts of Convergence

A review of the literature reveals that the term *convergence* has been used to mean many different things, some of them only distantly related to others.[2] The contents of this book are no exception. To avoid contributing further to any resulting confusion, we will describe some of the pertinent concepts. It should be clear from the ensuing discussion that none of these concepts is inherently superior to the others and that each can be put to good use if its user is careful to define the terminology clearly and to employ the selected concept only where it is appropriate. It is also important to recognize that the convergence concept selected should determine the choice of measuring tool, for example, the coefficient of variation, the range, the ratio of the value of the critical variable for a particular country to the corresponding value for the leader country, or the regression coefficient between the initial values of the pertinent variable for a set of countries and their subsequent growth rates, which is, of course, taken to be negative in a case of convergence.

There appear to be (at least) seven different convergence concepts in fairly widespread use. They will be referred to here as *homogenization, catch-up, gross convergence, explained convergence, residual convergence, asymptotically perfect convergence,* and *bounded convergence.* Let us consider them in turn.

The first pair of concepts, *homogenization* and *catch-up,* are of particular importance for this book, because about half of the chapters focus on one of them and the remaining chapters concentrate on the other. One of these groups uses statistical measures such as variance, calculated for certain countries, without any particular attention to the identity of the leader or to the makeup of the remainder of the pack. The other group, in contrast, is concerned primarily with the identity of the leader at some particular time, with the sources of that economy's leadership, and with the relationships between the leader and the remainder of the group.

1. *Homogenization* refers to a reduction in the dispersion among some set of countries (or regions or industries) in terms of some measure of performance. For example, if a study shows that there has been a steady decline in the coefficient of variation of the levels of labor productivity for some set of countries, the conclusion that their productivity has been converging means that their labor productivity is becoming homogenized. It means, simply, that on average, the percentage spread in the productivity levels of the countries in question has been narrowing. This happens when those countries' productivity levels that had started out furthest behind then experienced percentage growth rates faster than those of the countries that had started out furthest ahead. Thus, a negative correlation between the percentage growth rate and the initial level of the variable in question (e.g., productivity) is both a necessary and a sufficient condition for homogenization in terms of that variable.

2. *Catch-up* refers to a narrowing in the percentage gap between the leading country's performance in the variable in question and that of the other countries in the pertinent set. For example, if the average level of the OECD countries' labor productivity had been 45 percent of that of the United States in 1950 but had risen to 80 percent of the U.S. figure by 1990, we would conclude that they had caught up with the United States, assumed here to be the leader in productivity. Note that homogenization is neither necessary nor sufficient to catch-up. The average productivity of the

set of countries could have moved closer to that of the United States, and yet the performance of the other countries might have grown more diverse. Similarly, a decline in the differences among the performances of those other countries need not bring them closer to that of the United States. Thus, although both homogenization and catch-up are concepts of considerable importance, they are not equivalent. Indeed, much of the earlier literature, as well as a good part of the current policy discussion, seems more concerned with catch-up than with homogenization. This appears to be true of the writings that discuss how the countries of continental Europe caught up with Britain, the erosion of the United States' competitive superiority, and the forging ahead of Japan's economy. In particular, much of the recent literature that describes its subject as "convergence" seems to be concerned primarily with catch-up in the form of the dwindling U.S. lead rather than with homogenization. In at least some cases, however, the measurements and criteria the literature has employed relate to homogenization and so are relatively poor indicators of catch-up.

Of course, reality is likely to provide cases in which the relationships are more complex than either pure homogenization or pure catch-up. For example, as may have happened soon after the Industrial Revolution or during World War II, the leader can pull ahead of the pack, with the others resuming their attempt to catch up only after a considerable delay. Or most of the countries in the second tier may pull closer to one another, but not to the leader. Such cases are obviously of considerable interest, but we should probably take care to distinguish them from cases in which some uncomplicated form of convergence is present.

Finally, homogenization and catch-up usually seem to have gone hand in hand, at least among the OECD countries since 1950.

3. *Gross* (or *unconditional*) *convergence* is a term that can apply to either homogenization or catch-up. It refers to those countries that have been shown to have experienced some degree of convergence in the variable in question, without correcting for the influence exercised by other pertinent variables. For example, if the coefficient of variation in the labor productivity levels of a set of countries has increased between 1960 and 1990, we can say that those countries' productivity levels have undergone gross divergence (heterogenization). We can say this even though further calculation indicates that the divergence can be ascribed to growing disparity in their investment in capital equipment and that after correcting for that disparity, there was clear homogenization (in TFP) throughout the period in question.

4. *Explained convergence* is, of course, the counterpart of the preceding concept. It refers to statistical evaluation of the role of pertinent and measurable variables that can reasonably be expected to influence the time path and degree of convergence experienced by some economies. These include variables such as expenditures on capital equipment, outlays for education, strength of commitment to freedom of trade, and political stability. The study of explained (or, perhaps, statistically explainable) convergence is clearly important to the design of policy. If it is found, for example, that investment in equipment is a key variable in determining whether or not a country can attain membership in the convergence club, growth planners in a country that has been falling behind will have a very valuable piece of information.

5. *Residual convergence* refers to the possibility that after a statistical removal of the effects of the variables estimated in the explained convergence calculation, the remaining—and statistically unexplained—residue in the behavior of the dependent

variable (such as productivity or GDP per capita) will itself prove to display convergence among the countries studied. That is, for example, after correcting for differences in their expenditures on equipment, Country A's productivity may catch up with that of Country B. One of the chapters in this volume reports on a number of studies indicating that there are many more countries in which residual convergence has occurred than there are in which gross convergence was present. These studies indicate that many poorer countries benefited from residual convergence, even though they fell behind in investment and other pertinent variables condemned them to gross divergence from most of the world's economies. This suggests that if these countries adopt policies that improve their performance on the explained convergence front, they can be comforted by the evidence that these measures will probably not be undermined by the residue's divergent behavior.

The evidence also suggests that even for the most prosperous countries, the period since the mid-1970s has been one of gross divergence, despite the continuing residual convergence.

Residual convergence is not to be interpreted as a measure of convergence that is formulated in terms of total factor productivity, in contradistinction to labor productivity. Any adjustment for influences such as degree of freedom of trade or political stability clearly has no connection with the distinction between the two measures of productivity. Rather, residual convergence should be interpreted as a black box containing any residual forces creating homogenization or catch-up, after identifying and separating the effects of the individual influences on convergence for whose role there is strong empirical evidence or at least a convincing presumption.

Residual and explained convergence would appear to be concepts more analytically satisfying than gross convergence, because they recognize that any convergence process must be subject to disturbance by a number of "ancillary variables," themselves perhaps of considerable importance, and that the premise that convergence is generated by a relationship that encompasses only a single independent variable is the height of implausibility. It is clear that we probe more deeply by taking account of the role of the ancillary variables, evaluating their influence and then netting out that influence, as the concept of residual convergence requires.

Explained and residual convergence may also be the concepts that prove to be useful for the design of growth policy. Thus, for example, suppose the evidence indicates that Country X benefits from a strong tendency toward residual convergence in the form of catching up to those ahead of it but that impediments to freedom of trade and low investment in education have effectively offset its effects. This analysis then suggests two reasonable priorities for that country's policy: It indicates that a modified trade policy and a shift in the budget toward improved education may be able to release the underlying forces of convergence and permit them to help move the economy upward in the direction of countries more prosperous than itself.

As a measure of the welfare of the countries in question, it is surely gross convergence, and not residual convergence, that matters. It can provide little pleasure to the impoverished inhabitants of a less developed land to find that even though they have fallen still further behind the income levels in the industrialized countries, several variables can explain their misfortune and that after correcting for the effects of those variables, they were still enjoying the fruits of residual convergence. Residual convergence is simply not a good indicator of what is happening to standards of living. Indeed, one commentator has characterized a residual convergence approach as one that proceeds by first removing most of the layers pertinent to convergence and then peering underneath to see whether anything that remains merits notice as a pure manifestation of the phenomenon.

In addition, one may well have reservations about the prospects for success in breaking up the sources of growth with the aid of an exercise in growth accounting. As will be emphasized in the next chapter, there is reason to suspect that many of the sources of growth are complementary and interact strongly. It may therefore not be feasible statistically or even illuminating to attempt to divide up the attribution of growth among them. This is particularly daunting when the list of influences with which one tries to deal is open-ended, including not only the set of variables usually taken as "proximate causes" but also a vague and ill-defined group of factors that are assumed to lie behind the proximate causes. When the list is taken to include institutions—the organization of industrial and financial enterprise and their interrelation to one another and to political institutions—the complexity of any attempt to relate them to total factor productivity should be clear enough.

We turn next to the stronger and weaker variants of some of the convergence concepts that have already been offered. Before providing the two corresponding definitions that remain to be added to our set, we should make a few preliminary remarks. Most of the statistical studies carried out so far employ one or another of what can be referred to as *weak criteria*. One such criterion, which we could call *weak catch-up*, was described by Barro and Sala i Martin (1990, p. 11): "Convergence applies if a poor country tends to grow faster than a rich one, so that—other things equal—the poor one tends to catch up with the rich one in terms of the level of per capita income or product." They cite as users of this definition "Barro [1984] Chapter 12, Baumol [1986], De Long [1988], [and] Barro [1991]." The second of the weak criteria (call it *weak homogenization*), according to Barro and Sala i Martin, "concerns cross-sectional dispersion. In this context, convergence occurs if the dispersion—measured say by the standard deviation of the logarithm of per capita income or product across a group of countries or regions—declines over time." They tell us that this second definition has been used by "Easterlin [1960], Borts and Stein [1964, chap. 2] Streissler [1979], Barro [1984, chap. 12] Baumol [1986] and Dowrick [and] Nguyen [1989]." These conditions are weak in that the dispersion, though declining, can approach a rather large lower bound. Or it is possible that even after such a "convergence" process has run its course, the poor countries will still remain extremely impoverished relative to the wealthier ones. One might well have reservations about saying that two countries, A and B, are converging if B's per-capita income, initially 45 percent of A's, is asymptotically approaching, say, 52 percent of the latter.

To avoid such an anomaly, Bernard and Durlauf (1990) and Quah (1990) proposed a far stronger criterion. In general terms, although their criterion allows two economies to differ temporarily, "all per capita output deviations are transitory" (Bernard and Durlauf 1992, p. 13). In other words, they are proposing a convergence concept that is something like the following.

6. *Asymptotically perfect convergence* refers to two economies that are converging if in the long run the pertinent variables for the two countries (such as their per-capita incomes) asymptotically approach precisely the same level.

To make the concept usable in empirical studies, Bernard and Durlauf envision the growth of per-capita income or any other pertinent variables as a process in which disturbances give rise to stochastic trends. According to their definition, "Convergence requires that output deviations between countries i and j . . . obey a zero mean stationary stochastic process" (Bernard and Durlauf 1992, p. 13). If two economies whose convergence is being studied are subject to stochastic trends and if the trends in the two economies bear a linear stochastic relationship to each other, then the per-capita outputs in the two countries are said to be "cointegrated." Finally, if the cointegrated income levels of the two economies differ only by a random term corresponding to a zero mean stationary process, then Bernard and Durlauf characterize the process as "stochastic convergence" (Bernard and Durlauf 1990, pp. 4–6).

This strong definition contributes considerably to our understanding of the complexities of the convergence issue, and of the role of innovation, which is interpreted as a random shock. But because this definition in effect requires the economies in question to approach precisely the same levels, it should hardly be surprising that tests of the data have shown very few country pairs to be converging. It is equally predictable that after a few appropriate adjustments, several country pairs have been found to meet the weaker criteria, as they have been described so far. This suggests that neither of these definitions quite meets the needs of economic historians or policy analysts, one concept perhaps being too demanding and the other insufficiently so. Accordingly, this list of convergence concepts will end with an attempt to outline a criterion of intermediate strength that may come closer to what is needed to analyze the messy data describing the performance of real economies.

One obvious way to arrive at such a criterion is to select an arbitrary maximum difference, say 5 or 10 percent, between the limits that, say, the per-capita GNPs of two countries are approaching, and to define any difference greater than this as not constituting a case of convergence. This gives us the last of the concepts to be offered here:

7. *Bounded convergence* means that two countries are undergoing a process of bounded convergence if the time paths of the pertinent variables are heading toward destination points that are not necessarily identical but that can be deemed to be reasonably close to one another on some explicit and preselected criterion.

As we have already said, none of the seven convergence concepts offered here is inherently superior or inferior to the others. Each has a role to play, and each can be used without apology. We need merely take the trouble to ensure that our readers have been adequately informed about the identity of the concept they have chosen to use, perhaps along with some indication of the reason that the selected concept is appropriate to the subject at hand.

Looking Forward

As areas of economic investigation go, the study of convergence is still quite new. It should not be surprising, therefore, that there are many questions in the field remaining to be examined. The implied research agenda should keep several investigators busy for a long time. A few examples will show the magnitude of the remaining tasks.

1. Perhaps the major analytical problem that remains to be explored is how the convergence process changes as the members of the convergence club draw closer together in their average productivity. Does this mean that the engine that drives the

process has exhausted itself, and if so, where can the affected economies be expected to go from here?

2. Moses Abramovitz predicts that among a group of countries, forces of divergence as well as influences leading to convergence may always be present. When one of these weakens or is exhausted, the other is apt to take over. The forces that lead to divergence appear to include national characteristics and institutions that affect technological congruence and social capability. This viewpoint may have much to tell us about the evidence of divergence in the past two decades among the leading industrial countries, as well as about the widening gap between the LDCs and the more advanced countries. A study of the influences that lead to divergence and their apparently evolving identity and changing role can contribute valuable knowledge.

3. By now there already has been so much convergence among the OECD countries that its forces may have been largely exhausted. For those countries, the concept may retain relatively little explanatory power, perhaps because the disparity in what any one OECD country has to learn from the others has all but disappeared. Even if this is so, however, for the LDCs there still remains enormous scope for convergence. Nonetheless, we understand relatively little about the means that can be used to encourage participation in the process by the poorer countries and the obstacles that beset it.

4. We know relatively little about the relation between the rate of convergence and the rate of growth of productivity in the leading countries. Is it really easier to catch up with a leader if the frontier is expanding slowly? The answer may have significant implications for the relationship between the productivity slowdown of the 1970s and the subsequent speed of the convergence process.

5. The diversity of the political systems that govern the countries that have succeeded in catching up suggests that the relation between political system and catch-up is complex. The subject clearly merits more systematic investigation.

6. The role of the ancillary variables included in studies of net convergence has yet to be spelled out. In particular, no study seems to have distinguished between those influences that affect the speed of convergence and those that affect membership in the "convergence club." This is surely a matter that deserves some priority.

7. The process of catch-up does not occur smoothly across the industries or sectors of an economy. In a country whose aggregate productivity is catching up with that of the leader, some industries may pull ahead of the leader, and others may fall further behind. What are the factors and forces that influence the choice of industries that move ahead and those that remain behind?

This is only a sample of the many important topics that remain to be studied. Convergence analysis also raises issues of at least initially greater importance for theory, for example, the relationship between convergence and factor price equalization, the emphasis of endogenous growth theory on endogenous innovation, and the role of the externalities of proximity in research and production activity. Does the convergence phenomenon mean that this literature has overvalued the role of these influences? In regard to the phenomenon of feedback in the growth process and path dependency, do such relationships stimulate convergence or impede it?

The chapters in this book touch on many of these questions, and some of them go considerably further than that. Still, it would be misleading to state that any of the preceding questions is answered definitively. Rather, they would be better considered as an entry to the agenda for future research.

Organization of the Book

Part I of this volume contains chapters by the three authors who, arguably, have had most to do with inspiring the recent writings on convergence. Angus Maddison has provided both much of the empirical grist for the mill and much of the broad analysis that has shaped the discussion. His 1982 book, *Phases of Capitalist Development,* and his update of that work in his 1991 book, *Dynamic Forces in Capitalist Development,* are monumental achievements.

Maddison's chapter in this volume beautifully summarizes many of the empirical data he has gathered and lays out much of the analysis that he has put forth. He is concerned with both of the broad orientations, homogenization and catch-up, the main branches of convergence analysis discussed earlier in this introduction. He is concerned, first, with changes in national economic leadership, with Britain taking the flag from the Netherlands in the late eighteenth century and, in its turn, the United States taking the lead toward the close of the nineteenth century and holding it up to the present. His chapter shows that the United States actually extended its lead over the rest of the pack throughout the first half of the twentieth century, with that lead dwindling only after 1950.

Maddison also examines patterns of convergence in the statistical sense of variance, noting that convergence in this latter sense certainly was not in the past, and is not now, a phenomenon that holds among the complete set of countries in the world. Although since 1950 there has been convergence among the OECD countries (though at a slower pace recently than early in the postwar period), only a few of those that were less developed in 1950 have since then joined the "convergence club." Many of the economies that lagged behind in 1950 are now even further behind.

Both in his own work and in his collaborative work with Wolff and Blackman, William Baumol has been another central instigator of and contributor to the recent literature on convergence. For the most part he has been concerned with whether there has been convergence, in the sense of diminishing variance, and, if so, over what time periods and including what group of nations. It is fair to say that most of the recent writings by other authors that share this analytic orientation were stimulated by Baumol's 1986 piece, "Productivity Growth, Convergence, and Welfare: What the Long Run Data Show." Baumol's chapter here is a brief summary of this literature.

In his chapter Baumol looks at two important issues, first, the country-specific variables that seem to be associated with whether or not a country is a member of what might be called the "convergence club." He observes that over the full set of countries for which we now have data, the overall tendencies toward convergence are relatively weak. On the other hand, if one considers countries that have relatively high levels of educational attainment, that have achieved high rates of investment in new plant and equipment, or that have been blessed by political stability, one notices that there are strong tendencies toward convergence among this group. What Baumol is offering here is the beginning of an empirically based theory of what it takes to be a member of the convergence club.

Baumol next sketches two different "models" of convergence. One contains common influences that stimulate growth in different countries and that are subject to diminishing returns or erosion with the passage of time once they are embarked on their role in a particular country. Convergence results because the stimulants peter out in the leader countries before they do in the laggards. A second "contagion" model contains a leading nation that is pioneering new technology and also a group of followers. Convergence is associated with the transfer of the technology from the leader to the laggards, a stimulant that spreads growth from the leader to the followers but tends to peter out after the followers have acquired the bulk of the leader's technology.

The third contributor to Part I, Moses Abramovitz, has been a pioneer in empirical research on economic growth and in forging an understanding of what lies behind the key processes involved. His contributions in this area date back to the 1950s. Abramovitz's article "Catching Up, Forging Ahead, and Falling Behind" clearly was a major stimulus to the recent convergence literature. Although it was not published until 1986, drafts of the paper had circulated for some years before that. To a considerable extent Abramovitz's article was based on Maddison's data, and in turn, Baumol's 1986 piece takes off from Abramovitz's analysis.

Although Baumol's orientation toward convergence has not concentrated explicitly on the relationships between a leader nation and a follower group, the latter has been the central issue for Abramovitz. In his chapter here, Abramovitz draws on Maddison's data and other sources to show that although there was convergence among the major industrial nations during the first half of this century, in the sense of declining variance, there was no tendency by the pack behind the United States to close that gap. Abramovitz examines what has been different about the period since World War II that has caused the rapid convergence (up until the mid-1970s) of the OECD countries. In his elegant analysis, he weighs various explanatory factors, ending up highlighting the great differences in international trade and investment between the postwar and prewar eras, and the growing commonality of technological knowledge. Abramovitz notes that after the middle 1970s, convergence slowed (although the rest of the pack crept closer and closer to the United States) and that economic growth also slowed in all of the major industrial nations. He concludes by speculating on the reasons for this and then peers into the future.

The two chapters in Part II are on the sources of national economic and technological leadership and the reasons for their erosion. The chapter by Nelson and Wright argues that there were two relatively distinct sources of U.S. manufacturing leadership in the period immediately after World War II. American leadership in mass production industries, like automobiles and steel, they contend, goes back at least as far as the turn of the century. That American advantage, they maintain, stems in large part from the fact that by that time the United States was the world's largest common market and also, compared with Europe, was remarkably well endowed with raw materials. Also by that time, American wages were higher than those in the United Kingdom and far higher than those on the Continent. This combination led American industry to adopt a scale-intensive, capital-intensive, and resource-intensive mode of production that gave it significantly higher levels of output per worker than Europe's mode of production did. This advantage continued through the interwar period, mainly because of the sharp increases in trade barriers that marked that period. European firms lacked both the incentive and the capability to adopt American-style mass production methods. Nelson and Wright argue that in contrast, the United States' postwar lead in high-technology industries was new. It was associated with massive investments in scientific and engineering education and in research and development spending that far outstripped those of other countries.

The analysis by Nelson and Wright of how and why the U.S. lead diminished after 1950 is similar to Abramovitz's. Open world trade in manufactured goods and raw materials made the world a common market and eroded the long-standing American advantages in mass production industries when other countries began to match American investments in scientific and engineering education and in research and development.

William Lazonick's chapter takes American technological dominance from the early twentieth century until about 1970, using the latter as its benchmark, and looks backward and forward. He looks backward at Great Britain—the economic and technological leader during much of the nineteenth century—and asks why Great Britain lost its lead to the United States in the early twentieth century. Lazonick puts great stock in the differing ways in which companies were managed and, in particular, in the relationship between owners and managers. Citing Chandler, Lazonick observes that by the early twentieth century, American companies (and also German firms) were beginning to be run by a cadre of professional hired managers who had a stake in the company's future. In contrast, the owners of British companies did not make the same investments in professional management, and increasingly they paid the price. Lazonick also finds that in the United States, management gained control over activity on the shop floor, whereas in Great Britain, skilled labor continued to have its way, thereby preventing the development in Great Britain of the "scientific management" that grew up in the United States.

Lazonick also looks forward from the era of American economic dominance, and explores what it is about Japanese firms that has enabled them to be more efficient than American enterprises in a wide range of industries. He argues that a central factor is that Japanese firms have managed to bring shop-floor labor into the group that considers itself committed to the firm and its future, whereas in the United States, labor remains uncommitted to the particular firms in which it happens to be working.

The three chapters in Part III investigate some of the factors that are responsible for the convergence in productivity levels among advanced nations and the failure of the LDCs to close the productivity gap. The first chapter, by David Dollar and Edward Wolff, studies the role of capital formation in the convergence in both labor and total factor productivity on the industry level among OECD countries since the early 1960s. Earlier work by them (1988) explored how convergence in aggregate productivity is manifested in specific manufacturing industries. Dollar and Wolff concluded that the proximate cause of the convergence in aggregate manufacturing labor productivity was the convergence of labor productivity within industries.

In this chapter they find evidence of the convergence (homogenization) of total factor productivity and capital–labor ratios for both aggregate manufacturing and individual manufacturing industries in OECD countries between 1963 and 1985, though this process of convergence was much faster before 1972 than after. The convergence of TFP has been the main source of labor productivity convergence. Dollar and Wolff also discover that cross-country variation in the state of technology (as measured by TFP) and capital intensity was greater in individual industries than in aggregate manufacturing. The greater similarity among countries in their aggregate productivity than in their productivity in particular industries indicates that countries differ from one another in the identity of the industries in which they excel, so that on average, aggregate productivity levels among countries are closer than are their productivity levels within industries. The same is true for capital intensity. Thus, these results indicate that countries have specialized in different industries, particularly since the mid-1970s. This also helps explain the process by which several countries took over productivity leadership from the United States in certain industries. Dollar and Wolff conclude that changes in international comparative advantage may be attributed to a combination of worldwide shifts in technology leadership and investment strategies.

Another influence that appears to be vital to the convergence process is education. Previous work on the subject has suggested that next to capital investment, education may be the most important contributor to the convergence process (see, e.g., Baumol, Blackman, and Wolff 1989, chap. 9). One of the principal reasons, besides low investment rates, for the relatively weak catch-up performance of the less developed countries over the postwar period was apparently the failure of the lagging countries to keep up with, absorb, and use new technological and product information and to benefit from the international dissemination of technology. One of the elements that explains an economy's ability to absorb information and new technology is the education of its people, in which the LDCs are well behind the industrialized countries.

The next chapter, by Frank Lichtenberg, in Part II provides new evidence for the role of education in the productivity convergence process. Most of the simple models of aggregate production imply that productivity depends on the "quality" of the labor force in general and on the distribution of the work force by educational attainment in particular. International differences in both the level and the growth rate of education should explain some of the differences observed in both productivity levels and growth rates among countries. Lichtenberg finds, first, that both educational enrollment and attainment rates have converged among countries—more so for the former than the latter and more so at lower than at higher educational levels. Using an augmented growth model of the Solow type, however, he discovers (rather paradoxically) no evidence that educational convergence has led to convergence in per-capita income among nations.

The third chapter in Part II, by Magnus Blomström, Robert Lipsey, and Mario Zejan, focuses on another important element in the convergence process, commercial interchanges with foreign countries. Several previous studies have documented that trade openness is a significant ancillary variable in the conditional convergence process: more open economies, other things being equal, have higher rates of per-capita income growth than do less open ones (see, e.g., Dollar, 1992).

This chapter examines the role of foreign direct investment and the imports of machinery and transportation equipment in the process of per-capita income convergence. The authors speculate that both may be sources of the diffusion of new technology. They view the former as a possible measure of the inflow of disembodied technology and the latter as a possible indicator of the inflow of technology as embodied in new machinery. Using the Summers–Heston database, they focus on countries in the developing category between 1960 and 1985. Their principal finding is that the inflow of foreign direct investment had a significant positive influence on income growth rates among middle-income countries but no significant effect among low-income countries. Moreover, they find that imports of machinery and transportation equipment, when combined with other explanatory variables, were not statistically significant.

Part III shifts to newly industrialized countries (NICs), middle-income economies, and less developed countries (LDCs). The first chapter in this part, by Magnus Blomström and Edward Wolff, is related to the previous one and explores the effects of multinational corporations (MNCs) on productivity growth at the industry level among Mexican manufacturing industries in the 1970s. They argue that the presence of multinational firms may yield positive productivity spillovers to locally owned firms in an economy, for three reasons: (1) the added competition from the MNCs; (2) the training of labor and management provided by the multinationals, which may then become available to the general economy; and (3) the influence of the foreign subsidiaries in the host economy on their local suppliers, through their insistence on standards of quality control, delivery dates, prices, and so forth.

Blomström and Wolff find, first, that both labor productivity levels and TFP levels of locally owned firms in Mexico have converged on those of foreign-owned firms. Second, both the rate of labor productivity growth of local firms and their rate of catch-up to the multinationals are positively related to an industry's share of foreign ownership. Their results support the argument that local firms in Mexico have benefited from productivity spillovers generated by multinational firms in the Mexican economy.

In the second chapter in Part III, Takashi Hikino and Alice Amsden argue that the experience of what they call the "late industrializers" represents a departure from the experience of the earlier industrializers—the United Kingdom, the United States, and Germany. The earlier industrializers were creators of new technology, whereas the later industrializers—most notably Japan, South Korea, and Taiwan—were borrowers or learners. They had to industrialize primarily by learning from others. Hikino and Amsden's principal argument is that such differences in technology acquisition determine the role played by the government in the growth process.

They also contend that there was less need for the government to intervene in shaping the course of the early industrializers, as its role was limited to providing infrastructure, a legal and administrative framework, an educational system, and tariff protection to infant industries. In contrast, they suggest, more government intervention has been required for the late industrializers, because business requires extensive subsidies to compensate for the lack of pioneering technology that gave the early industrializers an advantage over rival economies.

Almost all work in this field has used measures of purely economic accomplishments, such as productivity (output per employee, hours worked, or total factor productivity) or income per capita to measure convergence or catch-up. In the last chapters in this book, Gregory Ingram looks at a wide range of social indicators (measures of human welfare) to evaluate the relative progress of the less developed countries. His main finding is that whereas the LDCs have achieved little or no gain relative to the advanced countries in terms of income or productivity, they have made substantial relative gains in important social arenas. Among the most significant of these are life expectancy, caloric intake, educational enrollment rates (particularly at the primary school level), and degree of urbanization and, to a lesser extent, in the share of GNP devoted to social purposes. There is also evidence of catch-up between middle-income and high-income countries in the number of newspapers, hospital beds, doctors, telephones, and cars per capita. The most telling result is that for several of these variables, the well-being of the inhabitants of middle-income and even low-income countries has been gaining on that of the residents of advanced countries, even though their per-capita income has not risen in tandem. Interestingly, this finding is similar to one by Mayer and Jencks (1993), indicating that during the 1980s, low-income Americans gained ground on other Americans in regard to these social indicators, even though they lost ground in regard to income.

Notes

1. Indeed, the collapse of the Communist regimes in the Soviet Union and Eastern Europe provides some evidence for the importance of relative incomes. In general, the standards of living in those countries had been improving. But they had been falling behind those of Western Europe, which surely contributed to public discontent (e.g., see Wolff, 1993).

2. In addition to the connotations that will be discussed here, this term has a more venerable use in the sociological literature. As Gavin Wright points out in a letter, it refers

> to the Weberian conception that societies evolve from disparate cultural backgrounds toward some common patterns dictated by technology and the spread of rationality. It is related to the concept of "modernization," the notion that there is a flow in history from tribalism and traditionalism to rationalism.... I don't think the economic version is entirely removed from the older and less rigorous thinking.

References

Abramovitz, Moses. (1986). "Catching Up, Forging Ahead, and Falling Behind." *Journal of Economic History* 46:385–406.

Barro, Robert J. (1984). *Macroeconomics.* 1st ed. New York: Wiley.

————. (1991). "Economic Growth in a Cross Section of Countries." *Quarterly Journal of Economics* 106:407–43.

Barro, Robert J., and Xavier Sala i Martin. (1990). "Economic Growth and Convergence Across the United States." National Bureau of Economic Research, Working Paper no. 3419, August.

Baumol, William J. (1986). "Productivity Growth, Convergence, and Welfare: What the Long Run Data Show." *American Economic Review* 76:1072–85.

Baumol, William J., Sue Anne Batey Blackman, and Edward N. Wolff. (1989). *Productivity and American Leadership: The Long View.* Cambridge, MA.: MIT Press.

Bernard, A. B., and S. N. Durlauf. (1990). "Convergence of International Output Movements." Paper, Stanford University.

————. (1992). "Interpreting Tests of the Convergence Hypothesis." Paper, Stanford University.

Borts, G. H., and J. L. Stein. (1964). *Economic Growth in a Free Market.* New York: Columbia University Press.

De Long, J. Bradford. (1988). "Productivity Growth, Convergence, and Welfare: Comment." *American Economic Review* 78:1138–54.

Dollar, David. (1992). "Outward-oriented Developing Economies Really Do Grow More Rapidly: Evidence from 95 LDCs, 1976–85." *Economic Development and Cultural Change* 40:523–44.

Dollar, David, and Edward N. Wolff. (1988). "Convergence of Industry Labor Productivity Among Advanced Economies, 1963–1982." *Review of Economics and Statistics* 70:549–58.

Dowrick, Steve, and Duc-Tho Nguyen. (1989). "OECD Comparative Economic Growth 1950–85: Catch-up and Convergence." *American Economic Review* 79:1010–30.

Easterlin, R. A. (1957). "Regional Growth of Income: Long Run Tendencies." In S. Kuznets and D. Thomas, eds., *Population Redistribution and Economic Growth in the United States.* Philadelphia: American Philosophical Society, pp. 141–99.

————. (1960). "Interregional Differences in per Capita Income, Population, and Total Income, 1840–1950." *Conference on Research in Income and Wealth, NBER Studies in Income and Wealth* no. 24.

Gerschenkron, Alexander. (1952). "Economic Backwardness in Historical Perspective." In Bert F. Hoselitz, ed., *The Progress of Underdeveloped Areas.* Chicago: University of Chicago Press, pp. 3–29.

Kuznets, Simon. (1973). *Population, Capital, and Growth: Selected Essays.* New York: Norton.

Maddison, Angus. (1982). *Phases of Capitalist Development.* Oxford: Oxford University Press.

————. (1989). *The World Economy in the 20th Century.* Paris: OECD, Development Centre.

Mayer, Susan E., and Christopher Jencks. (1993). "Recent Trends in Economic Inequality in the United States: Income vs. Expenditures vs. Material Well-Being." In Dimitri B. Papadimitriou and Edward N. Wolff, eds., *Poverty and Prosperity in the USA in the Late Twentieth Century.* London: Macmillan.

Quah, D. (1990). "International Patterns of Growth: Persistence in Cross-Country Disparities." MIT Working Paper.

Streissler, E. (1979). "Growth Models as Diffusion Processes: II. Empirical Implications." *Kyklos* 32:571–86.

Summers, Robert, and Alan Heston. (1988). "A New Set of International Comparisons of Real Product and Price Levels: Estimates for 130 Countries." *Review of Income and Wealth* 34:1–25.

Wolff, Edward N. (1993). "International Convergence in Productivity Levels: Has Central Planning Mattered?". In Pierre Pestieau ed., *Public Finance in a World of Transition,* vol. 47. The Hague, Netherlands: International Institute of Public Finance, pp. 122–37.

2

Explaining the Economic Performance of Nations, 1820–1989

ANGUS MADDISON

The aim of this chapter is to establish how Western countries became rich and to understand why the rest of the world is poorer. I first measure the extent of real-income disparities to see how they have changed since 1820. I examine the causal role of quantifiable factors—natural resources, raw labor, human capital, and physical capital—and speculate on their interaction with demographic change, the growth and diffusion of technology, the growth of international trade and capital flows, and changes in economic structure. There are also deeper and less tangible layers of causality related to the character of basic institutions, the degree of social conflict, the international order, ideology, and the nature of economic policy. These underlie, interact with, and complement the "proximate" causality.

The Unit of Analysis

As in most growth analyses, the unit considered here is the nation-state. Since 1820, the constellation of states has varied as countries have split up, merged, or changed their boundaries. It is therefore not possible to identify all of them or to monitor their experience over the past 17 decades.

The maximum number of states has probably been below 200 over the whole period. Writing in 1951, Kuznets counted 85 independent states (including "such curiosities as Monaco, the Vatican and Andorra") and 111 non-self-governing units. In 1992, we have 175 member countries of the United Nations and a much smaller number of non-self-governing units.

The type of economic reasoning that is appropriate to such a restricted universe is different for that which is normally used to analyze the behavior of individual economic "agents" (about 5.5 billion people), "firms" (several million), or "regions" (several thousand).

When we consider economic agents or firms, it is legitimate to disregard the institutional or policy context and assume that resource allocation, resource accumulation, transmission of information, and technology occur through disembodied competitive market forces. But the performance of nation-states is strongly influenced by governments with coercive power. These governments have widely differing institutions, policies, interests, traditions, and beliefs, and the degree of freedom they permit for economic transmission mechanisms to operate across their borders is usually much more limited than the freedom for homogenizing forces to operate internally.

This, of course, is a rather self-evident point and fully reflected in what I consider to be the mainstream literature on economic growth, for example, by analysts like Kuznets or Denison. However, some of the new growth theory that has emerged since 1986 does not adequately acknowledge the specificity of the nation-state as the basic unit of analysis, and it tries to assimilate the problem of explaining the growth performance of nations to that of explaining the equilibrium behavior of individuals or firms. Paul Romer's (1986 and 1990) influential essays are a good example of this. His analytical model concentrates on the behavior of "profit-maximizing agents" or modes of transmission of knowledge and technology between "firms."

Establishing the Basic Facts About Income Growth and Its Dispersion

Table 2-1 gives a representative portrayal of comparative growth performance and income dispersion between nations since 1820, that is, for the whole period of modern economic growth.[1] It measures the gross domestic product (GDP) per capita. The logic of national accounts was developed by some of the finest minds in the economic profession, and there is wide agreement as to the scope, coverage, and boundaries of this indicator. Nevertheless, to measure output over such a long period means comparing the present situation with that of dead ancestors who had no experience of air and motor transport, radio, television, cinema, or household electrical appliances. Similarly, it means comparing incomes across countries whose life-styles are vastly different, so one cannot hope to get more than rough estimates covering such large interspatial and intertemporal distances.

The estimates of Table 2-1 merge four kinds of information: (1) historical national accounts built up mainly by academic research; (2) postwar official national accounts that are based on the UN/OECD/Eurostat standardized system but whose quality is often weak in poor countries; (3) purchasing power parity (PPP) converters provided by the joint International Comparisons Project (ICP) of Eurostat/OECD and the United Nations; and (4) estimates of population that are still subject to significant error in the poor countries (most egregiously so in Nigeria).

For the former communist countries and the African countries, we must use GDP estimates that are a good deal weaker than those for the OECD countries. We must also include some countries for which the historical record does not reach earlier than 1950. In order to express GDP in a common currency (1985 dollars at U.S. relative prices), we have to splice the results for the 1980 and 1985 ICP rounds and make some use of the proxy PPP converters developed by Robert Summers and Alan Heston (1988 and 1991).

Our sample covers 43 countries in 1989 and 21 in 1820. It represents about three-

Table 2-1. GDP per Capita in Our Sample of 43 Countries, 1820–1989
($ at 1985 U.S. relative prices)

	1820	1870	1890	1913	1950	1973	1989
The West European capitalist core and its offshoots (14 countries)							
Austria	1,048	1,442	1,892	2,683	2,869	8,697	12,519
Belgium	1,025	2,089	2,654	3,267	4,229	9,417	12,875
Denmark	980	1,543	1,944	3,014	5,227	10,527	13,822
Finland	639	933	1,130	1,727	3,481	9,073	14,015
France	1,059	1,582	1,955	2,746	4,176	10,351	13,952
Germany	902	1,251	1,660	2,506	3,295	10,124	13,752
Italy	965	1,216	1,352	2,079	2,840	8.631	12,989
Netherlands	1,308	2,065	2,568	3,179	4,708	10,271	12,669
Norway	856	1,190	1,477	2,079	4,541	9,347	15,202
Sweden	1,008	1,401	1,757	2,607	5,673	11,362	14,824
United Kingdom	1,450	2,693	3,383	4,152	5,651	10,079	13,519
Australia	1,250	3,143	3,949	4,553	5,970	10,369	13,538
Canada		1,330	1,846	3,515	6,112	11,835	17,236
United States	1,219	2,244	3,101	4,846	8,605	14,093	18,282
Average	1,055	1,723	2,191	3,068	4,813	10,298	14,228
European periphery (7 countries)							
Czechoslovakia	836	1,153	1,515	2,075	3,465	6,980	8,538
Greece				1,211	1,456	5,781	7,564
Hungary		1,139	1,439	1,883	2,481	5,517	6,722
Ireland				2,003	2,600	5,248	8,285
Portugal		833	950	967	1,608	5,598	7,383
Spain	900	1,221	1,355	2,212	2,405	7,581	10,081
Soviet Union		792	828	1,138	2,647	5,920	6,970
Average	868	1,028	1,217	1,641	2,381	6,089	7,931
Latin America (6 countries)							
Argentina		1,039	1,515	2,370	3,112	4,972	4,080
Brazil	556	615	641	697	1,434	3,356	4,402
Chile			1,073	1,735	3,255	4,281	5,406
Colombia				1,078	1,876	2,996	3,979
Mexico	584	700	762	1,121	1,594	3,202	3,728
Peru				1,099	1,809	3,160	2,601
Average	570	785	998	1,350	2,180	3,661	4,033
Asia (9 countries)							
Bangladesh				519	463	391	551
China	497	497	526	557	454	1,039	2,538
India	490	490	521	559	502	719	1,093
Indonesia	533	585	640	710	650	1,056	1,790
Japan	609	640	842	1,153	1,620	9,524	15,336
Korea			680	819	757	2,404	6,503
Pakistan				611	545	823	1,283
Taiwan			564	608	706	2,803	7,252
Thailand		741	801	876	874	1,794	4,008
Average	532	591	653	712	730	2,284	4,484

	1820	1870	1890	1913	1950	1973	1989
Africa (7 countries)							
Côte d'Ivoire					888	1,699	1,401
Ghana				484	733	724	575
Kenya					438	794	886
Morocco					1,105	1,293	1,844
Nigeria					608	1,040	823
South Africa				2,037	3,204	5,466	5,627
Tanzania					334	578	463
Average	400[a]	400[a]	400[a]	580[a]	1,044	1,656	1,660

Source: OECD countries from A. Maddison 1991 at 1985 U.S. relative prices, using Paasche PPPs supplied by Eurostat from the ICP V exercise. For non-OECD countries, from sources indicated in Maddison (1989 and 1990b) whose figures were in 1980 international dollars with PPPs derived mainly from UN/Eurostat (1986, pp. 7 and 8). I have converted them into dollars at 1985 U.S. relative prices, using a multiplier of 1.343. This crude adjustment reflects both the rise in price level between 1980 and 1985 in the United States (the numeraire country) and the average difference between the Paasche PPP and the Geary–Khamis PPP for the OECD countries. For China, Taiwan, and Mexico, the 1980 levels were derived as described in Maddison 1989, p. 111. For Czechoslovakia and the Soviet Union, the 1980 levels were derived from Summers and Heston 1988 relative to per-capita product in Hungary and, for Ghana, from their figure relative to Nigeria. The figures are adjusted to eliminate the effects of boundary changes.

[a]Rough guesses, assuming no progress in the nineteenth century.

quarters of the world population and an even larger share of the world product. In terms of income spreads, the sample is fairly complete. Summers and Heston (1991) record only 4 countries with an income level somewhat below that of Tanzania (Ethiopia, Mali, Uganda, and Zaire) and only 1 (United Arab Republics) with an income level marginally higher than that of the United States.

The following facts emerge from the evidence of Tables 2-1 through 2-5.

1. Between 1820 and 1989 there was a substantial increase in real income in all countries outside Africa (see Figure 2-1).

2. The rates of growth in these countries varied considerably, and there was a clear divergence in performance over the long run. In 1820 the intercountry income spread was probably about 4:1; in 1913 it was 10:1; in 1950 it was 26:1; in 1973 it was 36:1; and in 1989 it was 39:1. Between 1913 and 1950, not only was there increasing divergence on the global level; there was also an increase in the proportional gap between the lead country and 30 of the 37 follower countries for which we have evidence. However, the widening in the spread between 1950 and 1989 was due entirely to disappointing performance in very poor countries. The percentage gap between the lead country, the United States, and 30 of the 42 follower countries was reduced and often very significantly reduced between 1950 and 1989 (i.e., in all 18 European countries, in Australia and Canada, in 8 Asian countries, and in 2 Latin American countries). Clearly, there was a good deal of "catch-up" within a global framework of "divergence" (see Table 2-3).

3. Our 43 sample countries are divided into five separate groups. Except for Asia, their in-group performance has had some degree of homogeneity.

The capitalist core countries have had the highest incomes and the fastest long-term growth. Already in 1820 these countries had a clear lead, because of their slow but significant growth in the protocapitalist period.[2] Between 1820 and 1989 their average real income rose thirteenfold, and there was intergroup convergence from an income spread of 2.3:1 in 1820 to 1.5:1 in 1989.

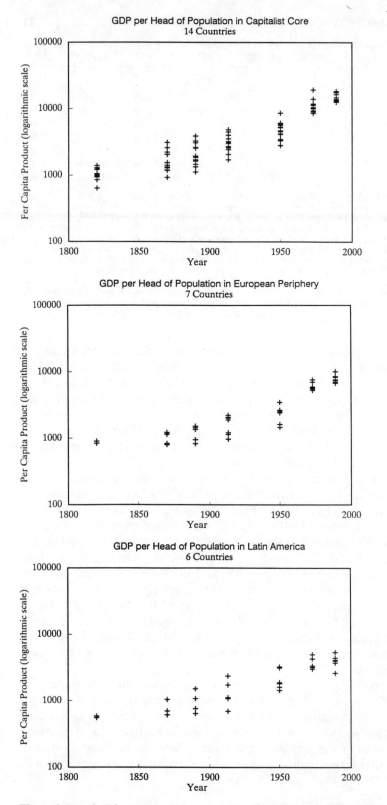

Figure 2-1. a–f: Divergence and convergence in GDP per capita, 1820–1989.

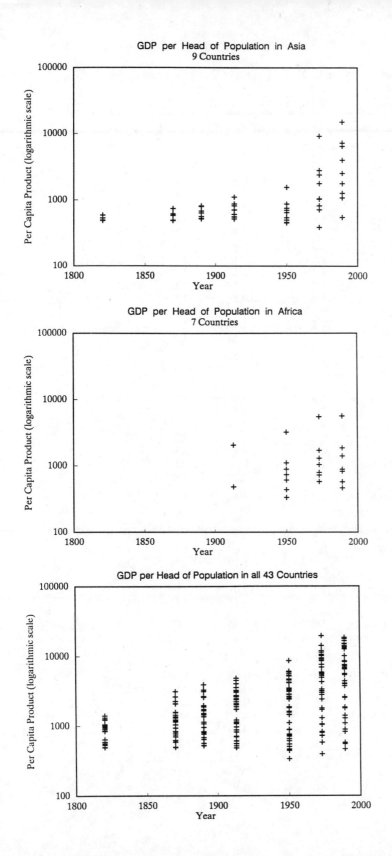

Table 2-2. Rates of Growth of GDP per Capita in Our 43-Country Sample, 1820–1989
(annual average compound rate of growth)

	1820–70	1870–1913	1913–50	1950–73	1973–89
The European capitalist core and its offshoots					
Austria	0.6	1.5	0.2	4.9	2.3
Belgium	1.4	1.0	0.7	3.5	2.0
Denmark	0.9	1.6	1.5	3.1	1.7
Finland	0.8	1.4	1.9	4.3	2.8
France	0.8	1.3	1.1	4.0	1.9
Germany	0.7	1.6	0.7	5.0	1.9
Italy	0.4	1.3	0.8	5.0	2.6
Netherlands	0.9	1.0	1.1	3.4	1.3
Norway	0.7	1.3	2.1	3.2	3.1
Sweden	0.7	1.5	2.1	3.1	1.7
United Kingdom	1.2	1.0	0.8	2.5	1.9
Australia	1.9	0.9	0.7	2.4	1.7
Canada		2.3	1.5	2.9	2.4
United States	1.2	1.8	1.6	2.2	1.6
Average	0.9	1.4	1.2	3.5	2.1
European periphery					
Czechoslovakia	0.6	1.4	1.4	3.1	1.3
Greece			0.5	6.2	1.7
Hungary		1.2	1.2	3.5	1.2
Ireland			0.7	3.1	2.9
Portugal		0.3	1.4	5.6	1.7
Spain	0.6	1.4	0.2	5.1	1.8
Soviet Union		0.8	2.3	3.6	1.0
Average	0.6	1.0	1.1	4.3	1.7
Latin America					
Argentina		1.9	0.7	2.1	−1.2
Brazil	0.2	0.3	2.0	3.8	1.7
Chile			1.7	1.2	1.5
Colombia			1.5	2.1	1.8
Mexico	0.4	1.1	1.0	3.1	1.0
Peru			1.4	2.5	−1.2
Average	0.3	1.1	1.4	2.5	0.6
Asia					
Bangladesh			−0.3	−0.7	2.2
China	0.0	0.3	−0.5	3.7	5.7
India	0.0	0.3	−0.3	1.6	2.7
Indonesia	0.2	0.5	−0.2	2.1	3.4
Japan	0.1	1.4	0.9	8.0	3.0
Korea			−0.2	5.2	6.4
Pakistan			−0.3	1.8	2.8
Taiwan			0.4	6.2	6.1
Thailand		0.4	0.0	3.2	5.2
Average	0.1	0.6	−0.1	3.5	4.2

	1820–70	1870–1913	1913–50	1950–73	1973–89
Africa					
Côte d'Ivoire				2.9	−1.2
Ghana			1.1	−0.1	−1.4
Kenya				2.6	0.7
Morocco				0.7	2.2
Nigeria				2.4	−1.5
South Africa			1.2	2.3	0.2
Tanzania				2.4	−1.4
Average			1.2	1.9	−0.3

Source: Data derived from Table 2-1.

The European periphery has the second-highest level of income. Since 1820 its average real income has risen ninefold, and the intercountry income spread within this group was probably similar in 1820 to what it is now, that is, about 1.5:1.[3]

Latin America was the third most prosperous group for most of the period, and its average per-capita income rose sevenfold. The 1989 income spread within our Latin American sample was about 1.6:1, which is probably similar to that in 1820.[4]

Table 2-3. Rates of Catch-up on the per-Capita GDP Level of the Lead Country (the United States), 1913–89
(annual average compound rate of growth)

	1913–50	1950–89		1913–50	1950–89
Austria	−1.4	1.9	Argentina	−0.8	−1.2
Belgium	−0.9	0.9	Brazil	0.4	0.9
Denmark	−0.1	0.6	Chile	0.2	−0.6
Finland	0.3	1.7	Colombia	0.0	0.0
France	−0.4	1.2	Mexico	−0.7	0.3
Germany	−0.8	1.7	Peru	−0.2	−1.0
Italy	−0.7	2.0	Bangladesh	−1.8	−1.5
Netherlands	−0.5	0.6	China	−2.1	2.5
Norway	0.6	1.2	India	−1.8	0.1
Sweden	0.6	0.5	Indonesia	−1.8	0.7
United Kingdom	−0.7	0.3	Japan	−0.6	3.9
Australia	−0.8	0.2	Korea	−1.7	3.6
Canada	−0.1	0.7	Pakistan	−1.9	0.3
Czechoslovakia	−0.2	0.4	Taiwan	−1.1	4.1
Greece	−1.0	2.3	Thailand	−1.5	2.0
Hungary	−0.8	0.6	Côte d'Ivoire	n.a.	−0.8
Ireland	−0.8	1.0	Ghana	−0.4	−2.6
Portugal	−0.2	2.0	Kenya	n.a.	−0.2
Spain	−1.3	1.8	Morocco	n.a.	−0.6
Soviet Union	0.7	0.6	Nigeria	n.a.	−1.2
			South Africa	−0.3	−0.5
			Tanzania	n.a.	−1.1

Source: Data derived from Table 2-1, taking rates of growth between the standing of the country relative to the United States in the years in question.

Table 2-4. Population of Our Sample of 43 Countries, 1820–1989
(000s at midyear, adjusted to 1989 boundaries to exclude impact of frontier changes)

	1820	1870	1913	1950	1973	1989
The European capitalist core and its offshoots						
Austria	3,189	4,520	6,967	6,935	7,586	7.624
Belgium	3,424	5,096	7,666	8,640	9,739	9,938
Denmark	1,155	1,888	2,983	4,269	5,022	5,132
Finland	1,169	1,754	3,027	4,009	4,666	4,964
France	31,250	38,440	41,690	41,836	52,118	56,160
Germany	15,788	24,870	40,825	49,983	61,976	62,063
Italy	19,000	27,888	37,248	47,105	54,779	57,525
Netherlands	2,355	3,615	6,164	10,114	13,439	14,846
Norway	970	1,735	2,447	3,265	3,961	4,227
Sweden	2,585	4,164	5,621	7,015	8,137	8,493
United Kingdom	19,832	29,312	42,622	50,363	56,210	57,236
Australia	33[a]	1,620	4,821	8.177	13,505	16,807
Canada	657[a]	3,736	7,582	13,737	22,072	26,248
United States	9,656[a]	40,061	97,606	152,271	211,909	248,777
European periphery						
Czechoslovakia	7,190	9,876	13,245	12,389	14,560	15,643
Greece		5,425		7,566	8.929	10,033
Hungary	4,571	5,717	7,840	9,338	10,426	10,587
Ireland			3,110	2,969	3,073	3,515
Portugal	3,420	4,370	6,001	8,441	8,316	9,793
Spain	12,958	16,213	20,330	27,977	34,810	38,888
Soviet Union	50,392	79,354	158,371	180,050	249,800	288,887
Latin America						
Argentina	534	1,796	7,653	17,150	25,195	31,883
Brazil	4,507	9,797	23,660	51,941	99,836	147,473
Chile	885	1,943	3,491	6,082	10,012	12,961
Colombia	1,206	2,392	5,195	11,597	22,916	32,335
Mexico	6,587	9,219	14,971	27,376	56,481	84,330
Peru	1,317	2,606	4,507	7,630	14,347	21,142
Asia						
Bangladesh			31,786	43,135	74,368	106,510
China	350,000	350,000	430,000	546,815	881,940	1,105,000
India	172,383	208,674	251,826	359,943	579,000	811,820
Indonesia	16,443	26,528	48,150	72,747	124,189	179,140
Japan	31,000	34,437	51,672	83,662	108,660	123,120
Korea			10,277	20,557	34,103	42,894
Pakistan			20,007	37,646	66,669	109,950
Taiwan			3,469	7,882	15,427	20,050
Thailand	4,665	5,775	8,690	19,553	39,527	55,450
Africa						
Côte d'Ivoire				3,091	6,235	11,713
Ghana	885	1,403	2,085	4,368	9,388	14,425
Kenya				6,556	12,770	23,277

	1820	1870	1913	1950	1973	1989
Morocco				9,142	16,511	24,567
Nigeria				40,588[b]	71,361[b]	113,665[b]
South Africa			6,214	13,863	24,158	34,925
Tanzania				8,341	14,927	24,728

Source: Maddison 1989, OECD Development Centre data bank, World Bank, *World Tables,* and national sources. As far as possible, the figures are adjusted to refer to populations within the 1989 boundaries, although this was not possible for Indonesia. The 14-country sample for Group 1 had a 1989 population of 580 million, or 98 percent of the population of the 18 countries in this category; the 7 countries in the European periphery had 377 million, or 79 percent of the 13 countries in this category; the 6 countries in Latin America had 330 million, or 75 percent of the population of the 33 countries in this category; the 9 Asian countries in our sample had a population 2,554 million, or 83 percent of the population of the 44 countries in Asia; the 7 countries in our African sample had 217 million, or 38 percent of the population of the 53 countries of Africa in 1989 (see *Population et sociétés,* July–August 1989).

[a]Excludes indigenous populations.

[b]*Population et sociétés,* October 1992, suggests revising the figures for Nigeria in the light of the 1991 census: 1950 would become 36,147; 1973 would become 56,450; and 1989 would become 82,244.

Table 2-5. Rates of Growth of Population in Our 43-Country Sample, 1820–1989
(annual average compound growth rate adjusted to 1989 boundaries to exclude impact of frontier changes)

	1820–70	1870–1913	1913–50	1950–73	1973–89
Capitalist core					
Austria	0.7	1.0	0.0	0.4	0.0
Belgium	0.8	1.0	0.3	0.5	0.1
Denmark	1.0	1.1	1.0	0.7	0.1
Finland	0.8	1.3	0.8	0.7	0.4
France	0.4	0.2	0.0	1.0	0.5
Germany	0.9	1.2	0.5	0.9	0.0
Italy	0.8	0.7	0.6	0.7	0.3
Netherlands	0.9	1.2	1.3	1.2	0.6
Norway	1.2	0.8	0.8	0.8	0.4
Sweden	1.0	0.7	0.6	0.6	0.2
United Kingdom	0.8	0.9	0.5	0.5	0.1
Australia	8.1[a]	2.6	1.4	2.2	1.4
Canada	3.5[a]	1.7	1.6	2.1	1.1
United States	2.9[a]	2.1	1.2	1.4	1.0
European periphery					
Czechoslovakia	0.6	0.7	−0.2	0.7	0.4
Greece			0.9	0.7	0.7
Hungary	0.4	0.7	0.5	0.5	0.1
Ireland			−0.1	0.1	0.8
Portugal	0.5	0.7	0.9	−0.1	1.0
Spain	0.4	0.5	0.9	1.0	0.7
Soviet Union	0.9	1.6	0.3	1.4	0.9
Latin America					
Argentina	2.5	3.4	2.2	1.7	1.5
Brazil	1.6	2.1	2.1	2.9	2.5
Chile	1.6	1.4	1.5	2.2	1.6

Table 2-5. Rates of Growth of Population in Our 43-Country Sample, 1820–1989 (*continued*)

	1820–70	1870–1913	1913–50	1950–73	1973–89
Colombia	1.4	1.8	2.2	3.0	2.2
Mexico	0.7	1.1	1.6	3.2	2.5
Peru	1.4	1.3	1.4	2.8	2.5
Asia					
Bangladesh			0.8	2.4	2.3
China	0.0	0.5	0.7	2.1	1.4
India	0.4	0.4	1.0	2.1	2.1
Indonesia	1.0	1.4	1.1	2.4	2.3
Japan	0.2	0.9	1.3	1.1	0.8
Korea			1.9	2.2	1.4
Pakistan			1.7	2.5	3.2
Taiwan			2.2	3.0	1.7
Thailand	0.4	1.0	2.2	3.1	2.1
Africa					
Côte d'Ivoire				3.1	4.0
Ghana	0.9	0.9	2.0	3.4	2.7
Kenya				2.9	3.8
Morocco				2.6	2.5
Nigeria				2.5[a]	3.0[a]
South Africa			2.2	2.4	2.3
Tanzania				2.6	3.2

Source: Data derived from Table 2-4.

[a]With INED revisions (see note b to Table 2-4), these rates become 2.0 and 2.5, respectively.

The Asian sample is much more heterogeneous than any of the others. Its income spread in 1820 was rather narrow but since 1950 has widened very sharply and in 1989 was 27:1. The average income of the group has risen eightfold since 1820. Originally this group was poorer than the first three, but the average income is now above that in Latin America, and it contains one country, Japan, whose income has risen above the average for the advanced capitalist group.

The African group has the lowest income level. The average now is not very different from that of the capitalist core 120 years ago. The quality and quantity of evidence for this group are weaker than for all the others. The divergence in performance within the group is higher than in the first three groups but narrower than in Asia. The current spread of income within the group is about 12:1.

4. The pace of growth over the 17 decades has not been steady. In all areas and in all countries (except Bangladesh, Chile, and Ghana) the years between 1950 and 1973 were a golden age when the growth in real income per capita was much faster than ever recorded before. The acceleration was most marked in Asia and least so in Latin America and Africa. Since 1973 this growth has slackened appreciably in all areas except Asia, and in Africa, income actually declined (see Table 2-2 and Figure 2-2).

5. The in-group homogeneity of the long-run performance record suggests that the countries in each group had common institutional or policy characteristics that distinguished them from the members of the other groups. The universality of the

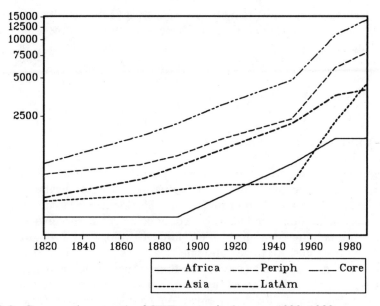

Figure 2-2. Comparative growth of GDP per capita by area, 1820–1989.

acceleration in the golden age does suggest, on the other hand, that there are some ecumenical influences powerful enough to have had a global effect. These forces generally originated in the first group and diffused their negative influences between 1913 and 1950 and their positive impact between 1950 and 1973.

6. The first group has provided "leadership" in productivity and technology for the past six centuries. Northern Italy and Flanders played this role from 1400 to 1600, the Netherlands from 1600 to 1820. Since 1820, there have been two successive "leaders." The United Kingdom had the highest level of labor productivity from 1820 to 1890, and the United States in the century since then.[5] To a significant degree, at least in the twentieth century, the lead country has determined the potential performance of the other countries. In most sectors of activity, the technical frontier has been in the United States. The other countries have been followers, and their performance over the past century has been substantially influenced by the diffusion of technology from the lead country.

7. Population growth in Western Europe has been modest over the long run. The long experience of declining mortality was matched by gradual reductions in fertility, although family tradition had already imposed constraints on fertility before the mortality rate began to fall. For several hundred years, Europe has had a later marriage age and a greater incidence of celibacy than Africa, Asia, or Latin America have had, and more widespread, checks on fertility within marriage. Australia, Canada, and the United States have had higher population growth because of their large-scale immigration and higher fertility, but their fertility is now low by Asian, African, or Latin American standards. In the European periphery, demographic growth has been near the West European range. With the exception of Japan, whose demographic experience lies within the European range, the Asian countries have had a much faster nat-

ural rate of increase since 1950 than Europe or Japan have ever had. The sharp decline in mortality, due to rising living standards, better sanitation, and the rapid impact of improved medical technology, was not matched by a falling fertility rate, though there was some decline after 1973. The significant demographic differences between the rich and poor countries have undoubtedly had some impact on their per-capita growth potential, though the relationship has not always been clear-cut.

Causal Analysis, Ultimate and Proximate

When assessing the reasons for nations' differing growth performance, one can operate at two levels: "ultimate" and "proximate" causality.[6] An investigation of ultimate causality involves consideration of institutions, ideologies, socioeconomic pressure groups, historical accidents, and national economic policy. It also involves consideration of the international economic "order," foreign ideologies or shocks from friendly or unfriendly neighbors. All these "ultimate" features are part of the historians' traditional domain (e.g., Gibbon on the Roman Empire) or sociologists (e.g., Max Weber on the Protestant ethic). They are virtually impossible to quantify, and thus there will always be legitimate scope for disagreement on what is important. However, it is a mistake to ignore causality at this level, particularly if one is tackling such a wide range of experience in time and space.[7] The serious problems that the Soviet Union and Eastern Europe have had in switching to capitalism have made it abundantly clear that the capitalist model is not simply a reliance on market forces but has a complex institutional underpinning.

"Proximate" areas of causality are those where measures and models have been developed by economists, econometricians, and statisticians.[8] Here the relative importance of different influences can be more readily assessed. At this level, one can derive significant insight from comparative macroeconomic performance accounts (i.e., growth accounts, level accounts, and acceleration and slowdown accounts; see Maddison 1987). The most difficult problem at the "proximate" level of explanation is analyzing the role of technical progress, which interacts in myriad ways with other items in the growth accounts.[9] Hence technical progress must be treated separately from other elements of proximate causality, because it is almost as difficult to quantify satisfactorily as are the elements of ultimate causality.

I have tried to illustrate the operation of ultimate causality in two major respects: (1) "institutional" features of advanced Western capitalist economies which enabled them to embark on modern economic growth and do better than the rest of the world and (2) the changes in policy and circumstance underlying the postwar acceleration of growth.

Socioinstitutional Basis for the Early Western Lead and Greater Dynamism Until 1950

The fact that the West established an early lead which reached such gigantic proportions by 1950 is due in part to distinctive socioinstitutional characteristics that the Western countries acquired gradually during the Renaissance and the Enlightenment.

The most fundamental of these was the recognition of human capacity to transform the forces of nature through rational investigation and experiment. By the seventeenth century, Western elites had abandoned superstition, magic, and submission to religious authority. The Western scientific tradition that underlies the modern approach to technical change and innovation had clearly emerged and impregnated the educational system. Circumscribed horizons were abandoned, and the quest for change and improvement was unleashed. This characteristic of the West is brought out clearly by David Landes (1969), who rightly contrasts this European spirit with that in Asian countries.

The ending of feudal constraints on the free purchase and sale of property was followed by a whole series of developments which gave scope for successful entrepreneurship. A nondiscretionary legal system protected property rights. The development of accountancy helped further in making contracts enforceable. State fiscal levies became more predictable and less arbitrary. The growth of trustworthy financial institutions and instruments provided access to credit and insurance, which made it easier to assess risk and to organize business rationally on a large scale over a wide area. Techniques of organization, management, and labor discipline were also improved.

A third distinctive feature of Western Europe was the emergence of a system of nation-states in close propinquity, which had significant trading relations and relatively easy intellectual interchange in spite of their linguistic and cultural differences. This stimulated competition and innovation. Migration to or refuge in a different culture and environment were options open to adventurous minds; printing presses and universities added to the ease of interchange.

The Western family system was different from that in other parts of the world. It involved controls over fertility and limited obligations to more distant kin, which reinforced the possibilities for accumulation.

Since 1820, the institutional arrangements of advanced capitalist countries have not stood still. The degree of democratic participation and the socioeconomic role of government have changed a good deal in ways that have generally been positive for growth. In the postwar period, interrelations between these countries have involved articulate cooperation and some rudiments of a managed international order. This, too, has been favorable to economic growth.

The European "periphery" has an institutional heritage which is not the same as those of the advanced European countries. There are quite separate kinds of periphery. In the east, Russian traditional institutions were as much Asian as European and were further differentiated from the Western model from 1917 onward by the advent of communism. The East European countries had dirigiste central planning imposed on them for more than 40 years. In the Czech and Hungarian cases, they were plucked from the advanced capitalist group to be put into the communist camp. Some other East European countries with lower incomes (Albania, Bulgaria, Greece, Romania, and Yugoslavia) were part of the Ottoman Empire until the nineteenth century and so were isolated from the West European mainstream. This was also true of Poland, most of which was part of Russia until 1918.

The Western European periphery consists mainly of the two Iberian countries. Spain and Portugal were institutionally different from the advanced capitalist group in their degree of religious bigotry, censorship, neglect of popular education, and fiscal irresponsibility. Their colonization policy in Latin America reordered indigenous institutions very much in their own image.

Although Latin America became independent in the 1820s, it retained many of the Iberian institutional characteristics. The Latin American heritage of peonage and slavery led to very wide disparities in income, wealth, and economic opportunity, with neglect of popular education, heavy-handed regulatory tendencies in government, and fiscal irresponsibility. The last characteristic has led to chronic inflation, which in the past decade has brought Latin America close to societal collapse.

Historically, the performance of the Asian and African countries has been hampered by two types of constraint. Indigenous institutions were less favorable to growth than those in the West and most of them were colonies of the West in ways which also hampered their development (see Maddison 1990a). By Western standards, all of these countries except Japan remained relatively stagnant until 1950.

In China, bureaucratic control and excessive respect for tradition impeded the emergence of a modern scientific approach and held back a civilization that had earlier shown greater promise than Europe's had. The Chinese experience in this respect is laid out in Needham's huge multivolume study (1954). The essentially defensive and static character of India's social institutions also exerted a depressive influence on growth potential (see Lal 1980 and Maddison 1971).

Within Asia, Japan was unique in its early mimicry of Western institutions in the Meiji reforms of 1867, and its growth performance is the most striking in our whole array of 43 countries. Its per-capita income level has risen twenty-six-fold since 1820 and is now well within the range of the advanced capitalist countries.

Policy and Circumstances Underlying Postwar Growth

The Capitalist Core

The postwar boom in Western Europe was not due to an acceleration of technical change but was to a large extent a catch-up phenomenon. Over several decades, European productivity had fallen behind that in the United States, which was the country closest to the frontiers of technology. However, there was no automaticity or inevitability about the catch-up. It did not happen after the first world war, and its importance after the second depended strongly on policy improvements. With the stimulus of Marshall aid and new forms of international cooperation, liberal policies were reapplied to international trade, and international capital markets were reopened. High levels of domestic demand promoted full employment, better internal resource allocation and led to an unparalleled investment boom. This European boom—together with enlightened international economic policy in the United States, the abandonment of colonialism, and its replacement by aid programs—was basically responsible for the worldwide diffusion of the postwar golden age.

The long postwar boom in Europe was due, in large part, to the exploitation of once-for-all opportunities that had been missed earlier because of two world wars and the protectionist, dirigiste, and otherwise defensive policies of the interwar years.[10] The boom was biggest in those countries that had suffered most from these policies. By the end of the boom, the productivity gap between the advanced European countries and the United States had been considerably reduced. There was a convergence in levels of per-capita income and productivity that was normal for countries with close cooperation, similar institutions, similar human capital, and convergent economic policies. If there had indeed been a postwar acceleration of technical progress, one would have expected the postwar supergrowth in the advanced European countries to continue. But the fact that there was no postwar acceleration in productivity growth in the United States—the frontier country—meant that the advanced European countries would eventually reach a point at which the payoff for such high levels of investment was bound to falter.

The slowdown after 1973 was quite general and quite sharp. It did not simply reflect a gradual erosion of supergrowth possibilities. Its sharpness was due to three closely clustered and interactive developments that forced major changes in policy: the acceleration of the inflationary momentum that accompanied the prolonged boom, the collapse of the postwar monetary order—the dollar-based, fixed exchange-rate system established at Bretton Woods—and the OPEC shocks. By any reasonable accounting, the most sophisticated governments could be expected to lose output when dealing with these shocks in such open economies, because they involved new risks and transition problems in devising and learning to use new policy weapons, such as floating exchange rates. This was equally true of entrepreneurial and trade union decision makers whose reactions significantly affect macroeconomic outcomes.

Another influence that reinforced the sharpness of the slowdown was the basic change in the "establishment view" of economic policy objectives. The new consensus emerged as a response to events, but it also helped mold them. The shock of inflation, the new wave of payments problems, and speculative possibilities brought a profound switch away from Keynesian type attitudes toward demand management and full employment. Most countries gave overriding priority to combating inflation and safeguarding the balance of payments. Unemployment was allowed to rise to prewar levels. Even when oil prices collapsed and the momentum of world inflation was broken in the early 1980s, the new orthodoxy continued to stress the dangers of expansionary policy in spite of widespread unemployment and strong payments positions. It looked to a self-starting recovery rather than one induced by policy. A further reason for the cautiousness of policy compared with that of the golden age is the greater vulnerability to speculative capital movements in a world without exchange controls, and a dichotomous monetary order—the precariously frozen parities of European countries within the European monetary system, on the one hand, and the floaters (the United States and Japan), on the other.

The European Periphery

The postwar growth acceleration in the "capitalist" part of the European periphery had much the same causes as in the European core, but the results were better, partly because the starting point was lower and partly because the degree of institutional modernization was bigger. These economies benefited greatly from their proximity to the European core, which provided them with booming export markets and very large earnings from tourism and emigrants' remittances. More recently they have received large grant aid from the European community.

The sharp slowdown after 1973 was due to some of the same reasons as that in the core, and the close integration of the European economies meant that the periphery felt the full retarding influence of the slowdown in the core. The peripheral countries had even bigger problems in controlling inflation and dealing with payments disequilibria than did the core.

The performance of the communist economies is less well documented than that of OECD countries. Their own yardsticks for measuring growth and levels of performance have hitherto differed from those in the West. We have had to rely on the skill of Kremlinologists for measures of performance comparable in kind to those we use for OECD countries, and the CIA growth estimates (which I use here) have now come under challenge for exaggerating growth and levels of performance.[11] The communist countries did not benefit from the Marshall Plan and were relatively isolated from the new liberalism in the world economy. The acceleration in their growth involved a government effort to mobilize very high rates of investment. The poorer results were due to less efficient resource allocation, greater diversion of resources to military spending, and the deleterious effect of censorship and thought control on processes of innovation.

After 1973, the performance of these economies deteriorated sharply. Their slowdown was influenced to some extent by that of the capitalist countries, but it also reflected the increasing problems of running a command economy efficiently at increasingly sophisticated levels of demand. More recently (since 1989, when our tables end) they have fallen into a condition of deep crisis with some similarities to the Latin American situation (hyperinflation, fiscal crisis, indebtedness), plus the unprecedented problems of switching from a command to a market economy, dismantling the old apparatus of power (party, secret police, armed forces, and administration), and privatizing economies in which virtually all assets belonged to the state.

Latin America

Between 1913 and 1950, the Latin American countries performed very well compared with most of the rest of the world. They did not suffer significantly from the two world wars, and they offset the effects of the 1930s depression by successful import substitution and industrialization. In the early postwar years they had advantageous terms of trade.

Because they had no wartime backlogs to make good, were fairly content with the dirigiste and corporative policies of the 1930s and 1940s, and were not influenced by the liberalism that went with the Marshall Plan, Latin American countries chose to remain fairly isolated from the world economy for a fairly long time after the war. They did not have a postwar golden age. Although their experience between 1950 and 1973 was better in per-capita terms than that before 1950, it was not on the scale seen in Europe and Asia.

Latin American growth did not deteriorate sharply in 1973 as did that of the capitalist core, and Latin America generally did not react with the same caution as did most of the world to the OPEC shocks. The governments felt they could accommodate high rates of inflation, and they were able to borrow on a large scale to cover payments deficits incurred as a result of their expansionary policies. The crunch came in the

1980s, after the Mexican suspension of debt service, when their supply of new foreign funds dried up and service costs of existing debt soared because of rising interest rates. Since 1982 most of Latin America has had negative real income growth.

The dramatic Latin American slowdown was not caused by a sudden drying up of supply potential or by any unfairness in the operation of the international economy. Rather, it was the result of misguided domestic policies. The Latin American economies suffer from four basic problems:

1. *Heavy foreign debt.* Amortization payments generally stopped, but interest payments are a very heavy burden for the balance of payments and governmental budgets. The bleak outlook here led to major capital flight and undermined the governments' domestic and international creditworthiness.
2. *Fiscal crisis.* Governments find it very difficult to maintain revenues or borrow.
3. *Hyperinflation* and the exhaustion of a whole menu of heterodox methods of dealing with it.
4. *Distortions in resource allocation* due initially to excessive government intervention and protectionism, which were further complicated by hyperinflation.

Asia

The great postwar acceleration in Asian growth can be traced to several influences:

1. The rise to power of new national elites, and the development of an indigenous capitalist class willing to keep their savings at home and free to pursue their own interests.
2. Virtually all the Asian countries followed the advice of development economists like Arthur Lewis, Walt Rostow, and Paul Rosenstein Rodan in mounting a big push in investment rates and an even bigger acceleration in the growth of capital stock.
3. They also followed the advice of Theodore Schultz to improve human capital. In 1950 their educational stock was a quarter of that in Europe, but it has grown prodigiously and, in some of the supergrowth countries, is now close to European levels.
4. The colonial drain was replaced by a new inflow of foreign capital and aid. In prewar years Asia had big trade surpluses, which have now become deficits. Between 1913 and 1938, the average Asian ratio of exports to imports was 1.22, whereas between 1950 and 1986 it was .85.
5. The postwar period was one of buoyant world trade, thanks to the faster growth in the capitalist core and the reduction of trade barriers. Many Asian countries, particularly those with supergrowth, took advantage of those new trade outlets by remaining competitive and aggressively seeking new markets. The opening up of their economies improved their efficiency and facilitated their growth.
6. Many of the Asian countries have had high per-capita labor inputs, with working years much higher than those in other parts of the world.

7. Finally, Asian countries were able to get a large catch-up bonus because their starting levels of productivity were so low and they were so far from the productivity frontier.

The continuation of the Asian countries' fast growth since 1973 (except in Japan, which is the nearest to the productivity frontier) makes one realize that there were other elements in their menu of progrowth policies whose importance was not so obvious in the golden age. These Asian characteristics now stand out more clearly because they were so lacking in Latin America.

8. Inflation was actually better controlled in the Asian countries after 1973 than between 1950 and 1973. Their average annual rate of price increase dropped from 17 percent a year between 1950 and 1973 to 11 percent between 1973 and 1982, and 6 percent between 1982 and 1987. In Latin America, by contrast, inflation accelerated from an average of 21 percent a year to 110 percent between 1973 and 1982 and 122 percent a year between 1982 and 1987.
9. The fiscal and monetary policies of the Asian countries were generally more prudent than those of the Latin American countries.
10. The Asian countries' foreign borrowing was more judicious. On a per-capita basis their borrowing averaged only a third of that of Latin America, and so with the exception of the Philippines, they remained creditworthy and did not face the crunch that hit Latin America in the 1980s. Furthermore, less of their debt to commercial bank lenders was incurred on a floating-rate basis.
11. They generally maintained their export competitiveness.
12. Most of the conunrties' economies had more flexible wage and price structures than did those of the capitalist core or Latin America.

It is the combination of these macropolicy virtues with continuing catch-up possibilities that has been the basis of Asian success since 1973. It should also be remembered that the Asian countries generally do not have as extreme inequalities in income and wealth as do the Latin American countries. This fact probably gave them greater sociopolitical coherence and meant that they were less subject to short-term vagaries in populist policies.

In terms of more proximate growth accounting there is nothing mysterious or miraculous in the postwar Asian experience (see Maddison 1989 for the relevant growth accounts). Asian growth has required fast-growing labor and capital inputs. Except for Japan, total factor productivity even in the supergrowth countries was not out of line with that of some of the European countries in the golden age, and this has been true since 1973 (see Maddison 1989).

Africa

In the postwar golden age, economic growth in Africa was much slower than in any other major world area. In the slowdown since 1973, their average incomes have actually fallen (see Table 2-2). African countries were the last to emerge from colonialism, and their education, health, and infrastructure are very poor. Their populations are growing twelve times as fast as those in the advanced capitalist countries of Europe are, and they are still accelerating. Another major problem is the newness of the nation-states whose rulers have often tried to forge a national unity by creating one-party regimes. This has reinforced a tendency for dirigisme that has led to big market distortions, artificial exchange rates, and policies harmful to agriculture. It was also a major barrier to corrective changes in policy. Sub-Saharan Africa has already received much foreign aid, and it is likely that it will continue, but a real turnaround in growth prospects will depend heavily on changes in domestic policy.

Proximate Influences on Economic Performance

We can now turn to proximate growth causality, an area that has attracted more precise technocratic analysis, because the important elements can be more readily measured. The degree to which they can be accurately measured leaves a good deal to be desired, however, and it should be stressed that these proximate influences are not independent of what I have called ultimate causes. Rather, to a significant degree they are dimensions through which ultimate causes can be seen to operate.

Table 2-6 compares the major characteristics that generally figure in growth accounts. We concentrate on a 1989 cross-section view and try to see what we can deduce about causality from this in an illustrative way. It would, of course, be useful to be more rigorous and to have all these indicators on a historical basis as well, but this is too big an exercise for this chapter.

Table 2-6. Comparative Characteristics of Economic Performance Near 1989 (U.S.A. = 100)

	Level of GDP per Capita	Labor Input per Capita	GDP per Hour Worked	Education per Capita	Land Area per Capita	Gross Capital Stock per Capita	Exports per Capita	Scale of Economy
Austria	68.5	91.2	75.1		29.6	106.2	286.5	2.1
Belgium	70.4	79.5	88.6	84.9	8.7	80.8	663.2	2.8
Denmark	75.6	114.2	66.2	78.1	22.6	89.9	374.6	1.6
Finland	76.7	109.8	69.9		166.6	110.9	321.1	1.5
France	76.3	80.1	95.3	84.7	26.6	90.8	218.5	17.2
Germany	75.2	95.4	78.8	70.9	10.6	101.7	376.5	18.8
Italy	71.0	88.2	80.5	59.1	13.9	79.3	167.1	16.4
Netherlands	69.3	75.0	92.4	73.2	6.3	81.1	503.0	4.1
Norway	83.2	100.1	83.1	77.6	197.3	154.5	437.8	1.4
Sweden	81.1	100.5	80.7	77.8	132.6	88.6	417.8	2.8
United Kingdom	73.9	91.0	81.2	79.8	11.4	69.9	182.1	17.0
Australia	74.1	95.5	77.6		1,231.8	91.1	153.3	5.0
Canada	94.3	103.5	91.1	84.7	954.6	102.0	313.3	10.0
United States	100.0	100.0	100.0	100.0	100.0	100.0	100.0	100.0
Czechoslovakia	46.7	124.3	37.6		21.7		63.2	2.9
Greece	41.4	87.3	47.4	61.2	35.3		51.4	1.7

Table 2-6. Comparative Characteristics of Economic Performance Near 1989
(U.S.A. = 100) (*continued*)

	Level of GDP per Capita	Labor Input per Capita	GDP per Hour Worked	Education per Capita	Land Area per Capita	Gross Capital Stock per Capita	Exports per Capita	Scale of Economy
Hungary	36.8	111.4	33.0		23.6		65.0	1.6
Ireland	45.3	69.6	65.1		53.3		402.2	0.6
Portugal	40.4	98.0	41.2	48.3	25.5	34.3	89.3	1.6
Spain	55.1	78.5	70.2	57.4	34.8	51.7	78.1	8.7
Soviet Union	38.1	123.9	30.8	68.1	209.5		25.7	44.5
Argentina	22.3	86.1	25.9	59.3	233.2	19.5	20.5	2.9
Brazil	24.1	100.1	24.1	36.8	155.7	25.5	15.9	14.4
Chile	29.6	73.4	40.3	61.6	157.1	17.4	43.2	1.5
Colombia	21.8	77.0	28.3	39.4	87.2		12.1	2.8
Mexico	20.4	73.4	27.8	46.3	62.0	21.8	18.7	7.0
Peru	14.2	82.5	17.2		164.4		11.3	1.2
Bangladesh	3.0	82.6	3.6		3.5		0.8	1.3
China	13.9	140.2	9.9	37.2	22.8		3.3	61.9
India	6.0	115.9	5.1	25.9	10.1		1.4	19.6
Indonesia	9.8	109.3	8.9		27.4	5.0	8.5	7.0
Japan	83.9	129.9	64.6	83.1	8.4	92.2	152.2	41.5
Korea	35.6	131.1	27.2	78.3	6.3	23.7	99.5	6.1
Pakistan	7.0	87.0	8.1		19.0		2.9	3.1
Taiwan	39.7	157.8	25.2	87.4	4.9	28.1	173.2	3.2
Thailand	21.9	145.2	15.1		25.0		24.8	4.9
Côte d'Ivoire	7.7	70.3	11.0		73.6		16.1	0.4
Ghana	3.1	71.6	4.3		43.2		3.6	0.2
Kenya	4.8	75.7	6.4		66.6		2.9	0.5
Morocco	10.1	57.2	17.6		49.5		9.2	1.0
Nigeria	4.5	67.7	6.6		21.7		4.7	2.1
South Africa	30.8	64.5	47.8		94.8		43.5	4.3
Tanzania	2.5	89.6	2.8		97.3		0.8	0.3

Source: Column 1 from Table 2-1, Column 2 from Table 2-8, Column 3 from Columns 1 and 2, Column 4 from Table 2-9, Column 5 from Table 2-7. The estimates of capital stock in Column 6 were made by cumulating investment at constant national prices for 30 years and converting it to 1985 dollars at U.S. relative prices, using same sources for investment as for the GDP estimates in Table 2-1. This measure of capital stock is very rough indeed compared with the estimates cited in Table 2-10. Exports were taken from IMF, *International Financial Statistics,* February 1992. Scale of economy was derived from Tables 2-1 and 2-4.

    I deal first with the role of the traditional factors of production, land, labor, and capital and then turn to influences on the efficiency with which they are used, that is, the degree of openness to international trade and economies of scale.

Natural Resource Endowment per Capita

In the early literature on economic growth, and particularly in the work of Thomas Malthus, the fixed character of natural resources was regarded as a major constraint that would ultimately result in a stationary state because of population pressure. Natural resource constraints have also been strongly emphasized by military thinkers, who regard them as an important problem in wartime when foreign trade is difficult.

No measures of aggregate natural resources are available, and as a crude proxy, Table 2-7 shows the comparative endowment of land per capita. Within our 43 countries, there is a very wide dispersion of land availability. Australia is the most favored with nearly 350 times as much per capita as Bangladesh, which has the poorest endowment. However, there is no discernible relationship between contemporary incomes per capita and natural resources per capita. Australia is 150 times better endowed than Japan is, but it has a lower per-capita GDP. The Netherlands has 0.23 hectares per capita, but it also has an extremely high labor productivity in agriculture, closer to that of the United States than any of the other advanced countries. Argentina has 46 times as much land per person as Taiwan does, but its per-capita product is half that of Taiwan. It is clear (see Figure 2-3), therefore, that in contemporary circumstances, natural resource endowment has a negligible effect on the growth potential of different nations, and the inexorable decline in the ratio between resources and population has little effect on contemporary per-capita growth performance. This does not mean, however, that we can ignore the historical role of natural resources, which were in fact influential in fostering the early dynamism of the United States and Australia.

Table 2-7. Land Area per Capita in 1989
(hectares per capita)

Capitalist core		Latin America	
Austria	1.09	Argentina	8.58
Belgium	.32	Brazil	5.73
Denmark	.83	Chile	5.78
Finland	6.13	Colombia	3.21
France	.98	Mexico	2.28
Germany	.39	Peru	6.05
Italy	.51	*Asia*	
Netherlands	.23		
Norway	7.26	Bangladesh	.13
Sweden	4.88	China	.84
United Kingdom	.42	India	.37
		Indonesia	1.01
Australia	45.33	Japan	.31
Canada	35.13	Korea	.23
United States	3.68	Pakistan	.70
		Taiwan	.18
European periphery		Thailand	.92
Czechoslovakia	.80		
Greece	1.30	*Africa*	
Hungary	.87	Côte d'Ivoire	2.71
Ireland	1.96	Ghana	1.59
Portugal	.94	Kenya	2.45
Spain	1.28	Morocco	1.82
Soviet Union	7.71	Nigeria	.80
		South Africa	3.49
		Tanzania	3.58

Source: Land area from FAO, *Production Yearbook,* Rome 1988. Population from Table 2-4.

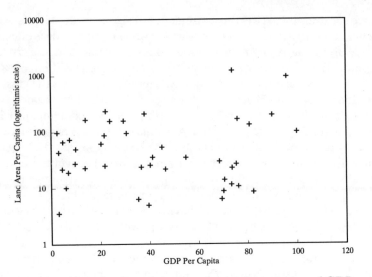

Figure 2-3. Relationship between endowment of natural resources and GDP per capita in 1989 (43 countries).

Labor Input per Capita (Raw Labor Input)

There is a significant variation in labor input per capita (though the intercountry variance in this characteristic is modest compared with that for the other characteristics shown in Table 2-6). This measure is rough even for the advanced countries, which have regular labor force surveys, but whose statistics on working hours are of varying quality. The lower down we go in the income scale, the worse the quality of the information is. However, the figures are robust enough to demonstrate that the advanced capitalist countries, the communist countries, Japan, Korea, and Taiwan have a much higher proportion of employed people than is the norm elsewhere. To some extent these variations in activity rates are a reflection of social institutions (with regard to female employment) or of deliberate policy to promote participation (e.g., in the communist countries), but a predominant influence is simply the age structure of the population as a result of demographic trends.

The demographic pattern in Europe and Japan increases the relative size of the active population by reducing the proportion of children and freeing women to enter the labor force. Thus in Japan 20 percent of the population are children under the age of 15, which is about half the share in the Third World, and about 40 percent of the labor force are women, compared with under 30 percent in the Third World. As a result, about half the Japanese population are employed, compared with 29 percent in Mexico, which is the extreme case of low activity rates. These differences in demographic structure and labor force activity help explain why Japan can save such a high proportion of its income, why a greater proportion of investment can go to capital deepening rather than providing for social infrastructure and capital widening, and why it can afford to educate its population so well.

The other dimension of labor input is the number of hours worked by those who are economically active. Not many countries have effective surveys of working hours for the whole economy, but one can get a reasonable representation of the situation in the advanced countries as well as the three Asian countries with the most rapid growth—Japan, Korea, and Taiwan. These figures demonstrate unequivocally that these three Asian countries have much longer working hours than does the capitalist core. It also seems that this is true of most Asian countries. For Africa, there is no real evidence on working hours, and so I have simply assumed that they are lower than elsewhere.

When we combine the two elements of labor input to get the average labor input per capita, there is a large variation, from 1,188 in Taiwan to 431 in Morocco, that is, a range of 2.8:1.

The estimates of hours in Table 2-8 have been used in conjunction with the per-capita GDP figures of Table 2-1 to produce the estimates of labor productivity.

Table 2-8. Labor Input per Capita, 1987

	Proportion of Population Employed	Average Annual Number of Hours per Person Employed	Annual Number of Hours Worked per Capita
Capitalist core			
Austria	43.0	1,595	687
Belgium	37.0	1,620	599
Denmark	51.6	1,669	860
Finland	49.7	1,663	827
France	39.1	1,543	603
Germany	44.3	1,620	718
Italy	43.5	1,528	664
Netherlands	40.8	1,387	565
Norway	50.8	1,486	754
Sweden	51.6	1,466	757
United Kingdom	44.0	1,557	685
Australia	44.1	1,631	719
Canada	46.6	1,673	779
United States	46.8	1,608	753
European periphery			
Czechoslovakia	49.9	1,875	936
Greece	36.5	1,800	657
Hungary	48.5	1,730	839
Ireland	30.8	1,700	524
Portugal	43.4	1,700	738
Spain	31.1	1,900	591
Soviet Union	52.1	1,791	933
Latin America			
Argentina	34.1	1,900	648
Brazil	39.7	1,900	754
Chile	29.1	1,900	553
Colombia	30.5	1,900	580

Table 2-8. Labor Input per Capita, 1987 (*continued*)

	Proportion of Population Employed	Average Annual Number of Hours per Person Employed	Annual Number of Hours Worked per Capita
Mexico	29.1	1,900	553
Peru	32.7	1,900	621
Asia			
Bangladesh	28.3	(2,200)	622
China	48.0	(2,200)	1,056
India	39.7	(2,200)	873
Indonesia	37.4	(2,200)	823
Japan	48.4	2,020	978
Korea	38.4	2,570	987
Pakistan	29.8	(2,200)	655
Taiwan	47.5	2,500	1,188
Thailand	49.7	(2,200)	1,093
Africa			
Côte d'Ivoire	37.8	1,400	529
Ghana	38.5	1,400	539
Kenya	40.7	1,400	570
Morocco	30.8	1,400	431
Nigeria	36.4	1,400	510
South Africa	34.7	1,400	486
Tanzania	48.2	1,400	675

Source: A. Maddison 1989 and 1991, ILO, and national sources. For the African countries, the employment ratios are in fact ratios of labor force to population as recorded in World Bank, *Social Indicators of Development 1989* (Baltimore: Johns Hopkins University Press, 1989), and the figures on working hours are a guess. For the first 14 countries and Japan, the figures refer to 1987 and for the other countries, to 1986.

Education and Skills per Capita

A significant characteristic of the advanced capitalist countries is the effort they have made over the long run to raise the level of education of their populations. In 1820, their average education level[12] for both sexes combined was probably about 2 years, and by 1989 this figure had risen about sevenfold (see Table 2-9). Furthermore, education is now more evenly spread, thanks to universal attendance in the primary and some of the secondary school years.

The higher the average level of education is, the easier it is for a working population to understand and apply the fruits of technical progress (see Figure 2-4). It is difficult to be at all precise about the impact of rising educational standards on productivity, but most growth analysts consider it to have been substantial, and levels of education have a significant positive relationship to the economic distance betewen nations. Within the advanced countries, differences in income and levels of education are now not too large by international standards, but the lead country, the United States, has a clear lead over the rest. The educational gap between the rich and the

Table 2-9. Levels of Formal Education per Person Aged
15 and Over, 1913–87
(average for both sexes, in equivalent years of primary
education)

	1913	1950	1987
Belgium	n.a.	9.85	14.34
Denmark	n.a.	10.44	13.19
France	6.99	9.58	14.31
Germany	8.37	10.40	11.97
Italy	n.a.	5.49	9.99
Netherlands	6.42	8.12	12.37
Norway	n.a.	8.44	13.10
Sweden			13.14
United Kingdom	8.12	10.84	13.47
Canada	n.a.	9.84	14.31
United States	7.86	11.27	16.89
Soviet Union	n.a.	4.10	11.50
Greece		4.16	10.34
Portugal	n.a.	2.49	8.15
Spain	n.a.	4.76	9.69
Argentina	n.a.	4.80	10.01
Brazil	n.a.	2.05	6.22
Chile	n.a.	6.09	10.41
Colombia		3.93	6.65
Mexico	n.a.	2.60	7.82
China	n.a.	2.20	6.28
India	n.a.	1.35	4.38
Japan	5.36	9.11	14.04
Korea	n.a.	3.36	13.22
Taiwan	n.a.	3.62	14.76

Source: See sources cited in Maddison 1989, p. 136. Primary education is
given a weight of 1, secondary 1.4, and higher 2.

poorer countries of the world is significant (even though the divergence is smaller than
for some other characteristics). In Asia, the link among education, real income levels,
and rates of growth is also striking, with India being the worst off and Taiwan, Japan,
and Korea in the lead. In 1950, the average educational levels in India were well below
those in Europe in 1820, as were its income and productivity levels. In the poorer
countries some people never go to school, and many drop out very early, so that these
countries' dispersion around the averages in Table 2-9 is greater than that of the
advanced countries. In addition, the quality of education is generally worse in the
poorer countries.

Physical Capital Stocks and Level of Investment

A necessary condition for exploiting the possibilities offered by technical progress is
an increase in the stock of machinery and equipment in which this technology is
embodied, and in the buildings and infrastructure in which they operate. There is a

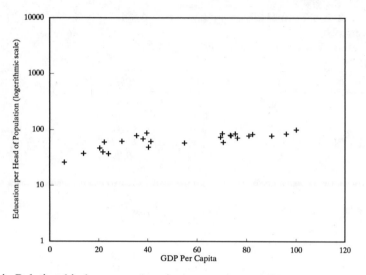

Figure 2-4. Relationship between education per capita and GDP per capita in 1989 (25 countries).

clear positive relationship between the level of GDP per capita and the level of capital stock: It is stronger than for the other inputs we have considered (compare Figure 2-5 with Figures 2-3 and 2-4).

All the advanced countries of Group 1 have accumulated huge stocks of physical capital. In the lead country, the United States, the capital stock has, until recently, been much higher per capita than in the other advanced countries, which have had lower productivity levels. This characteristic of the U.S. economy has been clearly discernible since it took over as the lead country in around 1890 (see Tables 2-10 and 2-11).

Over time there has been a rise in the capital output ratio in the advanced capitalist countries other than the United States, with the most marked rise in Japan, the country whose growth was fastest. This can be seen clearly in Table 2-12, which shows the sharp long-term rise in the capital output ratio in Japan compared with its relative

Table 2-10. Gross Fixed Nonresidential Capital Stock per Capita for Selected Countries, 1820–1989 (at 1985 U.S. relative prices)

	1820	1890	1913	1950	1973	1989
France	n.a.	n.a.	n.a.	6,861	17,925	33,210
Germany	n.a.	n.a.	n.a.	7,410	24,672	41,500
Japan	n.a.	568	1,068	2,994	17,373	44,064
Netherlands	n.a.	n.a.	n.a.	11,502	24,262	34,213
United Kingdom	1,203	3,399[a]	4,243	6,038	17,010	27,174
United States	1,016	8,221	14,421	19,438	28,999	40,913

Source: Maddison 1992c.

[a] 1891.

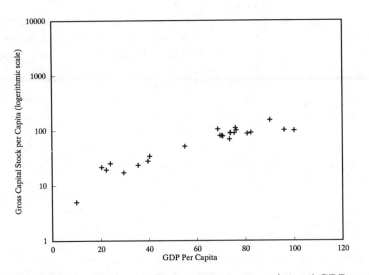

Figure 2-5. Relationship between gross capital stock per capita and GDP per capita in 1989 (24 countries).

Table 2-11. Rate of Growth of Gross Fixed Nonresidential Capital Stock per Capita, 1820–1989
(annual average compound growth rate)

	1820–90	1890–1913	1913–50	1950–73	1973–89
France				4.3	3.9
Germany				5.4	3.3
Japan		2.8	2.8	7.9	6.0
Netherlands				3.3	2.2
United Kingdom	1.5	1.0	1.0	4.6	3.0
United States	3.1	2.3	0.8	1.8	2.2

Source: Maddison 1992c.

Table 2-12. Ratio of Gross Nonresidential Fixed Capital Stock to GDP, 1820–1989
(at 1985 U.S. relative prices)

	1820	1890	1913	1950	1973	1989
France	n.a.	n.a.	n.a.	1.64	1.73	2.38
Germany	n.a.	n.a.	n.a.	2.24	2.44	3.01
Japan	n.a.	0.74	0.93	1.85	1.82	2.87
Netherlands	n.a.	n.a.	n.a.	2.44	2.36	2.70
United Kingdom	0.86	1.05	1.06	1.06	1.69	2.01
United States	0.83	2.77	2.96	2.26	2.06	2.24

Source: Maddison 1992c.

stability in the United States. This intensified capitalization of the economy is a characteristic of countries engaged in the process of catch-up. It also applied to the United
States when it was overtaking the United Kingdom as leader. But in the lead country,
which is the closest to the frontier of technology, capitalization cannot be sharply
increased without running into diminishing returns.

The information on the developing countries' capital stocks is more rudimentary
than that on the advanced countries, because their construction requires very long
series of investment data, and it is more difficult to estimate differences in the relative
price of investment goods. There is nothing in this past history of capital formation,
however, to suggest that fast growth can be attained without a major effort to sustain
high rates of capital formation.

Structural Change

Economic growth has been accompanied by massive changes in economic structure
whose long-term pattern has been similar in most countries. There has been a steady
decline in the share of agriculture in employment and value, and a rise in the share of
services, which was sharpest in countries with the highest income levels. Industry has
shown a bell-shaped pattern of development, with an increasing share as incomes rose
in the nineteenth and twentieth centuries and a fall in the advanced capitalist countries
in the past two decades (see Table 2-13).

Levels of labor productivity are generally much lower in agriculture than in the
rest of the economy, so some analysts treat the structural changes as an independent
source of growth due to improved resource allocation. But, it is necessary to treat the
role of structural change with caution, as many of the apparent gains from resource
reallocation are in fact due to increased inputs of physical and human capital in the
nonagricultural sectors.

Table 2-13. Long-Term Changes in the Structure of Employment and Output
(percentages of total employment and GDP)

	Employment			Value Added		
	Agriculture	Industry	Services	Agriculture	Industry	Services
	OECD countries					
1870	49	27	24	39	26	35
1950	25	36	39	15	41	44
1987	6	30	64	4	36	60
	Latin America					
1950	50	22	28	23	30	47
1986	24	28	48	11	38	51
	Asia					
1950	73	8	19	49	15	36
1986	57[a]	17[a]	26[a]	25	34	41

Source: A. Maddison, *The World Economy in the Twentieth Century* (Paris: OECD, 1989), p. 20.
[a]1980.

Structural changes reflect two basic forces that operate in all the countries when they reach successively higher levels of real income and productivity. The first of these is the elasticity of demand for particular products, which has been similar at given levels of income (particularly as relative price structures have moved in a similar direction). These demand forces have reduced the share of agricultural products in consumption and have raised the demand for the products of industry and services. The second force is the various sectors' differing pace of technological advance. Productivity growth has been slower in many services than commodity production has been, partly because of the intrinsic character of many personal services and partly because of measurement conventions that exclude the possibility of productivity growth in some services. Structural change has also been affected by other influences such as the size of government activity, the share and pattern of foreign trade, the rate of investment, and natural resource endowments and their rate of depletion (see Maddison 1980).

Foreign Trade

There are many ways in which nations interact with one another, and their degree of openness has an important impact on their growth potential. The main ways in which they interact are through the exchange of goods and services, migration of people, exchange of ideas and skills or tourism, and movements of capital, private or public. Foreign contacts and foreign trade are a major source of new technology, and they help determine the degree of economic specialization and economic structure, particularly for the follower countries. The state of the world economy also affects the level of demand, the rate of inflation, and fashions in economic policy. Although we cannot consider here the impact of all these external influences on growth, we can note some basic facts about the relationship of trade and growth of real income.

Over the long run, trade has grown faster than output, but the impact has varied over time. For instance, 1913 to 1950 was a period of neomercantilism, with the blockades imposed during the two world wars and the discriminatory policies, higher tariffs, quantitative restrictions, exchange controls, and other autarkic measures sparked off by the world depression of 1929–32.

After the second World War, the golden age was characterized by a revival of liberalism in commercial policy that was concentrated in the advanced countries but had

Table 2-14. Comparative Size of Manufacturing Plants in Six Advanced Capitalist Countries Around 1987 (number of persons engaged)

	France 1988	Germany 1987	Japan 1987	Netherlands 1985	United Kingdom 1988	United States 1987
Average size	19	30	16	34	30	49
Median size	146	318	166	254	240	263

Source: B. van Ark, "International Comparisons of Output and Productivity" (Ph.D. diss., University of Groningen, 1993), Table 6.6. Plant is a somewhat narrower definition than establishment. Plant is a local unit at a single postal address. Median is defined here in relation to total manufacturing employment. Half the employees are in smaller plants than the median, half in plants above that size.

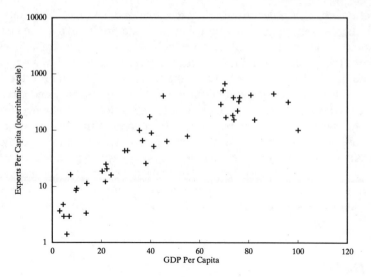

Figure 2-6. Relationship of exports per capita and GDP per capita in 1989 (43 countries).

worldwide effects in those countries that chose to benefit from the opportunity. Some of this growth-stimulating impact faded after 1973, as the effect of trade liberalization was absorbed, but international trade has continued to rise faster than output and has contributed to growth. Figure 2-6 shows the relationship between exports per capita and GDP per capita in 1989. Compared with some of the other characteristics, the positive relationship is rather strong.

Economies of Scale

There is a very wide range (500:1) in the size of our 43 economies, but there is no significant relationship between their size and their per-capita income performance (see Figure 2-7). Some small economies, like those of Norway and Sweden, have much higher per-capita incomes than large economies, like those of the Soviet Union or China. Most of the benefits of specialization and scale can be obtained by small countries through international trade.

In fact, the average size of productive establishments in advanced capitalist countries is much smaller than is often imagined (see Tables 2-14 and 2-15). In the private sector of the U.S. economy, there were 5.8 million establishments in 1986, and on average they employed 14 people; manufacturing had the largest establishments, with an average employment of 54 persons. The median size is much bigger than the average. In 1987 the median U.S. manufacturing plant employed 263 people (half those employed worked in bigger plants, and half worked in smaller plants). The median size of a U.S. plant was only marginally different from that in the Netherlands and the United Kingdom, and it was smaller than that in Germany. There is thus little evidence that big countries have much of a scale advantage, and again, small countries

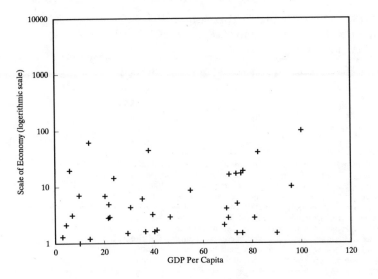

Figure 2-7. Relationship between size of economy and GDP per capita in 1989 (43 countries).

can get most of the benefits of specialization between firms through international trade.

Between 1899 and 1986 the average U.S. manufacturing establishment rose in size from 24 to 54 employees (see Table 2-16). The rise in median size may well have been bigger, although there is little evidence in these numbers that scale economies played more than a modest role in U.S. productivity. The United States' GDP per person employed rose almost fourfold between 1900 and 1989; the proportion of people with higher education rose ninefold; and the stock of machinery and equipment per person employed rose about fifteenfold. It is not easy to give a summary statistic on research activity, but according to the evidence presented in Mowery and Rosenberg (1989), it seems likely that it rose as fast proportionately as did inputs of machinery and equipment. Despite this evidence, many authors, for example, Kaldor and

Table 2-15. Average Number of Establishments, Employees, and Employees per Establishment in the United States in 1986

	Agriculture	Contract Construction	Private Services	Transportation	Mining	Manufacturing	Total
Establishments (thousands)	68	492	41,960	210	35	355	5,807
Employees (thousands)	412	4,659	55,524	4,884	847	19,142	83,380
Employees per establishment	6.1	9.5	13.2	23.3	24.2	53.9	14.4

Source: U.S. Department of Commerce, *Statistical Abstract of the United States 1989* (Washington DC: U.S. Government Printing Office, 1989), p. 523.

Table 2-16. Average Number of Establishments,
Employees, and Number of Employees per Establishment
in U.S. Manufacturing, 1899–1986

	Employees	*Establishments*	*Employees*
1986	53.9	355	19,142
1980	66.3	319	21,185
1950	55.6	260	14,467
1929	46.7	207	9,660
1899	23.7	205	4,850

Source: Data for 1980 and 1986 are the same as for Table 2-15; data for 1899
to 1950 from *Historical Statistics of the United States: Colonial Times to
1970, Part 2* (Washington, DC: U.S. Government Printing Office, 1975), p.
666. The rise in the size of establishments between 1899 and 1929 is exaggerated because the cutoff point for inclusion in the census was raised in 1921
from annual shipments of $500 to $5,000. This source also gives figures for
1840–99 that suggest that the average establishment size rose by about 28
percent between those dates. Note that there was a substantial rise in the
share of administrative and supervisory personnel. In 1899 "nonproduc-
tion" workers made up 7 percent of the total, and in 1970 this had risen to
25 percent.

Chandler, have held scale economies to be of major importance, though they usually
mix up scale economies with other influences.

Alfred Chandler (1990) argues that the growth of large multiunit firms has been
the major force underlying economic growth in the United States and that the greater
degree of corporativeness in the USA has been the major source of the U.S. productivity advantage over that of the United Kingdom. He puts considerable emphasis on
scope, that is, the vertical and horizontal integration of multifold activities within big

Table 2-17. Comparative Levels of Labor Productivity in
the Economy as a Whole, 1913–89
(U.S. GDP per labor hour = 100)

	1913	*1950*	*1973*	*1989*
Austria	48	27	59	75
Belgium	61	42	64	89
Denmark	58	43	63	66
Finland	33	31	57	70
France	48	40	70	95
Germany	50	30	64	79
Italy	37	31	64	81
Netherlands	69	46	77	92
Norway	43	43	64	83
Sweden	44	49	76	81
United Kingdom	78	57	67	81
Australia	93	67	70	78
Canada	75	75	83	91
United States	100	100	100	100
Japan	18	15	46	65

Source: Data for 1913–73 from Maddison 1991, p. 53; data for 1989 from
Table 2-6. GDP is measured in 1985 U.S. relative prices (Paasche PPP con-
verter).

corporations. This is, of course, contrary to the usual view that specialization is important. Chandler's analysis of scale and scope is not based on quantitative evidence, nor does he separate the impact of organizational advance from the role of improvements in technology and increases in physical and human capital inputs. His comparison with the United Kingdom ignores the fact that until recently Britain had much less capital per worker than did the United States. Furthermore, the evidence that Prais and associates (1981) and Caves and Krause (1980) found suggests that British firms have been too big rather than too small. In the 1980s, the size of British firms fell, and their productivity accelerated.

My own view is that scale economies are rather modest and that government efforts to promote bigness have generally been a failure, particularly so in Eastern Europe and the Soviet Union where industrial and agricultural establishments have been much bigger than in the West (see Ehrlich 1985).

Technical Progress

Technical progress is the most essential characteristic of economic growth. If there had been no technical progress, the whole process of capital accumulation would have been much more modest. Massive investment in transport was rational when railways, automobiles, and aircraft brought progressively bigger possibilities for reliability, speed, and comfort at low cost. Massive investment in horse-drawn carriages obviously would not have produced the same result.

A substantial part of technical progress must be embodied in new capital goods to be exploited effectively;[13] some of it becomes operational mainly through improvements in the skill and knowledge of the labor force; and some progress is due to improvements in management and organization. Because technical progress is continuous and substantial, economies never function at a technical optimum. There is a continuous process of learning by doing in which those using a new machine become familiar with its potential. By the time the new technique has been fully mastered in a given establishment, new and better techniques will become available and will be used in competitive establishments that will begin the process of learning by doing all over again. Firms vary in the vintages of capital they can deploy and in their level of organizational skill. Thus, the average level at which all advancing economies operate is below feasible best practice, and they have a variety of techniques in operation.

If labor productivity is used as a crude proxy measure of average technological levels, it is clear that the United States has been the lead country for all of the twentieth century. We can make such measures with any semblance of accuracy only for the countries in Group 1 and for Japan, but if the United States was unequivocally the productivity leader among these countries, it must also have been the world leader. Table 2-17 shows clearly that the United States was still the lead country in 1989, though its leadership edge had greatly eroded since 1950.

From the information we have by industry of origin, it seems probable that the U.S. lead prevailed in all major sectors of the economy and in virtually all branches of manufacturing. This is still the case, except for Japan. Japan's overall productivity standing is not impressive compared with that of the European countries, but its economic performance by sector and branch is more uneven than that of the European

Table 2-18. Comparative Levels of Labor
Productivity in Manufacturing, 1950–89
(U.S. manufacturing output per labor hour
= 100)

	1950	1973	1989
Germany	39	75	80
United Kingdom	40	52	61
Brazil	18	36	26
Mexico	18	32	30
India	5	5	6
Korea	5	11	20
Japan	18	56	80
United States	100	100	100

Source: B. van Ark 1993. Output was measured using a
Fisher PPP (geometric average of Paasche and Laspeyres
measures).

countries. Its manufacturing productivity was 80 percent of that of the United States
in 1989, and its productivity in the machinery and equipment sector was above that
of the United States (see Tables 2-18 and 2-19).

The reasons why the United States has been the lead country in the twentieth
century are that it had the highest levels of capital per capita until very recently (Table
2-10), it has had and still has the most highly educated labor force (Table 2-9), and it
had an even larger lead in expenditures on research and development (Table 2-20),
which it still maintains.[14] All of these characteristics interacted to make the United
States the technical leader and to produce a steady stream of technical improvement
at a faster pace than the United Kingdom (the old leader) produced in the nineteenth
century.

It seems legitimate to describe U.S. technical progress as steady, because U.S.
labor productivity growth was rather steady over the long haul from 1890 to 1973 (the
slowdown of 1929–38 being compensated in 1938–50). Since 1973 the rate of U.S.
productivity growth has decelerated markedly. As this slowdown has now lasted for
two decades, there are some grounds for thinking that the rate of technical progress
has decelerated particularly because the other advanced capitalist countries are now

Table 2-19. Comparative Levels of Labor Productivity in Branches of
Manufacturing, 1988

	Germany	United Kingdom	Japan	United States
Food products	69	49	24	100
Textiles	86	69	64	100
Chemicals	68	75	69	100
Basic metals	84	78	90	100
Machinery	80	62	114	100
Other	80	57	56	100

Source: Update of D. Pilat and B. van Ark 1991. Output was measured using Fisher PPP converters.

Table 2-20. Research and Development
Expenditure per Person Employed, Six
Countries, 1960–87
($ in 1985 U.S. relative prices)

	1960	1973	1987
France	207	448	761
Germany	179	475	848
Japan	89	342	757
Netherlands	291	514	687
United Kingdom	343	480	650
United States	809	814	1074

Source: Maddison 1991, p. 152.

much nearer to U.S. levels of performance and have stepped up their own research and development efforts, which one would normally have expected to reinforce the rate of technical progress.

One of the most ambitious analysts of technical progress (Schmookler 1966) argued that the development of new processes and products is induced by demand. "We are, and evidently for some time have been able to extend the technological frontier perceptibly at virtually all points" (p. 210). He buttresses his argument with evidence drawn from U.S. patent statistics (and chronologies of major inventions) covering a period of a century and a half "A million dollars spent on one kind of good is likely to induce about as much invention as the same sum spent on any other good" (p. 172). In effect, Schmookler says that there are constant returns to inventive effort, a viewpoint that may have seemed plausible in the 1960s but is much less so today.

Rosenberg (1976) challenged Schmookler's view on this issue and argued that science and technology are not omnicompetent, that certain obvious human needs "have long gone either unsatisfied or very badly catered for in spite of a well-established demand" (p. 267) and that attempts to quicken, or even maintain, the pace of technical progress may run into decreasing returns because the necessary process of trial and error imposes constraints on the pace of development of knowledge.

As productivity growth has slowed down in all the countries of Group 1 and in Japan as well, there is some reason to believe that the pace of technical progress has slowed down. One can subscribe to this proposition without being an adherent of the Kondratieff–Schumpeter hypothesis about the presence of long waves in technology.

The main burden of innovation in new processes and products has been borne by the advanced countries, and with some lag, follower countries can usually mimic the technology and copy the leaders. The advantage to a backward country is that it can grow faster than the leader when it is catching up and can mount a bigger investment effort without running so easily into a zone of diminishing returns. However, the Japanese experience shows that a substantial degree of catch-up requires great effort sustained over a long period to build up human capital, to accumulate physical capital, and to adapt technology to its own needs (see Hayami and Ruttan 1985, who show why the difference in factor endowment between Japanese and U.S. agriculture made it necessary for Japan to develop an idiosyncratic technology path in this sector).

Mimicry of the lead country's technology by follower countries is too facile a description of the process. Most technology needs to be carefully adapted to local needs and local skills, so it cannot be transplanted successfully without a reasonable level of education and skills in the follower country and some experience in adaptive R&D and in the installation of new capital. It requires a fair degree of what Abramovitz calls "technical congruence."

The Outlook for Growth and Convergence

In all the countries we have surveyed here, the major engine of growth has been advancing knowledge and technical progress, which needs to be embodied in human and physical capital in order to have an impact. There is no reason to suspect that this will change.

At the frontiers of knowledge and technology, economic progress is necessarily rather gradual, and there have been no big leaps forward in productivity. The United States—the lead country for a century in terms of living standards and level of performance—had a rather steady pace of advance in both labor and total factor productivity until the 1970s, at which time there was a distinct slowdown, which has persisted now for nearly two decades. If it continues in the long term, it will have a major influence on the pace of growth in the twenty-first century because the slowdown has also affected productivity growth in all of the other advanced countries and there is no clear prospect of a new leader emerging.

Within the world economy, there are large spreads in per-capita income and productivity. Some countries that were well below the frontier of technology at the beginning of the century were able to grow much faster than the lead country when they mounted the necessary effort in terms of human and physical capital. Japan, Korea, and Taiwan did a fair amount of catching up, but they are still significantly below U.S. productivity levels. Japan's experience suggests that supergrowth cannot be sustained indefinitely, for its productivity growth has not surpassed that of the top European performers in the past decade. Countries like Korea and Taiwan also seem likely to converge to slower growth paths within the next two decades.

Progress in many of the poor countries, particularly in Asia, was faster in the second half of the twentieth century than it was in the first, partly because the abolition of colonialism gave these countries greater freedom to control their destiny, a freedom that they generally used in a very positive manner. Progress was also helped by buoyancy in the world economy, better opportunities for trade and the transfer of technology, and, to a modest extent, because the advanced countries provided some aid for development. Nevertheless, despite significant gains in income and productivity, many of these poorer countries are not catching up to or keeping up the pace of growth in the advanced countries. Convergence in per-capita income levels is by no means inevitable, particularly in countries with a rapidly growing population.

It is clear that the eighth and ninth decades were not the twentieth century's best. Only the Asian countries grew rapidly. Latin America, Africa, Eastern Europe, and the former Soviet Union are in the middle of complex "adjustment" crises, and the performance of Western and Southern Europe is well below that of the postwar golden age.

The slowdown in the advanced countries was due in part to the erosion of once-for-all elements in the postwar golden age. It is nearer to being satisfactory than that in some other parts of the world economy. But growth and employment are below their potential because of caution about inflation and balance-of-payment risks, induced in part by problems of living in a world with unrestricted freedom for international capital movements and fluctuating exchange rates. Growth did not accelerate significantly in the 1980s despite the waning of inflation and the reduced power of OPEC. Mutual consultation has been successful in avoiding beggar-your-neighbor policies but very slow in getting remedial action to reduce payments disequilibria or to induce changes in the U.S. fiscal–monetary policy mix.

The general economic situation in Latin America is one of major crisis—worse than anything previously experienced in the twentieth century. Since 1982 these countries have had 10 years in the wilderness trying to tackle a multiplicity of problems with desperate remedies. There are four characteristic and interrelated problems: a fiscal crisis, galloping inflation, very heavy external indebtedness, and distortions in resource allocation that derived originally from excessive protectionism, subsidies, and dirigisme and have been complicated by inflation and depression. To solve all of them by means of orthodox policy measures has proved very painful, but heterodox alternatives have proved disastrous.

In the former Soviet Union and in Eastern Europe there is also a crisis of a different origin. The Stalinist model of authoritarian centralized controls has lost its legitimacy, because it produced low growth, shoddy products, queues, and shortages. The transition to a more market-oriented economy, with private ownership of means of production, more consumer choice, and scope for entrepreneurial initiative is being held back by both vested interests remaining from the old system and the inherent difficulty of the task. The remarkable results of liberalization in China are not much of a guide to what can be expected from changes in Eastern Europe and the former Soviet Union, because they were applied to a much more primitive economy. As Russia liberalizes, its problems will probably resemble more closely those of Latin America.

Notes

I am grateful to Gjalt de Jong for help in preparing the graphs and to Moe Abramovitz, Bart van Ark, William Baumol, and André Hofman for comments on the text. I also benefited from comments received during the two seminars organized by W. Baumol, R. Nelson, and E. N. Wolff, Historical Perspectives on the International Convergence of Productivity, in November 1991 and April 1992.

1. The importance of getting a representative sample of countries is clear from the exchange between Baumol (1986) and De Long (1988), which opened up the recent discussion on convergence. Baumol concentrated on evidence for 16 rich countries from Maddison (1982), and De Long pointed out that convergence was much weaker when the sample of countries was expanded. One of the striking features of the new growth economics that has emerged since 1986 is the fact that it takes a global view of economic growth and jettisons the old dichotomy between "growth" (of advanced countries) and "development" (of poor countries).

2. Simon Kuznets (1966) put the turning point for "modern economic growth" at 1750, but in the light of recent evidence suggesting that growth in the eighteenth century was slower than previously thought (Crafts 1985), I prefer to put the turning point at 1820. Furthermore, I think recent evidence has falsified the earlier view (espoused most strongly by Rostow 1960 and Gerschenkron 1965) that there was a long, drawn-out sequence of staggered "takeoffs" in West European countries throughout the nineteenth century. It now seems clear that growth was generally much faster after 1820 than it was in the "protocapitalist" period from 1500 to 1820, when Western Europe was slowly pulling ahead of the rest of the world. For evidence on the pace of growth in Flanders for 1500 to 1812, see van der Wee and Blomme (1992) who estimate a growth rate in GDP of 0.2 percent per year over these three centuries.

3. Within the European periphery, the countries excluded from our sample (Albania, Bulgaria, Poland, Romania, and Yugoslavia) probably have income levels below those of the Soviet Union, and so the degree of convergence is somewhat exaggerated by our sample.

4. Our Latin American sample excludes the Caribbean area where there are several countries below the income range in our 6 sample countries. In Latin America proper, some countries, like Bolivia and Ecuador, are below the level of Peru (the poorest of our sample countries), and two countries may have a higher income than our sample (Uruguay and Venezuela). See Summers and Heston 1991, pp. 351–52 for rough 1988 estimates for 29 countries in the region.

5. In defining productivity leadership, I have ignored the special case of Australia, whose impressive achievements before the first World War were due largely to its natural resource advantages rather than to its technical achievements and the stock of man-made capital.

6. For a more elaborate statement of my causal schema, see Maddison 1988 and 1991, p. 12. Maddison 1970, chap. 2, was an attempt to measure the interaction of different layers of causality.

7. This "ultimate" level of causality is generally missing in the new growth theory, which seeks to find comprehensive explanations by sticking to the proximate domain (see the contributions to the May 1991 issue of the *Quarterly Journal of Economics*). Lucas (1988, p. 5) is the most straightforward in recognizing these limitations:

> The term "theory" is used in so many different ways, even within economics, that if I do not clarify what I mean by it early on, the gap between what I think I am saying and what you think you are hearing will grow too wide for us to have a serious discussion. I prefer to use the term "theory" in a very narrow sense, to refer to an explicit dynamic system, something that can be put on a computer and *run*.

Adam Smith and Simon Kuznets, the fathers of modern growth analysis, clearly operated across a broader spectrum of causality. Kuznets did not claim to have a general theory but stuck to rather simple presentations of quantitative evidence, avoided econometrics, and made very sparing use of regressions. He used his imagination to fill empty economic boxes and to make strategic interconnections (see Lundberg 1971). Abramovitz (1989) approaches growth in the same way and refers frequently to the "ultimate" domain in terms of nations' differential "social capability," different degrees of "technical congruence," or differences in institutions and policy. See also Cipolla 1991 for a contrast between the approach of economists and that of economic historians.

8. There are two main schools of "proximate" analysis. The first consists of the growth accountants, whose guru is Ed Denison. Denison's (1967) analytic framework contains some neoclassic elements, particularly in his use of factor weights, but he is eclectic in his procedures. The new growth economists either ignore his work (as Paul Romer does) or label it without adequate qualification as neoclassic (as Lucas does). The advantage of the growth-accounting approach as Denison developed it is that the accounts are completely transparent and great care is given to what exactly the measures mean. The other school of proximate analysis is econometric, as represented by Chenery or Barro who tend to be "maximalist" in their willingness to use data of widely varying reliability. They also use less transparent procedures. Jorgenson falls somewhat between the two approaches. He is more strictly neoclassical than Denison, makes greater use of econometric techniques, and is less transparent, but he is generally more fastidious about the data he uses than are the maximalists.

9. See Abramovitz (1989, p. 23) for a cautionary note on interactive causality:

Growth accounting—holds that the sources it measures act independently of one another so that each makes its own contribution. There are good reasons, however, to question that claim. The growth sources feed from one another. The most important interactions are those between technological progress and the accumulation of tangible capital and between technological progress and the build-up of human capital through education and training.

10. See Maddison 1991 for the relevant growth accounts and a more detailed analysis of policy. Kindleberger 1992 provides an excellent survey of the variety of interpretations of the golden age.

11. It is too early to try to improve on the old CIA estimates until we have better evidence. However, it is now clear that the East German Statistical Office deliberately misrepresented economic growth. The same is probably true of Romania. In other East European countries the problem appears not to have been cheating but the inappropriateness of the data collection system for generating the statistics needed to estimate real GDP. For revisionist estimates for the Soviet Union, see Bergson 1991 and Khanin 1988. I have dropped the estimates for Bulgaria, Poland, Romania, and Yugoslavia that I included in Maddison 1990.

12. I have measured human capital characteristics in terms of the stock of formal education embodied in the population. I think this is preferable to flow data on educational enrollments which some analysts use as a proxy measure, for example, Easterlin 1981 or Barro 1991.

13. The interaction of investment, capital stock, and technical progress is shown most clearly in Salter 1960.

14. The R&D effort of the United States compared with that of the United Kingdom is analyzed and documented with great clarity in Mowery and Rosenberg 1989. They also show that the U.S. educational system and the direction of research in U.S. universities was well designed to foster the acquisition of technical skills and to nurture technical progress.

References

Abramovitz, M. (1989). *Thinking About Growth.* Cambridge: Cambridge University Press.

van Ark, B. (1993). "The ICOP Approach—Its Implications and Applicability." In A. Szirmai, B. van Ark, and D. Pilat, eds., *Explaining Economic Growth.* Amsterdam: North Holland.

Barro, R. J. (1991). "Economic Growth in a Cross Section of Countries." *Quarterly Journal of Economics,* May, pp. 407–43.

Baumol, W. J. (1986). "Productivity Growth, Convergence and Welfare: What the Long-Run Data Show." *American Economic Review,* December, pp. 1072–86.

Baumol, W. J., and Wolff, E. W. (1988). "Productivity, Convergence and Welfare: Reply." *American Economic Review,* December, pp. 1155–59.

Bergson, A. (1991). "The USSR Before the Fall: How Poor and Why." *Journal of Economic Perspectives,* Fall, pp. 29–44.

Caves, R. E., and L. B. Krause. (1980). *Britain's Economic Performance.* Washington, DC: Brookings Institution.

Chandler, A. D., Jr. (1990). *Scale and Scope: The Dynamics of Industrial Capitalism.* Cambridge, MA: Harvard University Press.

Chernery, H. and M. Syrquin. (1975). *Patterns of Development, 1950–1970.* Oxford: Oxford University Press.

Cipolla, C. M. (1991). *Between History and Economics: An Introduction to Economic History.* Oxford: Basil Blackwell.

Crafts, N.F.R. (1985). *British Economic Growth During the Industrial Revolution.* Oxford: Oxford University Press.

De Long, J. Bradford. (1988). "Productivity, Convergence and Welfare: Comment." *American Economic Review,* December, pp. 1138–54.

De Long, J. Bradford, and L. H. Summers. (1991). "Equipment Investment and Economic Growth." *Quarterly Journal of Economics,* May, pp. 445–502.

Denison, E. F. (1967). *Why Growth Rates Differ.* Washington, DC: Brookings Institution.

Dosi, G., C. Freeman, R. Nelson, G. Silverberg, and L. Soete. (1988). *Technical Change and Economic Theory.* London: Francis Pinter.

Easterlin, R. (1981). "Why Isn't the Whole World Developed?" *Journal of Economic History,* March, pp. 1–19.

Ehrlich, E. (1985). "The Size Structure of Manufacturing Establishments and Enterprises: An International Comparison." *Journal of Comparative Economics* 9:267–95.

Gerschenkron, A. (1965). *Economic Backwardness in Historical Perspective.* New York: Praeger.

Hayami, Y., and V. W. Ruttan. (1985). *Agricultural Development: An International Perspective.* Baltimore: Johns Hopkins University Press.

Hofman, A. A. (1991). "The Role of Capital in Latin America: A Comparative Perspective of Six Countries for 1950–1989." Working Paper no. 4, ECLAC, Santiago, December.

Khanin, G. (1988). "Ekonomicheski rost, alternativnaia otsenka." *Kommunist* 17:83–90.

Kindleberger, C. (1992). "Why did the Golden Age Last So Long?" In F. Cairncross and A. Cairncross, eds., *The Legacy of the Golden Age.* London: Routledge & Paul Kegan.

Kuznets, S. (1951). "The State as a Unit in Study of Economic Growth." *Journal of Economic History*, pp. 25–41.

Lal, D. (1988). *The Hindu Equilibrium.* Vol. 1. Oxford: Oxford University Press.

Landes, D. S. (1969). *The Unbound Prometheus.* Cambridge: Cambridge University Press.

Lucas, R. E. (1988). "On the Mechanics of Economic Development." *Journal of Monetary Economics* 22:3–42.

Lundberg, E. (1971). "Simon Kuznets' Contribution to Economics." *Scandinavian Journal of Economics*, pp. 444–61.

Maddison, A. (1970). *Economic Progress and Policy in Developing Countries.* New York: Norton.

————. (1971). *Class Structure and Economic Growth: India and Pakistan Since the Moghuls.* London: Allen & Unwin.

————. (1980). "Economic Growth and Structural Change in the Advanced Countries." In I. Leveson and J. W. Wheeler, eds., *Western Economies in Transition.* London: Croom Helm, pp. 41–66.

————. (1982). *Phases of Capitalist Development.* Oxford: Oxford University Press.

————. (1987). "Growth and Slowdown in Advanced Capitalist Economies: Techniques of Quantitative Assessment." *Journal of Economic Literature*, June, pp. 649–98.

————. (1988). "Ultimate and Proximate Growth Causality: A Critique of Mancur Olson on the Rise and Decline of Nations." *Scandinavian Economic History Review* 36:25–29.

————. (1989). *The World Economy in the Twentieth Century.* Paris: OECD Development Centre.

————. (1990a). "The Colonial Burden: A Comparative Perspective." In M. Scott and D. Lal, eds., *Public Policy and Economic Development.* Oxford: Oxford University Press, pp. 361–75.

————. (1990b). "Measuring European Growth: The Core and the Periphery." In E. Aerts and N. Valerio, eds., *Growth and Stagnation in the Mediterranean World in the 19th and 20th Centuries.* Leuven University Press.

————. (1991). *Dynamic Forces in Capitalist Development.* Oxford: Oxford University Press.

————. (1992a). "A Long-Run Perspective on Saving." *Scandinavian Journal of Economics*, June, pp. 181–213.

————. (1992b). *The Political Economy of Poverty Equity and Growth: Brazil and Mexico.* New York: Oxford University Press.

————. (1992c). "Standardised Estimates of Fixed Investment and Capital Stock at Constant Prices: A Long Run Survey for Six Countries." Paper presented at IARIW meetings, Flims, September.

Mowery, D. C., and N. Rosenberg. (1989). *Technology and the Pursuit of Economic Growth.* Cambridge: Cambridge University Press.

Needham, J. (1954–). *Science and Society in China.* Cambridge: Cambridge University Press.

Pilat, D., and B. van Ark. (1991). "Productivity Leadership in Manufacturing, Germany, Japan and the United States, 1973–1989." *Research Memorandum* no. 456, Institute of Economic Research, University of Groningen.

Prais, S. J., A. Daly, D. T. Jones, and K. Wagner (1981). *Productivity and Industrial Structure.* Cambridge: Cambridge University Press.

Pratten, C. (1988). "A Survey of Economies of Scale." Department of Applied Economics, Cambridge University, October.

Romer, P. M. (1986). "Increasing Returns and Long-Run Growth." *Journal of Political Economy* 94:1002–37.

————. (1990). "Endogenous Technical Change." *Journal of Political Economy* 98:S71–S102.

Rosenberg, N. (1976). *Perspectives on Technology.* Cambridge: Cambridge University Press.

Rostow, W. W. (1960). *The Stages of Economic Growth.* Cambridge: Cambridge University Press.

Salter, W.E.G. (1960). *Productivity and Technical Change.* Cambridge: Cambridge University Press.

Schmookler, J. (1966). *Invention and Economic Growth.* Cambridge, MA: Harvard University Press.

Summers, R., and A. Heston. (1988). "A New Set of International Comparisons of Real Product and Prices: Estimates for 130 Countries, 1950–1985." *Review of Income and Wealth*, March, pp. 1–25.

————. (1991). "The Penn World Table (Mark 5): An Expanded Set of International Comparisons, 1950–1988." *Quarterly Journal of Economics,* May, pp. 327–68.

United Nations/Eurostat. (1986). *World Comparisons of Purchasing Power and Real Product for 1980.* New York: United Nations/Eurostat.

van der Wee, H., and J. Blomme. (1992). "The Belgian Economy in the Very Long Run: A Case Study of Economic Development in the Flanders/Brabant Region 1500–1812." Paper presented at IARIW meetings, Flims, September.

3

Multivariate Growth Patterns: Contagion and Common Forces as Possible Sources of Convergence

WILLIAM J. BAUMOL

The homogenization form of the convergence hypothesis can be described as the proposition that there are economic forces leading different countries' productivity levels (and thus their living standards) gradually to close ranks. Recent empirical research provides substantial support for this conjecture, at least for the performance of the more affluent economies over the last half-century and, very probably, for an interval more than twice that length of time. The primary purpose of this chapter is to survey the substance of this recent literature rather than to offer any new contributions.

The persistence of the homogenization phenomenon in the leading industrialized countries poses something of a puzzle. It is reasonable to assume that the economic growth records of different countries depend on many different influences—cultural patterns, institutional arrangements, governmental policies, and so on—and the empirical studies offer evidence confirming that a number of variables do play a role in economic growth. Moreover, it is clear that the behavior of these variables differs among the countries that have participated in the convergence process. If so, how does one account for the apparent fact that these countries all seem to be heading, more or less consistently, in the same direction?

This chapter suggests some possible reconciliations of the two phenomena. Using the term *ancillary variables* to refer to influences that play no direct role in the convergence phenomenon, I will summarize recent evidence supporting the common-sense belief that such variables do matter for the absolute and relative growth performance of a particular economy. As a result, in any one period, some countries turn in a notably superior growth performance, and others may be fairly consistent under-achievers. I will suggest, however, that growth may be "catching," that is, that there seem to be strong forces that fairly rapidly spread the "contagion" of rapid growth from the high-achiever economies to those that have performed relatively poorly but are in most characteristics not vastly different from the high achievers. And the contagion process can, with some lag, offset a considerable portion of any differentials in the performance of these economies resulting from differences in the ancillary variables, thereby revealing the forces of convergence. Contagion of rapid growth can thus limit what unwise government policy or deleterious cultural influences can do to impede productivity growth. If true, this means that even though those nations more favorably situated for growth—institutionally or in other respects—may benefit from their felicitous circumstances, their success will draw other economies along with them in the growth process, enabling the "advantages of (moderate) backwardness" to do much of the remainder of the job of achieving convergence.

This chapter will begin by reviewing some of the data that have been used to examine the convergence hypothesis and summarize what they show, at least superficially. That is, using the terminology of the introductory chapter, we will discuss the implications of the data on *gross* convergence. Then, we will review the more recent and more probing investigations of the data, both to learn the nature and magnitude of the role they estimate the ancillary variables to play and to see what they indicate about the reality and pervasiveness of *residual* convergence, that is, convergence after netting out the effects of the ancillary variables. Finally, we will turn to the contagion conjecture, discussing in a priori terms the nature of the mechanism that may account for it and the extent to which one can expect it to reconcile the influence of the ancillary variables and the forces of convergence. We will contrast the contagion hypothesis with a model that may prove to be either an alternative or a supplement: the view that much of such convergence as has occurred should be attributed to the presence of a set of *common forces,* that is, variables that simultaneously make their influence felt among the members of the "convergence club" and promote convergence by pushing all those countries in a roughly similar direction.

The Data and Their Apparent Implications for Convergence

The studies of convergence among the economies of different nations are based largely on five sets of data. The longer-term studies use data compiled by Maddison (1982, 1989), who provides carefully derived estimates going back more than a century for some 20 countries, most of them among today's industrialized economies. A few studies have used Bairoch (1976), who deals with a sample similar to Maddison's but for a somewhat longer period.[1] Others have worked with the far more extensive sample of countries available for the period beginning in 1950. Most of these later studies rely on the sophisticated and painstaking database assembled by Summers and Heston (1988), who provide purchasing-power–parity evaluations of per-capita GDP for a sample of 72 countries between 1950 and 1985 and for a considerably larger sample for more limited time periods. As a check on the Summers–Heston calculations, some investigators have also used data provided by the World Bank (various years), generally with no significant difference in results from those obtained from the Summers–Heston data. In addition, there is a rich body of data available from the U.S. Bureau of Labor Statistics, much of it unpublished.

It is not difficult to summarize the qualitative results obtained by studies that simply examine the patterns manifested by the data themselves, without any attempt to probe statistically what lies beneath them, for example, by explicitly including ancillary variables in the regressions. Such calculations were carried out by a number of economists (e.g., Alam and Naseer 1990, Baumol 1986, Baumol, Blackman, and Wolff 1989, De Long 1988,[2] Ram 1991). It seems useful to divide the conclusions of these studies into two parts: those relating to the timing of such convergence as has occurred and those relating to the intertemporal behavior of the income levels (as a proxy for level of development) of the countries studied.

In regard to the timing of development, the evidence seems to suggest the following pattern: From the beginning of the Industrial Revolution in Great Britain until sometime near the middle of the nineteenth century, the economies of what are now the leading industrial countries seem to have diverged, though the statistical evidence for this period is, understandably, quite weak. Still, it is plausible that after its takeoff, the United Kingdom pulled ahead of the other economies in question and that then Belgium, the Netherlands, France, the United States, and (perhaps a bit later) Germany began to grow rapidly in labor productivity and per-capita income (the two variables studied), thereby creating a growing gap between themselves and the rest of the world. The United States leapt ahead of the pack toward the end of the nineteenth century. Nevertheless, roughly between 1870 and 1929, there was convergence, in the sense of homogenization, among perhaps the top eight or ten economies in the group, with both the range and the coefficient of variation in the two variables narrowing steadily and markedly. During this period, however, there was relatively little if any catch-up toward the leader, the United States. The third pertinent period is that encompassing the Great Depression and World War II, an era of divergence so sharp that it may have offset the bulk of the convergence achieved during the preceding 50 or 60 years, though for this period the data are clearly contaminated with so much noise that any formal convergence test becomes questionable. The postwar period from 1950 to 1970 (the "golden age" of growth) was one of unprecedented convergence in terms of homogenization and catch-up to the leader, as well as the size of the group of countries participating in the convergence process (the group numbering perhaps somewhere between 20 and 40 countries, depending on the criteria used). Finally, after 1970 a trend of relatively mild gross divergence began.

As we just indicated, the group of countries undergoing gross convergence has been relatively small throughout the period studied. The membership of what has been called the *convergence club* seems to have been growing more or less steadily since sometime before 1850. Nevertheless, even today it is clear that the most impoverished group of countries for which pertinent data are available have been excluded from the club. On the average, the less developed countries have been falling further behind the most prosperous economies and, even among themselves, have been experiencing some divergence, though it has been relatively weak and does not generally satisfy the relevant tests of statistical significance. Thus, if we use as the criterion of convergence the regression relationship between the growth rate of a country's per-capita income and the initial level of that same variable, taking a negative slope of this relationship to indicate convergence (the richer the country is, the more slowly it will tend to grow) and a positive slope to correspond to divergence, then quadratic regressions will show that the poorest of the less developed countries have generally shown divergence, whereas the relatively affluent among them have experienced some convergence over the period after World War II. The wealthier countries, on the other hand, have generally converged, with perhaps some divergence among the top few members (for the quadratic regression results, see Alam and Naseer 1990, Baumol and Wolff 1988, and Ram 1991).

This, then, is what the data show about gross convergence, that is, when no attempt is made to get at the individual influences to which the growth patterns can be ascribed. In sum, the figures suggest that gross convergence has been limited to a fairly small but growing number of wealthier economies and that when looked at in the long term, it has generally become more intense with the passage of time. These patterns are not inconsistent with what intuition and general observation have led a number of commentators to expect. Taking the speed and effectiveness of technology transfer to be a prime engine of convergence, they have concluded that the LDCs are at a disadvantage in the process because they lack the skilled technicians, engineers, and scientists to enable them to take advantage of technology transfer opportunities, and their output is composed only to a minor extent of products for which sophisticated techniques are helpful.

For those countries that are in a position to benefit from technology transfer, the laggards have more to learn from the leaders than the leaders can learn from them— hence the advantages of *moderate* backwardness. The increasing pace of the resulting convergence process has been ascribed to the growing internationalization of the marketplace, which has in turn raised the penalty for lagging behind in the acquisition of the latest technology, and to the improvements in means of communication, which have reduced the cost of transfer of information while increasing its speed. Of course, there is much more to be said on the matter, and we will therefore return to the subject. The purpose of the superficial discussion of this paragraph has merely been to show that the patterns exhibited by the data do no violence to our intuitive views on the subject.

The Multivariate Empirical Analyses

Several recent quantitative empirical studies have probed the convergence hypothesis more deeply. For example, Bernard and Durlauf (1990) and Quah (1990) explored the issue using the strong convergence criterion described in the introductory chapter. Dowrick and Nguyen (1989) sought to separate out the consequences of expansion of the capital stock and the labor force in the growth of output from the effects of changes in (residually defined) total factor productivity. Barro (1991) evaluated the separate contributions of the population's education, government expenditure, distortion of prices from their free-market values, and political stability to the growth rate of labor productivity. Barro and Sala i Martin (1990) related the results to those obtained from a comparative study of convergence in the economies of the individual states of the United States. We next shall recapitulate the results of these and several other such recent studies.

Let us begin with Bernard and Durlauf and their use of the strong (stochastic) convergence criterion that, in order for the economies of two countries to be deemed to be converging, "requires that income disparities eventually vanish" (Bernard and Durlauf 1990, p. 8). Bernard sums up their results: "Looking at annual log real per capita output for 15 OECD countries from 1900–1987, I find that the individual country series are well described as difference stationary processes with substantial stochastic trends" (pp. 3–4). "For most groupings of countries the [strong] convergence hypothesis is rejected, yet so too is the hypothesis of no common trends" (pp. 27–28).

As the introduction to this book pointed out, it should hardly be surprising that so few cases have been found that seem to meet the requirements of strong stochastic convergence. However, a good deal is suggested by the fact that cointegration appears to be common, that is, that many economies that have similar general circumstances are also characterized by linearly related stochastic trends in their labor productivity. This can be regarded as a significant and remarkable conclusion, indicating that the growth patterns of the different countries either affect one another indirectly or are subject to some common influences such as similar technology. This certainly also leaves open the possibility that such economies satisfy the requirements of a weaker criterion of convergence. Thus, even though it may be considered unlikely that many countries could pass the test of strict stochastic convergence, it is clear that examining the data with the aid of this criterion can be highly illuminating.

We turn next to the work of Dowrick and Nguyen (1989). Their analysis draws on the observation that if poorer countries were to invest more—relative to employment and output—than richer countries did (as the less affluent countries might be led to do by relatively low capital stocks that increased their relative marginal product of investment), the convergence in labor productivity might be sharper and more rapid than that in TFP, as faster capital accumulation helped the LDCs catch up with the industrialized economies. Of course, the study finds that the opposite is in fact true, that investment rates are higher in the wealthier economies and that the growth of labor force participation in the latter is more rapid to boot. As a result, "it appears . . . that income convergence has been somewhat *slower* than the underlying rate of TFP catchup" (p. 1018).

Dowrick and Nguyen's study uses the Summers–Heston data for 1950 to 1980 supplemented by OECD data for 1980 to 1985. The sample studied is the full set of Summers–Heston *market* economies, as well as the smaller set composed of the 24 OECD countries, with Japan sometimes excluded to determine whether the presence of this apparent outlier case substantially affects the calculations. Dowrick and Nguyen's basic finding is that TFP convergence (residual convergence) has been considerably stronger and far more widespread than gross convergence (convergence in per-capita GDP uncorrected for changes in capital stock or employment). In their words,

> We have [carried out] our analysis on a variety of samples from the Summers and Heston (1984) data set, using 1950 relative income levels as the basis for an *ex ante* selection of groups of capitalist economies. . . . The results . . . are startling. When we regress the trend growth rate of per capita GDP on initial income alone, we find a marginally significant negative coefficient only for the richest of our samples (with initial income at least 25 percent of U.S. per capita income in 1950). For the wider samples, convergence in per capita GDP levels has not occurred to any significant extent. Indeed, for the widest sample of 63 countries, income levels appear to have diverged. This matches the findings of Baumol (1986), De Long (1988) and Baumol and Wolff (1988). . . . When, however, population growth and investment ratios are included as explanatory variables, we find that the coefficient on initial income levels is negative and statis-

tically significant for all samples. . . . The apparent implication is that although income levels have not converged for the wider sample, TFP catch-up has been operating for all but the very poorest of the non-OECD economies, and at a rate very similar to that observed in the OECD group. (p. 1021)

Dowrick and Nguyen also found that the widely noted slowing or disappearance of convergence after 1973 does not apply to convergence in TFP, which seems to continue with little letup. Using the three subperiods 1950–60, 1960–73, and 1973–85 they discovered that "In each sub-period TFP catch-up is significant at the 1 percent level. Although catching up appears to be slightly weaker after 1973, the difference is not statistically significant. Indeed, we cannot reject the hypothesis that all slope coefficients are equal across the three sub-periods" (1989, pp. 1022–23). This suggests that the slowdown in convergence of per-capita incomes after 1973 can be attributed to a relative decline in investment rates by the poorer countries and also to most of the pertinent studies' failure "to correct for cyclical bias," as Dowrick and Nguyen did.

Finally, Dowrick and Nguyen concluded, as Baumol, Blackman, and Wolff (1989) did, that once one corrects for the relatively slow growth that convergence requires tautologically of the wealthier countries, their apparently poor performance often disappears and that a number of countries with seemingly poor records seem to have done reasonably well:

> A number of richer countries which, on the record, appear to have grown substantially slower than the OECD average are seen to be average performers once account is taken of catch-up: the USA, Canada, Luxembourg and Australia. Conversely, the high growth rates in some of the poorer countries are largely accounted for by catching up: Greece, Italy, Portugal, and Spain. The countries which emerge as the best performers on adjusted growth rates are Japan, Germany, Norway and France, while the serious under-performers are Turkey, Ireland, New Zealand and the U.K. . . . Certainly Germany's "miracle"—as measured by growth above our regression predictions—was restricted to the period 1950–60. . . . Japan's "miracle" was evident up until 1973, since when it seems to have disappeared altogether (after account is taken of its remarkably high investment ratio). (pp. 1025–27)

We may summarize our discussion of the Dowrick–Nguyen study by saying that their work in separating out the effects of capital accumulation and growth in employment relative to population appears to lend strong support to the (residual) convergence hypothesis, by simultaneously throwing light on the workings of the process and showing that it is much more widespread and persistent through time than earlier studies indicated.

Dowrick and Nguyen, however, devoted little attention to the role of what one may refer to as the "ancillary variables proper." For information on this subject, we must turn to the work of Barro and Sala i Martin. Barro employs the Summers–Heston (1988) set of data to study convergence for 98 countries (those for which the requisite data are available) between 1960 and 1985. Together with Sala i Martin, Barro studies the same issue for individual states of the United States, ranging in number from 29 in the earlier periods to 48 in more recent times. The sources of the information are the U.S. Department of Commerce and Easterlin (1957, 1960). Barro and

Sala i Martin examine, first, a simple (one independent variable) relationship between the growth rate and the initial level of per-capita income and, second, the corresponding multivariate relationship with a number of ancillary variables taken explicitly into account. Those variables are not quite the same for the country and the state studies because several of those that seem pertinent to the former are clearly irrelevant to the latter and because the available types of data were not the same for the two studies. The intercountry comparison included the following four ancillary variables:

> primary and secondary school–enrollment rates in 1960, the average ratio of government consumption expenditure (exclusive of defense and education) to GDP from 1970 to 1985, proxies for political stability based on numbers of revolutions, coups, and political assassinations, and a measure of market distortion based on purchasing-power–parity ratios for investment goods. (Barro and Sala i Martin 1990, p. 30)

These authors summarized their principal conclusions:

> The main finding [for the 98-country sample] . . . is the lack of a close [single-variable] relationship between [per-capita income growth rate and its initial value]. In fact, the convergence coefficient has the wrong sign, that is, there is a small tendency for the initially rich countries to grow faster than the poor ones after 1960.
>
> These cross-country results contrast sharply with the findings . . . for the U.S. states . . . [in which], particularly over the longer samples, there is a clear and substantial negative correlation between starting per capita income or product and the subsequent growth rate. (pp. 30–31)
>
> We find evidence of . . . convergence for a sample of 98 countries from 1960 to 1985 only if we hold constant a number of additional variables . . . then we estimate [convergence] coefficients that are similar—roughly 2% per year—to those found for the U.S. states. (pp. 34–35)

Evidence of the Role of Ancillary Variables

At least six studies have focused on the influence of what one may consider to be purely ancillary variables (in contrast with the role of growth in the capital stock and the labor force that was investigated by Dowrick and Nguyen).[3] The study by Barro and Sala i Martin (1990) has already been noted. In addition (roughly in chronological order) there is a study by Baumol, Blackman, and Wolff (1989), a second by Mankiw, Romer, and Weil (1990), a third by De Long and L. H. Summers (1990), a fourth by Dollar (1991), and a briefer piece by Ram (1991).

Barro and Sala i Martin (1990) studied a sample of 98 countries between 1960 and 1985. We have already described ancillary variables they took into account and so proceed directly to their results:

> Given the level of initial per capita GDP, the growth rate is substantially positively related to the starting amount of human capital. Thus, poor countries tend to catch up with rich countries if the poor countries have high human capital per person (in relation to their level of per capita GDP), but not otherwise. . . .

Per capita growth and the ratio of private investment to GDP are negatively related to the ratio of government consumption expenditure to GDP. An interpretation is that government consumption introduces distortions, such as high tax rates, but does not provide an offsetting stimulus to investment and growth. On the other hand, there is little relation of growth to the quantity of public investment.

Measures of political instability (proxied by figures on revolutions, coups, and political assassinations) are inversely related to growth and investment. These relations could involve the adverse effects of political instability on property rights and the linkage between property rights and private investment. The correlation could, however, also reflect a political response to bad economic outcomes.

A proxy for price distortions (based on purchasing-power–parity numbers for investment deflators) is negatively related to growth. (p. 20)

These results all follow patterns that intuition leads us to expect, but what is still more important to our discussion here is the strength of the relationships or, rather, their statistical significance, lending support to the judgment that the pure forces of convergence constitute only some of the influences determining the paths of growth in per-capita incomes in the industrialized countries.

De Long and Summers (1990) concern themselves only with investment in equipment (as distinguished from more general investment) as a determinant of growth in per-capita GDP. Using data sources largely overlapping those of the other studies we have discussed, they employ a sample of 61 countries and a smaller sample, "of the 25 nations with 1960 levels of GDP per worker greater than 25 percent of the U.S. level" (p. 11). They concluded:

We demonstrate a clear, strong and robust statistical relationship between national rates of machinery and equipment investment and productivity growth. Equipment investment has far more explanatory power for national rates of productivity growth than other components of investment and outperforms many other variables included in cross-country equations accounting for growth. High rates of equipment investment can, for example, account for nearly all of Japan's extraordinary growth performance. (p. 3)

We interpret our results as implying that the social rate of return to equipment investment is 30 percent per year, or higher. . . . The gains from raising equipment investment through tax or other incentives dwarf losses from any non-neutralities that would result. (pp. 46–47)

Baumol, Blackman, and Wolff (1989, pp. 204–6 and appendix to chap. 9) explored the role of education in the convergence process using the Summers–Heston data, data from the *World Development Report* on per-capita GDP, and data from the latter source on the proportion of the population in the pertinent age group attending school in each country:

The results were dramatic . . . for the nonindustrialized world with no education variable included the [convergence] statistical relationship degenerated into a pattern of confusion. However, with the education variable added, orderly behavior was restored. That is, *in effect, countries with similar educational levels were shown quite consistently to be converging among themselves in terms of RGDP, though not catching up with countries whose educational levels were higher.* The obvious statistical tests were almost always passed uniformly; that is, they had the numerical values required for convergence (the initially lower RDGP countries growing faster) and these numerical values almost always passed a reasonably demanding test of statistical significance. (pp. 205–6) (italics in original)

The role of education was also explored by Mankiw, Romer, and Weil (1990), basing their work on an expansion of the Solow growth model and using the Summers–Heston data supplemented by figures for secondary-school education from the UNESCO yearbook. As described in National Bureau of Economic Research (1991, pp. 2–3):

[The authors] examine a sample of 98 countries and find that 80 percent of the variation in income per capita can be explained by population growth, saving and schooling. They further find that the importance of saving and schooling are approximately equal: an increase of 1 percent in either the fraction of output saved or the fraction of output devoted to education leads to an increase of approximately 1 percent in the level of GDP per worker.

Mankiw, Romer, and Weil find that countries would converge if they all had similar rates of population growth, saving, and education.... Mankiw, Romer, and Weil estimate that when countries become similar in these respects, about half of the difference in their incomes can be eliminated over a 35-year period.

The authors recognize explicitly (1990, p. 21) that their results are consistent with those of Dowrick and Nguyen.

In a very recent paper (1991) Dollar investigates the convergence hypothesis using a set of ancillary variables somewhat different from those employed in the other studies and adding several variables which seem a priori likely to play an important role. These include the 1960 primary school enrollment rate for each country and its average investment as a share of GDP between 1960 and 1985, both of which clearly have counterparts in earlier investigations. But in addition, Dollar uses two variables—the variability of the country's real exchange rate and an index of distortion in the country's exchange rate measured as a deviation between the exchange rate and the Summers–Heston exchange rate—both calculated for the period 1960 to 1985. These last two variables are intended as indicators of the country's openness to trade, whether its institutions and policies permit full freedom of trade, at the one extreme, or keep the economy close to a state of autarky, at the other. Dollar concluded:

All of the variables that help explain growth are correlated with income level in 1960. In particular, the poorest countries in terms of 1960 income were characterized in the subsequent period by low rates of investment in human and physical capital, as well as by a tendency toward overvalued exchange rates that retarded trade. After controlling for the effects of these other sources of growth, there is a statistically significant, negative relationship between income level and growth, which may be capturing the advantage of being backward envisaged by

Gerschenkron and Veblen. For very poor countries, any such advantage that may exist in principle tends to be overshadowed in practice by weak investment and inward orientation.

[There is an interesting] interaction between outward orientation and exploiting the advantages of backwardness . . . [dividing] developing countries into two groups . . . [a]mong outward oriented countries, the middle income group has grown distinctly faster than developed countries, tending to converge on the latter. Inward-oriented developing countries of middle income, on the other hand, have not grown as rapidly as the developed countries. These results suggest that an open regime for trade and investment is one of the institutional supports that facilitate the acquisition of new technology and enable backward economies to catch up.

The outward-oriented low-income countries have not grown as fast as developed countries. Nevertheless, they have grown more successfully than their inward-oriented counterparts. (pp. 3–4).

Ram (1991) studied 59 economies for the period 1950 to 1985, using the Summers and Heston data. He emphasizes the importance of his use of a regression function that is quadratic in income and his inclusion for each country of a measure of the average schooling of the labor force, which leads to "a dramatic increase in the model's explanatory power. . . and [yields a] highly significant positive effect of labor-force schooling on per-capita income growth." He sums up by observing:

The main conclusion is that full-sample estimates do not support the convergence thesis in conventional models that do not include the schooling variable, but the estimates do support the hypothesis when labor-force schooling is added to the specifications. In models without education, one observes the phenomenon of initial divergence and later convergence: with education, the estimates clearly show cross-country convergence in GNP per capita even in this extremely diverse sample. (pp. 7–8)

Clearly, the empirical studies differ on the relative importance of the various ancillary variables, but they seem to agree strongly that these variables do matter substantially, all working in the directions that one would expect. They also agree that it is to differences in the values of these variables that one must attribute deviations from a pattern of gross convergence. The studies indicate that education, investment (particularly in equipment), openness of the economy, and political stability all do matter and that policies that neglect the critical role of these variables can undermine the pervasive forces of residual convergence that seem to embrace all but the very poorest of the nations of the world.

Hypothesis: Why the Similar Results of the Multivariate Studies?

A striking feature of the multivariate studies is the dissimilarity in the ancillary variables they include and the great similarity in their qualitative results. The variables included are equipment investment in one case, education in another, measures of political stability in another, and an index of openness of the economy in still another.

Yet all of them seem to show that convergence applies to far more countries than is indicated by studies that omit any ancillary variables. They also seem to show that there has been little or no slowdown in convergence in the two most recent decades, as was previously suggested by studies with the ancillary variables left out.

The similarity in the results of the various models may, perhaps, be entirely coincidental. But there is a hypothesis that offers an alternative explanation. As mentioned elsewhere in this chapter, Wolff and I are exploring the view that productivity growth is inherently a feedback process, with variables such as investment, education, and stability affecting productivity growth and with the level of productivity, in turn, affecting all of those variables. There is good reason to believe that many of these variables are affected by the level of productivity, and also in a manner that follows a roughly common pattern. Clearly, education, investment, and (probably) stability all initially increased with the sharp rises in productivity. But all of them ultimately begin to level off. Education ceases to rise substantially as what appear to be saturation levels are approached. Greater political stability with growing national wealth also begins to level off as instability approaches disappearance. Finally, growth in investment seems to be slowed by a combination of diminishing returns and a greater propensity to consume as traditional consumption patterns are eroded by growing incomes. The similarity in behavior of these ancillary variables means that each can substitute statistically for the others in any regression analysis, and so it becomes difficult to determine by econometric means any difference in the strength or, more important, the difference in their influence on the productivity growth process.

Common Forces Versus Contagion as Source of Convergence and the Role of Ancillary Variables

To arrive at a hypothesis that can explain the interaction of the ancillary variables and the forces creating convergence, it is first necessary to ruminate in somewhat broader terms than has perhaps been done before on the nature of the engine that can drive a convergence process. We will refer to two general types of such engines, the *common-forces mechanism* and the *contagion mechanism*. Only a study of the facts can provide evidence indicating which of these plays a greater role in reality or whether both are equally important. We will see that the two work in very different ways and that they assign a very different place to the ancillary variables, both in the part they play and in their consequences.

The common-forces mechanism is perhaps the more obvious intuitively, and it has the longer history in the literature on formal growth models. The hypothesis is that at some stage or in some circumstances inherent in the growth process, a set of variables influences a number of economies and drives them all in the same general direction. It is as though a common terminal point (the steady state) is equipped with something analogous to a magnet that draws toward itself all the economies whose histories it affects. The unusual feature of this magnet is that it exerts the greatest force not on the economies closest to the terminal point but on those that are currently furthest from it. Hence, convergence occurs—the economies initially furthest from the terminus are driven to move toward it most rapidly, which is, of course, a defining characteristic of a convergence process. Thus, we can define a *common-forces convergence model* as one in which a number of economies are subject to common influences that push each of them toward a (nearly) common steady state and whose strength varies inversely with the distance of the current state of the economy in question from the common steady state.

An example of such a construct is the neoclassical growth model of Solow (1956), Swan (1956), Cass (1965), and Koopmans (1965). In this, the central common force is that of diminishing marginal and average returns to capital. Economies are assumed to grow by means of accumulating capital. But those economies that are ahead in the process are automatically subjected to several handicaps to further growth, at least in comparison with those behind them. Lower average returns to capital reduce the resources available for further investment, and lower marginal returns reduce the incentive for investment. In open economies, capital flows from the richer to the poorer countries to take avantage of the higher marginal returns to investment, and labor flows in the opposite direction, lowering the relative capital–labor ratios in the richer countries and thus further handicapping their growth. Diminishing returns slow down the growth process in any country, and if all countries have identical technology, saving propensities, and so on, it can move them all toward a common steady state. This, together with the stronger impediment to growth that diminishing returns impose on the wealthier economies, constitutes a clear and well-known convergence process.

In contrast, a *contagion model of convergence* requires no common technology or psychological propensities in the participant economies, nor does it rest on the assumption that they all are being driven by the same forces. In such a model, circumstances—which may be fortuitous as far as the model is concerned—either inaugurate a growth process in one or more countries or serve as a disturbance that accelerates this growth. However, the market mechanism or some other arrangement makes it difficult for other economies to refrain from such a growth pattern for very long. Because of contagion, growth thus tends to gravitate toward the laggards, who are affected more than are the wealthier economies from whom they caught the infection (because the laggards have more to learn from the leaders than the leaders do from the laggards, and so the laggards can quickly make up for lost time). Thus this constitutes another convergence mechanism in which a number of countries are driven in a similar direction, and the laggards usually move in that direction more rapidly than do those in advanced positions. In sum, we may define such a model as one in which the growth process need not initially affect every economy, or at least not affect it to a comparable degree, but in which unusually rapid growth in one economy elicits even more rapid growth in others that have lagged behind it.

A contagion model is more commonly found in discussions by economic historians, and technology transfer is the most frequently cited means of contagion. The story is one in which substantial innovation occurs initially in one or several economies in which culture, government policy, and other particular influences are especially propitious for such a development. But, new technology does not long remain the exclusive property of the innovating countries. Enterprising exporters of technology profit by finding new geographic locations in which the inventions can be employed effectively, whereas the laggard countries, with their export markets threatened, are forced to imitate and, having more to learn from the leaders than the latter can learn from them, grow more rapidly than do those who initially embarked on the process of rapid growth. Later, we will say more about the contagion model, but at this point our main objective is to contrast the two convergence mechanisms.

Perhaps the clearest distinction between the two mechanisms is the degree of interdependence that they assume in order to characterize the different economies. According to the common-forces model, if some exogenous development causes growth to cease in Leader-country A, it need have no effect on the rate at which Follower-country B moves toward the steady state. So long as the original set of common influences continues to drive B as before, there is no reason to expect B to slow down. There can, of course, be such an effect—for example, if there is a consequent decline in the export of capital from A to B—but such a cross-country effect is not essential to the mechanism. In contrast, in a contagion model, since B's growth is at least for some substantial period driven by A's (at least until B has itself attained a position of leadership), the cross partial derivative between A's and B's growth rate cannot be close to zero.

There is also a basic difference in the role of the ancillary variables in the two models. For example, in the common-forces model, a difference in culture that leads to a sharp divergence between the two countries' savings propensities or a great difference in the behavior of government can lead to disparities in the steady states toward which the common forces drive the two economies and to differences in their time paths, which consequently never disappear. In the contagion model, in contrast, the ancillary variables determine which countries will embark on the growth process earliest and most strongly, but that is likely to be a transitory disparity as growth is transmitted from one economy to another. In other words, in economies driven toward convergence by a contagion mechanism, the ancillary variables can exercise considerable influence over relative growth trajectories in the short run, but their effect tends to vanish with the passage of time. A change in their values can markedly affect the transitory component of the solution of the underlying dynamic model, but it will have no influence on the equilibrium portion of the solution.[4] In a common-forces regime of convergence, strong convergence can occur only if the ancillary variables also take the same values for all the economies in question. Otherwise, each economy will have its own steady state, and the pertinent variables will never converge completely.

The preceding discussion suggests a number of testable implications that we may investigate empirically to determine which of the two models is a better description of reality or whether they both play a substantial role and, if so, whether we can evaluate their relative influence.

Because the neoclassical model, the prime example of a common-forces approach, has been discussed so extensively—particularly in the literature connected with the work of Paul Romer (1986)—we shall next discuss plausible mechanisms for the alternative approach—the contagion model.

Mechanisms of Contagion: Technology Transfer

Among the influences that determine an economy's growth, we usually see listed its rate of innovation, the rate at which the economy absorbs transferred technology, its rate of investment, the education of its labor force, and its political stability. We have already noted that technology transfer is one of the influences most commonly cited when implicitly discussing a contagion model. We will examine this view in this section, but I will suggest in later sections that some of the other growth-determining variables can also promote contagion.

It would seem clear from the standard discussions that from the point of view of growth promotion, the optimal speed of technology transfer entails a trade-off between two desiderata. On one side, excessive speed in dissemination impedes growth by undermining the incentives for innovative efforts, doing so by hastening the date at which the innovator's profits are eroded by the competition of imitators. On the other hand, excessive delay in dissemination handicaps growth by extending the period during which every producer except the original innovator is forced to operate with obsolete technology. In international terms, the statistics indicate that some 20 countries (including even Luxembourg) each contribute thousands of patents per year. A protracted delay in the transfer of the technology represented by these patents means that on the average, each country is deprived over the period in question of the use of 95 percent of the new products and processes that become available during this time. This appears to suggest that—in contrast with the economic efficiency that the market is said by economic theory to be able to achieve in terms of static resource allocation—in the domain of technology transfer the market mechanism performs rather poorly on two counts. First, because imitation is more rapid than might be hoped from the point of view of the stimulation of innovative activity, the free-rider problem leads to less investment in invention and innovation than required by the public interest. On the other hand, through the use of patents, secrecy, and other devices, innovating firms may generally succeed in raising the cost of imitation and in delaying the time at which an invention will become available to others. The implication that the market mechanism is an impediment to innovation and its dissemination is startling, given the widespread impression that the market's achievements in the field of technological change are unparalleled in human history.

The evidence on the speed of dissemination in practice implies that if the typical innovative firm is determined to prevent or at least delay the spread of its proprietory technology, it has proved remarkably ineffective in achieving its goal. Estimates of the time in which recent innovations have become available to economies other than that of the country of origin suggest that the typical lag ranges somewhere from 1 to 2.5 years (see Mansfield 1985, Tilton 1971; see also the rich body of information provided in the Yale survey, Levin et al. 1987). I believe that the market mechanism does provide elements that promote and speed dissemination, thereby serving as automatic and effective instruments of contagion. Not only do these avenues of dissemination hasten the availability of inventions to others besides those who introduced the initial innovation, but by providing a suitable reward to the innovator for sharing the proprietary knowledge, they also mitigate the innovation-deterring free-rider problem and perhaps in some cases eliminate it altogether.

How, then, does one account for the apparent failure of innovators to prevent the rapid diffusion of their ideas? Although it is undoubtedly not the entire story, the theory of entrepreneurship offers two components of such an explanation.

The Imitative Entrepreneur

The evidence going back at least to the Renaissance suggests that the principal instrument of dissemination of new technology at that time (and one that has by no means disappeared today) is the enterprising technology exporter. Such persons are themselves entrepreneurs who, rather than specializing in the initial innovation (including the financing of the requisite R&D and the other necessary activities), seek instead to find promising new markets for techniques that have already proved their economic viability in their country of origin.

Ever since the beginning of the Industrial Revolution and undoubtedly earlier, there has existed a group of innovative entrepreneurs who have found it profitable to use their talent for the innovative *dissemination* of technology. As Joseph Schumpeter implies, finding a new place in which to use an invention is itself an innovative act, and frequently the resulting transfer must be accompanied by product or process innovation, as when an item is adapted to a different climate or to a new market with its particular consumer tastes, and so on. Indeed, it has been common for some of the product modifications thereby introduced to be transferred back as product improvements into the country where the initial innovation took place.

Economic historians document the movements of the peripatetic imitating entrepreneurs who came from England and made their fortunes by rapidly disseminating British innovations throughout Europe and North America. And England was by no means alone. The Du Ponts, for example, brought to the United States the knowledge and skills of French chemistry, particularly in making gunpowder. Often the original innovators acted as their own dissemination agents, such as when Robert Fulton tried (but failed) to sell his steamboat (as well as his submarine and his torpedo) successively to Napoleon and to Napoleon's British enemies. The point is that money can be made from enterprising technology transfer, and therefore some entrepreneurs have concentrated on that task. With capable and energetic individuals engaged in this lucrative occupation, it is easier to see why the market has in fact achieved such a remarkable record in speed of dissemination. Still, this view assumes that such transfer activity serves principally to thwart the determined attempts of innovating firms to maintain the proprietary character of the new knowledge acquired by their own efforts. But there is both empirical and theoretical evidence suggesting that this view of the innovating firm's goals is, at best, an oversimplification.

Historically, we know that sometimes the enterprising exporters of technology were the very same persons as the innovating entrepreneurs, indicating that in at least these cases, rather than constituting a profit-eroding manifestation of the free-rider problem, dissemination actually promised to enhance the profitability of innovation, thereby providing an additional incentive for entrepreneurs to undertake the effort of innovation in the first place. Still, we should recognize that this was hardly always the case and that quick and easy dissemination could therefore serve as a substantial disincentive for innovation by private enterprise.

This situation changes when dissemination is channeled through the second of the two mechanisms to be discussed here, the arrangement to which I have referred elsewhere as a *technology-sharing cartel*. This second explanation for the market's record of rapidly spreading technology that emerges from the theory of entrepreneurship is the argument that market forces do not merely encourage firms (even those in direct competition with one another) to share their technological advances. Rather, these market forces often may offer those firms literally no other option and may severely punish enterprises that refuse to participate in such an information exchange.

Technology-Sharing Cartels

An example shows how the pressures of competition can force firms to share their technology by reciprocally licensing their patents or through other more or less flexible arrangements. Imagine an industry containing nine firms, initially identical in size and offering identical products, with each company investing the same amount per year in cost-reducing R&D. The yield of such outlays is uncertain, but assume that for each firm the expected yield of the process innovations is a half-percent reduction in unit cost from that of the preceding year. Suppose that eight of the firms decide to form a "technology-sharing cartel," in which each firm makes available to the other members the results of its own research, expecting in return full access to the results obtained by the others. The ninth firm, however, decides to stay out of the cartel and to retain proprietary control over whatever information its own research yields.

Clearly, any member firm, A, will acquire an enormous competitive advantage over the holdout firm, X. First, although both firms' R&D activities will have the same expected yield, A will automatically acquire at zero cost what amounts to an insurance policy against a failure of its own efforts in any particular year, since it will be privy to not only its own results but also those of its seven cartel partners, and the probability of all eight firms' failing is considerably lower than that of any one of them. Obviously, Firm X benefits from no such insurance. More important, the cost reduction expected by Firm A will not be 0.5 percent but will be closer to $4 = (8 \times 0.5)$ percent because A can use the inventions contributed by all eight cartel members.[5] And in this scenario, Firm A is likely to enjoy the near 4 percent rate of reduction in cost year after year. In contrast, holdout Firm X can expect a cumulative rate of cost reduction of just 0.5 percent a year. It should be obvious that unless something else happens to save it, Firm X cannot hold out very long against this competitive pressure. It simply will find it increasingly difficult to match the constantly declining prices of its rivals and so will be forced to join the cartel (if the cartel is willing, belatedly, to admit it), or it may face insolvency.

A moment's consideration will confirm that there is nothing pathological about this scenario. Although it need not hold universally, for reasons that space prevents me from discussing here, it should be clear that the story has wide applicability. Hence, it should not be surprising that empirical researchers such as Von Hippel (1988) have confirmed that there is, indeed, a considerable amount of technology-exchange activity among firms.

Thus, the cartel-organizing entrepreneur contributes in this way to the efficiency of the market as a mechanism of technology transfer and thereby helps account for the intertemporal efficiency of the market mechanism. For one thing, such a cartel deals effectively with the innovator's free-rider problem by transforming the revelation to others of its own technological contributions into its own ticket of admission to using the innovations introduced by the other members of the cartel. Therefore, rather than cutting down the profit return to investment in innovation, dissemination actually serves to enhance its profitability. In other words, the cartel helps ameliorate both of the market mechanism's alleged shortcomings in dealing with innovation: It reduces or eliminates free-rider disincentives to investment in innovation, and at the same time, it also weakens or destroys barriers to the rapid dissemination of innovation that makes the latest techniques widely available.

It seems clear that the contagion of growth from one economy to another is promoted by enterprising disseminators of technology and technology-sharing cartels. These two institutions are driven by the profit motive to transmit technological improvements quickly and effectively from one economy to another. To the extent that innovation is a (and possibly is *the*) main long-term instrument of growth in productivity and per-capita income, we may have described much of the mechanism of contagion, in which the performance of the growth leaders is transmitted to the laggards.[6]

This discussion also suggests why the advantages of backwardness may extend only to economies that are *slightly* backward. Those countries that are very far behind in the growth process are likely neither to be very attractive to exporters of technology nor to be in a position to take advantage of the prospective benefits that the latest and most sophisticated technology can promise to economies that are closer to industrialization. Because the least developed countries are typically short of trained engineers, technicians, and scientists, they lack the personnel needed to make sophisticated technology run with competitive effectiveness and efficiency. Because their economies often specialize in the export of raw materials, handicrafts, and either few manufactures or manufactures of the simplest varieties, their production processes ordinarily do not provide much scope for the use of complex technological developments. These and other handicaps tend to make the poorest countries immune or at least relatively resistant to growth contagion. Moreover, these same impediments, along with the poverty that makes them unpromising as markets, also mean that these countries are unlikely to offer the most attractive profit opportunities to entrepreneurs or firms that are prepared to arrange or at least participate in the export of technology. The most promising customers for technology exports are surely those whose technology currently is only slightly behind that of the leaders. This, then, is another reason that one may reasonably expect the convergence club to include as members the industrial leaders and those who are only a little behind them, occasionally admitting a "miracle economy" that is able to break out of its LDC status, while effectively keeping most of the poorer economies outside its doors.

Mechanisms of Contagion: Migration of Inputs

It is widely recognized (see, e.g., Barro and Sala i Martin 1990, pp. 9–11, and Wolff 1991) that in a world of open economies, growth in one country tends to be transmitted to another through the export of capital from the former to the latter. A rapidly growing economy is apt to generate substantial savings, particularly in the early years following its takeoff, when persistence in consumption habits is apt to restrain consumption outlays and prevent them from staying abreast of output. Although a considerable proportion of the resulting abundance of savings is likely to be invested at home, the saved resources also seek promising outlets elsewhere, and a laggard economy often is the beneficiary. Thus, capital accumulation—the variable other than technical change usually taken as the principal source of growth in labor productivity—may well serve as a second instrument of transmission of growth from one economy to another. As the neoclassical model makes clear, this is particularly likely to be so where diminishing returns to capital prevail, because then expanded investment at home in a country with an outstanding growth performance soon decreases the returns expected from additional domestic investment, and the initial scarcity of capital in the laggard countries shores up the marginal return to investment there. That obviously strengthens the incentive to export capital from the rapidly growing economy to those growing more slowly.

Capital is not the only input whose export makes growth more contagious. If impediments to the migration of individuals are weak or nonexistent, disparities in growth among economies will usually lure the poor and the ambitious members of the labor force to leave the laggard economies and migrate to the leaders. For obvious reasons, this movement will raise both wages and the marginal product of labor in the laggard economies and hold back the advance of both of these in the leader economies.

At the same time, the migration of skilled labor from the leaders to the laggards has historically also served as a significant conduit for the transfer of technology, because the migrants carry with them the information and training needed to make innovative technology work. Thus the migration of labor, too, serves to facilitate growth contagion, thereby contributing further to a convergence process.

Mechanisms of Contagion: Feedback in Productivity Growth

There are other means through which growth contagion can occur. For example, lagging countries may be led to deliberate imitation of the leaders, partly as a means to achieve respectability if not prestige. For example, probably partly for this reason, the period after World War II witnessed the widespread dissemination of elementary education, along with a considerable increase in the secondary-school and college-educated proportions of the populations of laggard economies, thereby adding to the stock of human capital invested in the labor force. This has undoubtedly helped erode one of the advantages for productivity growth that the leader economies previously possessed. The increase in human capital is not, however, the source of contagion on which I intend to focus in this section, though this example does point us in the desired direction.

The literature commonly cites a number of variables as major influences on the rate of growth of an economy's productivity. The point I want to make here is that once growth contagion is under way, these variables can both increase its intensity and offer, to the slightly backward economy, advantages relative to the growth leaders, advantages that contribute to a process of convergence. This process entails two general attributes of the mechanism of productivity growth: its feedback properties and the presence of a variety of relationships, not unlike diminishing returns, that affect some of its main components.

The feedback structure of productivity growth is easy to describe. We have already listed the variables commonly taken to be the main stimulants of labor productivity growth in an economy—capital accumulation, investment in R&D, education of the labor force, and, with it, the ability to absorb technological developments imported from abroad. Growth in productivity is believed, on the basis of some evidence, to be stimulated by an increase in the magnitude of any of these variables. But a moment's reflection will indicate that each of these variables, in turn, normally rises in response to either higher productivity or a faster rate of growth. It is not difficult to document that investment per member of the labor force tends to be higher among countries whose labor productivity and per-capita income is near the top of the range than it is among countries less successful in this arena. We have also noted that there is reason to believe that speeding up the growth of per-capita income enhances savings per person because persistence in consumption habits causes outlays in consumption to lag behind income (see Baumol, Blackman, and Wolff 1989, pp. 180–84). It also is true that both outlays on R&D per capita and real expenditures on education vary directly with an economy's level of labor productivity or its output per capita. In other words, those variables that encourage productivity growth themselves increase in value as the productivity rise that they helped bring about later materializes. Thus, productivity growth, perhaps as clearly as any relationship in economics, is characterized by all the elements that constitute a feedback process—one set of variables influences the value of another, and that other, *after some lag,* affects the values of the variables by which it was previously stimulated.[7] In the absence of a serious disturbance, one can expect these steps to be repeated, certainly not forever, but for several such feedback "rounds."

One may suspect that the feedback relationship includes more than the productivity-stimulating variables already listed. For example, as we noted earlier, Barro includes variables such as the stability of the government as a likely stimulant of productivity growth, but at least an impressionistic correlation seems to suggest that the political stability of countries tends in turn to be strengthened by an increase in their per-capita incomes.

In what way are the feedback attributes of the growth process pertinent to our central concern here—the mechanism of contagion of productivity growth? Although feedback itself does not seem to be a source of contagion, it can strengthen the process once it is under way. If a lagging economy has "caught" a mild case of growth from one of the leaders, which in turn stimulates capital accumulation, R&D investment, and education in the laggard, then with the passage of time the weak growth process may accelerate through the endogenous feedback mechanism and be transformed into something far more substantial. To strain the medical metaphor yet further, feedback can thus make the affected economy more susceptible to contagion, transforming what might otherwise have been a case of growth that hardly merited notice into one that is comparable to that of the leader.

One other force that appears to contribute powerfully to convergence still needs to be considered. This is the mechanism of international competition, which requires the producers of a common product in two different countries to stay abreast of each other in terms of both product attributes and (if input prices do not differ much in the two economies) productivity levels. To the extent that factor price equalization applies in the two economies, the country that permits itself to fall behind the other in productivity level will find itself at a cost disadvantage (see Dollar, Wolff, and Baumol 1988). To retain a place in the market, it will be driven to take measures to improve its productivity performance and the attributes of its products to the extent required for competitiveness. This means that managements in economies lagging in productivity will be under constant pressure to take whatever steps they can to bring themselves closer to the leaders. The market mechanism simply does not permit relative inefficiency to go unpunished, and this is as true for intercountry competition as it is for the markets of a single economy. Ultimately, then, we may well consider competition to be the main instrument of productivity growth contagion among economies that share many export products, that is, the leading industrial countries and those that are only slightly behind.

Convergence and Common Forces Analogous to Diminishing Returns

This completes our discussion of the contagion models of convergence. We turn, finally, to some brief remarks related to the other models—the common-forces models of convergence. Here we note that other influences seem to play a role analogous to that of diminishing returns. They do so in the sense that they promote convergence by eventually slowing the rate of productivity growth in the leader economies. A few illustrations will indicate how this can happen.

We noted that a takeoff toward more rapid growth in a laggard economy can increase its savings rate because ingrained consumption habits lag behind the expansion of income. But experience indicates that such a lag is apt to be only temporary. Even if the population cohort that was present at the takeoff does not greatly change its consumption patterns, the next generation or the generation after that usually demands living standards commensurate with its higher income levels, and as this consumption becomes more energetic, savings rates are likely to be driven down toward the levels that prevailed in the old leader economies. Thus, the savings advantages enjoyed by the slightly backward economies may well evaporate as they approach the level of attainment of the leaders.

Similarly, any special incentives to R&D expenditure enjoyed by the laggards are likely to erode over time, as a consequence of what I have elsewhere referred to as the "cost disease of the handicraft services." The labor content of several personal services—among them education, medicine, law, and the live performing arts—is difficult to reduce; that is, their labor productivity is particularly resistant to improvement. As a result, labor productivity in the remainder of the economy typically grows with far greater rapidity than it does in these arenas. Since real wages throughout the economy tend to be pulled upward more or less in step with the economy's average productivity performance, the consequence is that in an economy with rapid productivity growth, the cost per unit of output of such personal, stagnant services is likely to rise persistently and cumulatively at a rate faster than the average rate of inflation.

Research is an example of a labor-intensive activity, at least those parts that are not readily amenable to increases in labor productivity. This means that in an economy with rapidly growing productivity, the cost of R&D can be expected to rise relative to that of manufactured inputs such as capital equipment. To the extent that investment in R&D can substitute for investment in capital goods—considering both to be inputs into the production process—the rise in the relative cost of the former can be expected to inhibit the business demand for it. Thus, the free-enterprise system may be characterized by the secular erosion of the superior R&D outlays of the leader economies (see Baumol and Wolff 1983).

We could provide still other examples of diminishing advantages for the leader. For instance, education, besides being susceptible to the cost disease that was just described, has evident limits in the number of years that the typical member of the population wants to devote to it. It is not accidental that few people, even in the wealthiest countries, spend more time on their education than is required for a medical or a law degree. From the point of view of contribution to output, it would clearly be absurd for the labor force to spend most of its employable years in school. Consequently, as educational standards rise in the slightly backward economies, they normally draw closer to those in the leader countries, where time devoted to education is approaching some sort of ceiling.

All of these examples suggest that although during the feedback process, productivity growth itself tends to lead to increases in the values of the variables that are its prime stimulants, this may well be subject to erosion that helps the lagging economies catch up with the leaders, that is, that facilitates the process of convergence.

Concluding Comments

Fortunately, from the point of view of our job security, many questions associated with the convergence hypothesis remain to be explored. For example, there seems to be little definitive evidence on which one can base a defensible judgment between the contagion model and the common-forces model of convergence. Although the studies of the role of the ancillary variables are surely competent and impressive, they are far from conclusive.

Still, the body of empirical studies has contributed much persuasive evidence. It seems quite clear that stripped of disturbing influences, the evidence supports the convergence hypothesis rather strongly, at least after the influence of ancillary variables has been removed, that is, after the hypothesis has been translated into terms of *residual* convergence. It also seems clear that convergence does not apply to the poorest of the world economies, though the line separating those eligible for membership in the convergence club and those foreclosed from membership has not been determined definitively. There apparently are ancillary variables that do materially affect the relative performance of the converging economies, at least in the short run, and these ancillary variables may be the most promising focus of rational growth policy, particularly for the LDCs.

Finally, it seems to follow from the evidence that it makes no sense to judge the relative growth performances of the different economies except in relation to their expected positions in the convergence hierarchy. If it is true, as the evidence seems to show, that the forces of convergence are among the dominating influences on an economy's productivity growth, then a nation can be judged to have performed well or badly only to the extent that it exceeds or falls short of the ranking that the forces of convergence, acting alone, would have awarded it.

In closing, we may also note that although we have cited a number of forces that seem likely to drive the more successful economies toward convergence, it is possible that these forces may drive the economies in question only toward *close proximity* to one another's performance. None of the mechanisms that we have described here seems capable of ensuring that any two economies will be driven to an identical limiting position. Thus, the strong convergence concept discussed earlier in this chapter corresponds to a hypothesis that is probably far too demanding on any grounds of plausibility. It is not surprising that the results of the empirical test of this hypothesis offer it little support.

Notes

I am extremely grateful to the Alfred P. Sloan Foundation, the Price Institute for Entrepreneurial Studies, and New York University's C. V. Starr Center for Applied Economics for support of the research for this chapter.

1. This is not quite accurate. Maddison (1982) does provide estimates of per-capita income for three countries beginning in 1700, far earlier than the starting date of Bairoch's series. We should also note that the construction of Bairoch's series has been subject to some criticism.

2. This somewhat mischaracterizes the work of De Long, who does attempt to take account of the influence of differences in religion. However, the bulk of his illuminating discussion relates to the influence of the particular sample selected, correctly criticizing my earlier work for having been based on a sample of economies selected retroactively, so as to be composed largely of cases of successful growth performance, a procedure biasing the calculation toward the appearance of convergence. For this purpose there was no need for De Long to probe deeply into the multivariate elements of the growth process.

3. There is also a study by Kendrick (1990) that displays his wisdom and long experience in the field. However, since it deals primarily with a small number of industrialized countries, it is not directly comparable to the other investigations.

4. This statement is probably somewhat exaggerated. For example, cultural differences in attitudes toward education may affect the efficacy with which transferred technology is used in different countries, and such differences may well persist for considerable periods. Still, there is reason to believe that economic circumstances affect culture and that in the longer run the homogenization of living standards will diminish cultural differences and perhaps make them nearly disappear.

5. It is likely to be somewhat lower than that, both because there may be some duplication of the research results obtained by different cartel members and because technology transfer is not quite free. It takes time, and it is likely to require special staff training and entail the cost of getting rid of the "bugs" that almost always plague innovations during the period immediately following their introduction.

6. Note that technology cartels can also serve as an instrument of a common-forces model of convergence. In every industrialized economy, if firms find themselves forced by market pressures to enter into technology-sharing arrangements, each country's productivity growth rate may be sped up as a result. It is not clear, however, why that should offer a greater growth advantage to the moderately backward members of the group as they would need in order to converge toward the leaders.

7. For an early discussion suggesting the importance of such feedback relationships, see Nelson 1964, especially pp. 591, 595–97. For formal models of the feedback processes and an examination of their behavioral implications, see Baumol and Wolff 1983, and Baumol and Wolff, forthcoming.

References

Alam, M. S., and A. Naseer. (1990). "Convergence and Polarization: Testing for an Inverted-U Relation Between Growth Rates and GDP Per Capita." Paper, Northeastern University.

Bairoch, Paul. (1976). "Europe's Gross National Product, 1800–1973." *Journal of European Economic History* 5:213–340.

Barro, R. J. (1984). *Macroeconomics.* 1st ed. New York: Wiley.

———. (1991). "Economic Growth in a Cross Section of Countries." *Quarterly Journal of Economics* 106:407–43.

Barro, R. J., and Xavier Sala i Martin. (1990). "Economic Growth and Convergence Across the United States." Working Paper no. 3419. Cambridge, MA: National Bureau of Economic Research, August.

Baumol, W. J., S.A.B. Blackman, and E. N. Wolff. (1989). *Productivity and American Leadership: The Long View.* Cambridge, MA: MIT Press.

Baumol, W. J. (1986). "Productivity Growth, Convergence, and Welfare: What the Long Run Data Show." *American Economic Review,* December, pp. 1072–85.

Baumol, W. J., and E. N. Wolff. (1983). "Feedback from Productivity Growth to R&D." *Scandinavian Journal of Economics* 85:147–57.

———. (1988). "Productivity Growth, Convergence, and Welfare: Reply." *American Economic Review,* December, pp. 1155–59.

———. (Forthcoming). *Growth of Productivity as Feedback Process.* Cambridge, MA: MIT Press.

Bernard, A. B., and S. N. Durlauf. (1990). "A Test for Convergence Across National Economies." Working Paper in progress, Stanford University.

Borts, G. H., and J. L. Stein. (1964). *Economic Growth in a Free Market.* New York: Columbia University Press.

Cass, D. (1965). "Optimum Growth in an Aggregative Model of Capital Accumulation." *Review of Economic Studies,* July, pp. 233–40.

De Long, J. B. (1988). "Productivity Growth, Convergence, and Welfare: Comment." *American Economic Review,* December, pp. 1138–54.

De Long, J. B., and L. H. Summers. (1990). "Equipment Investment and Economic Growth." Working Paper no. 3515. Cambridge, MA: National Bureau of Economic Research, November.

Dollar, David. (1991). "Exploiting the Advantages of Backwardness: The Importance of Education and Outward Orientation." Washington, DC: World Bank, December (unpublished).

Dollar, David, E. N. Wolff, and W. J. Baumol. (1988). "The Factor Price Equalization Model and Industry Labor Productivity: An Empirical Test Across Countries." In R. Feenstra, ed., *Empirical Methods for International Trade.* Cambridge MA: MIT Press, pp. 23–47.

Dowrick, S., and D. Nguyen. (1989). "OECD Comparative Economic Growth 1950–85: Catch-up and Convergence." *American Economic Review,* December, pp. 1010–30.

Easterlin, R. A. (1957). "Regional Growth of Income: Long Run Tendencies." In S. Kuznets and D. Thomas, eds., *Population Redistribution and Economic Growth in the United States.* Philadelphia: American Philosophical Society, pp. 141–99.

———. (1960). "Interregional Differences in per Capita Income, Population, and Total Income, 1840–1950." In *Conference on Research in Income and Wealth, NBER Studies in Income and Wealth,* vol. 24. Princeton: Princeton University Press, pp. 73–140.

Kendrick, John W. (1990). "International Comparisons of Productivity Trends and Levels." *Atlantic Economic Journal,* September, pp. 42–54.

Koopmans, T. C. (1965). "On the Concept of Optimal Growth." In *Study Week on the Econometric Approach to Development Planning.* Amsterdam: North Holland, pp. 225–300.

Levin, R. C., A. K. Klevorick, R. R. Nelson, and S. G. Winter. (1987). "Appropriating the Returns from Industrial Research and Development." *Brookings Papers on Economic Activity.* Washington, DC: Brookings Institution, pp. 783–820.

Maddison, Angus. (1982). *Phases of Capitalist Development.* Oxford: Oxford University Press.

———. (1989). *The World Economy in the 20th Century.* Paris: OECD Development Centre.

Mankiw, Gregory N., David Romer, and David Weil. (1990). "A Contribution to the Empirics of Economic Growth." NBER Working Paper no. 3541, December.

Mansfield, Edwin. (1985). "How Rapidly Does New Industrial Technology Leak Out?" *Journal of Industrial Economics,* December, pp. 217–23.

National Bureau of Economic Research. (1991). *The NBER Digest,* March.

Nelson, Richard R. (1964). "Aggregate Production Functions and Medium Range Growth Projections." *American Economic Review,* September, pp. 575–604.

Quah, D. (1990). "International Patterns of Growth: Persistence in Cross-Country Disparities." Working Paper, MIT.

Ram, Rati. (1991). "Education and the Convergence Hypothesis: Additional Cross-Country Evidence," *Economia internazionale,* May–August, pp. 244–53.

Romer, P. (1986). "Increasing Returns and Long Run Growth." *Journal of Political Economy* 94:1002–37.

Solow, R. M. (1956). "A Contribution to the Theory of Economic Growth." *Quarterly Journal of Economics,* February, pp. 65–94.

Streissler, E. (1979). "Growth Models as Diffusion Processes: II. Empirical Implications." *Kyklos* 32:571–86.

Summers, R., and A. Heston. (1988). "A New Set of International Comparisons of Real Product and Price Levels: Estimates for 130 Countries." *Review of Income and Wealth,* March, pp. 1–25.

Swan, T. W. (1956). "Economic Growth and Capital Accumulation." *Economic Record,* November, pp. 334–61.

Tilton, John E. (1971). "International Diffusion of Technology: The Case of Semiconductors." Washington, DC: Brookings Institution.

Von Hippel, Eric. (1988). *The Sources of Innovation.* New York: Oxford University Press.

Wolff, E. N. (1991). "Capital Formation and Productivity Convergence over the Long Run." *American Economic Review,* June, pp. 565–79.

4

Catch-up and Convergence in the Postwar Growth Boom and After

MOSES ABRAMOVITZ

A central feature of the postwar growth boom is the convergence of the productivity levels of those relatively advanced industrialized nations that organize economic activity mainly by means of business enterprises and relatively free markets. The original members of the OECD, as organized in 1961, are the group of nations that share these characteristics, and this chapter focuses on their experience. It is the record of this group during the great postwar growth boom that, more than any other single consideration, brought to the convergence hypothesis the attention it enjoys today.

The experience of these nations during the postwar growth boom was unusual in two senses. First, the variance of their productivity levels declined more rapidly and with greater consistency across countries than ever before. Convergence in this sense was much stronger. Second, all the countries of the group quickly narrowed the productivity gaps separating them from the United States, which was and remained the productivity leader of the period. There was "catch-up" as well as "convergence." By contrast, during the prewar decades as far back as 1870, the average gap between the United States and the other members had been widening. Because productivity growth in the United States during the growth boom was itself at least as fast, perhaps faster, than it was before the war, it follows that the pace of growth of the group as a whole was much more rapid after the war than it was before.

With the end of the growth boom, say in 1973, the convergence experience of the group took another form. Decline in the variance of productivity levels became much slower. On the other hand, the productivity gaps between the United States and almost all the other members continued to narrow, and although the catch-up continued, it was at a slower pace than during the boom. Retardation in growth was the common fate of all the member countries, but that of the "followers" was more severe than in the United States, and so there was a very severe general slowdown.

The purpose of this chapter is to help us understand the postwar experience of the relatively rich group of industrialized capitalist countries in respect to both convergence among themselves and catch-up with the United States. So stated, this study has two serious limitations. Because it neglects the experience of the much larger group of poorer countries and of nations that organized their activities through different institutions and policies, the scope and the reliability of its generalizations about the convergence process are necessarily qualified. And because it does not attempt to explain the growth record of the United States itself, except insofar as that country responded to the same factors that governed the growth rates of followers, this chapter's account of the causes of the very rapid postwar growth and of the subsequent slowdown is restricted.

Convergence within a group of countries during a limited period of years is manifested in two main ways. One is in the degree of intercountry variance in the levels of some selected measure of economic performance, say national product per capita, labor productivity, or multifactor productivity. A second is the consistency with which individual countries take part in the convergent experience of the group. We can identify the latter with the degree of association between initial levels of per-capita product or productivity or whatever and subsequent growth rates. In regard to the indicators of levels and growth rates, this chapter depends mainly on labor productivity and, to a lesser extent, multifactor productivity. Besides convergence in the senses just explained, there is the related but distinct matter of catch-up, which I measure by the relative differences between the productivity levels of particular countries and that in the United States, which was the productivity leader during the period with which this study is primarily concerned.

My argument proceeds from the view that the factors governing the pace and international consistency of convergence may be usefully organized under two general headings. One is the *potential* for relatively fast growth that countries with comparatively low productivity enjoy. This is a potential that reflects these countries' greater opportunity to advance by borrowing and adapting the best-practice technology and organization of more productive economies, by accumulating capital faster, and by improving their allocation of resources. The opportunity for faster capital accumulation is part of potential because capital–labor ratios in laggard countries are relatively low, and new investment can embody larger technical leaps and yield higher rates of return. The chance for gain by better allocating labor is greater among laggards because their agricultural and petty trade sectors, in which productivity is relatively low, are larger. Gains from all these sources then carry a bonus insofar as they permit gains from economies of scale. The other heading covers the class of factors that may support or impede the pace of the *realization* of potential.

My preliminary index of potential is the relative gap that separates each country's productivity level from that of the productivity leader of the time. One can easily see that if that were the only variable of consequence in determining potential and if conditions for realization were equally favorable for all countries, both the variance of productivity levels and the gaps that separate national levels from a leader's would decline steadily; there would be a perfect, negative association between productivity growth rates and initial levels; the rate of convergence would decline as the gaps became smaller; and ceteris paribus, the growth rates themselves would decline as the gaps contracted.

Relative gaps, however, are not the only variable of consequence controlling potential. There are three additional conditions. One is the natural resource endowment of each country taken in relation to its labor force and reproducible capital stock, both physical and human. This is a factor that influences relative levels of labor productivity but is open to enlargement only in the degree—different in different countries—to which advanced methods of discovery and extraction can improve an underdeveloped supply. Access to crude materials depends heavily on the use of advanced methods to find and exploit a domestic supply. (David and Wright, forthcoming). It also depends on a country's proximity to sources in other countries and on costs of transportation. But finally, it also depends on what there is to find and develop in each country. Unequal endowments of natural resources are, therefore, necessarily reflected in levels of productivity, and the expected association between levels and growth rates must be weaker than it would be if growth depended solely on the ability to imitate or otherwise acquire better methods used elsewhere. A further complication is that the importance of differences in natural resource endowments is not itself a constant. Its importance has diminished over time with the worldwide discovery and exploitation of new sources of supply, with the fall in transportation costs, with the introduction of synthetic materials, and with the greater elaboration of processing, distribution, and producer and consumer services that has been a concomitant of modern economic growth (Nelson and Wright, forthcoming; also see Chapter 5). As an element of potential, their natural resource endowments have now become a minor concern for the more advanced group of countries, but I judge that they were of substantial importance a century and more ago, and they remain a matter of importance for less developed countries today.

Technological "congruence" is a second supplementary condition. By this I mean the relevance or usefulness to less advanced countries of the techniques and forms of organization that characterize the frontiers of productivity in a leading economy. If factor supplies, markets, and their scales differ substantially among countries, the opportunities open to countries of equal productivity to take advantage of the methods of more productive economies will also differ. And in general, the potential of smaller countries to catch up to a productivity leader much larger in size will be restricted.

"Social capability" is the third condition. This is a vague complex of matters, few of which can be clearly defined and subjected to measurement. It includes personal attributes, notably levels of education, an attribute that is subject to measurement, however imperfectly. But it also refers to such things as competitiveness, the ability to cooperate in joint ventures, honesty, and the extent to which people feel able to trust the honesty of others. And it also pertains to a variety of political and economic institutions. It includes the stability of governments and their effectiveness in defining and enforcing the rules of economic life and in supporting growth. It covers the experience of a country's business people in the organization and administration of large-scale enterprises and the degree of development of national and international capital markets.

Besides potential, the pace of convergence is also influenced by another complex of conditions that govern the pace at which potential can be realized. Here I merely suggest their nature. There are three main classes of factors. One refers to the conditions that control communication across borders and, more generally, the variety of matters that influence the international diffusion of technology. A second has to do with the conditions that bear on the mobility and adaptability of factors and that may impede or facilitate the pace of structural change. And a third covers the macroeconomic background of a period and, therefore, the stability and duration of conditions that support investment and the steady absorption of an expanding product.

With all this in mind, the general thesis of this chapter may be simply stated. A special conjuncture of circumstances during the first quarter-century following World War II made the potential for convergence unusually strong and enabled the presently developed countries to exploit that potential rapidly and in concert over a long period. Many of these favoring circumstances, however, were transitory. Some were transitory in their very nature, notably, but not exclusively, the opportunities for technological modernization and the other growth advantages inherent in the large productivity gaps of the early postwar years. They were bound to weaken as the convergence boom proceeded. Still other favoring circumstances, which were perhaps not inherently transitory, have nevertheless become weaker or disappeared. There were still other developments—the larger investments in research and development, the expansion of multinational corporate operations, higher levels of education and managerial competence, and the unification of the European economy—that favored convergence in the past and that are likely to persist into the future. Not all of these elements of modern growth, however, now work for convergence. As a larger number of countries approach the highest existing levels of average productivity, more of their effort takes the form not of catch-up but of pressure against the frontiers of technology and capital intensity. Tendencies to divergence come to accompany and offset the continuing efforts of all to modernize and keep abreast. All this will favor growth but will not necessarily make steadily for greater convergence.

The remainder of this chapter is organized as follows. First I provide a summary picture of the long-term record of convergence and catch-up. Then I deal with the extraordinary convergence experience of the first 25 or so years after World War II and its connections with the potential of the time and with the conditions controlling the pace of realization. Finally I take up the causes of the breakdown of the convergence boom and the subsequent record of weak convergence and retarded catch-up. I discuss the transitory basis of the convergence boom itself and of the forces making for both divergence and convergence in a new world of more nearly equal technological rivals.

The Record of Convergence

To appreciate the extraordinary character of the post–World War II convergence experience, one must compare it with the longer-term record. Here I summarize only the broad features of the record, but a more elaborate and detailed review is provided in Chapter 2 by Angus Maddison, on whose data I largely depend.

A clear tendency for productivity levels to converge, even among the group of presently advanced countries, did not appear until about 1870. During the earlier part of the nineteenth century, the records—in the few countries for which they exist—instead suggest divergence.[1] This is hardly surprising. Countries entered the process of modern economic growth at different dates and developed a potential for catch-up at different rates. The experience from 1870 onward, however, is one of convergence, and a compact summary of the record appears in Tables 4-1 and 4-2.

The tables are drawn from estimates by Angus Maddison (1982 and 1989 and

Table 4-1. Comparative Levels of Productivity, 1870–1989: Means and Relative Variance of the Relatives of 15 Countries Compared with the United States
(U.S. GDP per hour = 100)[a]

	Means			Coefficients of Variation		
	A	B	C	A	B	C
1870	77 (66)	—	—	.51 (.51)	—	—
1890	68 (68)	—	—	.48 (.48)	—	—
1900	—	52	—	—	.39	—
1913	61 (76)	52	54	.33 (.36)	.35	.37
1929	57	—	—	.29	—	—
1938	61	—	—	.22	—	—
1950	46	43	43	.36	.37	.37
1960	52	—	—	.29	—	—
1973	69	65	66	.14	.16	.14
1979	75	—	—	.15	—	—
1986	—	76	—	—	.14	.13
1989	—	—	81	—	—	—

Sources: A columns, based on Maddison 1982, Tables 5.2 and C.10; B columns, based on Maddison 1989, Table 7.3; C columns based on Maddison, Chapter 2 in this volume, Table 2-13.

[a]1870, 1890, and 1913. Figures in parentheses are based on relatives with the United Kingdom = 100. The data in the C columns are based on 14 countries relative to the United States.

Table 4-2. The Association (Rank Correlation) Between Initial Levels and Subsequent Growth Rates of Labor Productivity, 1870–1986
(GDP per hour in 16 countries)

Discrete Periods		Lengthening Periods	
	Based on Maddison 1982		
1870–1890	−.32	1870–1890	−.32
1890–1913	−.56	1870–1913	−.59
1913–1929	−.35	1870–1929	−.72
1929–1938	−.57	1870–1938	−.83
1938–1950	+.48	1870–1950	−.16
1950–1960	−.81	1870–1960	−.66
1960–1973	−.90	1870–1973	−.95
1973–1979	−.13	1870–1979	−.97
	Based on Maddison 1989		
1900–1913	−.51	1900–1986	−.96
1913–1950	−.18		
1950–1973	−.96		
1973–1986	−.53		

Sources: The same as in Table 4-1 plus Maddison 1982, Table 5.1, and 1989, Table 7.2.

Chapter 2 in this volume), referring to 16 advanced OECD countries (15 in the data from Chapter 2). The tables support several findings:

1. There was a consistent tendency for labor productivity levels in the group to converge. Coefficients of variation declined steadily, with only a single break in the period across World War II.

2. The tendency was systematic in that the less productive countries tended, on the whole, to advance at faster rates than did the richer countries. The correlation between the initial country levels in each period and their subsequent growth rates was always negative, subject again to the single exception of the World War II decade. The correlation, though negative, was indeed weak in some periods. The inverse association, however, stands out with special force in the cumulative record for longer and longer periods that appears in the right-hand column of Table 4-2. As the period is extended, the correlation grows stronger—except, again, for the effect of World War II. Countries that lagged to start with, or along the way, made up ground later if not sooner. The association between levels and growth rates between 1870 and 1979, or between 1900 and 1986, is well nigh perfect.[2]

3. There is, however, a distinct difference in the strength of the group's convergent tendency between the postwar boom and the prewar years. This is immediately apparent in the relatively high correlation coefficients for 1950 to 1960 and 1960 to 1973 and the lower coefficients for earlier periods. It is also the case that the pace of convergence, as measured by the rate of decline in coefficients of variation, was more rapid during the postwar boom than in earlier periods.[3]

4. With the end of the boom in 1973, all these evidences of convergence weakened. The association between levels and growth rates fell back to its more modest prewar strength, and the pace of convergence did so as well.

5. "Catch-up," the other aspect of convergence, is another story. The simple theory leads us to expect that the "followers" will grow faster than the "leader." Instead, it appears that from 1870 to 1913 the United States advanced faster than did the average of the followers. From 1913 to 1938, the United States maintained its relative lead and then, from 1938 to 1950, under the impact of World War II, enlarged it again. Only since 1950 have the followers, on average, begun to catch up. Between 1950 and 1973, the relative level of the followers rose by over 50 percent. And since the U.S. pace of advance was then at least as fast as it had been before, this meant that the progress in Europe and Japan was very rapid. Even after 1973, the process of catch-up continued, but less rapidly. The average productivity growth rate of the followers, which between 1950 and 1973 exceeded that in the United States by 2.2 percentage points a year, now exceeded the much reduced U.S. pace by only 1.1 percentage points.

The Roles of Potential and Realization in the Postwar Convergence Boom and in the Past

The Stronger Potential for Convergence and Catch-up: Enlarged "Gaps"

The enlarged gaps in labor productivity separating the "follower" countries from the United States in 1950 are one preliminary measure of the stronger potential for rapid advance enjoyed by these countries when the postwar period began. The enlarged variance of productivity levels is a second (see Table 4-1).

There are indications that the enlargement of the labor productivity gaps caused similar changes in both capital intensity and total factor productivity (TFP), which are the two most important channels of catch-up. Edward Wolff (1991) reported the figures in Table 4-3, which refer to a sample of five large countries (Germany, Italy, United Kingdom, Japan, and the United States).

In this small sample, both the average capital-intensity gap and that in total factor productivity increased over the whole period between 1880 and 1950. But the gap in capital intensity grew especially quickly between 1880 and 1913, when the United States was establishing itself as the world's leader in labor productivity. The American lead in TFP grew only slowly in these years. Between 1913 and 1950, however, mainly under the impact of World War II, the U.S. lead in TFP increased a great deal.[4] These figures suggest, therefore, that the postwar period opened with enlarged gaps that set the stage for the catch-up that followed. Changes in the variance of the two factors across countries were more modest, but there was a notable increase in the variance of TFP between 1913 and 1950—again a reflection of the uneven impact of the wars, the ensuing financial disturbances, and the Great Depression on different countries.

That both TFP growth and capital accumulation were systematic channels of convergence and catch-up in labor productivity is supported by the estimates of Steven Englander and Axel Mittelstädt (1988). On the basis of their data for the business sectors of the 16 advanced members of OECD, it appears that between the early 1960s and 1973, the rank order correlation between initial levels of labor productivity and subsequent growth rates was -0.86 for labor productivity itself; that between initial levels of labor productivity and the growth rates of TFP was -0.66; and that for labor productivity levels and the rates of capital–labor substitution was -0.70.

In this period, TFP growth and capital accumulation were not only systematic sources of convergence but also sources of labor productivity growth and of catch-up to the United States. Kendrick's data for 1960 to 1988 attribute about 65 percent of labor productivity growth to TFP growth and about 35 percent to capital accumulation per worker in both Japan and OECD Europe (1990, Table 6). For the same period, he found that about 70 percent of the difference between Japan and the United States in labor productivity growth was attributable to Japan's more rapid growth in TFP.

Table 4-3. Capital–Labor Ratios and Total Factor Productivity Levels: Coefficients of Variation in 5 Countries[a] and Mean Levels in 4 Countries Relative to the United States, 1880–1979

| | Capital–Labor Ratios | | Total Factor Productivity Levels | |
	Mean Level Relative to USA	*Coefficients of Variation*	*Mean Level Relative to USA*	*Coefficient of Variation*
1880	0.54	0.59	0.62	0.43
1913	0.38	0.62	0.59	0.38
1950	0.33	0.63	0.45	0.48
1970	0.50	0.40	0.77	0.14
1979	0.72	0.27	0.81	0.10

Source: Wolff 1991, Tables 1 and 2.

[a]Germany, Italy, United Kingdom, Japan, United States.

The remainder he attributes to capital–labor substitution. Between Europe and the United States, faster TFP growth accounted for about 64 percent of Europe's faster advance in labor productivity. On this showing, therefore, TFP growth was the more important source of catch-up, but capital accumulation was a second important source.

That gaps between followers and the United States in both capital–labor ratios and TFP increased between 1880 and 1950 and especially during the decade of World War II and its immediate aftermath is a relevant part of the background from which the postwar catch-up and convergence boom took its start. It would be a mistake, however, to emphasize unduly the separate roles of capital accumulation and TFP. The action of each and both is the outcome of an interactive process. The prospect of making speedy technological progress by introducing new, state-of-the-art capital equipment, which was an especially attractive prospect given the enlarged postwar gaps, supported high rates of investment and rapid capital accumulation. The accelerated rate of accumulation made the rate of introduction of modern technology faster than the advance of the best-practice frontier. In the growth accounts, this embodiment effect was registered in TFP. And there are other reasons that capital accumulation and technological progress support each other. In the period between the early 1960s and 1973, the rank order correlation between the growth rates of TFP and those of the capital–labor ratios of 16 advanced OECD countries was +0.51 (Abramovitz 1989, Englander and Mittelstädt 1988, Tables 1 and 2, Nelson 1964, 1981).

The decomposition of labor productivity growth into the contributions of capital–labor substitution and total factor productivity yields only a very gross analysis of the channels of convergence, because TFP is itself a broad cover for many diverse sources of growth.

The principal sources covered by the umbrella of TFP, besides technological progress itself, are, first, improvement in the quality of labor because of longer schooling and other such labor quality changes due to shifts in the age and sex composition of the work force; second, gains in productivity from the better allocation of labor as workers move from low productivity farm jobs and self-employment to higher productivity wage and salary work in industry and other nonfarm employment; and third, enlargements in market scale that permit a higher degree of specialization in the work that people do, in the tools and power that aid them, and in the organization of industry.

It appears, however, that in the postwar convergence boom, labor quality improvement was not a uniformly important source of catch-up for the laggard countries in the advanced group. The reallocation of labor, on the other hand, was such a source, at least for those countries that were especially laggard immediately after the war and in which the farm sectors were still relatively large. It did not count for as much in countries like the United Kingdom and the Netherlands which were higher up in the early postwar productivity scale and in which farm populations had already been sharply reduced in earlier decades. Finally, the enlargement of market scale was generally a source of convergence, but one of limited importance. I base these judgments on figures drawn from Maddison's growth account (1987, Tables 19 and 20. Also see Table 4-4 in this chapter, Abramovitz 1979, n. 2, and Denison 1967, Tables 21–24 and 21–26).

These observations lead to a simple conclusion. When one has allowed for the

Table 4-4. Excess Growth over the United States in Labor Productivity and Its Sources, 5 Countries, 1950–1973
(percentage points per annum)

	France	Germany	Netherlands	United Kingdom	Japan
GDP per hour	2.62	3.46	1.44	0.68	5.32
Capital–labor substitution	0.45	0.99	0.99	0.39	1.37
TFP	2.17	2.47	0.45	0.29	3.95
Labor quality	−0.01	−0.18	0.04	−0.27	0.16
Reallocation	0.53	0.44	0.14	0.17	1.29
Scale effect	0.08	0.11	0.07	0.02	0.04
Remainder	1.57	2.10	0.20	0.39	2.46

Source: Maddison 1987, Tables 19 and 20.

three principal components of TFP, the remainder of TFP is still its major part. Disregarding other minor elements that might still be in question, this remainder of TFP may be regarded as a rough measure of the convergence that took place through the modernization of capital equipment and of a disembodied technology. This, therefore, was the major channel of postwar convergence among the industrialized countries.

The general lesson so far is that the postwar period opened with Europe and Japan further behind the United States in labor productivity and in its components, total factor productivity and capital intensity. In addition, it appears that the enlarged TFP gap reflected a more serious degree of low productivity employment in farming in Japan and in some European countries (Abramovitz 1979, pp. 21–23, 26–28). In each case, an important part of the enlargement of gap can be traced to the war, which is a pointer to its transitory character. Its origins in the war, moreover, gave it a special connection with the potential for rapid productivity growth, and I will take this up later in this section.

It is necessary first, however, to recall that the enlarged gaps are only preliminary indexes of a stronger potential for growth. I will, therefore, discuss the three conditions, mentioned earlier, that qualify the significance of the gaps themselves. I argue that in each instance, these qualifications were less severe in the postwar years than they had been earlier in this century and were still less severe than before 1900.

Differences in Natural Resource Endowments

I suggested earlier that the differences among countries in the quantity and quality of their natural resource endowments were one source of variance in labor productivity levels and that such differences were, by their nature, not subject to complete elimination. Differences in natural resource endowment, therefore, would weaken the association between levels and growth rates of productivity and inhibit the decline of the variance in levels otherwise expected in the convergence process. The rich endowment of the United States gave it an advantage over Europe and Japan, whose poorer resources put for many years an obstacle in the way of catch-up (Wright 1990). The importance of such intercountry differences, however, has fallen over time (Schultze 1951; also see Chapter 5). There are several reasons for this:

- Both land and water transportation costs have dropped sharply.
- Resources have been discovered in many parts of the world whose existence was unknown a century and more ago, and they have been exploited more efficiently.
- Technological progress, by increasing farm yields per acre, has been of a land-saving character. It has raised the value of mineral deposits previously neglected and added new metals and synthetics to the metals and other materials on which production had earlier relied.
- Crude materials are now processed more elaborately than they used to be, and on this account too, primary products now make up a smaller fraction of the cost of finished goods.
- Services in which the crude materials component is small have become more important as incomes have risen, and food, in which the materials component is large, has become less important.

For all these reasons, differences in natural resource endowment have counted for less in recent decades than they did earlier. One striking recent example of these changes deserves special notice. When the postwar period opened, it was widely expected that the well-worked, high-cost coal resources of Europe and the more general lack of energy sources in Japan would pose serious obstacles to further industrialization for both. The rapid exploitation of cheap Middle Eastern petroleum, however, and the development of low-cost transport by supertankers changed the picture. Energy problems became much less severe in Europe and Japan, and this went far to eliminate what had been an important relative advantage of the United States.

Differences in "Congruence"

The technological path that the United States followed in the late nineteenth century, when it was rising to the top of the productivity ladder, and in the early decades of this century, when it was consolidating and increasing its lead, was resource intensive, scale intensive, and capital intensive (Wright 1990; also Chapter 5). Resource intensity was consonant with American resource abundance and with relatively early and technologically ingenious resource development (David and Wright, forthcoming). Scale intensity was consistent with a large domestic market. This was itself the product of a large and rapidly growing population, high levels of per-capita income, and a homogeneity of customs and tastes that reflected the country's brief history, its relatively egalitarian character, and its rapid settlement from a common source along the Atlantic Coast. Capital intensity derived from the opportunity to use expensive systems of power production and transmission and specialized equipment in large establishments and from the capital requirements of the transportation network that itself created the large national market. Behind these sources of American technology were other personal, governmental, and institutional characteristics and arrangements that I shall describe later under the heading of "Social Capability."

The scale-intensive and capital-intensive character of American technology was also supported by the direction taken by the composition of American consumer goods in the first three decades of this century. As incomes rose in the years before World War I and, still more, in the 1920s, American households became large users of new durable consumer goods. These included not only sewing machines, bicycles, and typewriters, which had come on the market earlier, but also automobiles, phonographs, gas and electric stoves, refrigerators, telephones, and radios. Some of the same products, of course, were equally important as producer goods, especially telephones, automobiles, tractors, and trucks. All these products gained large markets because they could be made by mass production methods at prices within the income limits of a large fraction of American households.

Countries less well endowed with natural resources and with smaller domestic markets could not easily adopt and exploit American technology. One symptom of this difficulty appears in Wolff's capital stock figures (see Table 4-3). Even by 1880, the level of capital intensity in the United States was far higher than the average level in the United Kingdom, Germany, Italy, and Japan. The U.S. lead then increased 35 percent from 1880 to 1913. As we have seen, during the decades before World War II, there was a considerable degree of convergence among the European countries but, on the average, no catch-up with the United States.

All these restrictions, however, were becoming less severe as time passed. The U.S. advantage in raw materials and power sources was becoming less important. The development of foreign trade between 1880 and 1913 helped the European countries overcome the limitations of their smaller domestic markets, and so did the general increase of their incomes, although per-capita incomes were not rising as fast as they were in the United States. Yet by 1913, the average per-capita incomes in the other advanced countries were as high as that in the United States in 1890. Seven of the 15 "laggard" countries in 1913 had higher incomes than the United States did in 1890. If, therefore, European income levels in 1913 were not yet high enough to support the industries whose scale-intensive methods had been and were being explored by the United States, they soon would have been if income growth had proceeded without the great disturbances that accompanied and followed the two world wars and the Depression. The postwar experience of Europe and Japan in developing scale-intensive and capital-intensive industries to produce both consumer and producer durables once prewar income levels had been regained supports this conjecture.[5] And the postwar extension of more liberal arrangements for trade and payments and the establishment of the European Common Market and the European Free Trade Area then carried this process further.

There are, therefore, good grounds for thinking that a variety of developments in the late years of the last century and in the opening decades of the present century were gradually strengthening the degree of congruence among the circumstances of Europe, Japan, and the United States. The ability of the "followers" to adopt and exploit the techniques of production and organization developed in the United States thus was growing. One might have expected that the rate of convergence would have accelerated and that the process of catching up to the United States would have begun in the 1920s and proceeded apace. This expectation, however, was blighted by the two great wars, by all the economic disturbance that followed, and by the Depression of the 1930s. It remained for the postwar decades to take advantage of the greater congruence that had been emerging for half a century or more. And because this congruence was greater, the postwar potential for convergence and catch-up was even stronger than the enlarged productivity gaps suggest.

Social Capability

Social capability is a class of factors that in some ways lie behind the degrees of technological congruence just discussed. The term itself comes from Kazushi Ohkawa and Henry Rosovsky (1973, esp. chap. 9). It is a large and still poorly defined subject that I will treat only briefly, partly for lack of space, but still more because no one knows the full scope of the subject or how to measure many of its elements.

In an earlier work (1986, p. 388), I identified a country's social capability with "technical competence, for which—at least among Western countries—years of education may be a rough proxy, and with its political, commercial, industrial and financial institutions, which I characterize in more qualitative ways." I had in mind mainly the stability and effectiveness of government and "experience with the organization and management of large scale enterprise and with financial institutions and markets capable of mobilizing capital for individual firms on a similarly large scale." In a later work I referred to matters connected with social attitudes toward wealth and growth and to problems of incentives and opportunities (1989, chap. 1).

With respect to all this, it is tempting, at least in hindsight, to say that in the postwar period and for the sample of advanced countries here in question, social competence was high enough to absorb and exploit the best-practice technology of the time. After all, productivity variance fell rapidly for more than two decades after 1950, and the gaps between the United States and the follower countries were quickly narrowed. This, however, leaves open some obtrusive questions, for example, how far Japan's extraordinary performance or Britain's poor showing can be attributed to differences in the elements of social capability and, if so, to which of them. It also leaves open the question whether a general rise over time in the social capability of the whole group of advanced countries helps account for the unusual strength of the convergence process in the first quarter-century following World War II.

I suspect that considerations falling under the rubric of social capability are important to both these questions. Pleading incompetence, however, I shall say nothing about the relation between social capability and international differences in performance. And pleading only a slightly smaller degree of incompetence, I shall say just a little about some general changes in social capability. In regard to them, I point to the following developments:

1. Levels of education rose steadily throughout the half-century preceding the postwar period. They did so even during the war and interwar years between 1913 and 1950. Insofar as the education of the general population and of a cadre of competent engineers and technicians are required to discover, assess, and acquire modern technology and to use it effectively, countries were better equipped after the war than they had been in earlier decades.

2. Although, on average, the followers failed to gain ground on the United States in the disturbed years from 1913 to 1938 and then fell back during World War II, both the European countries and Japan were then entering or expanding industrial sectors

that had greater capital and scale intensity or that involved higher degrees of technical precision than they had undertaken in the past. Examples are chemicals, steel, shipbuilding, automobiles, tractors, and optical goods. This was partly a consequence of increasing supplies of capital, closer "technological congruence," and higher levels of general and technical education, partly a reflection of the growing competence of the countries' cadres of industrial entrepreneurs and managers, and partly a concomitant of aggressive military policies and of preparation for war. In any event, the increasing experience in the follower countries with the organization and management of large-scale industry put them in a better position at the end of the war to borrow, adapt, and exploit the characteristic style of American business than they had been earlier.

3. Besides organizational experience, the establishment and expansion of large-scale enterprise requires access to an efficient capital market. This requirement arises from the need to overcome the well-known disjuncture between the types of assets that households, seeking safety and liquidity, are prepared to hold and the types of liabilities that industrial firms, operating with illiquid assets in a risky business environment, are prepared to assume. A modern capital market—with its outfit of limited liability corporations, efficient security exchanges and traders, a panoply of different sorts of intermediaries, and a public accustomed to its operations and confident of its safety and effectiveness—is needed to overcome this disjuncture. Yet countries in the early stages of industrialization are typically ill equipped in every aspect of an effective capital market. The process of technological catch-up is, therefore, inhibited.

Capital markets develop in a time-consuming process of challenge and response. Inadequate financial markets inhibit the pace of industrialization, but the unmet needs of business elicit financial development. This view suggests that one of the reasons for the relative weakness of the convergence and catch-up processes before 1913 was the limited development of capital markets in Japan and in many European countries, particularly those that were latecomers to industrialization. Financial markets, however, were becoming more effective in those years, and the process of financial development continued even during the hiatus in convergence from 1913 to 1950, and this development has been carried still further during the years since.

My more general conclusion is that the developments just sketched—in education, managerial experience, and the effectiveness of capital markets—combined to make the social capability of the followers greater in 1950 than it had been earlier. This is still another reason for thinking that the potential of these countries to catch up by means of technological borrowing and capital accumulation was then stronger than even the enlarged gaps in capital intensity and total factor productivity suggest.

The Special Effects of World War II

We have already seen that World War II produced a larger gap between the United States and the other advanced countries in labor productivity, in capital–labor ratios, and in total factor productivity and that it enlarged the variance of productivity levels. According to the reasoning of earlier pages, this increased the followers' potential for rapid advance and convergence. But the fact that the enlargements of gaps and of the variance of levels arose in good part as a result of the war raised the potential for growth and convergence in special ways not yet discussed. Some of this special power arose from causes that weakened after only a few years, but other causes were more persistent.

First, the wartime destruction or undermaintenance and shortages of materials produced unbalanced capital stocks. Lack of inventories or damage to mechanical components or parts of infrastructure (bridges, freight yards) made much larger amounts of capital useless or usable only in limited ways. It was possible, therefore, to bring large quantities of capital back into operation and to make large increases in output by making relatively small investments in repair, by replacing missing components, and by building up stocks of materials.

Second, because investment for civilian production was restricted during the years of preparation for war and still more during the war itself, the ratio of civilian capital to potential labor input was reduced. These effects were probably more severe in Japan and in the belligerent countries of Europe than in the United States. If so, the relevant civilian capital–labor gap between the United States and other countries in 1950 was larger than the figures for total capital indicate.

Third, partly overlapping with the first and second causes, the war, together with the Depression, the disturbed conditions of the 1920s and World War I itself, produced a large decline in the ratio of physical to human capital. Although the rates of physical capital accumulation had slowed during these disturbed years, the pace of advance of education and training continued relatively steadily. Rolf Dumke (1990), citing Walter Krug (1967), reports that in Germany, the ratio of physical capital to a measure of human capital, which stood at about 8:1 in 1913, fell to about 5.2:1 in 1925, to 4:1 in 1938, and to about 2.1:1 in 1950. The trends in this ratio in other countries were doubtless different in strength but probably similar in direction. If, as seems plausible, human and physical capital are complementary, the relative abundance of human capital in 1950 would have supported the rapid physical capital accumulation in forms embodying advanced technology. We may see this as a particular aspect of the improvement in the social capability of the followers already mentioned.

Fourth, the war had other effects that bore more on the pace of realization than on potential itself. I refer to the impact of war, and more particularly of defeat, on territorial adjustments, political regimes and policies, barriers to trade, financial disturbances, the organization of business (cartels, unions), business leadership, and the like. In some circumstances, the general effects of postwar reactions to war may be injurious to catch-up and growth, but in others they are supportive. The aftermath of World War I was probably injurious (Cf. Svennilson 1954), but I believe that the reactions to World War II were, on the whole, supportive. Consideration of these various special effects of the war indicates that they worked in ways that made the potential for rapid advance greater than it would normally have been, given the magnitudes of the productivity and capital intensity gaps and the opportunities to improve resource allocation. The Dumke study includes a number of econometric experiments that lend some statistical support to these observations. Dumke finds that the impact of the war (proxied by changes in per-capita output between 1938 and 1950 had an effect on postwar output growth that was complementary to that of the 1950 productivity gaps but that its effect quickly diminished and was no longer significant after 1960. In short, the war was a transient influence that strengthened the convergence process for some years but then weakened and disappeared.

Factors Supporting the Realization of Potential

Besides a stronger potential for growth and convergence, the decades following World War II were favored by a conjuncture of conditions that supported the fast, sustained, and concerted realization of potential. I discuss these conditions summarily under three general headings: technological effort and facilities for the diffusion of technology, structural change, and capital accumulation.[6]

Technological Effort and Facilities for Diffusion

It is now a commonplace that the exploitation of best-practice products and methods in use elsewhere is a costly process. It involves, first, awareness, then appraisal, then acquisition by purchase or reverse engineering, and finally, adaptation from the form in which the techniques may have been cast where first applied to one better suited to the resources, skills, scale of market, and style of products of the firms and markets to which it is to be transferred. This means costly investment. The scale and effectiveness of such effort were supported after the war by a number of developments.

As evidenced by expenditures on organized R&D, technological investment was much higher after the war than in earlier decades. In the follower countries generally, such expenditures started from low levels but grew quickly. By 1965, they had reached an (unweighted) average of 1.6 percent of GDP in the four major European countries plus Belgium and Japan. By 1970, the average in these countries was 1.8 percent and that in a broader sample of 14 OECD countries had reached 1.5 percent (Englander and Mittelstädt 1988, Table 14). These figures may be compared with the U.S. ratio in 1970—2.65 percent in all, but only 1.68 percent in spending for nondefense purposes.

One may presume that this allocation of investment was itself a response, at least in good part, to a perceived opportunity to acquire, adapt, and improve methods already in use elsewhere. The effort was further supported by a variety of conditions on the supply side, notably by more widespread general and technical education and by a larger presence of engineers in higher levels of management.

These efforts took place under conditions that came to be more strongly favorable to the diffusion of existing technology than had been the case in earlier decades. There was a much larger technical and business press. Air transport made international travel far faster and cheaper. The liberalization of international trade and payments acquainted managers throughout the industrialized countries with the products and techniques of firms in other countries, and competition impelled an early response. The Marshall Plan, with its arrangements for the exchange of American and European productivity missions, was an early opportunity to observe foreign production methods and focused attention on the superiority of the American methods then in use. The governments of the NATO and OECD countries encouraged the spread of knowledge about productivity-enhancing methods. When the growth of the European market became apparent, American firms became eager to obtain a share of the business through patent licenses, technology transfer contracts, joint ventures, and foreign subsidiaries. When the Common Market was established, it encouraged the same sort of activity among its members. By contrast with the portfolio investment that had dominated capital flows before 1914, these direct investments were carriers of technology and advanced capital goods pressing domestic firms to modernize. The revival of trade, supported by the successive GATT rounds, by the Common Market, and by EFTA worked to the same end.

Conditions Supporting Structural Change

The general principle that change in the structures of production, occupations, and locations is a necessary concomitant of economic growth is well established. After the war, a special conjuncture of conditions made labor supplies particularly responsive to demands and, therefore, facilitated the necessary transfers of labor.

In some countries, these conditions stemmed initially from high levels of unemployment (Denison 1967, Table 5-1A). Next, there were still large reserves of labor in farming and self-employment. (Abramovitz 1979, Kindleberger 1967). Repatriation of nationals added large numbers to the labor force in Japan, Germany, and France. And permanent immigration and guest workers added many people more, not only in Germany and France, but also in Switzerland and Scandinavia.[7]

The very rapid postwar rise of labor productivity in farming kept the level of redundant farm workers high for many years and so encouraged the movement of workers to industry and services. Angus Maddison (1982, Tables 5.11 and 5.13) provides the following estimates of prewar and postwar farm productivity growth in a small sample of large countries.

	1870–1950	1950–1973
	(percent per year)	
France	1.4	5.6
Germany	0.2	6.3
Japan	0.7	7.3
United Kingdom	1.4	4.7
United States	1.3	5.5

I have made rough estimates of the relation between the migration of workers off the farms (some of whom may have gone abroad, especially from Italy) and the number of workers added to nonfarm employment between 1950 and 1970 (see Abramovitz 1979, p. 26, no. 2).

United Kingdom	34 percent
Germany	51 percent
France	77 percent
Italy	100 percent
Japan	58 percent

The pronounced rise in farm productivity after the war was doubtlessly due in part to the augmented rate of transfer of partly redundant and low productivity labor out of farming to satisfy the growing demand for nonfarm labor. But it also reflected the effect of consolidation of small holdings, mechanization, electrification, better fertilizers, insecticides, and improved seeds.

The transfer of workers among sectors was also facilitated by the initial postwar weakness of labor unions that were less able to control entry into trades and industries. This condition, which lasted into the 1960s, may also have played a part in permitting the widespread use of guest workers.

There is one more point to be made about the relation between migration and the growth of nonfarm labor supply in Europe. It is an important point because it helps explain the fact that during the postwar boom, the countries of Europe and North America were able to enjoy accelerated growth in concert, rather than alternatively or in disjunct fashion, which was the rule before World War I. Before 1914, business cycle expansion in the United States and in other countries of recent settlement, and still more the investment booms connected with "long swings," attracted heavy immigration from Europe. On such occasions, workers from the farms of Europe went overseas, and the growth of the European nonfarm populations and labor supplies was correspondingly restricted. Growth acceleration overseas tended to be accompanied by retardation in Europe. The clearest example of this seesaw pattern was in the relation between the United States on the one side and Britain on the other, but there are indications that Germany, Italy, Norway, and Sweden also took part on some occasions.[8]

In the years after World War II, however, restricted immigration in the United States, Canada, and elsewhere made these countries only limited rivals for the supply of European reserve labor. Instead, the overseas countries, aided by large increases in agricultural productivity, drew heavily on their own farm populations and were aided by the entry of women into the labor force. At the same time, besides absorbing workers from their own farms, Northern and Western Europe and northern Italy gained labor by immigration from the East and from the less developed countries bordering the Mediterranean. The obstacle that population flows from Europe to North America and other countries overseas had posed to concurrent expansion on both sides of the Atlantic was largely removed. I shall refer to the conditions favoring concurrent expansion again in the next section.

Supports for Investment

Heavy investment was a central element in the rapid postwar catch-up and convergence process. It was needed by the laggard countries as the carrier of embodied technological progress, in order to build up their low levels of capital equipment, and, less certainly, as an instrument of learning by doing. By the same token, their war-damaged and unbalanced initial capital stock, its comparative obsolescence, and simply its limited quantity conferred on laggards the potential for rich rewards to investors and for quickly growing productivity—provided that finance could be obtained. In the background of the investment boom were also the new sources of heightened potential for growth by modernization that I summarized by reference to the diminished importance of restricted national endowments of natural resources, closer technological "congruence," and stronger social capability.

In the years immediately following the war, however, there were serious obstacles to investment. These stemmed partly from postwar financial and fiscal disorganization and inflation, partly from shortages of materials and inventories generally, and partly from balance-of-payments problems that restricted imports. These problems were gradually overcome in the late 1940s and early 1950s by monetary and fiscal reforms, by the Marshall Plan and other extraordinary aid, and by such transitional devices as the European Payments Union. As these obstacles were overcome, both Europe and Japan found that they enjoyed unusual and valuable supports for the investment needed to realize their strong potentials for growth. The question here is what the conditions and developments were that facilitated and sustained heavy investment for 20 years.

The Propensity to Save. A strong savings propensity emerged initially because both households and business firms had a pressing need to rebuild the cash assets and other liquid claims to money that had been depleted or entirely lost in the postwar inflations (Carré, Dubois, and Malinvaud 1975, Wallich 1955). Of longer-lasting importance, however, was the sharp rise of household incomes, business profits, and government revenues that were engendered by the investment and productivity advances themselves. Because the pace of income growth in many countries was unprecedentedly hasty, it also greatly exceeded expectations. It therefore outran the planned expenditures of governments and households and the dividend distributions of corporations and left all three with larger surpluses—or smaller deficits—than expected. This condition persisted into the 1960s. The "Julius Turm," where the Prussian kings had kept their war chest, became a familiar metaphor by which to characterize the cumulating surplus in the German federal budget, but it was a symbol of a much wider experience (Carré et al. 1975, chap. 9, Ohkawa and Rosovsky 1973, chaps. 6 and 8, Wallich and Wallich 1976, chap. 4).

The Initial Financial Condition of Firms and Households. As asset holders or creditors, the inflation depleted the financial positions of firms and households and encouraged savings. The same inflations, however, essentially wiped out the indebtedness of firms and households. In that sense, they improved the balance sheets of prospective investors. As soon as financial markets were again functioning, firms were willing and able to borrow with little concern for the debt burden, and lenders were correspondingly willing to extend credit. In most countries, therefore, credit rationing rather than concern for creditworthiness was the effective constraint on finance in the early postwar years. This initial freedom from debt supported investment for several subsequent years (Carré et al. 1975, pp. 313, 501).

Government Support for Investment

Private firms were the dominant agents of capital formation in all the advancing countries, but the governments participated in different ways and in different degrees. Government was less prominent in Germany, perhaps because large-scale industry was better established there than in other European countries. Also, German industry had enjoyed a recent period of profitable expansion in the 1930s and during much of the war under the stimuli of Nazi military preparation and war production. Elsewhere, large-scale industry was less well developed, and France and, to a lesser degree, Italy had suffered periods of stagnation more recently. These countries, as well as Japan, had traditions of regulation and protection that gave their governments postwar roles of great importance.

To appreciate this influence, one should recall that as late as the early 1950s, expectations of rapid growth were not common. Few people in Japan or Europe yet appreciated the growth potentials of their countries (Carré et al. 1975, pp. 278–79, 471, Ohkawa and Rosovsky 1973, p. 232). In this atmosphere of uncertainty and indecision, governments encouraged investment. By analogy with Schumpeter's "New Men," the dynamic innovators to whom he attributed recurrent expansions, there were again "New Men" after the war who got their chance in the train of war and defeat and who operated in and through government.

In these respects, France is a typical case. Spurred by Jean Monnet and the group who founded the plan, the government undertook unprecedentedly large programs to modernize transport, power, and heavy industry generally. The government's ability to act was stronger because postwar nationalizations had enlarged the scope of state-owned industry and because it had enough control over finance and trade to give priority to heavy industry not owned directly (Carré et al. 1975, pp. 477, 274–76, and, on French "planning" and its influence, chap. 14). In Italy, too, government takeovers under Fascism and after the war had enlarged the public sector. Grouped in umbrella organizations like ENI and IRI and led by forceful new personalities, these government-directed corporations also took an early lead in postwar capital investment.

In Japan, the government made itself felt partly through its own large investments in infrastructure and partly through its Ministry of International Trade and Industry. The ministry's purpose and effect were to provide guidance to private firms and to lessen the risks of innovation and investment faced by businesses venturing into new enterprises on a large scale. The government operated by selecting sectors for development, by supporting tariff protection, by choosing firms for the controlled importation and exploitation of foreign technology, and by helping arrange the industrial combinations needed to ensure a proper scale of operation. Its activities served to raise the sights of private business (Ohkawa and Rosovsky 1973, chap. 9).

The early importance of governments helps explain one of the otherwise puzzling features of the postwar catch-up process. Gaps in technology and capital intensity were significantly reduced during the decade of the 1950s. Yet the pace of convergence and catch-up did not decline in the 1960s as one might have expected; rather, it accelerated. The paradox is at least partly resolved if we consider that private business was at first hesitant and went forward more boldly only as the growth potential of the postwar economy became apparent. It was government that provided the early impetus, and this was carried forward only later by the rising confidence of private business. The same considerations meant that investment in the earlier years was more concentrated in the sectors under government ownership and special influence, that is, power, transportation, communications, and heavy industry generally. These demanded very large forward-looking investments that yielded their returns only slowly. The private investment of the 1960s could be more largely applied to equipment, the operation of which both raised the utilization rate of infrastructure capital and yielded more immediate returns to its owners and to the economy.

Labor Supplies Again. The redundant work force in farming and self-employment and the new conditions of international migration did more than foster labor mobility, occupational change, and regional shift. The availability of these supplies of cheap labor also inhibited the rise of nonfarm wages and so sustained the rates of return to investment in the face of large expansions of capital stock. By permitting large productivity gains to be achieved in both the industrial and agricultural sectors without provoking an unduly rapid rise in wages, it encouraged the expansion of industry and enlarged the scope for capital investment. The level of investment must have been raised and the investment boom prolonged instead of being cut short by falling profits.

These growth-supporting conditions, of course, could not be maintained indefinitely. Eventually, labor markets did become tighter and helped bring the boom to an end, but that is a story for later.

Payments Balances and Supplies of Money. The investment boom had both a monetary and a real side. Nominal income and thus the money supply normally grow at least as quickly as does the real output that the investment boom supports. In the postwar years, the conceivable alternative that a long-term price decline might provide was neither practical economics nor practical politics.[9] In the United States itself, the release of wartime suppressed inflation made a large postwar price rise inevitable, and inflation was then renewed by the Korean War and later by the Vietnam War.

The necessary growth of nominal income and money stock in the rest of the industrialized world, however, was more rapid than in the United States. Not only was real output growth faster than in the United States, but so was the rate of inflation. The reason is that in a fixed exchange-rate system, the process of balance-of-payments adjustment, although with a lag, forces up money wages faster in countries with relatively rapid productivity growth than in countries with slower productivity growth, like the United States. Prices, therefore, rose faster than in the United States, not so much in tradable goods whose productivity growth was relatively quick and over which international competition ruled, but in the less progressive nontradables (McKinnon 1971).

The implied growth of money stock involved a quick but by no means equal growth of reserve assets. And given the commitment to fixed exchange rates, a large part of those reserves had to have international currency. Under the Bretton Woods dollar-exchange system, this meant gold or short-term claims on dollars. When the war ended, however, the world's monetary gold stock was disproportionately concentrated in the United States, and foreign short-term claims on dollars were extremely small. Monetary growth in Japan and Europe, therefore, required a redistribution of the United States' gold stock and the accumulation in these countries of dollar claims.

Monetary growth in the industrialized world therefore came to depend on an arrangement of great delicacy, one that called for the simultaneous fulfillment of two basically contradictory conditions. The continuing redistribution of gold and the acquisition of dollar claims required a chronic balance-of-payments deficit in the United States and a cumulative deterioration of the U.S. reserve position. But it also required continued faith in the United States' ability to maintain convertibility and the gold par of exchange in order to avoid a flight from the dollar, the consequence of which would have been a U.S. monetary policy tight enough to halt American capital exports and to produce business contraction, first in the United States and then in the rest of the industrialized world.

The United States did maintain a chronic balance-of-payments deficit. By 1970, it had lost $13.5 billion in gold and $2.5 billion in other international reserves and had accepted some $41 billion of additional short-term liabilities. Meanwhile, the international reserves of other countries had risen by some $52 billion and those of developed countries alone by $42 billion, a quadrupling of their 1949 holdings (Abramovitz 1979, p. 29 and footnote).

The world's success in maintaining this process for two decades in the face of the cumulative deterioration of the U.S. reserve position constitutes a basic difference between the money-growth experience after the war and in earlier times. Before 1914, when investment booms and growth spurts overseas drew large capital exports from Britain, they had to be sustained in part by slower growth in Britain and, to some extent, in other parts of Europe that limited their loss of reserves. This, therefore, is a second reason that concerted growth in both Europe and the United States before World War I was difficult. Moreover, when Britain was the monetary leader, losses of exchange reserves even a fraction as large as those of the United States during the postwar boom would have caused the Bank of England to impose severe checks on monetary expansion and capital exports. The dollar basis of the postwar boom proved as durable as it did because of several transitory peculiarities of the postwar economy:

- The dollar was initially extremely strong. The United States at first had an enormous stock of gold and other international reserves and few liquid liabilities. The limited production capabilities of Europe and Japan in the early 1950s and their needs for imports meant an excess demand for dollars. The actual U.S. deficit, due to unilateral transfers, was discretionary, in a sense deliberate, and it was so perceived.
- Short-term claims on the United States accumulated, but some part of them was willingly held as working balances to support a growing trade denominated in dollars.
- The United States proved to be politically capable of exercising monetary and fiscal restraint for a dozen years after the Korean War. This lowered its own rate of inflation to a practical minimum and thereby limited the rate of inflation and demand for money in the rest of the world.
- When, at last, the United States' international position and prospects came to be viewed unfavorably, other countries faced a difficult choice. They might continue to amass dollar claims and thereby accept an increasing risk of loss by dollar devaluation. Or they could demand gold at once and so precipitate immediate devaluation and U.S. disfavor as well. The two risks were about equally unattractive. Countries, therefore, chose to postpone rather than hasten the event. The life of the system was, in this way, extended for several years.

How the monetary side of the great investment and productivity convergence boom came to an end and what this meant for later growth is again a story for later.

A Summary of the Basic Elements of the Convergence Boom

A conjuncture of numerous elements produced the convergence boom of the 1950s and 1960s.

The United States rose to productivity leadership and then extended its lead between 1870 and 1913 by its vigorous exploitation of advantages that other countries could not immediately match. One was its early development of a rich resource base. In a time of still high transportation costs and spotty resource exploitation elsewhere, this enabled the country to gain a lead in the development of resource-intensive industries. A second advantage was the emergence of a large national market that enabled the country to profit from the possibilities of an evolving power-driven, capital-intensive, and scale-intensive technology and organization. Behind these developments were the country's high level of income—a reflection, in part, of its rich resource base—the large population it attracted, its early investments in popular and technical education and in a national infrastructure of transportation and communication, and its equally early development of an effective capital market.

Few other countries, even among those now industrially advanced, could reproduce or offset these developments quickly. When the United States began its surge to leadership, some of its present rivals, for example, Italy and Japan, were still in the earliest stages of establishing their social and political bases of industrialization. Most others suffered, in one degree or another, because their economic circumstances were incongruent with the era's most promising path of technological progress then emerging in the United States. They lacked so rich a potential resource base, and their national markets were much smaller. These drawbacks, although they affected all other countries, differed in importance from one country to another. The upshot was not only that the followers fell further behind the United States but also that the convergence process among themselves, though clearly evident, went forward relatively slowly.

These drawbacks, however, became less important over time. The discovery and exploitation of resources in other parts of the world and the gradual decline of transportation costs were eroding the United States' advantage from the early exploitation of its own rich resource endowment. The rise of incomes and the development of international trade during the more liberal trading regime from 1880 to 1913 were opening the way for Europe and Japan to follow the United States more easily along its capital-, scale-, and power-intensive technological path. Technological congruence was becoming closer. And the ability to follow that path was rising with the spread of general and technical education, growing experience with large-scale industrial organization, and the development of capital markets both nationally and internationally.

The years following 1913 might, therefore, have witnessed a convergence and catch-up process rivaling in strength what actually took place only after World War II. This potential development, however, was blocked by the uneven effects of World War I, by the political and financial disturbances of the 1920s, by the Great Depression, and finally by the impact of World War II, which greatly widened the spread of productivity levels and enlarged the gaps separating other countries from the United States.

The great convergence boom of the 1950s and 1960s thus rested first on a potential for growth by catching up that had been gathering strength for a long time but whose realization had been frustrated by the troubles of the three decades between 1914 and 1945 as well as by those of the immediate post–World War II years. During the 1950s and 1960s, however, the strong potential for convergence was brought to realization by new circumstances, and these were the second basic element on which the convergence boom rested.

The postwar conditions that supported rapid realization of potential included some that facilitated the transfer and diffusion of technical knowledge, others that supported structural change, and still others that strengthened the public and private propensities to save and invest and that sustained a high level of business activity and employment. To some extent, these conditions arose from the policies of governments and the popular sentiments on which they rested. But they were also a response to the strong potential for growth itself. This was the case because conditions inherent in that potential promised large returns to R&D and technological effort generally, to physical investment, and to workers' transferring from farming and self-employment to larger-scale industry and commerce. There was, therefore, an interaction between the convergence potential of the time and the factors supporting rapid realization, and the two together produced the strong convergence of the postwar years.

After the Convergence Boom

The convergence experience of the 1950s and 1960s stands out as a unique episode, not only because it was preceded by many decades of slower and less systematic convergence, but also because it has again been followed by a period of slower growth and less systematic convergence that has now lasted for two decades and still continues. We now need to ask what brought the boom to an end and why the new period of weaker convergence persists.

My answer is that some of the more important elements that supported both the potential for convergence and its realization during the boom were inherently transitory. Others, though not necessarily transient, nevertheless weakened or disappeared. Finally, tendencies to divergence have come to accompany those that make for convergence. As the general levels of productivity in the followers rose, the levels in particular industries in some countries approached or even exceeded those in the same American industries. To be more precise, I suppose that the number of such instances increased. Technological effort then turned from borrowing, imitating, and adapting the existing best practice to pushing out the frontiers of technology. The relation between general levels of productivity and subsequent growth rates then tended to weaken (Hansson and Henrekson, 1991).

The remainder of this part of the chapter is a brief elaboration of these themes organized again under the headings of "Potential" and "Factors Supporting the Realization of Potential."

Potential

Developments that changed the potential for growth by catching up included some that strengthened potential as well as some that weakened it. I believe that on balance, those that weakened it were more important, and as suggested, these reflected the essentially transitory nature of these elements in the convergence process.

Recovery from the War

Productivity levels in Japan and in many European countries were initially very low because of the war. The nature of these losses was such as to make the marginal productivity of investment abnormally high. Relatively small investments in rebuilding stocks of goods and in repairing and replacing damaged facilities brought large quantities of undamaged but underemployed capital back into service. Foreign markets and supplies of imported materials were initially limited by shortages of foreign exchange and the resultant exchange controls. All these troubles were gradually overcome during the late 1940s and 1950s, and as they were, countries enjoyed a one-time or short-term boost. Thereafter, an important source of further rapid catch-up in productivity levels was lost.

The Diminished Gaps of 1973

The clearest and most important examples of the inherently transitory elements that supported the boom are the reductions in the various "gaps" that separated the followers from the United States and from one another. The figures in Table 4-5 indicate the importance of the declines in the gaps that resulted from the superior growth performance of the followers between 1950 and 1973. They also provide information about the continuing reductions in the gaps after 1973, when differences between growth rates in the United States and other countries were smaller. They bear on the continuing, if weaker, convergence in the 1970s and 1980s.

According to Table 4-5, the relative levels of labor productivity in the followers compared with the United States rose substantially between 1950 and 1973 and continued rising after 1973. Based on the experience of five large countries, this was also true of both components of labor productivity, capital per labor hour and total factor productivity (Frame I). To judge by the differences in growth rates, rather than in relative levels, there were similar changes in a much larger sample of countries (Frame III). In regard to productivity growth by resource transfer out of agriculture, I judge the decline in the potential for superior growth in the followers by the difference between the fractions of workers employed in farming in the followers and that in the United States (Frame II). Here again, it appears that there were large reductions in potential between 1950 and 1973 and that these kept on falling after that time.

Sources of the Reduced Growth Advantage of the Followers

Between 1950 and 1973, labor productivity growth in the follower countries was almost twice as fast as in the United States and exceeded the United States' pace by about 2.1 percentage points. Since 1973 the average rates in both the followers and the United States fell drastically, and the growth advantage of the followers dropped to 1.4

Table 4-5. Figures Bearing on the Decline in the "Gaps" Separating Follower Countries from the United States, 1950 to 1973 and After.[a]

I. Ratios of levels in follower countries to those in the United States.

	1950	1973	Latest
1. Labor productivity	.43	.66	.79 (1987)
2. Non residential capital per person employed	.30	.63[a]	.92 (1987)
3. Total factor productivity	.47	.79[a]	.84 (1979)

II. Excess of farm employment as a fraction of total employment in follower countries over the United States (percentage points).

	1950	1973	1987
1. Japan	35.3	9.3	5.3
2. 12 European OECD countries	11.8	5.6	3.2

III. Comparative growth rates (percent per year).

	Capital per Worker		Total Factor Productivity	
	1960s–73[b]	1973–86	1960s–73	1973–86
1. United States	1.9	1.5	1.5	0.0
2. 15 other OECD countries	5.1	3.6	2.9	1.0

Sources: Frame I, line:

1. Maddison 1991, Table 3.4 (15 OECD countries).

2. Maddison 1991, Table 3.10 (5 countries: France, Germany, Netherlands, United Kingdom, Japan).

3. Wolff 1991, Table 1 (5 countries: France, Germany, Netherlands, United Kingdom, Japan).

Frame II: Maddison 1991, Table C-5.

Frame III: Englander and Mittelstädt 1988, Tables 1 and 2.

[a]1970.

[b]Various dates in 1960s, as follows: United States 1960, Japan 1967, Germany 1961, France 1965, United Kingdom 1960, Italy 1961, Canada 1962, Austria 1961, Belgium 1961, Denmark 1960, Finland 1962, Netherlands 1962, Norway 1964, Sweden 1966, Switzerland 1963, Australia 1961.

percentage points (Maddison 1991, Table 3.3). The declines in the gaps indicated in Table 4-5 suggest that the major proximate sources on which convergence and catch-up depend would share in this drop in the followers' growth advantage. The growth accounts in Tables 4-6a and 4-6b (one based on Maddison's estimates, the other on Kendrick's), indicate that these expectations were generally satisfied (but this does not mean that the degree of response in the various sources corresponded in any clearly systematic way to that of the declines in the gaps).

Some comments on Tables 4-6a and 4-6b are in order. The results they report differ from each other in some respects, as one might expect. The two accounts cover different periods of time; Kendrick's sample of European countries is much larger (14 countries against 4); and their data sources and methods were not the same. They agree, however, that the drop in total factor productivity convergence ("output per unit of input" in the Maddison table) was the most important source of the decline in the pace of labor productivity convergence (see the columns on interperiod change in each table). It accounted for the whole of the decline in the pace of Japanese labor productivity convergence in the Maddison table. In Kendrick's account, capital accu-

Table 4-6a. Sources of Convergence in Labor Productivity, 1950–87 (differences in growth rates between follower countries and the United States)

	1950–73		1973–87		Interperiod Change	
	Europe[a]	Japan	Europe[a]	Japan	Europe[a]	Japan
Labor productivity	2.21	5.02	1.56	2.06	−0.65	−2.96
Capital per labor hour	0.93	1.40	0.74	1.44	−0.19	+0.04
Quality of labor	−0.15	0.17	−0.05	0.12	+0.10	−0.05
Output per unit of input	1.42	3.45	0.86	0.50	−0.56	−2.95
Structural effect	0.09	1.10	0.04	0.26	−0.05	−0.84
Scale and trade[b]	0.43	0.48	0.04	0.14	−0.39	−0.34
Other minor effects[c]	0.05	−0.01	0.12	0.06	+0.07	+0.07
Residual[d]	0.86	1.88	0.67	0.04	−0.19	−1.84

Source: Adapted from Maddison 1991, Table 5.22.

[a] Average of Germany, France, Netherlands, and United Kingdom.

[b] Trade effects combined with contribution of economies of growing scale on the ground that increased trade itself contributes to economies of scale.

[c] Includes two sources: "Energy effects" and "Natural resource windfalls."

[d] Includes "Quality of capital," "Technological diffusion," and "Unexplained convergence."

Table 4-6b. Sources of Convergence in Labor Productivity, 1960–88 (differences in growth rates between follower countries and the United States)

	1960–73	1973–88	Interperiod Change
USA–Japan differences			
Labor productivity	6.6	1.9	−4.7
Capital per labor hour	2.0	0.6	−1.4
Total factor productivity	4.6	1.3	−3.3
Scale and intensity	0.6	0.1	−0.5
Other nontechnical sources	1.4	0.0	−1.4
Technical residual	2.6	1.2	−1.4
USA–OECD Europe differences			
Labor productivity	2.2	1.1	−1.1
Capital per labor hour	0.7	0.3	−0.4
Total factor productivity	1.5	0.8	−0.7
Scale and intensity[a]	0.0	−0.5	−0.5
Other nontechnical sources[b]	0.5	0.0	−0.5
Technical residual	1.0	1.3	+0.3

Source: John W. Kendrick, "International Comparisons of Productivity Trends and Levels," Invited address to the Twenty-ninth Atlantic Economic Conference, Geneva, Switzerland, March 1990.

[a] A category that combines the contribution of economies of scale—taken to add 10 percent to the sum of the contributions from all other sources—with that of the change in the intensity of use of resources as indicated by changes in unemployment rates.

[b] A category that combines the contribution of changes in labor quality (education plus sex and age) with those of resource reallocation among industries and of some smaller sources. Kendrick's text makes it clear that only the reallocation of resources, mainly labor transfer out of farming, was most important.

mulation shared in the decline but was definitely the smaller source, as it was in Maddison's European account.

Within TFP, both tables tell us that a drop in the Japan–United States differential in the final residual, a crude indicator of relative rates of technological progress, was the most important source of slower labor productivity convergence. In Europe, however, the residual was far less important; in the Kendrick table, indeed, the European advantage over the United States even became somewhat larger. This finding, of course, does not mean that European residuals did not drop severely between the decades before and after 1973. They did, but the American residual utterly collapsed (Denison 1985, Table 8-1).

With one exception, the two accounts also agree that both the shifts of resources among sectors (the "structural effect") and the economies of scale played significant parts in lowering the rates of convergence of both Japan and Europe. In the Maddison account, however, the structural effect in Europe was not important.

The Embodiment of and Interaction Between Capital and Technology

The results yielded by the growth accounts, however suggestive, cannot be taken at face value. The various sources are interdependent. Here I shall try to take into account the fact that "embodiment" in new forms of equipment and structures or in capital in new locations is needed in order for some portion (presumably large) of newly discovered or newly available methods to be incorporated into production. Similar embodiment is also needed to take advantage of the economies of larger scale or of the potential gains from transferring farm labor to industry or the self-employed to dependent employment in industry or commerce. These three elements, in turn, are the main components of measured total factor productivity growth.[10]

There are two reasons that the embodiment effect may have been of substantial importance in helping account for the reduction in the rate of catch-up between the postwar boom period and the years following 1973. First, the growth rate of the gross capital stock between 1950 and 1973 was far more rapid than in previous decades, and so the average age of the stock was declining and was doing so faster among the followers than in the United States. This supported a high level of measured TFP growth and a large difference between such growth in the followers and that in the United States. After 1973, the growth rates of capital stock fell or, in some countries, stopped rising. The average age of capital increased, which slowed the rate of absorption of new technology, of economies of scale, and of resource reallocation. The difference between the rates in the two periods contributed to the large interperiod declines in the followers' measured TFP growth. The second element in the effect was the difference between the two periods in what one may call the "age-neutral" rates of embodied technological advance, those that would have obtained had the age of capital not changed. These were very high in the 1950s and 1960s and much lower thereafter. When age-neutral rates are high, this encourages a speedup in capital accumulation, and the consequent drop in capital's age makes a bigger difference to measured TFP than when age-neutral rates are lower.

I have used Richard Nelson's formulas (1964) to get a quantitative impression of the importance of differences in the rate of change of capital's age in accounting for the decline of measured TFP between the boom period and the years after 1973. The results appear in Table 4-7. When making these calculations, I took "measured residual growth" to be the sum of "economies of scale" and "reallocation of resources" as these appear in the growth accounts, plus their final residuals which for this purpose, I took to represent "advances in knowledge," whether by borrowing or innovation. My assumption in this experiment is that embodiment is required to incorporate only one-half of the advances in knowledge, economies of scale, and structural change. I regard this as a lower bound. If I am right, the true effects of changes in the age of capital are rather larger than the table suggests.

On my "one-half embodiment" assumption, the calculation based on the Maddison (1987) account tells us that of the interperiod decline in the difference between the United States and Japanese residual growth (−1.6 points), some 0.4 points were due to the greater slowdown in the Japanese rate of capital accumulation and the consequent relative increase in the age of Japanese capital stock (Column 3). Had capital's age remained constant in both Japan and the United States, Japan's advantage in residual growth would have fallen by only 1.2 points (Column 4) instead of the 1.6 points in Column (1). For the European countries, the difference made by the slowdown in capital accumulation was even larger relatively (0.3 out 0.8). The Kendrick-based data yield qualitatively similar results.

The general lesson to be drawn from these calculations is that if the causal connections between accumulation and technological progress run only from the former to the latter, then the usual growth accounts understate capital's role in accounting for the slowdown after 1973. By the same token, they overstate the importance of the slowdown in technological advance—and in the gains from economies of scale and resource reallocation. These distortions, moreover, would be all the greater if my 50 percent embodiment assumption is, indeed, unduly low.

Table 4-7. Change in Age of Fixed, Nonresidential Capital Stock as Source of Declines in Measured Residual Productivity Growth Between Growth Boom and Later Years (assuming one-half of residual sources require embodiment)

	Measured Residual Growth (percentage points) (1)	Capital Rate of Age-Change (years per year) (2)	Effect of Age-Change on Measured Residual Growth (percentage points) (3)	Age-Neutral Residual Growth (percentage points) (4)
I. Maddison-based data: Changes from 1950–73 to 1973–84				
United States	−1.4	+0.14	−0.1	−1.3
Japan	−3.0	+0.40	−0.5	−2.5
4 European countries	−2.2	+0.45	−0.4	−1.8
II. Kendrick-based data: Changes from 1960–73 to 1973–79				
United States	−1.1	+0.16	−0.1	−1.0
Japan	−3.6	+0.48	−1.0	−2.6
6 European countries	−1.9	+0.18	−0.3	−1.6

Source: See Appendix Note to Table 4-7.

These inferences, however, are only part of the story. The potential gains from capital investment are governed in substantial part by investors' perceptions of the productivity advances that can be realized from capital of new design or location.[11] So the slowdown in capital's growth between the boom and retardation and the consequent rise in capital's age were due in part—possibly in large part—to the substantial reductions in the "age-neutral" residuals that Table 4-7 reveals. There were also other reasons, however, for the slowdown in capital accumulation, and some of these will be noticed later.

More Considerations of the Potential for Productivity Growth After 1973

Three matters are noteworthy. First, differences in domestic endowments of natural resources (specifically energy resources) became more important for a decade or more than they had been for a quarter-century. The principal developments were the OPEC oil shocks of 1973 and 1979. Great increases in the price of petroleum followed and led to general increases in the prices of all energy sources. The effects in various countries differed partly because their domestic energy sources varied in importance and had a different impact on general inflation and partly because countries chose to react in different ways to the higher costs of energy and of rising inflation. These developments worked against a systematic association between aggregate productivity levels and subsequent growth rates. And this tendency toward divergence was somewhat strengthened by the offshore oil discoveries in British and Norwegian waters and of natural gas in the Netherlands.

Second, there was continuing progress toward closer technological congruence among countries and stronger social capabilities supported by rising levels of education, more ample supplies of capital per worker, convergence of consumer spending patterns, and the enlargement of domestic and international capital markets. These developments favored systematic tendencies toward productivity convergence.

Finally, stronger tendencies toward divergence arose as the catch-up of earlier years brought individual industries and firms in more countries up to the best practice of the time. National differences in technological and scientific networks, in entrepreneurial outlook and corporate organization, and in financial organization and practice then became more important.

These developments have been manifested in a number of ways. Expenditure for organized research and development has not only grown faster in virtually all the advanced countries than in the United States, but since the mid-1970s, industry-financed expenditures have also reached higher proportions of the value of industrial output in a number of countries. (Japan, West Germany, Netherlands, and Sweden; see Pavitt and Patel 1988, Table 3). Per-capita patenting in the United States (patents per million population) by Swiss applicants was considerably higher than those by American applicants. By this measure, patenting by Japanese, German, and Swedish applicants varied between 50 and 60 percent of the U.S. level[12] (Pavitt and Patel 1988, Table 4; the figures refer to the years 1980–85). Between 1967 and 1983, the growth rates of industrial R&D expenditures by Japan, France, Germany, Italy, and Sweden exceeded those of the United States by proportions varying from 24 to 161 percent (Pavitt and Patel 1988, Table 6).

These developments in R&D expenditures reflect the relatively high productivity levels achieved by the follower countries in a variety of industrial sectors. For example, in a comparison of gross value added per hour worked in Japan and the United States in 1987 (based on purchasing power parity equivalents), Japanese labor productivity substantially exceeded that in the United States in 2 out of 16 sectors and stood between 75 and 90 percent of the U.S. level in 3 more (Pilat and van Ark 1991, Table 3.6). In a similar comparison between the United States and West Germany, the same authors found that German labor productivity stood within 78 to 83 percent of the U.S. level in 7 out of 16 sectors (Pilat and van Ark 1991, Table 3.5). In joint factor productivity for manufacturing as a whole, the Japanese level, which had reached 72 percent of the U.S. level in 1973, rose to 82 percent in 1988 after peaking at 94 percent in 1982. The German relative level rose from 75 percent in 1973 to 91 percent in 1982 but then relapsed to 76 percent in 1988 (Pilar and van Ark 1991, Table 4.4).

It is, indeed, reasonable to think that as labor productivity and joint factor productivity levels approach that of the productivity leader in various broad industrial sectors, many narrower industrial groupings and many individual firms will find themselves operating at the technological frontier itself. Rivalry for market share and profits will then drive them to try to push the frontier outward, to seize the technological lead, and, if possible, to enlarge it. The bases of national success then tend to shift. National and firm differences in the organization of technological effort, in the relation between R&D and firms' manufacturing and merchandising activities, and in the connections between finance and industry appear to become significant factors influencing the pace of national progress. (Richard Nelson and Gavin Wright provide a more systematic and thorough treatment of this view in Chapter 5 of this volume.)

The orientation of management policy becomes more important. Contemporary students of international technological competition stress the importance of firm-specific and national industry–specific learning and knowledge in contradistinction to the knowledge that can be reduced to written description and blueprint or acquired by transfer agreement, reverse engineering, and the like. Such firm and national-industrial learning is the outcome of a continuing and cumulative process of interaction and feedback among research, development, production, and marketing, a process that follows technological paths that are, to a degree, peculiar to the firms and industries of particular nations (Kline and Rosenberg 1986, Nelson and Wright, forthcoming).

By its nature, the acquisition and development of such firm-specific and national industry–specific knowledge is the outcome of consistent work and investment pursued over a period of years. National markets that present managements with rewards that depend more immediately and largely on near-term increases in profits inhibit the pursuit of longer-term cumulative learning. National differences in the roles of financial markets and banks create differences in managements' perceptions of rewards and exert an influence on managerial doctrine and practice. The result is that the elements of social capability that help govern the potential for growth take a different shape and may encompass national differences in financial organization and practice that have no clear relation to existing or past levels of aggregate labor productivity. (Abegglen and Stalk 1986, Abernathy and Hayes 1980, Aoki 1988, 1990, Dertouzos et al. 1989, Hatsopoulos, Krugman, and Summers 1988, Landau 1990, Landau and Hatsopoulos 1986).

As such differences in national systems of technological organization, policy, and practice become more significant, they work to weaken tendencies toward productivity convergence, not only in the aggregate, but also to a greater degree in those industrial sectors in which past convergence has gone furthest and in those particular industries that have come to operate most closely to the frontier of international leadership. Results that bear on that interpretation are reported in a recent paper by Pär Hansson and Magnus Henrekson (1991). In a study of 14 OECD countries from 1970 to 1985, they found that in aggregate manufacturing—the sector that caught up most quickly relative to the United States during the preceding growth boom—there was neither a significant catch-up in TFP levels after 1970 nor convergence among countries.[13] On the other hand, both catch-up and convergence were stronger in 6 other industrial sectors in which the catch-up and convergence processes had not yet gone so far as in manufacturing (agriculture, mining, construction, trade, transportation, and finance).[14]

By way of conclusion, we should note that many, if not all, of these changes that helped weaken the potential for catch-up and convergence in the 1970s and 1980s are again consequences of the convergence process itself. They are another expression of the inherently transitory character of the preceding growth boom.

The moral to be drawn from these observations can be expressed differently. The final outcome of a process of convergence and catch-up is not necessarily, perhaps not even probably, a state of continuing technological equality, still less a state of equality in labor productivity. Rather, the outcome will be a state of rivalry in the extension of technological frontiers. In this competition, the opportunities for superior growth by catch-up will no doubt limit the size of the gaps that open up among advanced nations. But the future nature of technological advance cannot be predicted. It may make the frontiers of technology again incongruent with the economic circumstances and characteristics of the laggards, or of some of them. And the elements of national social capability needed to exploit the emerging technology may again inhibit the catch-up potential of some or many countries. In such eventualities, therefore, gaps may again appear and grow for extended periods of time.

Factors Supporting the Realization of Potential

The events that brought the postwar convergence boom to a definite end were the OPEC oil embargo of 1973 and the subsequent great rise of energy prices. The immediate result was the first serious international business contraction of the postwar years. Together with the second oil shock of 1979, the rise in energy prices contributed to a strong inflationary trend that was already under way for other reasons; and the efforts of governments to contain and offset the inflation reversed the thrust of government monetary and fiscal policies. Expansive earlier, they now became contractionary. They tended to support a condition of stagflation that was clearly discouraging to investment and innovation. And since both the impact of the energy crisis and the

policies of governments differed from country to country, the net result was an impediment to the convergence process.

These more dramatic and largely exogenous developments of the post-1973
years, however, were only one part of a less visible and more complicated set of changes
that, not in every respect but on net balance, weakened the factors supporting the realization of potential for growth by catch-up. Again, many of these changes in the background of events were themselves the outcome of the earlier convergence process.
They serve to reinforce the view that the convergence boom was an essentially transitory experience.

I deal with the subject of this section as (1) factors supporting the diffusion of
technological knowledge and practice, (2) those bearing on structural change, and,
most important, (3) those supporting investment and the stable expansion of business
activity and employment.

Diffusion of Knowledge

It is in this respect that the supports for the realization of potential have become
stronger. Industrial and governmental laboratories have increased in number, and the
scientists and engineers working to advance technology are more numerous both absolutely and in relation to total employment. Consonantly, the real expenditures for
R&D have become larger both absolutely and in relation to GDP (Englander and Mittelstädt 1988, pp. 34–37).

These measures of effort apply to the facilities for diffusion. A larger expenditure
for R&D means that technological rivals follow more closely the advances in other
firms and other countries. In addition, international licensing and technology transfer
agreements and joint ventures between firms in different countries have become more
numerous, and there is a larger volume of direct capital investment across national
borders (Nadiri, 1993, Sec. IV). Finally, the volume of international trade has continued to expand, although not at the same pace as during the boom years (Maddison
1991, Table F-8). For all these reasons, firms have become better able to keep up technologically, which makes for convergence—but they are also more concerned with
getting ahead, which does not.

Structural Change

The growth accounts in Tables 4-6a and 4-6b show that the contributions of structural
change to productivity convergence were much smaller after 1973 than before. Much
of this must have been due to the reductions in farm employment and self-employment that had already occurred during the convergence boom and that continued after
1973. The lower rates of capital accumulation needed to provide jobs in industry and
commerce is still another reason. Both point to the convergence process itself as a
cause of the slowdown in the rate of structural change as a source of further convergence. All this belongs under the heading of "Potential" already taken into account.

There also were, however, developments that hampered the mobility of labor that do belong under the heading of "Realization."

The permanent and temporary flows of foreign workers, who helped meet labor demands in Western Europe during the boom, gradually accumulated and became significant fractions of both populations and labor forces. Continued immigration, therefore, met xenophobic resistance. When unemployment rates vaulted, immigration was restricted, and guest workers were repatriated. Labor unions recovered from the disorganization imposed by the war and its aftermath. They became strong during the years of tight labor markets, and their members developed aspirations, not only for more rapidly rising wages, but also for a variety of protections against layoffs. Their influence persuaded governments to enact laws and regulations that increased the costs of layoffs or of relocation of plants and that provided more generous provisions for unemployment benefits. An additional result of these developments is that firms hesitate to hire new workers because their employment involves not only the high cost of wages, taxes, and fringe benefits but also the risks and costs associated with barriers to layoffs and relocation should they become necessary.

Investment and Capital Accumulation

We have already seen that the association between rates of capital accumulation per worker and initial levels of productivity became weaker after 1973 than it had been earlier. The rates of accumulation were also lower. The slower pace accounted for a substantial part of the decline in labor productivity growth both directly and because of its effect on the age of capital and thus on the rate of embodiment of improved methods, enlarged scale, and better industrial composition.

My earlier argument concluded that the lower rates of capital accumulation in the 1970s and 1980s stemmed in part from the strong catch-up process during the preceding decades and from the investment boom to which it had led. Capital–labor ratios, initially low, rose sharply in the 1950s and 1960s, and the technological advances that could be made by substituting modern for obsolete capital goods became smaller.

At issue here, however, is the possible effect of the earlier convergence process and its investment boom on the macroeconomic climate of the 1970s and later. This climate deteriorated for several reasons, but the connection with the catch-up process is quite obvious. If one is right in thinking that the smaller gaps in capital–labor ratios and technological levels meant a weaker demand for new investment, then the catch-up of the 1950s and 1960s stands as one cause of the poorer environment for business after 1973 and therefore as an additional factor that produced the lower rates of capital accumulation and thus the weaker support for the realization of potential since that time.

There is a second, less obvious, connection between the convergence and catch-up of the 1950s and 1960s and the weakened support for the realization of potential in the 1970s and later. The macroclimate of the 1950s and 1960s was favorable in part because the international monetary regime, taken in conjunction with U.S. economic policy, provided a world supply of money that grew fast enough to meet the requirements for expansion of real output together with the relative inflation that accompa-

nies relatively fast productivity growth without initiating serious inflationary upheav-
als. At the same time, under the fixed-rate, dollar-exchange standard of the 1950s and
1960s, prices of tradables and exchange rates remained relatively stable and interest
rates moderate (McKinnon 1971, McKinnon and Ohno 1989).

I have already argued that the success of these arrangements demanded that two
conditions be satisfied. One was the redistribution and expansion of the world's supply
of gold and other international reserve assets. Since gold was initially heavily concentrated in the United States and since other international reserve assets under the Bretton Woods regime were essentially short-term, liquid claims on dollars, this condition
implied a chronic U.S. balance-of-payments deficit and hence a cumulating deterioration of the reserve position of the key-currency country. The other condition was
continuing faith in the ability of the United States to maintain the gold convertibility
of the dollar at the established rates of dollar exchange.

The two conditions were, in the long run, mutually contradictory. The redistribution and expansion of monetary reserves in the "rest of the world" and the implied
U.S. deficit were embedded in the convergence process itself. Productivity growth in
Europe and Japan was faster than in the United States, and at the exchange rates initially fixed, the competitive position of the United States became steadily weaker. Its
balance-of-payments position was further damaged by the desire of U.S. business and
finance—once the bright prospects of Europe became apparent—to enlarge their positions in the expanding European market. There was a net flow of private U.S. capital
to Europe.

As things worked out, the collapse of the Bretton Woods system was speeded by
political developments: first the U.S. deficit finance during the Vietnam War and later
the oil crisis of 1973. The underlying cause of the breakdown, however, was the con-
tradiction between a fixed-rate system, whose keystone was dollar–gold convertibility,
and the productivity catch-up, which year by year produced the dollar deficits and
therefore the required expansion of international monetary reserves but whose cumulative effect was to undermine dollar convertibility.

This monetary breakdown left the industrialized world with an international
monetary regime that is distinctly less supportive of investment and capital accumulation than was Bretton Woods during the years when it worked. The floating-rate system that we have known since 1973 may or may not be the best that can now be
devised to meet present circumstances, but it has permitted far larger fluctuations and
international divergences in inflation rates, interest rates, and exchange rates than did
the Bretton Woods regime (McKinnon 1990). Schumpeter would not have regarded
our current arrangements as conducive to enterprise, innovation, and the realization
of technological potential.

The general lesson of this section is that in realization, as well as in potential, the
convergence boom itself produced conditions unfavorable to continued productivity
convergence at the boom's rapid pace or with the same high degree of systematic association between initial levels and subsequent growth rates. The convergence boom was
an inherently transitory experience. As far as potential is concerned, the support for
this view is largely, but far from entirely, implicit in even a simple theory of convergence. The deterioration of the conditions for the realization of potential, however,
added obstacles to the prolongation of the convergence boom that a simple theory does
not envisage.

Notes

1. A rank correlation between levels of output in 1830 and growth rates from 1830 to 1870 for 9 European countries and the United States yields a correlation coefficient of .32, a positive relation rather than the negative relation characteristic of later years (data from Angus Maddison 1990, Tables 1,a; 1,b; and 2,a).

2. Measures of the association between initial levels and subsequent growth rates present a biased picture of the true tendency toward convergence because of measurement errors or transient circumstances affecting the terminal productivity levels between which the growth rates for a period are measured. If the errors and transient circumstances at terminal dates are random and of equal magnitude, the inverse correlations between initial-year standings and subsequent growth rates will be biased upward. In the same circumstances, however, measures of variance provide unbiased estimates of the true tendency toward convergence (see Abramovitz 1979, n. 11; Milton Friedman, 1992, provides a systematic exposition of this problem).

If error and transient circumstances affect terminal-date standings randomly and with equal strength, the bias in the correlations between initial levels and subsequent growth rates will count for less the longer the period over which the association is measured. According to this account, one would expect that measures such as those in the right-hand column of Table 4-2 would decline as the length of periods are extended. They actually increase markedly and almost monotonically. I take these results to be evidence of a systematic tendency toward convergence that has strengthened over time.

There were at least three instances in which transient circumstances arising from war or cyclical contraction had an especially important impact on the productivity standings of a particular year and therefore on growth rates in which that year figured. The years were 1938, 1950, and 1979. The normal inverse correlation between initial standings and subsequent growth rates would have either weakened in those periods in which one of these years was a terminal date or strengthened in those periods in which it was an initial date. I take account of the circumstances of each date and of the periods they bound in the analysis of later pages.

3. The rate of decline in the coefficients of variation run as follows in percent per annum (based on Table 4-1, Columns B and C):

	Column B	Column C
1900–13	− .083	—
1913–50	+0.15	0.00
1950–73	−3.58	−4.23
1973–86	−1.02	—
1973–89	—	−0.46

Maddison's earlier volume (1982) makes it possible to measure rates of convergence over shorter periods. From these it appears that the rate in the first postwar decade (1950–60) was exceeded twice during similarly short periods:

1890–1900	−2.73 percent (12 countries)
1929–38	−3.08 percent
1950–60	−2.14 percent

But the rate of convergence from 1960 to 1973 was correspondingly more rapid, −5.60 percent a year.

The measures of the decline in variance may also be tainted by measurement error. Since the accuracy of economic data has generally improved over time, the observed decline in the variance of productivity levels may be due in part to fewer measurement errors. However, the particularly rapid drop after World War II, when economic measurements had already been greatly improved, is unlikely to be due to an acceleration in the rate of improvement.

4. The Wolff estimates of the change in relative capital capital–labor ratios, however, do not jibe with those for a similar and overlapping sample of countries (France, Germany, Japan, and United Kingdom) for 1913 and 1956 by Maddison (1991, Table 3.9). The average relative level in the 4 countries stands at 0.24 in 1913 and at virtually the same relative level, 0.25, in 1950. But Maddison's estimates of the growth of TFP amply confirm Wolff's estimate of a large increase in the gaps in TFP between 1913 and 1950 (Maddison 1987, Table 20; TFP calculated as the difference between the growth of the GDP and the contributions of labor quantity and capital quantity).

5. When incomes in the more well-to-do countries of northwest Europe had regained their prewar levels, households could afford to buy the new durables, and industries to satisfy the new demand were either established or quickly expanded. American methods were adopted, and the prices of consumer durable goods, which had been much higher than in the United States, fell markedly. The structures of consumption, production, and prices came to resemble more closely those in the United States. The same process took hold even in such poor countries as Italy and Japan where it was favored by their dual structure. Had earnings been distributed more equally in these low-income countries, the development of domestic markets for durable consumer goods would have proceeded more slowly. Nonetheless, families with a member employed in the modern sector had incomes and consumptions standards that soon approximated those of northwest Europe.

Denison argues persuasively that the convergence of consumption, production, and price patterns in the followers toward those in the United States is attributable to the high income elasticity of the consumer demand for durables. By creating large domestic markets for such goods, it enabled producers to increase the scale of output and to adopt the production methods explored earlier in the United States. The relative decline of European prices for durables followed (Denison 1967, pp. 235–50). The importance of this development is suggested by Denison's ingenious measure of "scale economies associated with income elasticities." Using this measure, he found that 34 percent of the difference between the average northwest European growth rate of national income per person employed (1950–62) and that in the United States may be attributed to this variety of scale economies. The same figure for Italy was 23 percent and for Japan (1953–71), 19 percent (for Europe, see Denison 1967, Tables 21–23; for Japan, see Denison and Chung 1976, Table 5-1).

6. My earlier paper (1979) contains a more extended discussion of some of the matters taken up in this section, as well as more extended references to supporting literature.

7. Between 1945 and 1948, Japan received some 6.1 million persons (half military, half civilian), amounting to 7.6 percent of the 1948 population and almost 18 percent of the gainfully occupied. Between 1945 and 1950, West Germany received some 9 million refugees from the east (Kindleberger 1967, p. 30). Between 1955 and 1961, about 150,000 workers per year came to West Germany from the east, accounting for 27 percent of the labor force growth in that period (OECD, *Economic Survey of Germany*, 1962). France repatriated 350,000 persons from Algeria in 1962 and had a net immigration of 180,000 per year between 1964 and 1968 (Carré et al. 1975, chap. 2 and App. Tables 3 and 4). Germany, France, Switzerland, and other northern countries enjoyed a large net immigration of foreign guest workers during the entire postwar period. The proportion of foreign workers in the German labor force rose from 1.3 percent in 1960 to 10 percent in 1971 (Statistisches Bundesamt, *Bevolkerung u. Wirtschaft, 1872–1972*, pp. 115–16).

8. A substantial literature deals with these relations between migration and growth patterns. See Abramovitz 1961, Easterlin 1968, Kuznets 1958, Kuznets and Rubin 1954, Thomas 1954.

9. A rise in velocity may make possible the needed growth of nominal income without an equal growth of money stock, but that in fact did not occur, except to some degree in the United States.

10. Questions may be raised about my inclusion of scale and structural change with that of technological advance more narrowly defined among the categories of change partly dependent on embodiment. My defense is as follows:

Re economies of scale. Exploiting the advantages of larger scale requires different and more specialized forms of capital equipment. These are devised as the enlargement of the market spurs the search for new forms of scale-dependent technology and as advances in knowledge generally suggest new possibilities. They form part of the stock of newly acquired knowledge whose pace of application depends on change in the pace of capital accumulation and on the consequent change in the age of capital stock.

Re structural change. The rate of absorption of partly redundant labor from low-produc-tivity farming and from self-employment and family help in other sectors into more productive occupations does not require the latest capital-embodying technology. But it does depend on the rate of expansion of the absorbing sectors, and that in turn depends heavily on the rate of advance of per-capita output and therefore on the pace of technological progress incorporated into pro-duction. This, in turn, is a function of the pace of embodiment and thus of the rate of change in the age of capital.

11. The interactions between potential technological progress and capital accumulation do not stop here. It may be argued that the potential rate of progress, and not only the realized rate, depends on the pace of accumulation. The reason is that learning depends in part on experience with the production and use of new capital goods, as Kenneth Arrow (1962) and Nathan Rosen-berg (1982) have urged. This is, indeed, a plausible hypothesis, especially in its application to long periods of time.

Learning, however, is a cumulative process. Its contribution to the technological potential of the post-1973 period would have derived a great deal from the experience of earlier years, during the investment boom of the 1960s, and during the years of slower accumulation that followed. So the effect of the slower rate of capital's growth on the technological potential of the period of retardation is quite uncertain.

12. For comparative purposes, however, the figure for the United States itself is exaggerated because "the propensity of US firms to patent in their home country is higher than that of firms from other countries" (Pavitt and Patel 1988, Table 4, n. 1).

13. The coefficient of variation decreased between 1970 and 1985, but only from 0.159 to 0.153. The average TFP level in the followers relative to that in the United States rose, but only from 0.726 to 0.738.

14. In electricity there was continuing convergence, but on average, the followers fell further behind the United States.

Appendix Notes to Table 4-7

A full explanation of the logic of the calculations can be found in Nelson (1964). A compressed and simplified explanation can be obtained from me on request.

Given my one-half embodiment assumption, the equation underlying the numbers in Table 4-7, Column 4, is

$$\frac{\Delta A}{A} = \frac{\dfrac{\Delta A}{2A}}{1 - \Delta \bar{a}} + \frac{\dfrac{\Delta A}{A}}{2}$$

Here $\frac{\Delta A}{A}$ is the rate of "measured residual growth," and $\Delta \bar{a}$ is the rate of change in the age of capital stock. The first term on the right-hand side is the "age-neutral" rate of embodied residual growth, that is, what the rate of embodied growth would have been if the average age of the capital stock had remained constant. In this term, $\Delta \bar{a}$ is the change per year in the age of the capital stock. The second term is the rate of disembodied residual growth, assuming that one-half of measured technological progress was disembodied. Their sum, therefore, is the "age-neutral" residual growth overall (see Column 4 in Table 4-7). The effect of age-change itself on measured residual growth in Column 3 is then the difference between Column 1 and Column 4 in Table 4-7.

Two statistics were required to obtain the figures in Column 4:

1. Measured residual productivity growth (to represent $\dfrac{\Delta A}{A}$ in the formula) over the designated periods. For reasons explained in the text, I treat residual productivity growth as corresponding to the sum of the following sources of growth as estimated in the growth accounts: advance of knowledge plus economies of scale plus reallocation of resources.
2. The change per year in the average age of the capital stock is derived from estimates of the average age of the capital stock in the terminal years of the periods. The necessary figures were obtained for each of the two sources, as follows:
   a. "Maddison-based" estimates for 6 countries, 1950 to 1973 and 1973 to 1984.
      i. Measured residual productivity from the figures is presented in Maddison 1987, Table 20. His figures refer to sources of growth in gross domestic product. The required residual productivity estimates were obtained as the differences between GDP growth and the sums of the contributions of
         • Change in capacity utilization.
         • Quantity of labor.
         • Quality of labor.
         • Labor hoarding.
         • Residential capital quantity.
         • Nonresidential capital quantity.
      ii. Age of capital is from Maddison 1987, Table 10. Maddison obtained estimates of capital stock in each year by cumulating constant price gross investment in nonresidential fixed capital for 30 previous years. Since this method revealed the size and age of each vintage of capital remaining in the stock in each year, the average age of the stock was easily obtained. The source notes to Maddison's table provide a more complete description of his method and identify the sources of investment data for each country.
   b. "Kendrick-based" estimates for 9 countries, 1960 to 1973 and 1973 to 1979.
      i. Measured residual productivity growth is from the figures in Kendrick 1981, Table 7. I obtained the required figure as the sum of his "Advances in knowledge and not elsewhere classified" plus "Economies of scale" and "Reallocation of labor." They refer to the sources of growth in real gross product per labor hour in the business economy.
      ii. Age of capital from Kendrick 1981, Table 13. The original data were obtained by Kendrick from the OECD.

References

Abegglen, James, and George Stalk, Jr. (1986). *Kaisha, the Japanese Corporation.* New York: Basic Books.

Abernathy, William J., and R. Hayes. (1980). "Managing Our Way to Economic Decline." *Harvard Business Review,* July–August, pp. 67–77.

Abramovitz, Moses. (1961). "The Nature and Significance of Kuznets Cycles." *Economic Development and Cultural Change,* April, pp. 225–48. (Also in Abramovitz 1989, chap. 8).

———. (1979). "Rapid Growth Potential and Its Realization: The Experience of Capitalist Economies in the Postwar Period." In Edmund Malinvaud, ed., *Economic Growth and Resources. Vol. 1: The Major Issues.* Proceedings of the Fifth World Congress of the International Economic Association, Tokyo. London: Macmillan, pp. 1–51. (Also in Abramovitz 1989, chap. 6).

———. (1986). "Catching Up, Forging Ahead, and Falling Behind." *Journal of Economic History,* June, pp. 385–406. (Also in Abramovitz 1989, chap. 7).

———. (1989). *Thinking About Growth.* Cambridge: Cambridge University Press.

———. (1993). "The Elements of Social Capability." In the *Proceedings of the Conference on the Economic Development of LDC's During the Five Decades, 1940's to 1980's.* Seoul: Korea Development Institute, forthcoming.

Aoki, Masahiko. (1988). *Information, Incentives and Bargaining in the Japanese Economy.* Cambridge: Cambridge University Press.

————. (1990). "Toward an Economic Model of the Japanese Firm." *Journal of Economic Literature,* March, pp. 1–27.

Arrow, Kenneth. (1962). "The Economic Implications of Learning by Doing." *Review of Economic Studies,* June, pp. 155–73.

Carré, J. J., P. Dubois, and Edward Malinvaud. (1975). *French Economic Growth.* Stanford, CA: Stanford University Press.

David, Paul A., and Gavin Wright. (Forthcoming). "Resource Abundance and American Economic Leadership." Center for Economic Policy Research, Stanford University, Discussion Paper no. 267.

Denison, Edward. (1967). *Why Growth Rates Differ.* Washington, DC: Brookings Institution.

————. (1985). *Trends in American Economic Growth.* Washington, DC: Brookings Institution.

Denison, Edward F., and William K. Chung. (1976). *How Japan's Economy Grew So Fast.* Washington, DC: Brookings Institution.

Dertouzos, Michael, Richard Lester, Robert Solow, and the MIT Commission on Industrial Productivity. (1989). *Made in America: Regaining the Competitive Edge.* Cambridge, MA: MIT Press.

Dowrick, Steve, and Duc-Tho Nguyen. (1989). "OECD Comparative Economic Growth, 1950–85: Catch-up and Convergence." *American Economic Review,* December, pp. 1010–30.

Dumke, Rolf. (1990). "Reassessing the *Wirschaftswunder:* Reconstruction and Postwar Growth in an International Context." *Oxford Bulletin of Economics and Statistics* 52:452–91.

Easterlin, Richard. (1968). *Population, Labor Force and Long Swings in Economic Growth: The American Experience.* New York: National Bureau of Economic Research.

Englander, Steven, and Axel Mittelstädt. (1988). "Total Factor Productivity: Macroeconomic and Structural Aspects of the Slowdown." *OECD Economic Studies,* no. 10 (Spring): 8–56.

Friedman, Milton. (1992). "Do Old Fallacies Ever Die?" *Journal of Economic Literature,* December, pp. 2129–32.

Hansson, Pär, and Magnus Henrekson. (1991). "Catching-up in Industrialized Countries: A Disaggregated Study." Trade Union Institute for Economic Research, Working Paper Series no. 92, October.

Hatsapoulos, George, Paul Krugman, and Lawrence Summers. (1988). "Competitiveness: Beyond the Trade Deficit." *Science,* July, pp. 299–307.

Kendrick, John. (1981). "International Comparisons of Recent Productivity Trends." *Essays in Contemporary Economic Problems:*

Demand, Productivity and Population. Washington, DC: American Enterprise Institute.

————. (1990). "International Comparisons of Productivity Trends and Levels." Invited address to the Twenty-ninth Atlantic Economic Conference, Geneva, Switzerland, March 17–23.

Kindleberger, Charles P. (1967). *Europe's Postwar Growth: The Role of Labor Supply.* Cambridge, MA: Harvard University Press.

Kline, Stephen, and Nathan Rosenberg. (1986). "An Overview of Innovation." In Ralph Landau and Nathan Rosenberg, eds., *The Positive Sum Strategy.* Washington, DC: National Academy Press, pp. 275–305.

Kuznets, Simon. (1958). "Long Swings in the Growth of Population and Related Economic Variables." *Proceedings of the American Philosophical Society,* February, pp. 25–52.

Kuznets, Simon, and Ernest Rubin. (1954). "Immigration and the Foreign Born." Occasional Paper no. 46, National Bureau of Economic Research.

Landau, Ralph. (1988). "USA Economic Growth." *Scientific American,* June, pp. 44–52.

————. (1990). "Capital Investment: Key to Competitiveness and Growth." *Brookings Review,* Summer, pp. 52–56.

Landau, Ralph, and George Hatsupoulos. (1986). "Capital Formation in the United States and Japan." In Ralph Landau and Nathan Rosenberg, eds., *The Positive Sum Strategy.* Washington, DC: National Academy Press, pp. 583–606.

Maddison, Angus. (1982). *Phases of Capitalist Development.* Oxford: Oxford University Press.

————. (1987). "Growth and Slowdown in Advanced Capitalist Economies: Techniques of Quantitative Assessment." *Journal of Economic Literature,* June, pp. 649–98.

————. (1989). *The World Economy in the 20th Century.* Paris: OECD.

————. (1990). "Measuring European Growth: The Core and the Periphery." In E. Aerts and B. Valerio, eds., *Growth and Stagnation in the Mediterranean World in the Nineteenth and Twentieth Centuries.* Leuven University Press.

————. (1991). *Dynamic Forces in Capitalist Development.* Oxford: Oxford University Press.

McKinnon, Ronald I. (1971). "Monetary Theory and Controlled Flexibility in the Foreign Exchanges." *Studies in International Finance* no. 84 (April). Princeton University.

————. (1990). "Interest Rate Volatility and Exchange Risk: New Rules for a Common Monetary Standard." *Contemporary Policy Issues* (April) 8:1–17.

McKinnon, Ronald I., and K. Ohno. (1989).

"Purchasing Power Parity as a Monetary Standard." In Omar F. Hamouda, Rubin Rowley, and Bernard Wolf, eds., *The Future of the International Monetary System.* Aldershot: Edward Elgar.

Nadiri, M. Ishaq. (1993). "Innovations and Technological Spillovers." C. V. Starr Center for Applied Economics, Economic Research Reports, RR #93–31, August.

Nelson, Richard R. (1964). "Aggregate Production Functions and Medium Term Growth Projections." *American Economic Review,* September, pp. 575–606.

———. (1981). "Research on Productivity Growth and Productivity Differences: Deadends and New Departures." *Journal of Economic Literature,* September, pp. 1029–64.

Nelson, Richard R., and Gavin Wright. (Forthcoming). "The Rise and Fall of American Technological Leadership: The Postwar Era in Historical Perspective." *Journal of Economic Literature.*

Ohkawa, Kazushi, and Henry Rosovsky. (1973). *Japanese Economic Growth.* Stanford, CA: Stanford University Press; Oxford: Oxford University Press.

Pavitt, Keith, and Pari Patel. (1988). "The International Distribution and Determinants of Technological Activities." *Oxford Review of Economic Policy* 4:35–55.

Pilat, Dirk, and Bart van Ark. (1991). "Productivity Leadership in Manufacturing: Germany, Japan and the United States, 1973–1989."

Research Memorandum no. 456, Institute of Economic Research, Faculty of Economics, University of Groningen, December.

Rosenberg, Nathan. (1982). *Inside the Black Box: Technology and Economics.* Cambridge: Cambridge University Press.

Schultz, Theodore. (1951). "The Declining Economic Importance of Agricultural Land Rents." *Economic Journal,* December, pp. 725–40.

Svennilson, Ingvar. (1954). *Growth and Stagnation in the European Economy.* Geneva: United Nations Economic Commission for Europe.

Thomas, Brinley. (1954). *Migration and Economic Growth.* Cambridge: Cambridge University Press.

Wallich, Henry C. (1955). *Mainsprings of German Revival.* New Haven, CT: Yale University Press.

Wallich, Henry, and Mabel Wallich. (1976). "Banking and Finance." In Hugh Patrick and Henry Rosovsky, eds., *Asia's New Giant.* Washington, DC: Brookings Institution, pp. 249–315.

Wolff, Edward N. (1991). "Capital Formation and Productivity: Convergence over the Long-Term." *American Economic Review,* June, pp. 565–79.

Wright, Gavin. (1990). "The Origins of American Industrial Success, 1879–1940." *American Economic Review,* September, pp. 651–68.

II
Technological Leadership

5

The Erosion of U.S. Technological Leadership as a Factor in Postwar Economic Convergence

RICHARD R. NELSON
GAVIN WRIGHT

The surge of research and writing on convergence in recent years has been motivated, in part, by a sharpening awareness of how rapidly other countries have been catching up to the United States, the clear twentieth-century world leader in productivity and technology (Figure 5-1). This chapter, certainly, was so motivated. We are concerned with two big questions. Where did the large lead come from, in the first place? And what have been the essential forces behind its erosion?

To tip our hand somewhat, we will argue that the postwar U.S. lead had two components. One was American leadership in mass production industries, and this had been around a long time, since at least the turn of the century. The other was American leadership in postwar "high-tech" industries, and this was the consequence of massive and unprecedented American investments in research and development after the war. Our analysis of the second question—why the two leads eroded—is tightly connected to our answer to the first. The U.S. lead in mass production dissolved as the world itself came to be a common market in manufactured goods and resources. The lead in high tech diminished as other countries came to match the United States in investments in advanced training and R&D in the relevant fields.

Thus our chapter is in the long-standing economic tradition of studies aimed at understanding why certain nations forge positions of technological and economic leadership in certain eras, and why this leadership is later relinquished to new insurgent countries. For many years that literature was mostly about Great Britain (Elbaum and Lazonick 1986). Now it is mostly about the United States. Some day it may be about Japan.

Although a share of the recent convergence literature is in this tradition, a good portion of it is oriented differently. Its focus is on measures of dispersion of income or

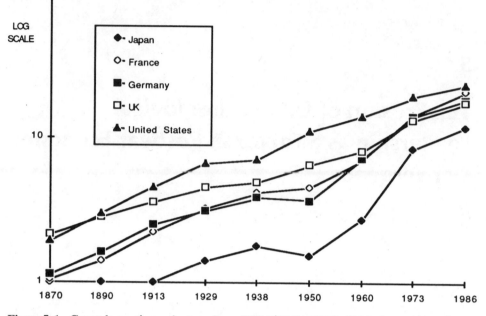

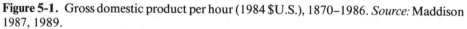

Figure 5-1. Gross domestic product per hour (1984 $U.S.), 1870–1986. *Source:* Maddison 1987, 1989.

productivity across a group of nations. The key questions are whether or not the dispersion measures have been diminishing, and if so, what the forces bringing nations together are, and if not, what the factors keeping them apart are. From this perspective, the nation that happens to be leading at any time deserves no special attention, nor does the question of whether or not other nations are catching up to this leader. Convergence understood as a reduction in dispersion tends to be associated with catch-up, but it may not be. Measured convergence may be attributable to the fact that nations below the leader are getting closer to one another, even though as a group they are not catching up with the leader. Indeed, this seems to have been the case for the period between 1890 and roughly 1950.

Although this chapter is mainly concerned with the sources of U.S. technological leadership and the reasons for its erosion, it bears on the convergence discussion in several ways. First, since 1950 or so, the European countries' and Japan's catching up to the United States has been an important part of the general story of convergence. The narrowing of the gap between the United States and other economies is a good part of the explanation for the rapid measured convergence over this period. In contrast, during the half-century before World War II, after the United States had established its position as leader, the other countries as a group were not overtaking it, even though they were growing closer to one another. This is the principal reason that the general reduction in international dispersion was smaller before World War II than after. Thus any explanation of why convergence accelerated after World War II must account for the contrast between these two epochs.

Second, our proposed answers to our own rather different questions have a bearing on the distinction between two different models of convergence laid out by Baumol in Chapter 3. In his first model there is, at any time, a lead nation that is ahead of the others for reasons intrinsic to itself. Forces for convergence lie in the ability of other nations to follow quickly and catch up with the leader, with obstacles to convergence taking the form of blockages to such imitation. In Baumol's second model, the lead nation plays a much less central role. Instead, it is a world frontier of technology that is advancing, and the lead nation at any time is simply the one whose firms are tracking this frontier most closely. Convergence occurs as firms become more equal in their tracking ability.

Our arguments suggest that before World War II, Baumol's first model was the more apt one for most fields of technology (though not all). Indeed, the United States was the techological leader with others following, because of certain special features, such as very large markets and cheap resources. The fundamental reasons that catch-up was limited at that time were the continuing differences between the economic environment in the United States and elsewhere. Some time after 1950, however, Baumol's second model becomes closer to the truth. Technical advance became less a matter of solving problems or seizing opportunities particularly salient to the U.S. scene, thus confronting other countries with a problem of adaptation. It became more a matter of tracking and implementing technological possibilities that were available to any country with the requisite capabilities. Although the United States was the first country to make the required investments, there was little that was intrinsically American about the technology. In contrast with the era of mass production, we argue, the United States has no unique advantages in advancing technology in today's economic world.

Reflection on the differences between Baumol's first and second models, in the light of the world's experience over the last century, suggests that they imply very different things about the economic and technological relevance of entities called *nations*. In the first model, nations are important, but in the second model, they are much less so. And this is our argument. A major world trend since 1950 is the decreasing importance of national boundaries or citizenship in defining technological and economic capabilities, and elaborating this theme is an essential purpose of this chapter.

Long-Standing American Strengths

In this section we deal with that part of the American postwar lead in manufacturing that had been there for a long time: mass production industries. We shall distinguish the reasons for the U.S. advantage in these industries from the factors behind U.S. dominance after World War II in fields like semiconductors and computers. But before we get into the discussion of American leadership in mass production, it is important to consider the senses in which we can talk at all about national technological capabilities. What does it mean to say that (firms in) one country has a technological lead over (firms in) other countries?

National Technologies and Technological Leadership

If technology were a pure public good, (including in the definition the attribute of nonexcludability—as economists are wont to assume in elementary versions of microeconomic theory—then the proposition that firms in certain countries are able to employ technologies that lie beyond the ken of firms elsewhere would make no sense. The input and output mixes of firms located in different countries might be different, but such divergence would merely reflect differences in market or other environmental conditions that influence what firms choose to do. Thus during the nineteenth century the special U.S. conditions of cheap resources, high wage rates, and large markets could be understood to induce the high labor productivity, large-scale, capital-intensive production methods that became known as characteristically American. But the contrast with European practice would be ascribable entirely to economic choices rather than to differences in technology choices.

Economists have long recognized that firms are sometimes able to bar others from using their technology, through threats of a patent infringement suit or by tightly held trade secrets. But there is little evidence that patent suits were effective barriers to technological transfer in the metalworking and mass production industries in which nineteenth-century American firms achieved their greatest advantage. Some American firms certainly tried to guard key trade secrets, but high interfirm mobility among technically informed personnel made firms into relatively leaky institutions for technical information that could be carried in the heads of knowledgeable individuals. Just as British restrictions in an earlier era did not stop Samuel Slater and a host of followers from carrying their understanding of textile technology across the Atlantic (Jeremy 1981), American firms of the late nineteenth and early twentieth centuries were seldom able to block technological secrets from international dissemination.

Nonetheless we argue that the concept of a "national technology" is a useful and defensible analytical abstraction, appropriate to much of modern history if decreasingly so in recent times. Our proposition rests on three intertwined arguments. First, the technologies in question were complex, involving different kinds of machines and a variety of learned skills and often requiring relatively sophisticated coordination and management. Although certain features of these complex operations were described in writing, or more generally were familiar to the experts in the field, to get the technologies under control and operating well generally required a lot of learning by doing by many interacting people, from engineers to managers to machine operators, as well as investment in plant and equipment. Thus "technology transfer" involved much more than what one or a few people could carry away in their heads or in a few drawings or models. These could provide a start on technology transfer, but a real command of the technology required a considerable amount of trial-and-error organizational learning. Thus the technology was not really a public good in the standard sense. American firms had a command of it that others did not and could not master without significant time and effort.

Second, to a considerable extent, technical advance in these fields was local and incremental, building from and improving on prevailing practice. The knowledge useful for advancing technology included, prominently, experience with the existing technology so as to be aware of its strengths and weaknesses and to know how it actually worked. Thus those at the forefront of the technology were in the best position to advance it. Economic historians have long been aware of this kind of technological learning. Nathan Rosenberg (1963) recounts the evolution of American machine-tool technology in the nineteenth century as a sequence of problem-solving challenges. At any given point, progress was considered by a particular bottleneck known mainly to those experiencing it, yet each new solution shifted the focus to another technical constraint or phase of production. With the frontier technology rapidly changing and new applications being spun off, a physical presence in the active area was virtually indispensable for anyone who hoped to improve on the prevailing best practice.

Third, sustained technological advance was not the result of one person or firm pushing things ahead but involved many interacting people and firms. One learned from another's invention and went a step further. R. C. Allen (1983) describes this process of "collective invention" in some detail, in his study of British Bessemer steel producers in the Cleveland district, and Morison (1974) describes a similar process among American Bessemer producers. The interdependencies went well beyond a more aggregation of achievements over time. As demonstrated in Ross Thomson's account of the origins and diffusion of the sewing machine (Thomson 1989), the success of new technical breakthroughs required that they mesh with prevailing complementary technologies and that they fit into a complex chain of contingent production and exchange activities, from raw material to final distribution. Any number of technically successful mechanical stitchers had been invented in the 60 years before Elias Howe's officially recognized invention of 1846, but none succeeded commercially. Howe's machine did succeed because it fit in with complementary technologies and skills and because it initiated a process in which new firms formed nodes in a communication network linked to other innovations. In turn, the principles and the networks of interdependence that came out of sewing machine development could be applied to a host of related industries.

In short, technological progress is a network phenomenon replete with "network externalities" of the sort that have now come in for intensive theoretical scrutiny (Katz and Shapiro 1985), by *path dependence,* that is, the dependence of successive developments on prior events (David 1975, 1988, Nelson and Winter 1982), and a tendency for particular systems to become "locked in" beyond a certain point (Arthur 1988, 1989). A striking historical feature of these networks of cumulative technological learning is that down to recent times their scope has been largely defined by national borders. Why should this have been so?

First is the reason of geographical proximity. The networks described by Allen, Morison, and Thomson all involved inventors and tinkerers living in the same general area and having intimate contact with one another's inventions, if not one another. Second, to the extent that technological communications networks follow in the tracks of previously established linguistic and cultural communities, it would be natural for technologies to have something of a national character. Such a primary basis might well be reinforced by the existence of centralized or uniform national institutions for technical training, though this was a less striking feature of American development than it was in European countries like France and Germany. Even in the absence of officially mandated uniformity, however, American scientists and engineers displayed early signs of national identity, rooted in the distinctness and commonality of their problem-solving environment: The resource base, the product market, and the legal/institutional conditions were marketly different from those in European countries.

The key elements of such networks are common terms and reference points, methods of measurement, and standards of technical performance. A Scottish visitor in 1849/50 complained that American mineralogists refused to label their formations with the names of European localities but insisted on an independent national terminology. Rosenberg (1985) points out that most of what we now call science-based progress did not deploy "frontier" scientific concepts but contained largely mundane and elementary tasks, such as grading and testing of materials, for which scientific training was needed but for which the learning was specific to the materials at hand. Standardizing such measurements and physically embodying them in instruments and apparatus (as well as procedures) were among the main tasks of the distinctly American scientific and engineering associations that emerged in this country at the end of the nineteenth century (Constant 1983). Critics of American capitalism complain that by the 1920s, American engineers themselves had become standardized commodities, through the close links between corporations and institutions of higher education (Noble 1977). Since the American technology was by that time the envy of the industrial world, however, aspiring young engineers could hardly have done better than to gain the training that would give them access to the national technological network.

Of course, not all countries had such indigenous national technological communities, for reasons of scale, political stability, or historical accident. We do not address ultimate questions of historical economic development in this chapter but focus instead on the narrower task of describing the emergence of a distinctive American technology from the end of the nineteenth century onward and tracing the course of that national characteristic in the twentieth century.

The Rise of Mass Production in the Nineteenth Century

American technology began to make a splash in the world at least as early as the mid-nineteenth century. Mechanical reapers, mass-produced firearms, and many other American novelties created a noticeable stir at the Crystal Palace exhibition in London in 1851. In this early period, however, the impressive technical achievements of the "American system of manufactures" pertained only to a small subset of industries, whereas in other major areas (such as iron making) the United States was clearly behind the European countries (James and Skinner 1985).

Nonetheless, during the nineteenth century the country did develop the sine qua non for advanced technological status, an indigenous technological community able to adapt European techniques to American conditions. The United States, like Japan more recently, became adept at acquiring technology from abroad and adapting it to American conditions, and in addition and perhaps just as important, it also effectively disseminated technology internally. This permitted the evolution of approaches that were widespread and thereby became characteristically American. It also contributed competitive strength to the country by enabling its firms to benefit from the technical achievements of many other U.S. enterprises.

Although the process of technological search was decentralized and competitive, flows of information through trade channels, printed media, and informal contacts established a distinctive American problem-solving network. An important early institutional manifestation was the emergence of a specialized machine-tool industry, which evolved from machine shops linked to New England textile mills in the 1820s and 1830s and became a "machinery industry" generating and diffusing new technologies for a wide range of consumer goods industries (Rosenberg 1963). Economic historians have traced remarkable threads of continuity in the histories of firms and individual machinists as steady improvements in machine speeds, power transmission, lubrication, gearing mechanisms, precision metal cutting, and many other dimensions of performance were applied to one industrial setting after another: textiles, sewing machines, farm machinery, locks, clocks, firearms, boots and shoes, locomotives, bicycles, cigarettes, sewing machines, and so on (Hounshell 1984, Thomson 1989). Whether the American approach then was more "advanced" from a technological standpoint, in comparison with British, German, and other producers, may be a meaningless question. But it was distinctively American and represented a type of collective learning that fed into the twentieth-century technologies that did form the basis of U.S. world leadership.

By the end of the nineteenth century, American industry had assumed a qualitatively different place in the world. A number of important innovations concentrated in the 1880s took advantage of the opportunities for mass production and mass marketing offered by the national rail and telegraph networks. These included new branded and packaged consumer products (cigarettes, canned goods, flour and grain products, beer, dairy products, soaps, and drugs), mass-produced light machinery (sewing machines, typewriters, cameras), electrical equipment, and standardized industrial machinery such as boilers, pumps, and printing presses (Chandler 1990, pp. 62–71). Although most of these products were developed for the domestic market, many of them became exports as well. The first wave of alarmist European books on "Americanization" dates from 1901 and 1902, with titles and themes about an "American invasion" that would again become familiar in the 1920s and 1960s (e.g., MacKenzie 1901). Particularly noteworthy were the growing American exports of industrial machinery, farm equipment, hardware, and other engineering goods, producers' goods that embodied mass production principles and that in many cases posed a new competitive challenge abroad. In addition, by 1900 the American steel industry had become a world leader, and the country was exporting an extensive array of iron and steel products (Allen 1977). This international standing was new. Before the 1890s, American steel rails would not have survived in the domestic market without tariff protection (Allen 1981).

These new turn-of-the-century achievements may be thought of as the confluence of two technological streams: the ongoing advance of mechanical and metalworking skills and performance, focused on the high-volume production of standardized commodities; and the process of exploring, developing, and utilizing the mineral resource base of the national economy. As surprising as it may seem from a modern perspective, the rise of American industry to world leadership was intimately connected with the rise of the country to world leadership in the production of coal, iron ore, copper, petroleum, and virtually every other major industrial raw material of that era. To cite one important example, the breakthrough in the steel industry coincided with the opening of the rich Mesabi iron range in the 1890s and to concomitant adaptations in technology and transportation (Allen 1977). An analysis of trade in manufactures reveals that intensity in nonreproducible resources was the most robust characteristic of American goods, and this relative intensity in fact increased across the critical period from 1880 to 1930 (Wright 1990). Cain and Paterson (1986) find that material-using technological biases were significant in 9 of 20 American sectors, including those with the strongest export performance.

It would be a mistake to imply that the country's industrial performance rested on resource abundance and scale economies as opposed to technology, because mineral discovery, extraction, and metallurgy drew on, stimulated, and focused some of the most advanced engineering developments of the time, as did mass production. The U.S. Geological Survey was the most ambitious and successful government science project of the nineteenth century, and the country quickly rose to world leadership in the training of mining engineers (David and Wright 1991). New processes of electrolytic smelting and refining had a dramatic impact on the industrial potential of copper, nickel, zinc, and aluminum. The oft-noted complementarity between capital and natural resources in that era was not merely an exogenous technological relationship but may be viewed as a measure of the successful accomplishment of a technology in which Americans pioneered. Mass production industries also intensively used fuels and materials. Not only did the capital stock itself embody domestic materials, but "high-throughput" methods, to maximize the sustainable rate of capacity utilization, imply high ratios of physical materials and fuels to labor.

For these reasons, although they were highly profitable given the economic conditions in the United States, American technologies were often not well adapted to other localities. Robert Allen (1979, p. 919) estimates that in 1907–9 the ratio of horsepower to workers was twice as large in America as in either Germany or Great Britain. On the other hand, American total factor productivity in this industry was only about 15 percent ahead of Great Britain and approximately equal to that in Germany. This statistic does not imply that German steel makers could have matched American labor productivity levels "simply" by operating at the American level of capital and resource intensity. Our central point is that there is nothing "simple" about the processes through which firms come to adopt and learn to control technologies that have been in use elsewhere for some time. Rather, the numbers illustrate the particular kinds of new technological developments that the Americans developed. Accounts of the course of technological progress in Germany suggest an entirely different orientation governed by "the desire to find substitutes for expensive and uncertain imports" (Hayes 1987, p. 1).

American manufacturing firms and their technologies not only were resource and capital intensive but also operated at much greater scale than did their counterparts in the United Kingdom and on the Continent. Large-scale operation was well tuned to the particularities of the large affluent American market. By 1900 the total national income in the United States was twice as large as that of the United Kingdom and about four times as large as that of France or Germany. Per-capita income had also surpassed that of Great Britain and was well ahead of continental Europe. American language and culture were reasonably homogeneous, and internal transportation and communications systems were well developed. Perhaps because of their relative freedom from traditional class standards, American consumers readily took to standardized products, a development that came much later in Europe. Further, this large American market was effectively off limits to European producers because of high protective tariffs. Although the size of the U.S. domestic market may have been partially offset by the greater relative importance of exports for the European countries, foreign markets were highly diverse and much less receptive to standardized goods than they later became. Oriented mainly toward the domestic market, American firms tended to produce a narrow range of product specifications. In the steel industry, for example, though the United States was dominant in mass-produced products, in specialty steels the U.S. performance was "a story of false starts, technological backwardness, commercial failures, and continued dependence on foreign steel" (Tweedale 1986, p. 221). American harvesting machinery and locomotives (like automobiles at a later point) were technically impressive but not suitable for most of the world's markets. Many European engineers held a low opinion of their American counterparts, for emphasizing production and speed over quality and durability (Headrick 1988, pp. 75, 84).

It has often been argued that the distinctive strength of American corporations lay less in technology per se than in organizational efficiencies associated with mass production and mass distribution. The success abroad of the Singer Sewing Machine Company, for example, was not based on highly sophisticated product design or factory technology, but on the efficiency of its production, sales, and service organization (Carstensen 1984, p. 26). Singer's ventures abroad came relatively early, but in general, the interest of American firms in foreign markets emerged belatedly, only after they had established national distribution networks (Wilkins 1970). Here again, we should not think of organizational strength as an alternative but as a complement to advanced technology. As Alfred Chandler has argued, modern corporate enterprise tended to arise in sectors that had earlier undergone technological transformation, and the new organizational form used more effectively these new technological possibilities (Chandler 1977). Chandler's new comparative work, *Scale and Scope,* emphasizes that the United States had much earlier and far more of these new technically and managerially advanced corporate institutions than did any other country. Chandler's account of the "organizational capabilities" within large American firms is compelling and persuasive, but we would place more emphasis than he does on systemwide features of the economy and on the ongoing development of the technology itself. The large American companies were not just efficiently streamlined organizations; they were part and parcel of an emerging technological network engaged in a collective learning process with a strongly national character. By the late nineteenth century, the management style in American manufacturing companies had become very different from those in Great Britain and continental Europe.

The concept and practice of "professional management" first arose in the United States, and by 1900 it was common for a large American firm to be staffed by a cadre of professional, educated, middle managers, a phenomenon that seems to have been almost exclusively American. In his recent book, Lazonick (1990) contends that American management increasingly took control of the job floor at this time, in contrast with Britain, where management had little control over the details of work. The "scientific management" movement was singularly American and closely associated with the professionalization of management. In a fascinating recent paper, Kogut (1992) stresses the importance of basic principles of management and organization, which he argues take on a strikingly national character, or at least used to. He proposes that it was the style of management and organization, far more than the simple economies of scale and scope, that led to the preeminence of American corporations in the early years of the twentieth century, although the former was essential to the latter. In his empirical examination of the character of American corporations that established overseas branches, Kogut found many large corporations but also some middle-sized ones. Almost all of them, however, were marked by strong adherence to the management and organizational principles just described, which formed a distinctly American style.

We note here that relatively little of the American performance during this era was based on science or even on advanced technical education. American technology was practical, shop-floor oriented, built on experience. The level of advanced training in German industry was substantially higher (Kocka 1980, pp. 95–96). As prominent an American engineer as Frederick W. Taylor, who played a major role in developing high-speed tool steel years before he invented "scientific management," had only an undergraduate degree and was deeply skeptical of the practical value of university training. The search for valuable petroleum by-products was carried out by people with only a smattering of chemical education (Rosenberg 1985, p. 43). Many of the industries in which American strength was clearest and strongest, such as nonelectrical machinery, steel, and vehicles, were distinguished well into the twentieth century by an aversion to organized science-based research. American universities did have areas of strength in certain applied fields, but an aspiring student who sought the best available academic education in scientific disciplines like physics and chemistry would have been advised to study in Germany, Britain, or France. As Figure 5-2 shows, the United States did not surpass these countries in scientific Nobel Prizes until long after World War II.

These observations are intended to delineate rather than to downplay the magnitude of what American industry had achieved by the early twentieth century. American firms were the clear leaders in productivity across the range of mass production industries. This lead in manufacturing combined with highly productive American

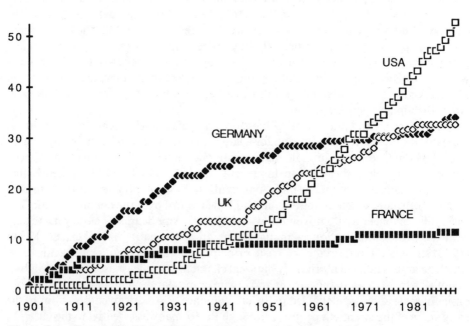

Figure 5-2. Cumulative Nobel Prizes in physics and chemistry, 1901–90.

agriculture to support wage rates and living standards higher than those in England and higher still than those on the Continent (Phelps Brown 1973). In turn, high wage rates and living standards induced and supported large-scale, capital- and resource-intensive production. And although the particular technologies and structures adopted by U.S. manufacturing firms reflected these unique aspects of the American scene, by and large where American industry went, Europe followed, if often with a pronounced lag.

Building the Infrastructure for Science-Based Industry

By the start of World War I, the United States had established a position of leadership in mass production and mass distribution industries, a technology characterized by scale economics, capital intensity, standardization, and the intensive use of natural resources. Although the United States was not the world leader in science or in the use of science-based technologies at that time, the country had developed much of the private organization and public infrastructure needed to operate effectively in the science-based industries that were coming into prominence.

Federal government support for university programs in agriculture and the practical arts dates from the Morrill Land Grant College Act of 1862. Even though this act led directly to the founding of several major state universities and the strengthening of others, little significant research could be credited to it before the Hatch Act of 1887, which provided each state with funding for an agricultural experiment station. The level of support for research was doubled by the Adams Act of 1906, and unique institutions for the dissemination of knowledge among farmers were in place with the establishment of the cooperative extension service in 1914. At this juncture the United States was well behind Europe in the deployment of "scientific agriculture"—soil chemistry, plant biology, and animal husbandry. But a generation later these investments in infrastructure had unprecedented payoffs in agricultural productivity.

The Morrill Act also provided a federal stimulus to engineering education; within a decade after its passage, the number of engineering schools increased from 6 to 70, growing further to 126 in 1917. The number of graduates from engineering colleges grew from 100 in 1870 to 4,300 at the outbreak of World War I (Noble 1977, p. 24). Like their agricultural counterparts, engineers and scientists at American universities were under continuing pressure to demonstrate the practical benefits of their efforts. "Merely theoretical" research was openly belittled, and the areas of applied science that did show some strength in the nineteenth century were mainly those linked to state-specific economic interests, such as geology and industrial chemistry (Bruce 1987). Nonetheless, by the turn of the century a network of research universities had come into being, striking an institutional balance between the demand for immediate usefulness and the ethos of academic independence espoused by the emerging scientific disciplines. According to Geiger (1986), the main elements in this balance were the provision of large-scale undergraduate teaching as a means of financing research and graduate training, and the successful mobilization of nationalistic sentiments in support of science. A watershed of sorts was passed with the founding of the American Association of Universities in 1900, to bolster academic standards, establish uniformity in requirements for the Ph.D., and achieve foreign recognition for U.S. doctorates. Although this business–university cooperation has continued to be an important part of American technological history, the prospect of world-class research universities came only after a certain social distance from industry had been established.

At the same time, American industry was building its own technological infrastructure. In the wake of the great merger wave in American business (1897–1902), which established many of today's well-known corporations in positions of national market power for the first time, there was an unprecedented expansion of private-sector research laboratories, a trend that accelerated over the next half-century (Figure 5-3). General Electric, Du Pont, AT&T, and Kodak all set up formal research laboratories before World War I. Here, too, the lasting institutional implications may have been very different from the founders' original motivations. Business historians have argued that these early firms were not looking to do pioneering research in new technologies, but to control innovation and protect an established patent position (Reich 1985, Smith 1990). Once established, however, a science-based research tradition evolved, often with considerable autonomy from the employer's immediate objectives.

Only in chemistry had there been any substantial use of scientifically trained personnel before 1900. In 1875 the Pennsylvania Railroad hired a Yale Ph.D. chemist to organize a laboratory for testing and analyzing materials brought from suppliers. As Rosenberg points out, much of the early use of science by industry was of just this sort, a relatively mundane application of laboratory procedures for testing materials, well within the frontiers of existing science. Institutionalizing such procedures, however, often led to unexpected results. The Pennsylvania Railroad laboratory, for example,

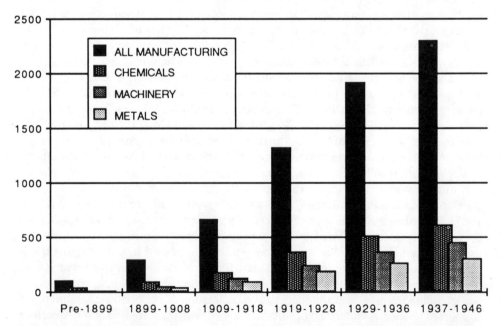

Figure 5-3. Laboratory foundations in U.S. manufacturing, 1899–1946. *Source:* Mowery and Rosenberg 1989, Table 4.1.

went on to develop an improved lubrication composition for locomotives. A Ph.D. chemist hired by the Carnegie Steel Company not only helped identify high-quality ores but also found ways to make better iron and steel. Increasingly, chemists came to play an important part in technological innovation in iron and steel making, in traditional inorganic chemicals like soda, and in new organic chemical substances like dyes and, later, plastics.

The German chemical industry was unquestionably the leader in dyestuffs, plastics, and other new products based on organic chemistry. Christopher Freeman's data show that through 1945, I. G. Farben was by far the largest patentor in plastics. By 1910 or so, however, the leading American companies like Du Pont, Dow, and Kodak had established R&D laboratories and had developed the capacity to produce a full range of industrial chemicals and a wide range of fine chemicals (Hounshell and Smith 1988, Noble 1977). These companies were able to draw on the newly emerging specialty of chemical engineering, an American professional hybrid. They were thus organizationally well positioned to take advantage of the cutoff of trade with the Germans during World War I and to respond to the need to provide a variety of products for the military. The abrogation of German patents brought the American companies close to technological parity with the Germans by the 1920s.

The story in the new electrical industry is similar, except that here American strength was apparent somewhat earlier. As in chemistry, performance was clearly not rooted in any American advantage in fundamental science; U.S. universities were significantly behind those in Germany and other continental countries in teaching and research in physics. But American industry had early access to trained personnel in electrical engineering. By the last decades of the nineteenth century in universities like MIT and Cornell, physics and mechanical engineering had been self-consciously combined as a field of training (Rosenberg 1984). Thomas Hughes observed that in the new electrical industries, the Americans excelled in the conception, design, development, and implementation of large-scale systems (Hughes 1987). In addition, the U.S. industry benefited from scientifically educated European emigres like Thomson, Tesla, Steinmetz, and Alexanderson.

Here again one may see the influence of the large, affluent American market, not as an alternative to technology, but as an influence on the directions taken by American technology and as a source of unique advantages in international comparisons. There are numerous examples of innovations that were European in origin but whose development progressed most rapidly in the United States because of the scale economies accessible in the American market (Braun 1983).

The Interwar Period

In the 1920s and 1930s, American industry consolidated its position of leadership in mass production industries while joining these longer-term strengths to organized research and advanced training in important new industries such as chemical and electrical engineering. Some of the circumstances were historically fortuitous. The United States escaped damage and even enjoyed industrial stimulation from World War I. After the war, the institutions of international trade and finance remained in disarray, stumbling toward their complete collapse in the 1930s. Industrial countries that depended on foreign markets had a hard time of it (though Japan managed to continue its industrial growth despite these obstacles). American industries were largely insulated from these problems. The country was highly protectionist from the time of the Civil War. In the 1920s, despite the emerging strength of American industry, import barriers were increased, first by the Fordney–McCumber Tariff of 1922 and then by the notorious Hawley–Smoot Tariff of 1930. But the domestic market was more than sufficient to support rapid productivity growth and the ongoing developnent and diffusion of new technologies and new products.

The Marriage of Old and New Industrial Strengths

The automobile industry was the most spectacular American success story of the interwar period, a striking blend of mass production methods, cheap materials, and fuels. The distinct lead of American producers over French and British rivals really only dates from the advent of the assembly line at Ford between 1903 and 1913, but the ascendancy was quick thereafter. Although the historical origins of this performance may be traced back to characteristics of the domestic market, the extent of American leadership is clearly indicated by the high volume of exports, notwithstanding the fact that the size and fuel requirements of American cars were poorly suited to foreign demand. Despite barriers to trade and weak world demand, U.S. cars dominated world trade during the 1920s, and motor vehicles dominated American manufacturing exports (Figure 5-4). Henry Ford's books were best-sellers abroad, and "Fordism" developed a cult technocratic following in both Germany and the Soviet Union (Hughes 1989). The components of the U.S. cost advantage are difficult to measure precisely, however, because the large-scale auto firm came as a package: organizational, managerial, financial, and technological. The branch plants of American firms were also dominant abroad, though during the interwar period they were not fully able to replicate performance at home (Foreman-Peck 1982). The process of global diffusion and adaptation of American methods would surely have continued, however, by either imitation or direct foreign investment, if it had not been interrupted by World War II.

In many ways a more lasting and significant basis for technological leadership was established in those industries that were able to marry mass production methods to organized science-based research, such as the electrical industries and chemical engineering. Even though the fundamental scientific breakthroughs in electricity had come earlier, the interwar period saw the realization of this potential through the full electrification of factories and households. Paul David (1989) recently called attention to electrification as an example of an innovation whose productivity impact was delayed for a full generation, because of the need to disseminate and adapt the underlying knowledge and to restructure physical plants and work routines. The percentage of factories using electrical power grew from 25 in 1910 to 75 in 1930 (Devine 1983), a development essential to the acceleration of productivity growth at this time. A similar diffusion occurred in the household, where the use of electric lighting rose from 33 percent of urban families in 1909 to 96 percent in 1939 (Lebergott 1976). Large firms like GE, Westinghouse, and AT&T established advanced research organizations that

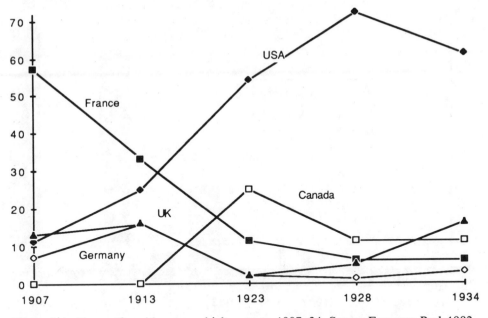

Figure 5-4. Shares of world motor vehicle exports, 1907–34. *Source:* Foreman-Peck 1982, p. 868.

generated an ongoing flow of innovative new electrical products, sometimes advancing the frontiers of science in the process.

The rise of chemical engineering was also a marriage of old and new strengths. Landau and Rosenberg (1992) point out that this professional category was an American innovation, combining chemistry with training in industrial processes. It was also relatively new, emerging as a course of study at MIT in the first two decades of the twentieth century and becoming a separate department in 1920. The American surge was also closely associated with a shift in the basic energy source for chemical plants from coal to petroleum, a primary product in which the United States dominated world production. As technology developed, the production of organic chemicals was carried on most effectively as a by-product of general petroleum refining, hence closely connected with the location of petroleum supplies. Before the 1920s, there was little contact between petroleum companies and the chemical industry. In that decade, however, important connections emerged, through mergers, research establishments, and industry–university associations. Working in close partnership with MIT, New Jersey Standard's research organization in Baton Rouge, Louisiana, produced such important process innovations as hydroforming, fluid flex coking, and fluid catalytic cracking (Landau 1990b). Here we have a remarkable blend of mass production, advanced science, and American resources. As the chemical engineer Peter Spitz wrote:

> Regardless of the fact that Europe's chemical industry was for a long time more advanced than that in the United States, the future of organic chemicals was

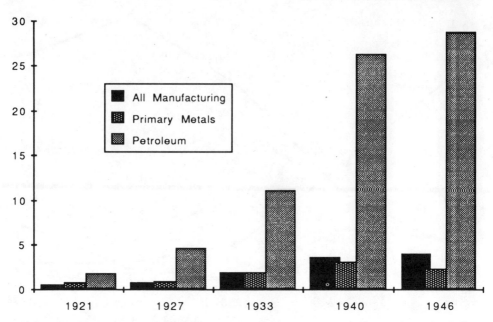

Figure 5-5. Scientists and engineers per 1,000 wage earners, 1921–46. *Source:* Mowery and Rosenberg 1989, Tables 4.2–4.6.

> going to be related to petroleum, not coal, as soon as companies such as Union Carbide, Standard Oil (New Jersey), Shell, and Dow turned their attention to the production of petrochemicals. (Spitz 1988, p. xiii)

Petroleum led the way in the use of scientifically trained personnel in the first half of the century (Figure 5-5).

Education and Technology

Sooner or later, discussions of American industrial and technological performance generally come around to the educational system. Americans seem to believe in a golden age during which the country led the world in mass public schooling and that this enlightened leadership in education was also closely associated with leadership in technology. There is some truth in this account, but the story is less straightforward than commonly imagined. It is true that the United States was an early leader in literacy and primary education, achieving close to universal elementary enrollment before the Civil War (outside the South), well ahead of France and Britain (Easterlin 1981). Only Germany (where in Prussia compulsory education dated from 1763) approached these levels. Since basic education has a clear effect on the capacity to conduct commercial operations and process written information (Schultz 1975), the diffusion of schooling among the American farming population undoubtedly had a positive influence on its responsiveness to new opportunities and its receptivity to innovations. But these benefits pertained largely to a population of farm proprietors, which for the most part was not the source of the labor for American factories during the country's surge to world industrial leadership. From the time of the Irish influx in the 1840s, the bulk of the industrial labor force came from immigration, mostly from non-English-speaking countries with far lower educational standards than those prevailing among the native born. In 1910 the foreign born and the sons of the foreign born made up more than 60 percent of the machine operatives in the country and more than two-thirds of the laborers in mining and manufacturing (U.S. Senate 1911, pp. 332–34). There is no reason to believe that this labor force was particularly well educated by world standards, but this may not have been a drawback. It has been argued that the work pace in American factories was uniquely high (Clark 1987), an intensity of effort that one might well associate with "high-throughput" production strategy, but not necessarily with high levels of education on the part of workers. To be sure, the educational background of overhead and administrative personnel undoubtedly contributed to rising productivity, but the combination of a well-educated staff at the top and hard-driving workers at the bottom is very different from the success formulas of today's world. The upgrading of educational standards for production workers came largely after the cutoff of immigration in the early 1920s.

Educational attainment did indeed increase rapidly, as much of the country moved toward the norm of a high-school degree. As job qualifications were raised and mechanization tended to eliminate jobs requiring mere brute strength and exertion, it is reasonable to hold that higher educational standards contributed to the remarkable rates of productivity growth maintained by American industry between 1920 and 1960, though we have no detailed understanding of this process. It is appropriate to note, however, that the expansion of secondary education in the twentieth century was not unique to the United States. Similar trends were recorded in virtually all of the "advanced" countries of the world, and as of 1950 there was no marked difference in average years of secondary education among the United States, France, and Britain, all of which were still well behind Germany (Figure 5-6). This does not deny the contribution of secondary education to American performance, but it underscores the point that broadly based education contributes to technological leadership only as these skills are effectively utilized by industrial employers. The disrupted conditions of world trade between 1914 and 1950 very likely constrained many countries from exploiting their educational potential.

The respect in which the United States was distinct among the nations of the world was the percentage of the population gaining access to a college education (Figure 5-7). As early as 1890, the ratio of university students per 1,000 primary students in America was two to three times that of any other country, and this gap widened during the period of American industrial ascendancy. After 1900, the surge in enrollment was particularly robust in applied sciences and engineering (Geiger 1986, p. 14); in new specialties like electrical engineering, American institutions such as MIT were reputed to be the best in the world by World War I. Advanced training in business management also grew rapidly after 1900 (Chandler 1990, p. 83). Even though university-trained engineers, scientists, and managers were only a small percentage of those employed in American industry, here if anywhere is a specific institutional basis for American technological leadership. The utilization of such personnel grew steadily

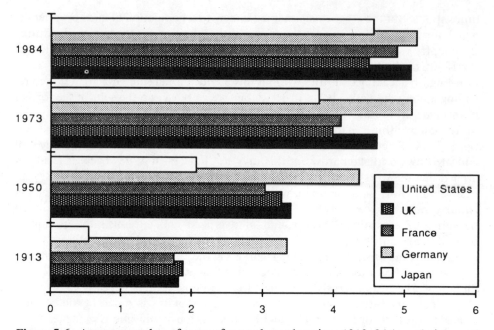

Figure 5-6. Average number of years of secondary education, 1913–84 (population aged 15 to 64). *Source:* Maddison 1987, Table A-12.

through the twentieth century (Mowery and Rosenberg 1989), as did the employment of college-trained people in a wide range of activities ancillary to R&D and production. Employment in marketing, accounting, legal service, finance, insurance, and communications grew quickly over the interwar period, some of it in manufacturing firms, some of it in other sectors. By and large, American organizations were able to tap a more highly educated population for these jobs than their European counterparts could.

There are some reasons to believe that the numbers somewhat exaggerate the American educational advantage "at the top." The elite grammar schools of the United Kingdom, the *gymnasium* of Germany, and the *lycée* of France tended to teach subjects beyond what was taught in all but the best American high schools, and Americans graduating from high school usually were younger and had had fewer years of education than had their European counterparts coming out of the secondary institutions just listed. A number of commentators (e.g., Geiger) have noted that American university faculty often complained that their students were not as well educated when they came to university as were students entering university in Europe. However, particularly with the advantage of hindsight, it is clear that long before the Europeans, the Americans developed a tradition in which a significant fraction of the sons (and later the daughters) of middle-class families went on to education beyond high school. And the American middle class wanted "practical education."

Although the significance of university education for technology may seem self-evident, we have to acknowledge that we lack a clear understanding of the specific link-

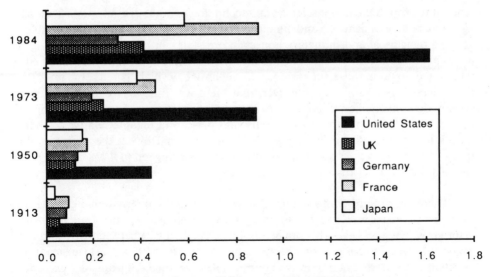

Figure 5-7. Average number of years of higher education, 1913–84.

ages. As with education more generally, what is important is not the sheer number of students or the quantity of their training but the effectiveness with which that training is integrated into improving the technology of operating firms. In interwar America that coordination was advanced to a high state of refinement as the curricula of educational institutions came to be closely adapted to the requirements of the "positions" that graduates would be taking, and vice versa (Lazonick 1990, pp. 230–32). A 1921 survey noted the "progressive dependence [of corporations] upon higher ecucation institutions as sources of employee supply . . . the prejudice of many businessmen to higher education as a factor in employment is being rapidly overcome" (quoted in Noble 1977, p. 243). Political critics have complained that the process of national standardization in the specifications for products and processes came to be extended to personnel, as engineers "automatically integrated professional requirements with industrial and corporate requirements" (Noble 1977, p. 168). In 1919, for example, MIT launched its cooperative course in electrical engineering, a program that divided the students' time between courses at the Institute and at General Electric, which hired one-half of the students after graduation. The program was later joined by AT&T, Bell Labs, Western Electric, and other firms (Noble 1977, p. 192). Whatever the merits of Noble's reservations about the close links between universities and private firms, what he describes is an effective network of training and utilization, operating efficiently at a national level because it was self-contained, internalizing the resource base and market demands of the national economy.

We have noted that in recent years a sizable literature on economic "convergence" has emerged, oriented around the proposition that large technological gaps between countries, and the associated gaps in productivity and income, cannot be sustained if the lagging countries have the requisite "social capabilities." Abramovitz (1986) has suggested that this means a well-educated work force, including competence at the top in the major sciences and technologies of the era, adequate firm management and organization, and financial institutions and governments capable of keeping their fiscal and monetary houses in order. It can be argued that during the interwar period the major European economies were not significantly outmatched by the United States in these dimensions, although we have highlighted some important differences. It is noteworthy, however, that there was little if any tendency toward systematic convergence in command of mass production technologies during this period, or in levels of labor productivity and per-capita income relative to that of the United States. Although the general dispersion narrowed, the mean productivity of Maddison's 15 successful countries was no higher in 1938 as a percentage of the U.S. level than it had been in 1929, 1913, or 1890 (Abramovitz 1986, p. 391).

There are a number of reasons. One was the chaotic international climate that affected most economies over this interval. Indeed, Maddison's data show a sharp drop in the growth of world exports from nearly 4.0 percent per year between 1870 and 1913 to about 1.0 percent per year on average between 1913 and 1950. The average ratio of merchandise exports to GDP in the countries he examined fell from 11.2 percent in 1913 to 8.3 percent in 1950, and the number was almost certainly even lower during the 1930s. Thus during the interwar period, nations were even more self-contained than they had been in the 30 years or so before World War I, and far more so than they became after World War II. This meant that the mass production methods used by American producers, which were highly productive and efficient on the American scene, were less attractive to European firms facing their own home markets. Convergence is far from an automatic phenomenon. It requires not only that the lagging nations have the requisite social capabilities but also that their firms face an economic and political environment conducive to adopting the technology used in the leading country. Rather than refining procedures for testing the "convergence hypothesis" as a widespread tendency at all times, it seems more fruitful to examine the new features of the postwar era that have encouraged and facilitated convergence among the world's leading countries.

The Postwar Era: The American Breakaway at the Technological Frontiers

Just as it did after World War I, the United States came out of World War II buoyant, with its technological capabilities extended by its wartime production experience, whereas Europe came out prostrate. In contrast with the 1920s, after World War II Japan, too, was a demolished economy and nation. But by the mid-1950s, most of the war-devastated countries had regained and surpassed their prewar productivity and income levels, but as Figure 5-1 shows, the United States' productivity and income edge remained enormous. Although some Europeans seemed surprised at the Americans' lead even after the European recovery, they should not have been. The U.S. productivity lead in general, and in mass production industries in particular, had prevailed since the turn of the century. What was new was U.S. dominance in the "high-technology" industries of the postwar era. Several intertwined but distinguishable reasons lay behind this development.

National Technology and National Leadership in Science-Based Fields

As are the mass production technologies, the newer "science-based" technologies are advanced through community efforts. But to a far greater extent, chemical and electrical technologies, and nowadays in fields like aircraft and semiconductors, technological advance requires university-trained scientists and engineers, engaged in teamwork aimed at new and better products and processes, through activities that have come to be called research and development. As a result, possession of university training and involvement in organized R&D define the relevant technological communities.

Put in another way, in science-based technologies the skills and experience needed to advance a technology usually include much more than those that can be acquired simply by working with that technology and learning from experience. In some cases the two components are completely separate. For example, a chemist working on a new drug in a laboratory owned by a pharmaceutical company may know little about how pharmaceuticals are produced or even how the drug works on the human body. In other cases both kinds of understanding are needed. Thus a chemical engineer working on a way to produce a new plastic must know both the standard production practice and a lot of formal chemistry. If the two types of understanding are separated too widely, problems of execution can easily result. But whatever the optimal mixture or practice, the industries in which the United States forged ahead after World War II required experience, specialized training, and organized research and development for effective advancement of the technology.

How then did the United States forge its new lead in high-technology industry? By investing more than other nations did in training scientists and engineers and in R&D in these technologies. The groundwork for these massive investments had been well laid earlier. We have described the rise of industrial R&D and the rise of higher education. By World War II the United States had a number of world-class firms in science-based industries, and several universities doing world-class research. But the United States was not dominant in high-technology industries.

The Surge of Investment in Research and Development

World War II changed the context. Victory brought a new sense of confidence and pride in America's strength, an awe for the power of science and technology engendered by its role in winning the war, and a burning belief in its capabilities for opening new horizons. The write-ups of wartime science clearly were designed to kindle this appreciation on the part of the public (e.g., Baxter 1946). Vannevar Bush's *Science, the Endless Frontier* (1945) gave the trumpet call, and the country was off to historically unprecedented levels of investment in science and technology.

Before the war Americans had, on average, roughly double the years of postsecondary education as did the Europeans, although as we have noted, the statistics may exaggerate the actual size of the educational gap. Between 1950 and 1973 the average number of years of American postsecondary education again doubled, further widening the gap. In part this was a simple consequence of affluence and a belief in the value of education. But the trend was also strongly encouraged by government policies. The G.I. Bill of Rights, which guaranteed educational funding to all qualified veterans, was both emblematic and an important factor in its own right. College fellowships became available through a number of other public programs. The state-supported part of the American higher education system provided significant additional funding and subsidy. Only a relatively small share of the new wave of university students went into natural science and engineering, but the sheer numbers meant that there was a large increase in the study of trained scientists and engineers.

The expansion of supply was also supported, and in part propelled, by major increases in demand, from several sources. A small but important fraction was employed by the rapidly expanding U.S. university research system. The scientists and engineers who had engaged in the war effort had striking success in their argument that university science warranted public support, and during the half-decade after the war the government put into place machinery to provide that support. The new research support programs of the National Science Foundation and the National Institutes of Health supplied public funding of university basic research across a wide spectrum of fields. However, the bulk of government support for university research came not from these agencies but from agencies pursuing particular missions and using university research as an instrument in that endeavor. Thus, the Department of Defense and the Atomic Energy Commission offered large-scale research funding in fields of particular interest to them. And the support was not just for basic research. These agencies funded research that involved applied science and engineering departments in work at the forefront of technologies in materials and electronics. By the middle 1950s the American research universities clearly were ahead of those in the rest of the world in most fields. Just as young American scholars had flocked to German universities to learn science during the late nineteenth century, so young students from Europe, Japan, and other parts of the world came to the United States for their training.

The largest share of the increased demand for engineers and scientists, however, came from a vast expansion in the number of American companies doing R&D and in the size of their R&D programs (Mowery and Rosenberg 1989). Figure 5-8 displays the number of scientists and engineers in R&D (including corporate, university, and other organizations) as a fraction of the work force. The U.S. lead in the early 1960s is striking. Figure 5-9 shows the same phenomenon in terms of R&D as a fraction of GNP. Between 1953 and 1960, total R&D expenditures (in constant dollars) more than doubled, and the ratio to GNP nearly doubled. The employment of scientists and engineers in industrial research grew from fewer than 50,000 in 1946 to roughly 300,000 in 1962. Other countries lagged in increasing these kinds of investments. As late as 1969, the total U.S. expenditure on R&D was more than double that of the United Kingdom, Germany, France, and Japan combined. But by then the slowdown in U.S. productivity growth had already begun.

The R&D figures exaggerate somewhat the increase in investments in technical progress (Soete et al. 1989). Although formal R&D is the principal vehicle for technological advance in the science-based industries, a good share of the work of improving manufacturing processes goes on outside formal R&D organizations and often is not included in the R&D statistics. For example, a major part of improvement is often in design, usually done in an engineering department and often not counted as R&D even though it involves comparable activities. Many small firms engage in inventing, design, and development work without a formal R&D department and often without

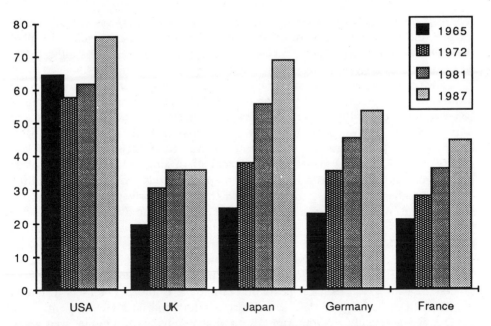

Figure 5-8. Scientists and engineers engaged in R&D per 10,000 workers, 1965–87. *Source:* National Science Board 1989, 1991, Appendix Table 3-19.

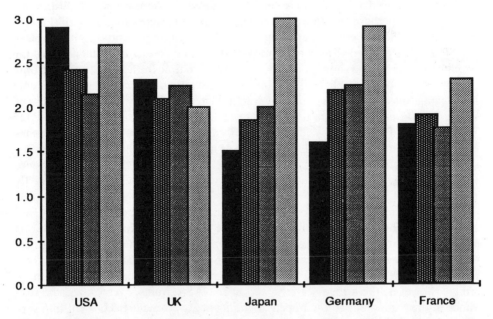

Figure 5-9. Expenditures for R&D as a percentage of GNP, 1964, 1971, 1978, 1989. *Source:* National Science Board 1989, Appendix Table 4-19; 1991, Appendix Table 4-26.

reporting any R&D. During the period in question, the term *R&D* was becoming fashionable, and it is likely that a growing fraction of that work was so labeled. With all of these qualifications, however, it is clear that the increase in resources allocated to advancing technology was massive and not matched in other countries.

The rise of corporate R&D in the United States had two sources. Partly it was the result of major increases in private corporate R&D funding, based on an optimistic belief in the profitability of such investments, a belief that by and large was well founded. Partly the rise came from large Department of Defense, and later NASA, investments in new systems. In the mid-1960s, private funds accounted for about half of corporate R&D, government funds the other half. In some industries, such as pharmaceuticals and other chemical industries, corporate funds provided almost all the support. In others, such as electronics, there was both strong private effort in such firms at AT&T and IBM, and large-scale Department of Defense funding. In industries like jet engines and space systems almost all the funding was from the Department of Defense or NASA.

American dominance in computer and semiconductor technologies gained the most European attention and concern during the 1950s and 1960s. These were considered the leading edge technologies of the era, and many foreign observers attributed the American advantage to defense support. Military and, to a lesser extent, space R&D support certainly was important. But military demands and money were going into an R&D system that was well endowed with trained scientists and engineers, had a strong university research base, and was populated with companies that were technically capable.

During the 1930s those concerned with the capabilities of the armed forces, both in Europe and the United States, were keenly aware of the advantages that could be gained by enhanced ability to solve complex equation systems rapidly. Ballistics calculations were perhaps the dominant concern, but there were others as well (Flamm 1987, Nelson 1982). Before and during World War II Germany and Britain as well as the United States funded research aimed at developing a fast computer. It is clear enough that during and shortly after the war, by which time the feasibility of electronic computers had been established, the United States vastly outspent other governments in bringing this embryonic technology into a form that was operational for military needs. Several major research universities were involved in the effort, notably MIT, and IBM and AT&T participated actively. Early assessments were that the nonmilitary demand for computers would be small. It was apparent by 1960, however, that the nonmilitary demand would be large, and it also turned out that the design experience that the major U.S. companies had had in their work on military systems was directly relevant to civilian systems.

The story regarding semiconductors is somewhat different (Malerba 1985, Nelson 1982). Although military funds had gone into semiconductor devices during World War II, it was the Bell Telephone Laboratories that came up with the critical discoveries and inventions, using their own money and motivated by the perceived technological needs of the telephone system. Once the potential had been demonstrated, however, the armed services, and later NASA, quickly recognized the relevance of the technology to their needs. Significant government R&D went into supporting technical advance in semiconductors, and perhaps more important as it turned out, the Department of Defense and NASA signaled themselves as large potential purchasers of transistors. The evidence is clear that major amounts of private R&D money went into trying to advance semiconductor technology, in anticipation of a large government market. And in the fields of both semiconductor technology and computer technology, design experiences with the transistors and later the integrated circuits that were of high value to the military established companies to produce items for civilian products.

By the mid-1960s the American lead in the new high-technology industries, like the old lead in mass production industries, was widely taken as a fact of life, a source of pride for Americans and of concern to Europeans, but not readily subject to change. J. J. Servan Schreiber pointed with alarm to the U.S. lead, arguing that if Europeans did not act quickly to catch up, they would be permanently subservient to the Americans. His diagnosis of the sources of American strength was rich and complex, if in places ironically amusing in the face of subsequent developments. He pointed not only to American investments in R&D and in science and engineering education but also to the overall quality of the American work force, its willingness to cooperate with management, and the skill, energy, and willingness to take risks that he believed characterized American management.

In its famous "technology gap" studies, the OECD provided a more systematic, nuanced, and variegated diagnosis. The OECD argued that there was little that American scientists and engineers knew that good Europeans ones did not know also. Instead, the "gaps" stemmed mainly from management, organization, and experience, just as we have stressed. Technology is partly in books and mind, partly in the fingers and organization. The information part is largely a public good for those with the requisite training and experience. But the latter part involves significant firm-specific investment and learning. Ironically, just at the time when American dominance was most visible, conditions were changing to undermine its sources. By the 1960s the U.S. lead was shrinking, both in the areas of long-standing strength and in the new high-technology fields.

The Closing Gaps

The period since the 1950s has seen a dramatic closing of the economic and technological gaps among the major industrial powers, largely ending a leadership position nearly a century old. The U.S. lead in high-technology industries was a more recent phenomenon. Interestingly, it appears to have held up better than the general U.S. economic lead. Figure 5-10 shows the share of the major industrial nations in exports of high-technology products since 1965. Contrary to popular belief, the U.S. share has diminished only slightly; the dramatic change is in the position of Japan relative to that of Europe. Figure 5-11 shows U.S. exports and imports of high-technology products since 1970. It has been the growth of U.S. imports, particularly since 1983, and not a decline of export performance, that has been the principal source of the erosion of the U.S. high-technology trade balance.

The data on patents reflect the same pattern. Since 1970 there has been a significant drop in the share of patents taken out in the United States and assigned to Americans. However, a large part of this decline reflects a rise in the fraction of inventions originating in other countries that are patented in the United States. From the middle

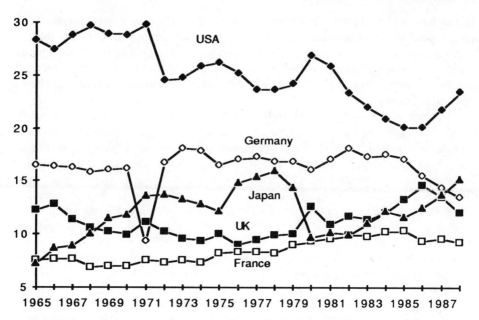

Figure 5-10. Country shares of world high-technology exports, 1965–88. *Source:* National Science Board 1987, Appendix Table 7-10; 1989, Appendix Table 7-10; 1991, Appendix Table 6-7. Note that the decline for Japan in 1980 corresponds to a shift in the basis of the calculation.

1960s to the middle 1980s, the share of all world patents given to Americans has been relatively constant. Japan's share has risen dramatically, mainly at the expense of Europe. A comparison of Japan's patent statistics with those of other countries is likely to be misleading, however, because of Japan's distinctive patenting laws, which require a multiplicity of patents for each invention in order to protect against copying individual features. Many analysts have noted that U.S. patenting has shown an absolute decline since the late 1960s. That is so, but it is also true of the major European countries, and the U.S. rate has partially recovered since 1980. We do not know what forces may account for these trends, but of the major industrial nations only Japan has experienced an increase in patenting (U.S. National Science Board 1991).

Within the group of industries in question, more finely grained analysis reveals a more varied picture regarding U.S. performance. Between the middle 1960s and the middle 1980s, the U.S. export share held up well in aircraft, aircraft engines and turbines, computing and other office machinery, and in several classes of chemical products. The U.S. export share fell significantly in professional and scientific instruments and in telecommunications. U.S. firms were routed in consumer electronics. The data on national patenting show a similar pattern. Generally, U.S. export shares have persisted in industries where U.S. patenting has held up and have fallen where patents by nationals elsewhere have risen relative to American patenting. This may entail a two-way relationship, with invention stimulating success and (as Schmookler argued) success stimulating patenting.

The definition of high-technology industries is somewhat arbitrary, as it is tied to

Figure 5-11. U.S. trade in high-technology products, 1970–87. *Source:* National Science Board 1989, Appendix Table 7-14.

R&D intensity exceeding a particular level. A number of industries are excluded from the definition, whose product and process technologies are complex and sophisticated and in which technical advance has been significant. Automobiles, machine tools, and other kinds of machinery are examples. By and large, the United States' export share and patenting have fallen significantly in these industries. Europe has done rather well. In contrast, the United States continues to be the export and patenting leader in many industries connected with agricultural products and others based on natural resources.

Thus beneath the surface of general productivity convergence, there is a much more complex picture. U.S. performance continues to be strong in several of the most R&D-intensive industries and in those connected to natural resources. It has declined in many of the industries—like automobiles, consumer electrical products, and steel making—in which the United States had had a dominant world position since the late nineteenth century. The interesting question, of course, is how this broad convergence came about. What were the forces behind it?

We would highlight four different developments. First, the drop in transportation costs and trade barriers has greatly expanded the flow of world trade, eroding the advantages in market size and raw material costs that U.S.-based firms used to have. Second, technology has become much more generally accessible to those with the requisite skills and willing to make the required investments, and hence it is much less respecting of firm and national boundaries than had been the case earlier. Third, the other major industrial powers significantly increased the proportion of their work forces trained in science and engineering and the proportion of their GNP allocated to research and development, thus establishing strong indigenous competence to exploit technologies from abroad, as well as to create new technology. Indeed, by 1980 a number of countries were outspending the United States in nonmilitary R&D as a fraction of GNP. This is important, because the fourth major factor behind convergence is, in our view, a decline in the importance of spillover from military R&D into civilian technology.

The period since 1960 has seen a significant rise in the percentage of manufactured products exported and imported in virtually all major industrial countries. Between 1960 and 1980, U.S. imports roughly doubled as a fraction of GNP. In France, Germany, and the United Kingdom taken as a group, the ratio of imports to GNP increased by about 50 percent. It grew by a quarter in Japan. All of these ratios were sustantially higher for manufacturing alone. This expansion of export markets opened up new opportunities for scale-dependent technologies in Europe and Japan, which had long been constrained by the limited size of their national markets (Caves 1989, pp. 1235–38). At the same time, trade in natural resources greatly expanded, and countries became less dependent on local materials. Postwar resource discoveries were far more dispersed around the globe than previously. Although the United States continued to be a large contributor to world mineral production, the country became a net importer of most major minerals, implying that the cost to industrial users was essentially the same as that in other countries. Thus the twin advantages long possessed by American mass producers—cheap raw materials and more-or-less exclusive access to the world's largest market—have dissolved. In combination with the growing domestic markets abroad, these international trends meant that by 1970 or so, supply and demand conditions among OECD countries had become quite similar. The economic environment of the United States was no longer distinct.

At the same time, business has become increasingly international. Technologically progressive American companies had established European branches even in the nineteenth century, but the scale of overseas direct investment surged dramatically during the 1950s and 1960s. In *The American Challenge,* Servan-Schreiber expressed concern that American companies were taking over the European economy at least as much by investing there as by exporting. By the late 1960s, Europe was beginning to return the favor by establishing branches or buying plants in the United States. Recently, Japanese companies have done the same, on a larger scale.

The internationalization of business has greatly complicated the interpretation of international trade statistics. For example, the nontrivial share of the rising U.S. imports in high-technology industries mentioned earlier originates in foreign subsidiaries of U.S.-owned companies (Langlois 1987, chap. 4). Although the U.S. share of world manufacturing exports (low and middle tech as well as high tech) fell somewhat from the middle 1960s to the middle 1980s, the export share of U.S.-*owned* firms held up, with gains in exports from foreign branches matching declines in exports from U.S.-based plants (Lipsey and Kravis 1987).

The internationalization of trade and business has been part and parcel of the second postwar development that we want to highlight—the erosion of firm and national borders as barriers obstructing or channeling access to technology. Modern science has been, from its beginning, an international activity. The ethos of science has for centuries stressed the public and international nature of scientific knowledge. British and French scientists continued to communicate during the Napoleonic wars, and attempts by national governments to define and keep separate a particular national science have often been condemned by the scientific community. Despite this ancient tradition, the real world of practical science has also displayed strong national elements, explicitly so in wartime and implicitly at other times in language, terminology, institutional structures, and objects of study.

In contrast with the universalist ethos of science, the notion that individuals and firms have proprietary rights to their inventions has been accepted for many centuries, and so too the idea that it is appropriate for a nation to gain advantage from the inventive work of its nationals. Nations have often tried to keep national technologies within their borders, however futile these efforts may often have been in many cases. Although technologists from different countries have communicated and formed something of an international community, until recently the notion that best-practice technology could be approached by any nation with the requisite resources was probably not correct. The technological advantage of the American mass market firms in industries like steel and automobiles did not derive from patents or well-protected secrets, but largely from experience gained well ahead of foreigners because of differences in the economic environment. With firms all over the world facing a common market for products and inputs, the forces that used to provide U.S. companies with incentives to get into certain technologies first have been largely eroded.

Even though the increasing similarity of economic environments may be the immediate reason for the convergence of technological capabilities, another important underlying development in the post–World War II era is that many technologies became more like sciences than before. Earlier we described the particular characteristics of science-based industries like chemical products and electronics. It is noteworthy that patents in these industries (and recently in biotechnology) cite scientific literature to a far greater extent than do patents in fields like steel and automobiles. Since 1960, however, the number of citations of scientific literature in patents has increased significantly in almost all technological fields, including steel and autos. In contrast with an earlier era, a larger proportion of the generic knowledge relevant to a technology now is written down, published in journals, discussed at national and international meetings, taught in schools of engineering and applied science, and so on.

Internationalization of business is an important part of this story. It is not just that foreigners can learn what American engineers can learn by going to American universities. European engineers can observe American technology in operation in their home countries and can purchase operating American firms. Companies like IBM have industrial research laboratories in a number of different countries, each employing a mix of nationals. In turn, scientists from IBM and scientists from Phillips, and Fujitsu, meet at conferences and exchange papers. Employees often move across national borders, within a firm or between firms. These are truly international networks, involving highly trained scientists and engineers, employed in universities and in industry, undertaking significant R&D efforts. The technologies emerging from such networks no longer have geographic roots, because horizons have become global and because material resource inputs more generally have declined in importance, relative to processing.

Generic technological knowledge, of the sort taught in graduate school, written down in books and articles, and exchanged among high-level professionals, does have strong public-good attributes. However, access is limited to those with the requisite training, and in many cases only someone who is actually doing research in a partic-ular field can understand the significance of publications in that field. To take indus-trial advantage of generic knowledge, or technology that is licensed from another com-pany, or more generally understanding what another company has done and how, usually requires significant inputs from trained scientists and engineers, plus expen-ditures on research and development aimed to tailor what has been learned to the spe-cific relevant uses (Nelson 1988, Nelson and Winter 1982, Pavitt 1987).

The other major industrial nations have, with a lag, followed the United States in making those big investments in education and training and R&D. The convergence in scientists and engineers in R&D as a fraction of the work force, and in R&D as a fraction of GNP, shown in Figures 5-8 and 5-9, is an essential part of, and a comple-ment to, the internationalization of technology. Convergence has occurred among those nations with modern educational systems, strong internal scientific and engi-neering communities, and sophisticated industrial enterprises. Nations without these attributes have tended to fall farther and farther behind the frontiers. There are now few important technological secrets, but it takes major investments of many kinds to command a technology.

Military technology has had a somewhat different history. The major military powers, prominently the United States, continue to make strong efforts to prevent mil-itary technology from leaking to potentially hostile nations or to nations that might serve as a conduit to hostile nations. But just as the political context of world conflict has changed with the end of the cold war, the economic context has altered completely. Whereas American dominance of the frontiers of military technology gave us signifi-cant civilian technology advantages during the 1950s and 1960s, today it buys us little outside the military sphere. In terms of access to technology that affects productivity in industry broadly defined, it does not hurt the Europeans or the Japanese that Amer-ican companies are engaged in military R&D to a much greater extent than they are and that the access to this technology is difficult, if not closed.

There are several reasons for the diminished importance of military R&D as a source of technological advantage outside the military field. First, although initially civilian demands for computers, semiconductors, and jet aircraft had lagged behind military demands, by the mid-1960s the civilian market for these products was as large or larger than the military; and in many dimensions, the performance demanded by the civilian market was actually higher. Companies responded by mounting their own R&D projects to meet these demands. Indeed, a strong case can be made that from the 1970s, the major direction of "spillover" was from the civil to the military. Thus the military bought the KC 10 as its tanker of choice, a plane that grew out of the McDonnell-Douglas DC 10, designed by the company for use by commercial airlines.

At the same time, military R&D increasingly focused on areas where its needs were specialized, engaging in specific product development efforts, as opposed to broadly applicable research. The share of military R&D that went into research and experimental development diminished significantly. With the end of the cold war, the outlook is for further decline in military R&D along with military spending more gen-erally, but at this point we do not foresee dire consequences for American technology as a result.

Conclusion

Much of the recent writing on convergence has not been directly concerned with the relationships between a leading economic and technological nation and its followers. But much of the stimulus for this new literature has been the eroding economic and technological lead of the United States, at least relative to the countries of western Europe and Japan. Indeed, this is a good part of the story behind the general convergence over the last 30 years shown by the statistical indicators. And this is what this chapter has tried to explain.

The stories we have told bear on Baumol's alternative theories about the sources of leadership and the nature of convergence. We first told the story of the rise in the late nineteenth century of a distinctly American technology and mode of business organization, stimulated and supported by features of the American economy that were different from conditions in other countries but that at the same time generated a level of American productivity and income to which other nations aspired. This component of the American lead was definitely connected with special conditions in America, and when the lead was generated in this way, the convergence of technologies depended on the convergence of economic conditions facing firms in different countries.

But we told another story as well, about the rise of industries with technologies based on inherently transnational science, and about how, after World War II, the United States came to dominate these industries not because of special attributes of the American economy but because we invested significantly more than other nations did in these technologies. Technology per se can rarely be contained for long within national borders. But the advent of science-based technologies has significantly increased the extent to which generic technological understanding is possessed by trained scientists and engineers, wherever they live. On the other hand, this same development has vastly increased the investment in education and in R&D that a nation, or a firm, must make to tap into and exploit generic technological understanding.

We argued that other countries have caught up to the United States partly because the economic environment facing firms in different countries became more similar, first as a result of increased opportunities for international trade and later because internal economic conditions became more similar. At the same time, other countries caught up with the United States in terms of their investments in scientific and engineering education and in R&D. These two broad developments went together. We contended, however, that they are anaytically separable, the first having to do with diminishing differences across countries in the incentives and the constraints bearing on the technologies that are profitable to develop and adopt, and the second having to do with other nations' doing what was required to tap into an increasingly powerful scientific basis for technology.

We believe that even though there may be temporary reversals, the world will continue to be one in which barriers to international trade and investment are much lower than they were before World War II. As we see it, developing technologies will increasingly have under them a codified body of formal science and engineering knowledge accessible to, and only to, those with formal training in the relevant fields.

As a result of both forces, the second theory articulated by Baumol will increasingly be the more apt.

Concepts like a "convergence club" make little sense under the first theory in which there is a clear national leader gaining and holding its lead because of special characteristics of that nation. This concept makes sense only if one posits that basic technological knowledge is transnational but that nations (or firms) need to make certain investments before they can effectively tap into it. We are not predicting that all nations within this club will have nearly identical levels of living and productivity, but we do suggest that the bounds for these variables will be tighter than they have been historically for nations that possess the requisite "social capabilities," to use the term that Abramovitz has made familiar. Nor are we proposing that there will be no significant differences among firms, in the same industry or among national groups of firms, in their ability to design and build first-class products. The performance of Japanese automobile producers relative to American firms is an obvious case in point. In this industry as in others, however, the differences do not arise from basic gaps in technological understanding. Rather, they reside largely in the organization of automobile production and design, that is, what the firms do with their technological knowledge. Even when interfirm differences in managerial performance are stubbornly persistent, their implications for *international* dispersion are ameliorated in today's world by the flow of direct foreign investment across national borders.

To be sure, we have stressed throughout the chapter that organization and management matter and that it has always been hard to separate these variables from command over technology. The early twentieth-century American advantage lay as much in the way in which firms were organized and managed as in their command of superior technology. The difference is that in that era much of the understanding of the technology itself was in the hands and fingers and hands-on experience; it was not in books, and little of it was taught in schools. Today much more is codified. The speed with which the Japanese, the Koreans, and the Taiwanese learned to command American-made technologies during the 1970s and 1980s—in many cases without much help from the Americans and without much experience in an American setting—demonstrates how much of today's technology can be found in books and learned in schools. These features of modern technology, together with the greater uniformity of market environments among nations, means that no nation will be able to take the kind of commanding technological lead that we have seen in the past.

Notes

This chapter is a reoriented version of our essay "The Rise and Fall of American Technological Leadership: The Postwar Era in Historical Perspective," written for the *Journal of Economic Literature,* December 1992. The original essay has been tailored to fit the subject matter of a conference on convergence.

Both authors of this chapter have been working for some time on the questions addressed here. Nelson's work was supported by the Sloan Foundation through its grant to the Consortium on Competition and Cooperation. Wright was supported by the Center for Economic Policy Research at Stanford. Both authors wish to express their debt to Moses Abramovitz. Moe has been a pioneer in charting this terrain and a generous adviser and critic for this chapter. We also thank William Baumol, Ralph Landau, Keith Pavitt, and Nicholas Von Tunzelmann.

References

Abramovitz, Moses. (1979). "Rapid Growth Potential and Its Realization: The Experience of Capitalist Economies in the Postwar Period." In Edmond Malinvaud, ed., *Economic Growth and Resources,* Vol. 1. London: Macmillan, pp. 1–51. Reprinted in Moses Abramovitz, *Thinking About Growth.* Cambridge: Cambridge University Press, 1989, pp. 187–219.

———. (1986). "Catching Up, Forging Ahead, and Falling Behind." *Journal of Economic History* 46:386–406. Reprinted in Abramovitz 1989.

Allen, Robert. (1977). "The Peculiar Productivity History of American Blast Furnaces, 1840–1913." *Journal of Economic History* 37:605–33.

———. (1979). "International Competition of Iron and Steel, 1850–1913." *Journal of Economic History* 39:911–37.

———. (1981). "Accounting for Price Changes: American Steel Rails, 1879–1910." *Journal of Political Economy* 89:512–28.

———. (1983). "Collective Invention." *Journal of Economic Behavior and Organization* 4:1–24.

Ames, Edward, and Nathan Rosenberg. (1968). "The Enfield Arsenal in Theory and History." *Economic Journal* 78:827–42.

Arthur, Brian W. (1988). "Self-reinforcing Mechanisms in Economics." In P. W. Anderson, K. J. Arrow, and D. Pines, eds., *The Economy as an Evolving Complex System.* Reading, MA: Addison-Wesley.

———. (1989). "Competing Technologies, Increasing Returns, and Lock-in by Historical Events." *Economic Journal* 99:116–31.

Barro, Robert J. (1991). "Economic Growth in a Cross Section of Countries." *Quarterly Journal of Economics* 106:407–44.

Baumol, William J. (1986). "Productivity Growth, Convergence, and Welfare." *American Economic Review* 76:1072–85.

Baumol, William J., Sue Anne Batey Blackman, and Edward N. Wolff. (1989). *Productivity and American Leadership.* Cambridge, MA: MIT Press.

Baxter, J. (1946). *Scientists Against Time.* Boston: Little, Brown.

Braun, Hans-Joachim. (1983). "The National Association of German–American Technologists and Technological Transfer Between Germany and the United States, 1884–1930." *History of Technology* 8:15–35.

Bruce, Robert V. (1987). *The Launching of Modern American Science, 1846–1876.* New York: Knopf.

Bush, Vannevar. (1945). *Science, the Endless Frontier.* Washington, DC: U.S. Government Printing Office.

Cain, Louis P., and Donald G. Paterson. (1986). "Biased Technical Change, Scale and Factor Substitution in American Industry, 1850–1919." *Journal of Economic History* 46:153–64.

Carstensen, Fred (1984). *American Enterprise in Foreign Markets.* Chapel Hill: University of North Carolina Press.

Caves, Richard E. (1989). "International Differences in Industrial Organization." In Richard Schmalensee and Robert Willig, eds., *Handbook of Industrial Organization.* Vol. 2. Amsterdam: North Holland, pp. 1226–50.

Chandler, Alfred D. (1977). *The Visible Hand.* Cambridge, MA: Harvard University Press.

———. (1990). *Scale and Scope: The Dynamics of Industrial Capitalism.* Cambridge, MA: Harvard University Press.

Clark, Gregory. (1987). "Why Isn't the Whole World Developed? Lessons from the Cotton Mills." *Journal of Economic History* 47:141–74.

Constant, Edward. (1983). "Scientific Theory and Technological Testability." *Technology and Culture* 24:183–98.

David, Paul A. (1975). *Technological Choice, Innovation and Economic Growth.* Cambridge: Cambridge University Press.

———. (1988). "Path-dependence: Putting the Past into the Future of Economics." *IMSSS Technical Report no. 533,* Stanford University.

———. (1989). "Computer and Dynamo: The Modern Productivity Paradox in a Not-Too-Distant Mirror." Center for Economic Policy Research Publication no. 172, Stanford University.

David, Paul A., and Gavin Wright. (1992). "Resource Abundance and American Economic Leadership." CEPR Publication no. 267, Stanford University.

De Long, J. Bradford. (1988) "Productivity Growth, Convergence, and Welfare: Comment." *American Economic Review* 78:1138–59.

Denison, Edward, with J. Puillier. (1967). *Why Growth Rates Differ.* Washington, DC: Brookings Institution.

Dertouzos, Michael, Richard K. Lester, Robert M. Solow, and the MIT Commission on Industrial Productivity. (1989). *Made in America.* Cambridge, MA: MIT Press.

Devine, Warren Jr. (1983). "From Shafts to Wires: Historical Perspective on Electrification." *Journal of Economic History* 43:347–72.

Dollar, David, and Edward N. Wolff. (1988). "Convergence of Industry Labor Productivity Among Advanced Economies, 1963–1982." *Review of Economics and Statistics* 70:549–58.

Easterlin, Richard. (1981). "Why Isn't the Whole World Developed?" *Journal of Economic History* 41:1–19.

Elbaum, Bernard, and William Lazonick, eds. (1986). *The Decline of the British Economy.* Oxford: Clarendon Press.

Field, Alexander J. (1983). "Land Abundance, Interest/Profit Rates and Nineteenth Century American and British Technology." *Journal of Economic History* 43:405–33.

Flamm, K. (1987). *Targeting the Computer: Government Support and International Competition.* Washington, DC: Brookings Institution.

Foreman-Peck, James. (1982). "The American Challenge of the Twenties: Multinationals and the European Motor Industry." *Journal of Economic History* 42:865–81.

Freeman, Christopher. (1987). *Technology Policy and Economic Performance: Lessons from Japan.* London: Francis Pinter.

Geiger, Roger L. (1986). *To Advance Knowledge.* New York: Oxford University Press.

Habbakuk, H. J. (1986). *American and British Technology in the Nineteenth Century.* Cambridge: Cambridge University Press.

Hatsopoulos, George, Paul Krugman, and Lawrence Summers. (1988). "United States Competitiveness: Beyond the Trade Deficit." *Science* 241:299–307.

Hayes, Peter. (1987). *Industry and Ideology: I. G. Farben in the Nazi Era.* Cambridge: Cambridge University Press.

Headrick, Daniel R. (1988). *The Tentacles of Progress: Technology Transfer in the Age of Imperialism 1850–1940.* New York: Oxford University Press.

Hounshell, David A. (1984). *From the American System to Mass Production, 1800–1932.* Baltimore: Johns Hopkins University Press.

Hounshell, David A., and John Kenly Smith, Jr. (1988). *Science and Corporate Strategy: Du Pont R&D, 1902–1980.* Cambridge: Cambridge University Press.

Hughes, Thomas P. (1987). "The Evolution of Large Technological Systems." In Wiebe E. Bijker, Thomas P. Hughes, and Trevor J. Pinch, eds., *The Social Construction of Technological Systems.* Cambridge, MA: MIT Press, pp. 51–82.

———. (1989). *American Genesis.* New York: Penguin Books.

James, John, and Jonathan Skinner. (1985). "The Resolution of the Labor-Scarcity Paradox." *Journal of Economic History* 45:513–40.

Jeremy, David. (1981). *Transatlantic Industrial Revolution.* Cambridge, MA: MIT Press.

Katz, Michael, and Carl Shapiro. (1985). "Network Externalities, Competition, and Compatability." *American Economic Review* 75:424–40.

Kennedy, Paul. (1987). *The Rise and Fall of the Great Power.* New York: Random House.

Kocka, Jurgen. (1980). "The Modern Industrial Enterprise in Germany." In Alfred D. Chandler and Herman Daems, eds., *Managerial Hierarchies.* Cambridge, MA: Harvard University Press, pp. 77–116.

Kogut, Bruce. (1992). "National Organizing Principles of Work, and the Erstwhile Dominance of the American Multinational Corporation." *Industrial and Corporate Change* 1:285–326.

Landau, Ralph. (1990a). "Capital Investment: Key to Competitiveness and Growth." *Brookings Review* 8:52–56.

———. (1990b). "Chemical Engineering: Key to the Growth of the Chemical Process Industries." In Jaromir J. Ulbrecht, ed., *Competitiveness of the U.S. Chemical Industry in International Markets.* American Institute of Chemical Engineers, Symposium Series no. 274, pp. 9–39.

Landau, Ralph, and Nathan Rosenberg. (1992). "Successful Commercialization in the Chemical Process Industries,." In Ralph Landau, David Mowery, and Nathan Rosenberg, eds., *Technology and the Wealth of Nations.* Stanford, CA: Stanford University Press, pp. 73–119.

Langlois, R. (1987). *Microelectronics: An Industry in Transition.* New York: Center for Science and Technology Policy.

Lazonick, William. (1990). *Competitive Advantage on the Shop Floor.* Cambridge, MA: Harvard University Press.

Lebergott, Stanley. (1976). *The American Economy: Income, Wealth and Want.* Princeton, NJ: Princeton University Press.

Lipsey, Robert E., and I. Kravis. (1987). "The Competitiveness and Comparative Advantage of U.S. Multinationals, 1957–1984." *Banca Nazionale del Lavoro Quarterly Review* 161:147–65.

MacKenzie, Frederick A. (1901): *The American Invaders.* New York: Arno Press, 1976 (first published 1901).

Maddison, Angus. (1987). "Growth and Slowdown in Advanced Capitalist Economies." *Journal of Economic Literature* 25:649–98.

———. (1989). *The World Economy in the Twentieth Century.* Paris: OECD.

———. (1991). *Dynamic Forces in Capitalist Development.* New York: Oxford University Press.

Malerba, F. (1985). *The Semiconductor Business.* Madison: University of Wisconsin Press.

Morison, Elting (1974). *From Know-How to Nowhere.* New York: Basic Books.

Mowery, David, and Nathan Rosenberg. (1989). *Technology and the Pursuit of Economic Growth.* Cambridge: Cambridge University Press.

Narin, F., and F. Noma. (1985). "Is Technology Becoming Science?" *Scientometrics* 7:369–381.

Nelson, Richard R., ed. (1982). *Government and Technical Progress: A Cross Industry Analysis.* New York: Pergamon Press.

———. (1988). "Institutions Supporting Technical Advance in U.S. Industry." In G. Dosi, C. Freeman, R. Nelson, G. Silverberg, and L. Soete, eds., *Technical Change and Economic Theory.* London: Francis Pinter, pp. 312–329.

———. (1990). "The U.S. Technology Lead: Where Did It Come from and Where Did It Go?" *Research Policy* 19:117–32.

Nelson, Richard R., and Sidney Winter. (1982). *An Evolutionary Theory of Economic Change.* Cambridge, MA: Harvard University Press.

Noble, David. (1977). *America by Design.* New York: Oxford University Press.

Pavitt, Keith. (1987). "The Objectives of Technology Policy," *Science and Public Policy* 4:182–88.

Pavitt, Keith, and R. Patel. (1987). "Is Western Europe Losing the Technological Race?" *Research Policy* 16:59–85.

Phelps-Brown, Ernest Henry. (1973). "Levels and Movements of Industrial Productivity and Real Wages Internationally Compared, 1860–1970." *Economic Journal* 83:58–71.

Piore, Michael, and Charles Sabel. (1984). *The Second Industrial Divide.* New York: Basic Books.

Reich, Leonard. (1985). *The Making of American Industrial Research: Science and Business at GE and Bell, 1876–1926.* Cambridge: Cambridge University Press.

Reich, Robert (1991). *The Work of Nations.* New York: Knopf.

Rosenberg, Nathan. (1963). "Technological Change in the Machine Tool Industry, 1840–1910." *Journal of Economic History* 23:414–43.

———. (1972). *Technology and American Economic Growth.* New York: Harper & Row.

———. (1985). "The Commercial Exploitation of Science by American Industry." In Kim B. Clark, Robert H. Hayes, and Christopher Lorenz, eds., *The Uneasy Alliance.* Boston: Harvard Business School Press, pp. 19–51.

Rosenberg, Robert. (1984). "The Origins of Electrical Engineering Education: A Matter of Degree." IEEE Spectrum, New York, 21:60–68.

Rothbarth, Edwin. (1946). "Causes of the Superior Efficiency of U.S.A. Industry as Compared to British Industry." *Economic Journal* 56:383–90.

Schultz, T. W. (1975). "The Value of the Ability to Deal with Disequilibria." *Journal of Economic Literature* 13:827–46.

Servan-Schreiber, J. J. (1968). *The American Challenge.* New York: Atheneum.

Smith, John Kenley, Jr. (1990). "The Scientific Tradition in American Industrial Research." *Technology and Culture* 31:121–31.

Soete, Luc. (1981). "A General Test of Technological Gap Trade Theory." *Weltwirtschaftliches Archiv* 117:638–660.

Soete, Luc, B. Verspagen, R. Patel, and K. Pavitt. (1989). *Recent Comparative Trends in Technological Indicators in the OECD Area.* Maastricht: Maastricht Economic Research Institute on Innovation and Technology.

Spitz, Peter. (1988). *Petrochemicals: The Rise of an Industry.* New York: Wiley.

Thomson, Ross. (1989). *The Path to Mechanized Shoe Production in the United States.* Chapel Hill: University of North Carolina Press.

Tweedale, Geoffrey. (1986). "Metallurgy and Technological Change: A Case Study of Sheffield Specialty Steel and America, 1830–1930." *Technology and Culture* 27:189–222.

U.S. National Science Board. (1987, 1989, 1991). *Science and Engineering Indicators.* Washington, DC: U.S. Government Printing Office.

U.S. Senate. (1911). *Report of the Immigration Commission.* Vol. 1. Washington, DC: U.S. Government Printing Office.

Wilkins, Mira (1970). *The Emergence of Multinational Enterprise: American Business Abroad from the Colonial Era to 1914.* Cambridge, MA: Harvard University Press.

Womack, James, Dan Jones, and Dan Rous. (1991). *The Machine That Changed the World.* Cambridge, MA: MIT Press.

Wright, Gavin. (1990). "The Origins of American Industrial Success, 1879–1940." *American Economic Review* 80:651–68.

6

Social Organization and Technological Leadership

WILLIAM LAZONICK

The Competitive Dynamics of International Leadership

This contribution to the convergence debate is dedicated to the propositions that as we reach the end of the twentieth century, the United States is falling behind both technologically and organizationally and that the United States, having fallen behind, will find it very difficult to put in place a mode of social organization required to catch up to the new leaders. Let me summarize the basic competitive dynamics involved. A national economy (say, Japan's) that rises to international industrial leadership does so on the basis of a mode of social organization that is capable of generating higher-quality products at lower unit costs than can be achieved on the basis of the mode of social organization that characterizes the old industrial leader (say, the United States). The old leader seeks to compete on the basis of what has now become a traditional mode of social organization. Indeed the old leader finds that by adapting to the new competition on the basis of the modes of organization and the types of technologies that made it successful in the past, it can continue to remain competitive for a time. Meanwhile, however, the new leader is continuing to use the social organization of its economy to generate innovation. By the time the old leader recognizes that it must change its mode of social organization in order to compete, the new leader has forged ahead.

Because the essence of social organization is the coordination of the abilities and incentives of numerous individuals toward a common goal, the old leader cannot simply decide to adopt the new and more powerful mode of social organization. Technical knowledge may transfer easily, but the social organization that is needed to develop and utilize this knowledge does not. Rather, to catch up, the old leader must begin a long process of social transformation, one that transforms the character of the relationships among those who participate in the nation's economy. In the absence of a commitment to engage in such social transformation, even the (now traditional)

modes of social organization that had brought the old leader to international prominence may begin to deteriorate, thus making catching up all the more difficult and
falling behind all the more likely.

This chapter summarizes a large and growing body of research, including my own
(Elbaum and Lazonick 1986, Lazonick 1990, 1991, 1992b), on the impacts of social
organization on technological change and productivity growth across the leading
national economies during the twentieth century. The empirial focus is on the social
organization that characterized two key changes in international industrial leadership:
the change in leadership from Britain to the United States in the first half of the twentieth century, and the change from the United States to Japan in the last half of the
century. Then I examine the evidence that suggests that over the past quarter-century,
in the face of increasingly intense global competition, the United States has been falling behind in its ability to develop and utilize technology.

The Rise and Decline of the British Economy

In *Productivity and American Leadership,* Baumol, Blackman, and Wolff (1989, pp.
21–22) recognized that the twentieth-century experience of the British economy was
one of falling further and further behind. But they made no attempt to explain either
Britain's long-term relative decline or, the other side of the same analytical coin, why
the United States and Germany were able to forge ahead.

The historical scholarship and debate on these issues are considerable. In the mid-
1980s, Bernard Elbaum and I, in conjunction with a number of other scholars, put
forth an analysis that rooted the British economic decline in the twentieth century in
the modes of social organization that had carried the British economy to industrial
leadership in the nineteenth century (Elbaum and Lazonick 1986). Central to the shift
of industrial leadership from Britain to the United States (particularly in consumer
goods) and Germany (particularly in capital goods) from the late nineteenth century
was a movement from market coordination to managerial coordination of economic
activity. In an era of less complex technological development, market coordination of
economic activity had the competitive advantage of avoiding the higher fixed costs of
managerial coordination. But through managerial coordination, the productive benefits that could be attained from more complex technologies more than offset the high
fixed costs of developing and utilizing these technologies (Lazonick 1991, chap. 3).

The problem for Britain in the twentieth century was that the very market-coordinated structures of industrial organization that had previously enabled its economy
to become the international industrial leader undermined the incentives and constrained the abilities of British enterprises and industries to make the transition to
managerial coordination. Without making such an organizational transition, the benefits of the more advanced technologies being developed elsewhere could not be
obtained within the British economy.

Although enterprise management had been important to the success of the pioneering factories in the early stages of the British industrial revolution, as the nineteenth century progressed, firms came to rely more on the external environment rather
than on internal planning and coordination to ensure access to the productive
resources required to generate (what were by the standards of the time) high-quality

products at low unit costs. The most important external resource that became available to British manufacturing firms in the nineteenth century was an ample supply of highly skilled and well-disciplined labor. Senior workers—known collectively as "the aristocracy of labor"—not only contributed their own skills to the building and operation of machinery but also recruited junior workers whom they trained and supervised on the shop floor (Burgess 1975, Harrison and Zeitlin 1985, Hobsbawn 1984, Lazonick 1990, chaps. 3–6).

Employers' reliance on skilled labor to organize work and train new workers had the advantage of low fixed costs not only for individual firms but also for the British economy as a whole. The progress of the British industrial revolution did not rely to any significant extent on state-supported or industry-supported education. The reproduction of an abundant and skilled labor force by means of worker-run, on-the-job training required little, if any, expense to either employers or the state.

These worker-run apprenticeship systems, moreover, yielded high levels of labor productivity. Eager to gain entry to the aristocracy of labor, the promise of promotion kept younger workers hard at work. The older workers, generally protected by union bargains that assured them shares of productivity gains were themselves not adverse to long and steady labor. Skilled workers' intimate practical knowledge of production methods meant that as by-products of shop-floor experience, they were able to keep imperfect machinery running steadily and to contribute to minor technological improvements.

As older workers trained younger workers, supplies of specialized labor expanded in certain localities during the nineteenth century. Given an industrialist's choice of business (itself typically a function of his own specialized training in a particular locality), he would tend to invest where labor with the necessary specialized skills was in relatively abundant supply. As a consequence, particular industries became increasingly concentrated in particular regions of Britain during the nineteenth century. The regional concentration of specific British industries meant that employers had access not only to large supplies of labor with the requisite skills but also to communication and distribution networks that supplied a regional industry with its basic inputs, transferred work-in-progress across the industry's vertically specialized productive activities, and marketed the industry's output.

The growth of a regionally concentrated industry facilitated the vertical specialization of constituent firms in a narrow range of activities, with these firms relying on other firms both to supply them with the necessary inputs and to purchase their outputs for resale downstream. The tendency toward vertical specialization was self-reinforcing because the growing availability of suppliers and buyers for intermediate products made it all the easier for new firms to become established as specialists. Hence the growth of a regionally concentrated industry was characterized more by the entry of new firms than by the growth of existing firms. Vertically specialized industries became horizontally fragmented industries (for a case study, see Lazonick 1983, reprinted in Lazonick 1992b).

The evolution of industry structures characterized by regional concentration, vertical specialization, and horizontal fragmentation as well as employers' ongoing reliance on skilled labor to organize work on the shop floor diminished the need for business firms to invest in the development of managerial structures. The lack of managerial organization in turn reinforced the tendency for industrial structures to be fragmented and specialized. Limited in their managerial capabilities, proprietary firms tended to confine themselves to single-plant operations, thus facilitating the entry of new firms into vertical specialties and hence increasing the extent of both the horizontal and the vertical fragmentation of industrial sectors. By reducing the managerial and financial resources necessary to run a business, the vertically specialized and horizontally fragmented industry structures permitted proprietary capitalists to avoid separating capital ownership from managerial control.

In the late nineteenth century, the leading economist of the era, Alfred Marshall, recognized the contribution to British industrial leadership of these regionally concentrated industries. Marshall (1920, pp. 283–88) eventually even coined a phrase—the "industrial district"—to describe these regional agglomerations. More than that, with his distinction between external and internal economies of scale, Marshall provided a theoretical perspective on the process of economic development that is exceedingly useful for understanding both the sources of British industrial leadership in the nineteenth century and its loss of industrial leadership in the twentieth century.

Economies of scale entail the spreading out of fixed costs over a larger output. These economies of scale are "external" when the growth of industry output occurs through an increase in the number of enterprises in the industry, and they are "internal" when it occurs through the growth of existing enterprises. Hence, given the business enterprise as the unit of analysis, external economies of scale imply industrial fragmentation and market coordination, and internal economies of scale imply industrial concentration and management coordination.

By themselves, however, economies of scale, whether external or internal, tell us nothing about why, at any given level of output, the resources employed in the industry are more or less productive (see Lazonick 1991, chap. 3). In other words, the existence of economies of scale does not explain the level of development of productive resources in an enterprise or industry.

Yet the sources of such development are critical to whether economies of scale will be internal or external to existing enterprises. For it is when existing enterprises within an industry develop superior capabilities that are enterprise specific that it becomes possible for these enterprises to gain a competitive advantage through internal economies of scale. Conversely, the attainment of competitive advantage on the basis of external economies of scale implies that the development of superior productive capabilities occurs more generally in the industrial district rather than in particular enterprises.

As I have already explained, the prime source of the development of productive capabilities in the industrial districts of nineteenth-century Britain was the skilled labor required to operate technologies that, even when mechanized, were highly imperfect. With the rise of managerial capitalism abroad in the twentieth century, the persistence of craft-based and market-coordinated industrial structures that had carried the British economy to international dominance in the nineteenth century impeded the development and utilization of advanced technology. In the staple industries—iron and steel, shipbuilding, mechanical engineering, and textiles—that had brought Britain to economic supremacy, more organizational capability resided in craft control on the shop floor than in the underdeveloped managerial structures (see Lazonick 1990, chap. 6).

Insofar as British craft workers continued to cooperate with their employers in the twentieth century, it was in squeezing as much productivity as possible out of the existing technologies, often by failing to maintain the quality of the product, driving their shop-floor assistants as well as themselves to supply more effort, and (as it became necessary in order to retain their jobs) accepting lower wages. Immobile because of their highly specialized skills, both workers and employers had the incentives to ensure the survival of the firms through which they gained their livelihoods. Many British firms in the staple industries were able to survive for decades by living off the plant, equipment, and infrastructures accumulated in the era of British industrial leadership (Elbaum and Lazonick 1986).

In some industries (mechanical engineering in particular), employers tried to use their collective power to break the crafts' control over the organization of work and the determination of remuneration. Even when employers rolled back prior union gains, however, craft control was not eliminated, in large part because proprietary capitalists, lacking managerial structures, had no organizational alternative to put in its place. What is more, even in a new machine-based industry such as automobile manufacture, in which the craft unions were not already ensconced, shop-floor control on the craft model became dominant in the first decades of the twentieth century as the automobile manufacturers tended to rely on craft workers to plan and coordinate the flow of work on the shop floor (for a summary, see Lazonick 1990, chap. 6).

Reliance on shop-floor workers to perform what we now consider to be managerial functions continued during the interwar period, even in firms such as Austin and Morris that were becoming dominant mass producers for the British market (see Lewchuk 1987). In the 1940s and 1950s, under conditions of tight labor markets combined with the limited opportunities for firms that relied on labor-intensive technologies to generate new sources of productivity, these workers used the shop-floor organizational responsibilities that had been delegated to them as the foundations on which to build specialized craft unions. The result was that by the 1960s one could find scores of separate craft agreements in place at any time in any one automobile plant, with the resultant fragmentation of employer–employee relations placing severe constraints on the managerial coordination of the specialized division of labor within the plant.

Yet the British automobile industry remained viable in global competition until the 1960s because of its low fixed costs (including the almost complete neglect of research and development) as well as the acceptance of relatively low returns by workers, managers, and owners. The 1960s and 1970s revealed, however, that like the staple industries of the nineteenth century, the British automobile industry had reached the technical and social limits of the utilization of its resources. Facing the continued development of the continental producers as well as the rise of the Japanese automobile manufacturers, the economic viability of the British industry could no longer be sustained.

The development of organizational capability was somewhat different in the science-based industries of the second industrial revolution—in chemicals, rubber, electrical equipment and appliances—in which it was impossible to enter into competition on the basis of technological capabilities inherited from the past. Largely through the efforts of dedicated and aggressive entrepreneurs (typically, although not always, owners as well as managers) who either developed new technologies or controlled foreign patents, a number of British firms such as Lever Brothers, Pilkington Brothers, Dunlop, Courtaulds, Crosfield's, Nobel's, and Brunner, Mond were able to become serious global competitors in the late nineteenth and early twentieth centuries (for business histories, see Barker 1977, Coleman 1969, Jones 1984, Musson 1965, Reader 1975, Wilson 1984).

Nevertheless, after the turn of the century the largest British firms were not only much smaller than the largest U.S. firms but also much more under the control of family ownership. In his recent book *Scale and Scope: The Dynamics of Industrial Capitalism,* Alfred Chandler (1990) attributed the relatively poor performance of British industry during the twentieth century to the persistence of "personal capitalism" in an era when managerial capitalism was making world leaders out of the economies of the United States and Germany. By personal capitalism, Chandler meant a system of corporate governance in which enterprise owners exercise control over capital-allocation decisions and hence over strategic decision making as well as day-to-day management of the enterprise. In short, ownership is integrated with control. By this definition, during most of the nineteenth century, personal capitalism was widespread in major industries, not only in Britain but also in all of the most advanced industrial economies, including those of the United States and Germany.

In speaking of "the continuing commitment to personal capitalism in British industry," Chandler (1990, chap. 7) meant that the British entrepreneurs who had transformed new ventures into going concerns in the capital-intensive industries of the second industrial revolution had "failed to make the essential three-pronged investment in manufacturing, marketing, and management" that could generate the economies of scale and scope being attained by their main international rivals. Most seriously deficient was investment in management: "The pioneers recruited smaller managerial teams, and the founders and their families continued to dominate the management of the enterprises" (Chandler 1990, pp. 236, 286).

In the twentieth century, British personal capitalism was successful in food, drink, and tobacco—industries in which brand-name recognition (i.e., assurance of product quality) was a source of competitive advantage but did not require large investments in complex technology and organization. "In branded, packaged products," Chandler (1990, p. 268) argued, "British entrepreneurs created national and international organizations that could still be personally managed by an extended family with a very few close associates." But such personal management was inadequate to global competition in standardized light machinery, electrical equipment, chemicals, and metals. In these industries, Chandler (1990, p. 275) contended, there was entrepreneurial failure in the last decades of the nineteenth century and the first decades of the twentieth century.

What accounts for this "continuing commitment to personal capitalism" in Britain in an era when managerial capitalism in the United States and Germany was on the rise? Chandler's basic answer to this question is the first-mover advantages of Britain's rivals. "As early as 1890," Chandler (1990, p. 284) pointed out, "the German and American first movers had already acquired powerful competitive advantages in their national markets, and this, in turn, provided a base for marketing abroad." Once the U.S. and German enterprises had achieved these economies of scale, it would have been irrational for British producers to try to compete. As Chandler (1990, pp. 285–86) summed up his argument:

Whatever the exact reasons for [British] entrepreneurial failure were, two points are clear. First, entrepreneurial failure in the new industries can be precisely defined. It was the failure to make the three-pronged investment in production, distribution, and management essential to exploit economies of scale and scope. Second, the time period in which that investment could have been made was short. Once first movers from other nations had entered the British market, often supplementing their marketing organizations by direct investment in production, the window of opportunity was closed.

But what can one say about the "exact reasons" for the failure of British enterprises to take advantage of the technological and market opportunities of the second industrial revolution? More specifically, what was it about the social environment in which British enterprises operated that led to their failure to make the necessary and timely investments in organization and technology? Was British "entrepreneurial failure" simply a cultural phenomenon that reflected a peculiarly British penchant for maintaining personal control over one's firm? Or was the failure of British industrialists to match U.S. and German investments in organization and technology conditioned by the social organization of the British economy, including the social organization of the enterprise itself, in the late nineteenth and early twentieth centuries?

My explanation for the persistence of "personal capitalism" lies in three interrelated systemic dimensions of the social environment in which the nation's industrial enterprises operated: the social system, the educational system, and the financial system (the following argument is elaborated, with references, in Lazonick 1986, reprinted in Lazonick 1992b, and Lazonick 1991, chap. 1). British industrialists of the late nineteenth century were generally middle class, with their home bases in the industrial districts of the Midlands and the North. Among those engaged in business, large accumulations of wealth and substantial political power were in the hands not of these industrialists but of financiers based in the City of London. Using upper-class educational institutions as means of entry and marriages as instruments of merger, wealthy financiers joined with the old landowning elite (many of them grown recently wealthy through rising land values) to form a new aristocracy. The wealth of this restructured upper class was not, as was increasingly the case in the United States and Germany, based on the application of science to industry and the resultant profits from technological innovation. Rather, the bases of wealth in financial activities were social connections and acquired reputations. Hence the importance for ultimate economic success of family connections and associations made at elite educational institutions— Oxford and Cambridge as well as public schools such as Eton and Harrow.

Lacking industrial roots, the aristocracy who controlled these elite institutions during the era of the second industrial revolution had no need for an educational system that developed technologists. They valued the study of science as a branch of sophisticated knowledge but had no interest in its application to industry. Indeed, the British elite positively resisted the notion that a concern with technology had any place in an aristocratic education. They wanted education to set them apart from the lower orders, not bring them in closer contact with them. For, as I have already outlined, in the rise of Britain to international industrial dominance during the first industrial revolution, technological knowledge had generally been in the possession of groups of workers—the so-called labor aristocrats—who gained this knowledge through the development and utilization of machinery on the shop floor.

Nor did successful industrialists who accumulated sufficient fortunes to contemplate joining Britain's upper class effectively challenge the anti-industry bias of Britain's elite educational system. Of middle-class, or even working-class, backgrounds, Britain's most successful industrialists sought to elevate their social standing by distancing themselves from the technological roots of their prior advance. They typically located their head offices in London and sent their sons to be educated at the elite public schools and, if possible, at Oxbridge. Thus they did not see it as in their interests to transform the nation's premier educational institutions into servants of industry. Their goal was, rather, to partake of aristocratic culture to serve their aspirations for upward mobility, which meant accepting the antitechnology bias of that culture. As the historian Donald Coleman (1973) put it in a well-known essay, successful industrialists sought to become "gentlemen" rather than "players."

In seeking to move up the social hierarchy, successful industrialists did not abandon industry for finance; barriers to entry into finance and related pursuits were high precisely because of the centrality of social connections and reputations to the success of the financial enterprise. Rather, as successful British industrialists sought to move up the social hierarchy, control over an established industrial enterprise remained the foundation of their material wealth and the most assured means of passing wealth on to their children. They brought in their sons and sons-in-law to manage their businesses, thus perpetuating the integration of family ownership and control. The larger owner-controlled firms that, because of enterprise expansion or a dearth of qualified family members, had to recruit top managers from outside the family gave highest preference to young men with a classical Oxbridge education. As a result, the most influential British industrialists put little pressure on the elite educational institutions to offer technical and organizational training even to the future captains of industry. Instead, the elite educational institutions became instrumental to the persistence of "personal capitalism."

By virtue of their educational backgrounds and social aspirations, those in control of British industrial enterprises in the first half of the twentieth century were not themselves well equipped or well positioned to lead their firms in the pursuit of technological innovation. Within the enterprise, the top managers of the most successful enterprises of the second industrial revolution set themselves apart as an elite social class, thus creating an organizational barrier between themselves as strategic decision makers and the technical specialists who were expected to implement enterprise strategies. Increasingly after the turn of the century, many of the technical specialists employed by science-based enterprises came from the newly established provincial universities that did try to cater to the educational needs of technologists. The second-class status of the graduates of the provincial universities was confirmed when they took up employment in a major British industrial enterprise. Because of the way in which the top managers of the personally managed enterprises were recruited, these technical specialists could not view their initial employment in even the larger enterprises as a first step up a managerial hierarchy that might ultimately lead to positions of control.

As a result of these barriers to social mobility within the enterprise, technical specialists were less committed than they might otherwise have been to furthering enterprise goals, and they were more likely than they would otherwise have been to view interfirm mobility as the main route to career progress. Such prospects of employee exit in turn reduced the incentive for the owner-managers of these enterprises to invest in the productive capabilities of these technical specialists. Even in the cases of trained scientists and engineers, therefore, leading British enterprises relied more on market coordination than management coordination in their employment of labor (see Dore 1990). In industries in which the development and utilization of technology depended on the development and utilization of highly specialized technical skills, enterprises that relied on market-coordinated employment relations could find themselves at a decided disadvantage in global competition.

But market-coordinated employment relations placed British enterprises at a competitive disadvantage only when foreign enterprises based on more management-coordinated employment relations were able to generate higher-quality products at lower unit costs. The key question, then, for understanding the social organization of the enterprise as a source of global competitive advantage is why, in a given industry, the social structures of enterprises in nations such as the United States and Germany were more management coordinated than they were in Britain. Put differently, why did a transition from "personal" (or proprietary or market) capitalism to managerial capitalism occur more rapidly and thoroughly in the enterprises of Britain's competitors than in British enterprises? Here I can only outline the answer to this question for the case of the United States. Nevertheless, the Anglo-American comparison makes clear the growing importance of social organization not only within the enterprise but more generally within the national economy as a source of industrial leadership and global competitive advantage in the first half of this century.

Organizational Capabilities and American Leadership

The Anglo-American comparison is worth making not only because British and U.S. enterprises competed in many industries but also because the two nations had a common cultural heritage. As late as the 1860s, the United States' system of higher education was based on the Oxbridge model. In both nations, moreover, the ideology prevailed in the nineteenth century that individualistic enterprise constituted the most powerful force for economic development.

As late as the 1890s in the United States, ownership of industrial enterprises remained integrated with managerial control. Yet over the next generation, there was a separation of ownership from control in the most successful and enduring U.S. managerial enterprises, and the U.S. system of higher education had been transformed to cater to the needs of U.S. managerial structures (Lazonick 1986, reprinted in Lazonick 1992b, Noble 1977). Why, by the early decades of the century, should such a change in enterprise governance have occurred on such a widespread basis in the United States, compared with Britain?

To comprehend how and why asset ownership was separated from managerial control in U.S. industrial enterprises requires answers to two questions. First, how was ownership transferred from the original owner-entrepreneurs who managed a company to the new owners who did not exercise managerial control? Second, how did it happen that the managers who were left in control of these companies after the transfer of ownership were both able and willing to apply science to industry in ways that generated technological innovation and, in many cases, global competitive advantage? As in the case of Britain, to answer these questions requires analyzing the dynamic interaction of the social system, the educational system, and the financial system in shaping the organizational evolution of the enterprise (the following argument, with references, is elaborated in Lazonick 1986, 1991, chap. 1, and 1992a).

Until the Great Merger Movement that began in the 1890s, a national market in industrial securities did not exist in the United States (Navin and Sears 1955). But by the 1890s a number of enterprises in the more capital-intensive industries had used retained earnings to finance continuous innovation that enabled them to capture dominant market shares. Key to the success of these enterprises was the willingness of owner-entrepreneurs to invest not only in production and distribution facilities but also in managerial personnel. These dominant enterprises were central actors in the Great Merger Movement, and the most successful mergers occurred in the industries of the second industrial revolution—industries in which enterprises gained competitive advantage through continuous product and process innovation and high-speed utilization of production and distribution facilities (Chandler 1990, chap. 3).

The Great Merger Movement did more than merely concentrate industry. With J. P. Morgan taking the lead, Wall Street financed the mergers by selling to the wealth-holding public the ownership stakes of the entrepreneurs whose companies were being merged. The ultimate result was the creation of a national market in industrial securities. Through the mediation of Wall Street, ownership of the assets of the newly merged companies was transferred from the original owner-entrepreneurs to a widely distributed population of wealth-holding households. After the turn of the century, a company that emerged as dominant in its industry could go public without merger and have its shares listed on the New York Stock Exchange.

In taking these enterprises public, the sale of common shares did not finance new investments in organization and technology. Rather, it financed the retirement of the old owners from the industrial scene. By purchasing these shares (increasingly on the secondary market), the new owners did not assume managerial control. What attracted these portfolio investors to the stock market was the fact that an ownership position in a company did not require any further commitments of time, effort, or finance to that company. When owners became dissatisfied with the performance of "their" companies, they could simply sell their ownership stakes on the highly liquid stock market to other, anonymous, portfolio investors who wanted to become owners for a while. Ownership had thus been separated from control (see Lazonick 1992a).

The managers now in control were not owners but salaried employees. Increasingly in the first decades of this century, the salaried employees who rose to positions of top management in the U.S. science-based enterprises had been recruited to their companies as university graduates in search of careers. The education that they received, moreover, provided them with the basic cognitive capabilities to apply science to industry, capabilities that they improved through in-house training and experience during their careers (Lazonick 1986, reprinted in Lazonick 1992b).

In Britain, as we have seen, the higher education most valuable for men destined for top management positions served to distance these future leaders from the application of science to industry rather than to immerse them in it. A classical college education, modeled after Oxbridge, had in the mid-nineteenth century also held sway in the United States at institutions of higher learning such as Harvard and Yale. With the coming of managerial capitalism, however, these educational institutions were transformed to meet the requirements of U.S. industrial enterprises for line and staff specialists. The pressure for educational change began to build in the mid-nineteenth century when the advocates of Jeffersonian democracy sought to establish institutions of higher learning that would elevate the social standing of the independent farmer and artisan while giving them advanced practical knowledge in agriculture and the mechanical arts. The ultimate legislative result of this movement was the Morrill Land Grant College Act of 1862 that funded the establishment of agricultural and mechanical arts colleges in every state in the nation.

As it turned out, individuals intent on being independent farmers or artisans had little use for the bachelor's degrees that the land-grant colleges offered. But the emerging system of managerial capitalism did. In current discussions of the rise of U.S. managerial capitalism, a much neglected industry is agriculture. From the 1890s the U.S. Department of Agriculture in effect transformed the land-grant colleges into operating divisions of a huge managerial bureaucracy that, in regional experiment stations attuned to improving the productivity of local crops, applied science to industry and, through extension services, sought to diffuse the resultant technologies to the mass of farmers who, in their combined roles as "plant" managers and "shop-floor" workers, transformed purchased inputs into salable outputs (Ferleger and Lazonick 1992). Also from the 1890s, U.S. manufacturing enterprises began to take an interest in the land-grant colleges—MIT among them—as a source of supply of scientists and engineers (Noble 1977; see also Servos 1980). This was a time when, for the sake of developing new technologies, the most prominent U.S. mass production enterprises were building in-house capabilities to apply science to industry (Hounshell and Smith 1988, Mowery and Rosenberg 1989, pt. II, Reich 1985) and, for the sake of utilizing these new technologies, were successfully eliminating craft control of production from the shop floor (Lazonick 1990, chap. 7, Montgomery 1987).

The growing importance of the land-grant colleges in American economic life in turn put pressure on the older colleges to make their scientific and educational activities relevant to the needs of industry. Especially after the turn of the century, when (largely through philanthropic foundations established by business fortunes) wealth accumulated in industry provided massive funding for education, managerial capitalism could use the entire system of U.S. higher education, whether privately or publicly funded. Industrial enterprises increasingly recruited managerial personnel from the system of higher education and then, through in-house training and on-the-job experience, developed the productive capabilities of these employees and promoted the best of them to middle-level and upper-level managerial positions. That there was room at the top for such career managers had been ensured, moreover, by the separation of ownership from control (Lazonick 1986, reprinted in Lazonick 1992b).

But why then did such a separation of ownership from control not occur in Britain during the first decades of the century? There were, after all, well-developed markets in industrial securities in Britain in advance of the United States. In my view, the key explanatory factor was the social segmentation that I have described between strategic decision makers and technical specialists within the owner-controlled British enterprise. By distancing themselves socially and often geographically from the technological activities of their enterprises, owners as strategic decision makers became unwilling to invest in the core capabilities of their enterprises and became less knowledgeable (if not ignorant) of what these core capabilities were. Hence a transfer of company ownership from owner-entrepreneur to wealth-holding public, as occurred in the United States, would not have left a qualified managerial team in its place.

The failure to invest in organizational capabilities, moreover, meant that British enterprises that had been successful in their entrepreneurial phases did not have the national or global competitive advantages that would have led the wealth-holding public to pay dearly for shares in these companies. The public sale of such a company, therefore, would have been less remunerative to the owner-entrepreneurs than was the case for their counterparts in the United States. R. C. Michie (1987) has shown that the London Stock Exchange was much less selective in listing companies than was the New York Stock Exchange, an organizational difference that may well have reflected the emergence of more markedly dominant enterprises in the United States than in Britain. Important, and perhaps paramount, sources of these cross-national differences in competitive advantage were differences in the social organization of U.S. and British enterprises that participated in the second industrial revolution.

Besides permitting the separation of ownership from control, the rise of managerial coordination in the United States had profound implications for the organization of work on the shop floor. Unlike Britain with its accumulations of skilled labor supplies in industrial districts, the interregional and interoccupational mobility of workers in the United States rendered skilled labor scarce throughout the nineteenth century. When U.S. industrialists wanted to engage in mass production, they had to look to skill-displacing technological change to overcome the constraints on labor supply that a highly mobile work force had imposed. To ensure the development and utilization of the skill-displacing technologies, U.S. industrialists had to invest in managerial structures. The result, by the middle of the nineteenth century, was the rise of a characteristic "American system of manufactures" (Hounshell 1984).

Nevertheless, during the rapid postwar expansion of American industry, U.S. manufacturing enterprises, and particularly those that sought to compete on growing national markets, found that they had to rely extensively on skilled labor to coordinate, and even in many cases plan, their production activities. By comparison with the persistence of craft control in Britain, however, American reliance on skilled shop-floor labor to coordinate production activities was generally short lived, as U.S. industrialists developed technological and organizational alternatives to leaving skills, and the control of work, on the shop floor. By employing unskilled immigrants from eastern and southern Europe, by investing in de-skilling technological change, and by elaborating their managerial structures to plan and coordinate the productive transformation, U.S. industrial capitalists attacked the craft control that workers—typically of British and German origin—had staked out during the 1870s and 1880s (Montgomery 1987).

The initial response of shop-floor workers to the exercise of managerial control was to form craft unions. When employers refused to bargain with these unions, shop-floor workers turned to restricting output in order to exercise direct control over the relation between the work effort they provided and the pay they received. During the first three decades of this century, employers used both political and economic power to eradicate and diffuse workers' attempts to assert shop-floor control. They relied on repression, instigated and financed both privately and publicly, to eliminate radical elements in the American labor movement. But having deprived their workers of militant alternatives, the leading industrial employers also gained the cooperation of their shop-floor workers by sharing some of the managerial surplus with them and by holding out (what during the 1920s at least appeared to be) plausible promises of employment security (see Brody 1980).

As I have argued elsewhere (Lazonick 1990, chap. 7), the phenomenal productivity growth in U.S. manufacturing in the 1920s could not have been achieved without managerial success in gaining control over work organization on the shop floor. At the same time, however, the decades-long managerial offensive against craft control—combined with the evolution of a highly stratified educational system that effectively separated out future managers from future workers even before they entered the workplace—left a deep social gulf between managers and workers in U.S. industrial enterprises. During the 1920s, even as many dominant industrial enterprises shared some of their surpluses with workers in the forms of higher wages and more employment security, U.S. managers, ever fearful of a reassertion of craft control, continued with their quest to take, and keep, skills off the shop floor.

The Great Depression, with its massive layoffs of blue-collar workers even by many of the most progressive employers of the 1920s, served to deepen the social separation of management from the shop-floor labor force. In response, the U.S. labor movement reorganized, but this time on an industrial rather than a craft basis, and used the crisis of the 1930s to wring from the state a measure of economic security for workers that private enterprise had shown itself incapable of providing. In the renewed prosperity of the 1940s, when the dominant mass producers once again sought to gain the cooperation of workers by offering them high wages and prospects of secure employment, they had to deal with powerful mass production unions.

These unions did not challenge the principle of management's right to plan and coordinate the shop-floor division of labor (see Lazonick 1990, chap. 9). In practice, however, the quid pro quo for union cooperation was that seniority be a prime criterion for promotion along well-defined, and ever more elaborate, job structures, thus giving older workers the best access to a hierarchical succession of jobs paying gradually rising hourly wage rates. In return, union leadership sought to ensure orderly collective bargaining, including the suppression of illegal work stoppages.

From the 1940s to the mid-1960s, union–management cooperation in the coordination of shop-floor relations permitted high enough levels of productivity to sustain a competitive advantage, despite the failure of the dominant mass producers to address the issue of de-skilled, monotonous, and hence alienating work. By sharing with blue-collar workers some of the gains that came with international dominance, U.S. mass producers exercised a substantial degree of control over the supply of effort on the shop floor. But just as the structures of cooperative labor–management relations that had served British employers well in the nineteenth century were to become barriers to organizational transformation in the twentieth, so too would the labor–management relations that prevailed in the U.S. era of economic dominance prove problematic when a more powerful mode of developing and utilizing technology came on the scene.

Organizational Capabilities and Japanese Leadership

Over the past two decades, Japanese manufacturing has outperformed U.S. manufacturing in the mass production of consumer durables, particularly automobiles and electronic equipment. These are the industries in which the United States had its greatest international competitive advantages in the first six decades of this century. Having gained competitive advantage in the consumer-durable industries, Japanese manufacturing has also made great progress in vertically related capital-goods industries: machine tools, electrical machinery, and semiconductors. Now in the 1990s, there is no doubt that Japanese manufacturing has taken the leading role in the microelectronics-based third industrial revolution.

As was the case historically in the United States, the Japanese state has played an important role in protecting the home market to permit business organizations to develop and utilize their productive resources to the point that they could attain a competitive advantage in open international competition. But the Japanese state has also gone further. It has maintained a stable macroeconomic environment, including high levels of employment and a relatively equal distribution of income across sectors, thus enlarging the extent of the Japanese market for manufactured goods. It has created incentives for consumers and businesses to purchase goods (e.g., televisions and computers) that embody state-of-the-art technologies. It has limited the number of firms competing in major manufacturing industries, thus creating incentives for these firms to incur the high fixed costs necessary to attain a competitive advantage. It has promoted cooperative research and development among major Japanese competitors. It has ensured manufacturing corporations access to inexpensive finance. And the Japanese state has provided industry with a highly educated labor force to fill blue-collar, white-collar, and managerial positions (Anchordoguy 1989, Best 1990, chaps. 5–6, Johnson 1982, McCraw 1986).

But however important the role of the Japanese state is in shaping an environment conducive to economic development, the formulation of investment strategies and the building of organizational structures to carry them out has been left to private-sector enterprises. Over the long run these organizations have outperformed and, in my view, will continue to outperform their U.S. counterparts because of management coordination that extends beyond the limits of the planned coordination of the specialized division of labor as practiced under U.S. managerial capitalism. First, management coordination in Japan extends across vertically related enterprises (or units of financial control) to a much greater extent than it does in the United States. Second, within the dominant Japanese enterprise, management coordination extends further down the organizational hierarchy to develop the skills of male production workers—the type of workers whom, historically, American managers have been loathe to entrust with skills (see Lazonick 1990, chaps. 7–10). Both these extensions of management coordination significantly enhance the organizational capability available to Japanese enterprises (Abegglen and Stalk 1985).

The combination of far-reaching management coordination within private-sector manufacturing and the activist role of the state in creating an economic and social environment conducive to the emergence of innovative capitalist enterprises represents a qualitatively new mode of business organization in the evolution of capitalism.

The extent of the collectivization of interests under Japanese capitalism contrasts with the more limited planned coordination of the specialized division of labor under U.S. managerial capitalism and the virtual lack of planned coordination that existed during the days of British proprietary capitalism. But in the light of the success of U.S. managerial capitalism earlier in this century, it must be recognized that the social organization of the Japanese economy is not a completely new model of successful capitalist development. Rather, it is a more thoroughgoing elaboration of the model of management coordination that brought the United States to global leadership earlier in this century.

A fundamental institution of Japanese collective capitalism is the enterprise group, or *keiretsu*. The original enterprise groups in modern Japan were the family-controlled *zaibatsu* that led the development of heavy industry—particularly iron and steel and shipbuilding—from the turn of the century until World War II. The abolition of *zaibatsu* control in the aftermath of World War II ultimately left the enterprise groups intact. Shares of individual enterprises were distributed across industrial and financial companies, both within and across groups. These companies act as "stable shareholders" that seek neither high yields nor capital gains on their equity positions. Rather, they hold the shares for the sake of ensuring reinvestment in industry in general, which over the long run generates more business for the companies in the activities in which their competitive advantages lie (Ballon and Tomita 1988, Gerlach 1989).

Since the end of World War II, the largest of these corporate entities—Mitsubishi, Mitsui, and Sumitomo—shorn of family control, have remained powerful corporate actors in the Japanese economy, along with a few other large groups built up by either powerful banks or industrial enterprises such as Toyota and Sony that, having emerged as dominant in the automobile and electronics industries, can take the lead in the planned coordination of group activities, including setting up new vertically related enterprises as the need arises. Enterprise groups permit the core companies to enjoy the advantages that the vertical integration of production and distribution creates for the borrowing of technology and the implementation of process and product innovation, without enduring the disadvantages of unmanageable bureaucracies that stifle technological and organizational change. By circumventing the intrafirm organizational structure through subcontracting arrangements with satellite firms, the core company can pursue new investment strategies that require entrepreneurial initiative and leaps in technological capability.

The growth of enterprise groups gives core companies an opportunity for strategically locating more labor-intensive activities in smaller firms in which the technical specialists have direct proprietary interests in enterprise performance and in which control of the terms of employment and work conditions need not be shared with the enterprise unions that have become central to labor–management relations in the dominant companies. Although as subcontractors for the core enterprises, the satellite firms can in principle act independently, in practice the very success of the innovative strategies of the dominant enterprises and their commitment to maintaining long-term relations with their subcontractors leads the smaller firms to view themselves as members of an integrated organizational structure (Best 1990, chap. 5, Dore 1986, Smitka 1991).

Over time, some of these "satellites," if successful, can take on lives of their own, as in the case of Fanuc, the company set up by Fujitsu to develop numerical control units for machine tools (Collis 1988). Even then, the very fact that one strong vertically related enterprise has emerged out of the development of another creates a continuing basis for cooperative investment policies while each builds its own internal organization. The organizational capability developed through intercompany cooperation within groups undoubtedly enhances the ability of firms from different groups to engage in cooperative research and development projects, as has been the case in the emergence of an internationally competitive Japanese computer industry (Anchordoguy 1989).

The ability to organize cooperative investment strategies *across* enterprises is enhanced by the structure of managerial decision making *within* enterprises. Consensus decision making—the *ringi* system—emphasizes the two-way flow of ideas and information up and down the corporate hierarchy. Consensus decision making grew out of the need of the rapidly growing *zaibatsu* of the early twentieth century to lure college graduates—products of a concerted effort by the state to create an educated elite—away from prestigious government posts. Considerable technical information was required from, and considerable authority had to be delegated to, these professional managers. Even in the cotton textile industry, which in Japan as in Britain and the United States played a major role in early industrialization, the recruitment of college graduates to serve as mechanical engineers was central to the achievement of high levels of productivity on the basis of inexpensive cotton and unskilled labor (Mass and Lazonick 1990, Morikawa 1989, Yonekawa 1984).

Ringi permits the knowledge and outlooks of the various division and department heads to become integral to the planning process itself. By formalizing a system of gathering input and approval from the various persons who will be responsible for overseeing the implementation of strategic decisions, *ringi* permits the identification and, if need be, accommodation within the organization of potential obstacles to the success of a strategy before strategic commitments have already been made. When operating effectively so that individual managers cannot circumvent the group process, consensus decision making eliminates competing centers of decision-making power within the organization that might otherwise undertake investments that have conflicting objectives. In effect, investment strategy and managerial structure are organizationally integrated.

At the same time, the process of consensus decision making not only provides a valuable source of information from below for top executives but also helps ensure that large numbers of more specialized managers on their way up the hierarchy are developing a general conception of organizational needs and capabilities. By promoting the transformation of technical specialists into general managers, consensus decision making enhances management coordination of the development and utilization of productive resources.

The institutional basis for the devolution of decision-making power from chief executives to a wider group that extends further down the formal hierarchy is permanent, or lifetime, employment. Japanese managers typically rise out of the ranks of "white-collar workers" who enter the firm after graduating from college. Like consensus decision making, the policy of permanent employment was extended to professional managerial personnel in the early twentieth century in order to attract them away from government service and to create the long-term attachments that would make it worthwhile for the business enterprises to invest further in the recruits' training (Daito 1986).

Over time, however, the offer of permanent employment has been extended further down the organizational hierarchy. Before World War II, permanent employment was used as a strategy to transform "key" skilled workers *(oyakata)*—who, as highly mobile labor contractors, had recruited, trained, and supervised shop-floor labor—into permanently employed foremen who now performed the same functions, but with a long-term commitment to one particular company (Gordon 1985, Okayama 1983). In the early 1950s a strategy of substituting cooperative enterprise unions for the militant industrial unions that had arisen after World War II resulted in the extension of permanent employment status to all male blue-collar workers in the larger enterprises (Cusumano 1985, chap. 3).

Some argue that permanent employment is not a critical economic institution in Japan because "only" some 30 percent of the Japanese labor force have permanent employment status. But this figure, derived from the present proportion of the Japanese labor force that is unionized, includes virtually all males working for the dominant industrial enterprises, whether as blue-collar or white-collar employees. Within these dominant industrial enterprises, the most prevalent form of labor force segmentation is between women, who are generally excluded from permanent employment (although in recent years some university-educated women have gained access to it), and men. Moreover, many male industrial workers who do not have permanent employment status enjoy substantial employment security often amounting to de facto permanent employment because the smaller-sized firms for which they work have long-term organizational ties with core companies that in part owe their organizational integration and dominance to the institution of permanent employment (see Cannings and Lazonick, forthcoming, Lazonick 1993).

The phenomenal successes of these dominant business enterprises have in turn made it economically viable for the government to implement policies that lead to employment stability in small-scale enterprises in agriculture and retailing, even though the workers in these sectors would not be counted among the ranks of "permanent employees." In dynamic historical perspective, permanent employment in what have emerged as the dominant business enterprises has been central to Japan's rise to industrial leadership.

Japan's permanent employment functions both as a training system that develops the skills of employees in a planned and coordinated way and as an incentive system that elicits efforts of high quality and quantity from individuals. During the first decade of an employee's career, promotion and pay increases occur by gradual steps and by seniority: "Fast tracks" have been rare in the Japanese corporate enterprise. During this initial period, the company invests in considerable specialist training of its permanently employed personnel. In contrast with the American practice of applying the terms unskilled, semiskilled, and skilled to different types of jobs to be filled by different types of workers, the Japanese have used these terms to apply to the stages through which a particular worker passes during the first 10 years of employment. The company also provides more general training by rotating employees to different technical specialties within the enterprise and, at times, even within the enterprise group. When qualitatively new investment strategies require qualitatively new skills, the permanent employment system gives Japanese companies the incentive to invest in the retraining of mid-career personnel (Koike 1987).

The existence of permanent employment and the emphasis on seniority in promotion and rewards, particularly in the early years of an employee's career, encourages personnel to cooperate with one another in pursuit of the business organization's goals. It is only in mid-career that promotion on the basis of individual performance becomes important, although even then seniority continues to have some influence on promotion decisions and remains the predominant determinant of salary increases. To encourage individual creativity and initiative, non-seniority-based incentives are also used, in particular the possibility of retaining an influential position in the company after the normal retirement age. But especially when the technology is complex and costly, economic success depends on not only individual initiative but also cooperative effort, and collective rewards may supply the appropriate incentive mechanisms. Backed by the bargaining power of enterprise unions, all permanent employees receive semiannual bonuses, which typically constitute one-third of an individual's annual earnings but are adjusted according to the profitability of the firm and thus its ability to pay (Abegglen and Stalk 1985, chap. 8, Dore 1987, chap. 4).

Through the organizational commitments inherent in permanent employment, the skills and efforts of male blue-collar workers have been made integral to the organizational capabilities of their companies, thus enabling the Japanese to take the lead in innovative production systems such as just-in-time inventory control, statistical quality control, and flexible manufacturing. Critical to the functioning of these production systems is the willingness of Japanese managers to develop the skills of shop-floor workers and then to depend on the initiative of these workers to exercise their skills. The recent success of Japanese mass producers in introducing flexible manufacturing systems owes much to the fact that for decades before the introduction of the new automated technologies, blue-collar workers were granted considerable discretion to monitor and adjust the flow and quality of work on the shop floor (Cusumano 1985, chaps. 5–6). Moreover, the ability of Japanese managers to develop the skills of blue-collar workers owes much to the existence for over a century of a national system of mass education designed specifically to ensure that the work forces of the future possess the general cognitive competence that advanced production technology requires (Dore and Sako 1989, Odagiri and Goto 1993).

Japanese practice is in marked contrast with the U.S. managerial concern with using technology to take skills and the exercise of initiative *off* the shop floor, a practice that goes back to the late nineteenth century when the success of U.S. mass production was dependent on breaking the power of craft workers and transferring to management the sole right to plan and coordinate the flow of work. Despite the existence of militant unionism in Japan at various points in the first half of the twentieth century, there was never any attempt by Japanese workers or their organizations to establish craft control on the shop floor (Gordon 1985, pt. 1). As a result, Japanese employers never had to confront the established craft positions of workers, as was the case with U.S. manufacturers around the turn of the century, nor did they have to resign themselves to simply leaving skills on the shop floor in the hands of autonomous craftsmen, as was the case in Britain.

Historically, the problem facing Japanese employers was not to rid themselves of skilled workers who might use their scarce skills to establish craft autonomy on the shop floor. Rather, their problem coming into the twentieth century was the absence of a self-generating supply of workers with industrial skills. To overcome this constraint, industrial capitalist employers had to make the investments that would transform unskilled workers into skilled workers and then retain them by integrating them into the organization. To be sure, these same employers generally accepted the institutionalization of permanent employment, enforced by enterprise unions, only when compelled to do so by the threat of militant unionism after World War II. In practice, however, out of the exigencies of developing and utilizing workers with industrial skills, the social foundations for the current permanent employment system were laid in Japan decades before the long-term commitment of the enterprise to the blue-collar worker became a recognized organizational feature of Japanese industry.

I must emphasize once again that the long-term relation between the business enterprise and its employees is not a social invention of the Japanese. Since the late nineteenth century, within managerial structures, such commitment of the organization to the individual, and of the individual to the organization, was essential to the foundation of the formidable productive powers of U.S. managerial enterprises. In a successful enterprise, the managerial structure represented a highly integrated community of interests that permitted a highly complex specialized division of labor to coalesce into a powerful collective force.

What the Japanese have done is to build on these communities of interest within the enterprise, by extending membership in the community not only to managers but also to nonmanagerial personnel. In contrast, to this day American managers cling to the ideology that the blue-collar worker is an easily dispensable "hourly" employee, even though the provision of stable long-term employment to these workers has been both cause and effect of the growth of major U.S. enterprises. What the Japanese have also done is to build these communities of interest across legally defined firms, thus tying the interests of the shareholders of any particular enterprise to the success of large groups of enterprises and, indeed, to the economy as a whole. In contrast, the prevailing managerial ideology in the United States is that the industrial corporations are run in the interests of shareholders, even though the separation of share ownership from managerial control has been both cause and effect of the growth of major U.S. enterprises.

The United States Is Falling Behind

In the 1960s and 1970s, as the Japanese mounted their global challenge in consumer electronics and automobiles, Americans were inclined to attribute Japan's competitive advantage to low-wage labor and long work hours. This response was reminiscent of British views of Japan's sources of competitive advantage in the 1920s, when the Japanese cotton textile industry was taking away market share from Britain's leading export industry. During the 1930s, however, as the Japanese cotton textile industry continued its rise to global dominance, foreign observers who visited Japanese textile mills noticed that its progress in cotton textiles depended on much more than cheap labor and long hours. Japan's success also depended on the development of an indigenous textile technology and its implementation within a highly managed structure of business organization (Mass and Lazonick 1990, Robertson 1990).

Indeed, the organizational capabilities that enabled Japan to gain a competitive advantage in cotton textiles in the decades before World War II bore a remarkable resemblance to the organizational capabilities that characterized Japan's consumer electronics and automobile industries in the decades after World War II. Low wages and long hours did not hurt Japan's competitive position in either of these periods. But foreign observers discovered as they visited Japanese automobile plants in the 1980s that the foundation of Japan's sustained competitive advantage was its ability to develop and utilize technology.

Now that Japan's wages have risen to U.S. levels and steps are being taken to cut the hours of labor (see various recent issues of the *Japan Labor Bulletin*), the dynamic interaction of organization and technology sustains Japan's competitive advantage not only in consumer durables and automobiles but also in vertically related capital-goods industries. A growing case-study literature on the sources of Japanese competitive advantage reveals that these industries did not catch up to the West simply by borrowing foreign technology (Anchordoguy 1989, Collis 1988, Cusumano 1985, 1991, Dore 1990, Tyson and Yoffie 1991, Vietor and Yoffie 1991, Womack, Jones, and Roos 1991; see also Mass and Lazonick 1990). Just as was the case with Britain in the last half of the nineteenth century and the United States in the first half of the twentieth century, the basis of Japan's competitive advantage over the past few decades has been the development and utilization of productive resources (Freeman 1987, Odagiri and Goto 1993).

I have already reviewed how, in the twentieth century, Britain failed to transform its educational, financial, and social systems to respond to the competitive challenges from abroad. The institutional structures that had enabled Britain to gain international industrial leadership in the nineteenth century no longer sufficed in the twentieth century. The British economy, of course, did not collapse. In the old staple industries, it continued to compete on the basis of traditional organizations and technologies (Elbaum and Lazonick 1986). In doing so, however, it failed to transform the educational, financial, and social systems to support the emergence and growth of managerial capitalism, thus constraining the development and utilization of technology even in new industries (Lazonick 1990, chap. 6). Even if the nation's fate was not a plunge into poverty, over the long run British incomes were lower on average than were those of its most successful international rivals.

Does a similar fate await the United States? The economic history textbooks of the mid-twenty-first century may give us the full explanation (although I should point out that even the standard economic history textbooks of the late twentieth century do not have a good explanation of the rise of the United States to industrial dominance in the first half of this century). But what can one say about what is happening to the competitive position of U.S. industry in the 1990s? (For recent surveys, see Dertouzos, Lester, and Solow 1989, Franko 1991, Kupfer 1992, U.S. Congress 1991.) In industries such as pharmaceuticals, forest and food products, aerospace, and chemicals in which the United States is still ahead, is it developing the technological and organizational capabilities required to sustain its existing competitive advantages in the future? And in industries such as electronics, metals, motor vehicles, and industrial machinery in which the United States has fallen behind, will its industrial enterprises be able to reorient their investment strategies and organizational structures toward generating technological innovations that can enable the United States to catch up? Or will strategic decision makers in these lagging industries be content with what I have elsewhere (Lazonick 1991, chap. 3) called *adaptive responses* that seek to reap the returns of past investments rather than invest in the technologies and organizations that can generate returns in the future?

In the concluding pages of this chapter, I shall provide only a broad outline of a number of apparent weaknesses of U.S. industrial enterprises engaged in global competition. In doing so, it is useful to distinguish between economic activities that *develop* productive resources and those that *utilize* them (see Lazonick 1991, chap. 3). The development of productive resources can generate superior technologies. But in doing so, the enterprise, industry, or national economy incurs fixed costs that can result in low unit costs only if the resources that have been developed are sufficiently utilized. Without the development of productive resources, one cannot have technological innovation. But without the utilization of productive resources, access to superior technologies cannot result in economic success.

The development of productive resources requires both long-term finance and highly specialized scientific and technical knowledge. Throughout the twentieth century, U.S. enterprises that have been in the forefront of global competition have been well endowed with both. I have already recounted how, as an integral element of the U.S. rise to industrial leadership during the first half of the century, the separation of ownership from control in major U.S. industrial corporations gave professional managers the power to retain earnings as the financial foundation for long-term investment strategies. When necessary, they leveraged these retained earnings by means of long-term bond issues at relatively low rates of interest.

From the 1950s, however, this commitment of internal finances to long-term growth began to erode as managers became owners and as institutional investors collectivized the power of shareholders (see Lazonick 1992a). The result was the shareholders' increasing ability to extract financial resources from the very industrial enterprises that were best positioned, financially, organizationally, and technologically, to undertake innovative responses to international competitive challenges. The proportion of after-tax corporate profits distributed as dividends was already high at 44 percent in the 1960s and 45 percent in the 1970s. Yet it rose to 60 percent in the 1980s. As total after-tax profits fell and total dividends climbed, the payout ratio rose to 72 percent in 1990 and 76 percent in the first three-quarters of 1991 (*Economic Report of the President 1992,* p. 397). In regard to external finance, real interest rates on Moody's Aaa corporate bonds rose from an average low of 0.39 percent in 1950–54 to an average high of 2.21 percent in 1965–69. In 1980–84, these yields were 5.43 percent, and in 1985–89, 6.15 percent. Although long-term interest rates have abated somewhat in the early 1990s, they are still at much higher real levels than for most years before the 1980s (*Economic Report of the President 1992,* p. 378).

The ability of portfolio investors to extract high yields from U.S. industry derives from the rise of a powerful market for corporate control. It is true that the much-publicized hostile takeovers of the 1980s did not affect industries that are R&D intensive, and some financial analysts have concluded, therefore, that the rise of the market for corporate control has had no adverse impact on the competitive performance of the highest value-added sectors of the U.S. economy. But to focus on these headline-making events is to misread what the market for corporate control has been all about. What it has not been about is using the ownership rights vested in shareholders to gain control over the *management* of enterprises. What it has been about is using those ownership rights to gain control over the *accumulated resources* of enterprises. The objective of participants in the market for corporate control is to extract existing value from industrial corporations, by either tapping what they call the "free cash flow" or selling off businesses. Their objective is not to create value for the future.

From this perspective, one can begin to understand how the financial environment of the 1980s adversely affected the long-term investment strategies of U.S.-based industrial enterprises in general, and especially those in high-technology industries in which technological innovation requires long-term financial commitment. During the 1980s all publicly traded U.S. industrial corporations felt under pressure to pay out a much higher proportion of their retained earnings as dividends than they had historically. Even a company as immune from hostile takeover as IBM has claimed that in the 1980s and early 1990s it was not able to retain sufficient earnings to finance the necessary long-term investments to compete globally.

This effusion and diffusion of critical industrial finance from the U.S. industrial enterprises best positioned to develop superior productive resources have gone forward not only under pressure from Wall Street but also with the cooperation of the top managers of industrial corporations. They have benefited handsomely from accommodating the rise of the market for corporate control. Although the real after-tax earnings of the average American worker fell by about 13 percent during 1970s and 1980s, the real after-tax compensation of the average CEO of a major U.S. company increased by 400 percent (Crystal 1991, p. 27).

The higher levels of compensation of U.S. executives are particularly evident when compared with their counterparts abroad. In 1990 the total compensation of CEOs of the 30 largest U.S. corporations was, on average, $3.1 million. For British CEOs, the comparable figure was $1.1 million, for French and German CEOs $0.8 million, and for Japanese CEOs $0.5 million (*New York Times,* January 20, 1992). Much more than in other nations (although much the same thing has been going on in Britain over the past two decades), the top managers of major U.S. corporations have been using their control over corporate revenues to benefit themselves at the expense of their organizations.

In terms of a commitment to innovation, the problem with the explosion in the pay of top managers is not so much the amount of financial resources that they extract from the enterprises that employ them. Rather, the problem is that, as the key decision makers on the investment strategies of their enterprises, the overcompensation of top corporate managers enables them to win economically even if their enterprises, and most of the people in them, lose.

We should also mention that such behavior is totally absent in dominant Japanese corporations. In Japan, strategic managers can benefit from neither the sale of stock nor, as was the case with "golden parachutes" in the United States in the 1980s, the sale of executive offices. Even if top managers in Japan own shares on their own account, their dividend income is minimal because Japanese companies use their financial resources to further the innovative capabilities of the organization, not to fill the pockets of their shareholders. The personal incomes of top managers are tied to the hierarchical structure of compensation within the enterprise, and their strategic behavior is disciplined by their career-long membership in the organization (see Abegglen and Stalk 1985, chaps. 7–8, Ballon and Tomita 1988, Dore 1987, chap. 6).

The financial revolution of the 1980s may have had adverse impacts on the organizational capabilities of U.S. corporations. While hostile takeovers and forced downsizings of the 1980s made career paths for technologists in industrial enterprises less secure, alternative employment opportunities arose in financial pursuits that highly educated entrants to the labor force found difficult to ignore (see, e.g., McCartney 1992). Even though Wall Street began laying off personnel after October 1987, salaries in the financial sector remained inordinately high. In 1989 the average compensation (salary and bonus) for the more highly paid stratum of corporate-finance and merger-and-acquisition specialists at the top ten securities firms was $450,000 if they had entered the firm in 1983, $300,000 if they had entered in 1986, just over $200,000 if they had entered in 1987, and about $140,000 if they had entered in 1988. The average compensation of the lower-paid specialists ranged from just under $300,000 if they had entered in 1983 to $100,000 if they had joined the firm in 1988 (*Wall Street Journal,* December 8, 1989, pp. C1, C5). During the 1980s it was not only with the Japanese that industrial America could not compete.

The recession of the late 1980s and early 1990s greatly accelerated the tendency that had been building since the early 1980s to terminate the employment of salaried personnel (Nussbaum 1992; see also Nussbaum 1986). To some (as yet undetermined) extent, this downsizing represents a necessary rationalization of overstaffed corporate bureaucracies. There is a danger, however, that forced downsizings might be diminishing the abilities of U.S. industrial enterprises to pursue innovative investment strategies. The inability of the enterprises to offer long-term employment security and income growth even to its salaried employees may reduce the organizational commitment of those salaried employees whom the company retains. As shown by the recent experience of many dominant U.S. companies (including IBM), the most able and experienced employees may look outside the company for employment. If and when they do in fact leave the company, they take with them skills acquired through in-house training and experience. Consequently, the company not only loses its investments in human resources but often finds that these resources are subsequently at the service of its competitors. The loss of human resources as well as competitive advantage makes the company reluctant henceforth to invest in the skills of its key personnel.

The long-term result of such responses is an erosion of organizational capabilities within the enterprise without any guarantee that the reduction of investment in human capabilities will be replaced elsewhere in the economy. Evidence of the extent of this perverse dynamic within U.S. industrial corporations, and its impact on enterprise performance, requires careful case studies of the organizational evolution of major U.S. enterprises (for well-researched journalistic studies, see Holland 1989, Keller 1989).

A failure of U.S. industry to invest in scientific and engineering capabilities is not, however, evident in the available aggregate data. In 1988, the employment of engineers in the United States stood at 2.7 million, an increase of 121 percent from 1970, and four-fifths of these engineers were employed by industry (U.S. Department of Commerce 1991, p. 595). From 1970 to 1988, the number of scientists and engineers employed in R&D in the United States increased from 544,000 to 949,000, or by 74 percent, and those employed specifically by industry increased from 376,000 to 717,000, or by 91 percent (U.S. Department of Commerce 1991, p. 594). Over this period, industry increased somewhat its expenditures (in real terms) per full-time equivalent scientist and engineer that it employed.

The number of scientists and engineers per 10,000 labor force participants in the United States was 65 in 1970 and 66 in 1986 (U.S. Congress 1991, p. 210). The Japanese, who had only half the number of scientists and engineers per 10,000 labor force participants as the United States in 1970, had caught up with the United States by the mid-1980s. During the last half of the 1980s, R&D expenditure as a percentage of GNP were about equivalent in these two nations, about 2.8 percent (U.S. Department of Commerce 1991, p. 591). By themselves, these data are consistent with the convergence hypothesis that the challenge to U.S. productivity leadership is just a matter of previously less advanced industrial nations catching up.

Even in terms of the aggregate data, however, the much greater role of the military in U.S. R&D expenditures (about 30 percent of the total for the United States and virtually nothing for Japan) reduces the impact of U.S. R&D investment because of a lack of spillover from military to civilian applications (see Nelson 1990). One reason for the lack of spillover in particular and of the decline in U.S. leadership in technological development more generally may be a neglect of long-term generic (or "precompetitive") research at the corporate level of major industrial enterprises, with the R&D focus devoted overwhelmingly to product and process development at the divisional level. To document the changing character of the U.S. R&D effort, more systematic research is needed (for the most useful surveys to date, see Mowery and Rosenberg 1989, 1990).

Evidence from Japan (based on lectures by Japanese research executives at Harvard's Kennedy School of Government) is that its major high-technology corporations that in the past emphasized applications of technology as part of the process of catching up are now using some of the returns from catching up to finance central research laboratories in which to generate knowledge about the technologies of the future. As for the present, analyses of patent citations by Francis Narin and his associates show that by the beginning of the 1990s, Japan was forging ahead in virtually every high-technology field (Narin and Olivastro 1991; see also Broad 1991).

If a reversal in long-term technological capability between U.S. and Japanese industrial corporations is taking place, it may also be affecting the different ways in which U.S. and Japanese industrial enterprises are using the unparalleled public-sector research capabilities of major American universities. Unlike the United States, where over a century ago, the U.S. federal government, through the Department of Agriculture, began funding basic research, the Japanese never developed universities for this purpose. Instead, as part of the process of catching up, Japanese companies applied scientific knowledge generated abroad to Japanese industrial requirements. But now that they have caught up, Japanese high-technology companies have been establishing close links between U.S. universities and their central research laboratories. U.S. industrial corporations, in contrast, appear to be increasingly interested in using university research capabilities for applied rather than basic research (for debate on these issues, see Etzkowitz 1991). If so, it may be that in the future Japanese companies will use the basic-research capabilities of U.S. universities to help them forge ahead in high-technology industries such as aerospace, medical equipment, chemicals, and biotechnology, and by failing to use these basic-research capabilities, U.S. companies will forgo a powerful means of catching up.

As for an industry such as automobiles in which the United States clearly fell behind in the 1980s, what the Japanese have shown in recent years is their ability to gain competitive advantage even when manufacturing in the United States, by transplanting the modes of shop-floor work organization that have already worked so well in generating exports from Japan (Kenney and Florida 1991). A key component to Japanese success in the United States has been the willingness of Japanese transplants to invest in the capabilities of shop-floor workers, as part of a broader investment strategy to build what Michael Porter (1990) calls a "home base" outside Japan (see also Lazonick 1993). Yet these are precisely the types of investments that dominant U.S. mass producers have been reluctant to make in the United States (see Lazonick 1990, chap. 9). In competition with the Japanese over the past quarter-century, the organization of work on the shop floor has been the Achilles heel of U.S. manufacturing (see Lazonick 1990; see also Florida and Kenney 1990). With its managerial structures in place, American industry may have entered the second half of the twentieth century in the forefront in the development of productive resources. But its weakness lay in the utilization of productive resources-manufacturing processes in which large numbers of shop-floor workers had to interact with costly plant and equipment.

Into the 1960s, U.S. enterprises dominated in the mass production of automobiles and consumer electronics by investing in special-purpose machinery that then required the cooperative efforts of masses of relatively unskilled labor to generate high levels of productivity. Aided by a centralized union movement, these enterprises secured a degree of shop-floor cooperation from production workers by offering them more employment security and better pay than could be found elsewhere in the U.S. economy. But the major industrial enterprises did not give these blue-collar workers substantive training. Nor, as we have seen, did they ever make explicit, and hence more secure, the long-term attachment of the "hourly" employee to the enterprise. Without this commitment of the organization to the individual, one could not expect the commitment of the individual to the organization that might have enabled U.S. mass producers to respond quickly and effectively to the Japanese challenge. In terms of the organization of work on the shop floor, the strength of that challenge derived in large part from investments in the skills of blue-collar workers (Cusumano 1985).

Production workers in the United States receive much less training and tend to be much less skilled than their counterparts in Japan or Germany (see Kazis 1989). As I have already stated, the de-skilling of shop-floor work in the United States arose out of successful managerial strategies to introduce mass production technologies that could take control over work organization out of the hands of craft workers and instead use inexperienced and untrained immigrant labor (see Lazonick 1990, chap. 7). The development and utilization of these mass production technologies required investment in skills. But those who received extensive training were better-educated technical specialists who were integrated into the managerial structure as salaried employees with the potential for rising up the managerial hierarchy. It was on this organizational and technological foundation that U.S. industrial enterprises achieved their positions of global industrial leadership.

The problem for the United States is that it has been in those mass production

industries in which it was once preeminent that the Japanese have changed the organizational and technological foundations of industrial leadership by developing and
utilizing the skills of production workers as well as technical specialists. They have
done so, moreover, on the basis of a mass education system that since the late nineteenth century has provided the preemployment cognitive foundations for the subsequent skill development of both production workers and technical specialists in the
workplace.

In the United States, the unskilled shop-floor worker is the product of an inferior
primary and secondary education that sufficed as long as the U.S. model of skilled
technical specialists and unskilled production workers yielded a global competitive
advantage. But the educational requirements of industrial leadership have changed.
Numerous comparisons of educational achievement among the OECD nations have
shown that the United States ranks at or near the bottom (see Ferleger and Mandle
1992, Kazis 1989).

One might expect that a nation such as the United States, with its historic commitment to equal opportunity through mass education, would quickly respond to the
changed educational requirements of global competition by upgrading the cognitive
capabilities of its future work force. In the past, the captains of industry have recognized the need to improve the education of the masses. Indeed, much of the funding
of mass schooling after the turn of the century came from the philanthropic foundations established by major industrialists, John D. Rockefeller and Andrew Carnegie
foremost among them. That was, however, an era when the U.S. economy was rising
to its position as global industrial leader. Despite a general consensus in the United
States that investments in mass education are the top priority for industrial regenera-
tion, the wealthiest Americans have shown little interest in making the funding available, through either philanthropic means or tax-financed government expenditures
(see Reich 1991, chap. 24).

The failure to provide high-quality mass education in turn constrains attempts
by industrial employers to develop the skills of production workers to complement
advanced process technologies. U.S. industry underinvests in the training of its shop-
floor workers, both relative to its own investments in managerial personnel and the
investments of its international competitors. Given this lack of in-house training and
the difficulty in utilizing advanced process technologies (e.g., robotics) on the shop
floor, U.S. industrial enterprises tend to search for alternative, less technologically
complex, investment strategies.

If present-day U.S. industrialists are unwilling or unable to take the lead in making the necessary educational and training transformations, one might expect that the
workers themselves, through their unions, would apply pressure on business and government to make such investments in human capabilities. In many Western European
nations and to some extent in Japan, unions play precisely this role, be it through
direct participation in investment decisions at the enterprise level or through political
representation in local and national governments. In the United States, however, the
1970s and 1980s witnessed a dramatic weakening of the labor movement at precisely
the time when unions needed to be brought into the investment decision-making process in both the private and public sectors. To do so, the adversarial business unions
of the 1950s and 1960s needed to be transformed into partners of industry. Instead,
through plant closings and legal rulings, the union movement was weakened. The

sharp decline of union membership from over 20.1 percent of wage and salary workers in 1983 to 16.4 percent in 1989 reflects a longer-run trend that manifests the erosion of organizational capabilities in the United States (U.S. Department of Commerce 1991, p. 425).

The weakening of the U.S. labor movement is also reflected in the decline in the real wages of U.S. manufacturing workers over the past two decades. Real hourly wages have been falling in manufacturing since the late 1970s, and from 1978 to 1990 real weekly wages declined by well over 10 percent (U.S. Congress 1991, chap. 1). This drop in the real wages of manufacturing workers manifests a growing inequality in income distribution that characterized the 1980s and persists in the 1990s. More than that, however, it also demonstrates an erosion of organizational capabilities. Within a major manufacturing enterprise (which was the type most apt to be unionized), well-established arrangements for sharing productivity gains with workers provide the social basis for generating the gains to be shared (Lazonick 1990, chaps. 8–10 and app.). The willingness of workers to supply high levels of effort increases productivity, and the cooperation of workers in the utilization of productivity-enhancing process technologies creates incentives for employers to invest in these technologies. A loss of control over the supply of effort on the shop floor, therefore, makes employers reluctant to invest in advanced machine technologies and in the skills of shop-floor workers needed to complement these machines. The long-run decline in real manufacturing wages reveals these perverse impacts of prevailing labor–management relations on shop-floor technological change and productivity growth.

In those industries in which the United States has fallen behind, therefore, the social organization of enterprise, industry, and the economy prevents it from catching up. In those industries in which the United States has remained ahead, more powerful modes of social organization abroad may lead to the emergence of new international leaders. A half-century after the fact, the British are now beginning to understand the role of social organization in their own long-run economic decline. Americans can wait, if they so wish, for future economic historians to document fully when, how, and why their nation entered into a long-term industrial decline. Or they can begin now to think seriously about the transformations in the social organization of the American economy that international competition requires.

References

Abeggelen, James C., and George Stalk, Jr. (1985). *Kaisha: The Japanese Corporation.* New York: Basic Books.

Anchordoguy, Marie. (1989). *Computers Inc.: Japan's Challenge to IBM.* Cambridge, MA: Harvard University Press.

Ballon, Robert J., and Iwao Tomita. (1988). *The Financial Behavior of Japanese Corporations.* Tokyo: Kodansha International.

Barker, T. C. (1977). *The Glassmakers: Pilkington—The Rise of an International Company, 1826–1976.* London: Weidenfeld & Nicolson.

Baumol, William J., Sue Anne Batey Blackman, and Edward N. Wolff. (1989). *Productivity and American Leadership: The Long View.* Cambridge, MA: MIT Press.

Best, Michael. (1990). *The New Competition: Institutions of Industrial Restructuring.* Cambridge, MA: Harvard University Press.

Broad, William. (1991). "In the Realm of Technology, Japan Looms Ever Larger." *New York Times,* May 28, pp. C1 and C8.

Brody, David. (1960). *Workers in Industrial America.* New York: Oxford University Press.

Burgess, Keith. (1975). *The Origins of British Industrial Relations: The Nineteenth Century Experience.* London: Croom Helm.

Cannings, Kathleen, and William Lazonick. (Forthcoming). "Equal Employment Opportunity and the 'Managerial Woman' in Japan." *Industrial Relations.*

Chandler, Alfred D., Jr. (1990). *Scale and Scope: The Dynamics of Industrial Capitalism.* Cambridge, MA: Harvard University Press.

Coleman, D. C. (1969). *Courtaulds: An Economic and Social History.* Vol. 1. Oxford: Clarendon Press.

————. (1973). "Gentlemen and Players." *Economic History Review,* 2nd series, 26:92–116.

Collis, David. (1988). "The Machine Tool Industry and Industrial Policy, 1955–82." In A. Michael Spence and Heather A. Hazard, eds., *International Competitiveness.* Cambridge, MA: Ballinger, pp. 75–114.

Crystal, Graef S. (1991). *In Search of Excess: The Overcompensation of U.S. Executives.* New York: Norton.

Cusumano, Michael. (1985). *The Japanese Automobile Industry.* Cambridge, MA: Harvard University Press.

————. (1991). *Japan's Software Factories.* Oxford: Oxford University Press.

Daito, E. (1986). "Recruitment and Training of Middle Managers in Japan, 1900–1930." In Kesaji Kobayashi and Hidemasa Morikawa, eds., *Development of Managerial Enterprise.* Tokyo: University of Tokyo Press, pp. 151–79.

Dertouzos, Michael L., Richard K. Lester, and Robert M. Solow. (1989). *Made in America: Regaining the Productive Edge.* Cambridge, MA: MIT Press.

Dore, Ronald. (1986). *Flexible Rigidities: Industrial Policy and Structural Adjustment in the Japanese Economy, 1970–1980.* Stanford, CA: Stanford University Press.

————. (1987). *Taking Japan Seriously: A Confucian Perspective on Leading Economic Issues.* Stanford, CA: Stanford University Press.

————. (1990). *British Factory–Japanese Factory: The Origins of National Diversity in Industrial Relations.* 2nd ed., including an Afterword by the author. Berkeley and Los Angeles: University of California Press.

Dore, Ronald P., and Mari Sako. (1989). *How the Japanese Learn to Work.* London: Routledge and Kegan Paul.

Economic Report of the President. (1992). Washington, DC: U.S. Government Printing Office, February.

Elbaum, Bernard, and William Lazonick, eds. (1986). *The Decline of the British Economy.* Oxford: Clarendon Press.

Etzkowitz, Henry. (1991). "Academic–Industry Relations." Photocopy.

Ferleger, Louis, and William Lazonick. (1992) "The Managerial Revolution and the Developmental State: The Case of U.S. Agriculture." Photocopy, Harvard University.

Ferleger, Louis, and Jay R. Mandle. (1992). "An International Comparison of Productivity Growth." Photocopy, Harvard University, March.

Florida, Richard, and Martin Kenney. (1990). *The Breakthrough Illusion: Corporate America's Failure to Move from Innovation to Mass Production.* New York: Basic Books.

Franko, Lawrence. (1991). "Global Corporate Competition II: Is the Large American Firm an Endangered Species?" *Business Horizons* 34:4–22.

Freeman, Christopher. (1987). *Technology Policy and Economic Performance: Lessons from Japan.* London: Francis Pinter.

Gerlach, Michael. (1989). "Keiretsu Organization in the Japanese Economy: Analysis and Trade Implications." In Chalmers Johnson, Laura D'Andrea Tyson, and John Zysman, eds., *Politics and Productivity: How Japan's Development Strategy Works.* New York: Harper & Row, pp. 141–74.

Gordon, Andrew. (1985). *The Evolution of Labor Relations in Japan: Heavy Industry, 1853–1955.* Cambridge, MA: Harvard University Press.

Harrison, Royden, and Jonathan Zeitlin, eds. (1985). *Divisions of Labour: Skilled Workers and Technological Change in the Nineteenth Century,* Sussex: Harvester Press.

Hobsbawm, Eric J. (1984). *Workers: Worlds of Labor.* New York: Pantheon.

Holland, Max. (1989). *When the Machine Stopped: A Cautionary Tale from Industrial America.* Boston: Harvard Business School Press.

Hounshell, David A. (1984). *From the American System to Mass Production, 1800–1932.* Baltimore: Johns Hopkins University Press.

Hounshell, David A., and John Kenly Smith, Jr. (1988). *Science and Corporate Strategy: Du Pont R&D, 1902–1980.* Cambridge: Cambridge University Press.

Johnson, Chalmers. (1982). *MITI and the Japanese Miracle: The Growth of Industrial Policy, 1925–1975.* Stanford, CA: Stanford University Press.

Jones, Geoffrey. (1984). "The Growth and Performance of British Multinational Firms Before 1939: The Case of Dunlop." *Economic History Review,* 2nd series, 37:35–53.

Kazis, Richard. (1989). "Education and Training in the United States: Developing the Human Resources We Need for Technological Advance and Competitiveness." In MIT Commission on Industrial Productivity, *The Working Papers of the MIT Commission on Industrial Productivity.* Vol. 2. Cambridge, MA: MIT Press.

Keller, Maryann. (1989). *Rude Awakening: The Rise, Fall, and Struggle for Recovery at General Motors.* New York: Morrow.

Kenney, Martin, and Richard Florida. (1991). "How Japanese Industry Is Rebuilding the Rust Belt." *Technology Review,* February–March, pp. 25–33.

Koike, Kazuo. (1987). "Human Resource Management and Labor–Management Relations." In Kozo Yamamura and Yasukichi Yasuba, eds., *The Political Economy of Japan.* Vol. 1. Stanford, CA: Stanford University Press.

Kupfer, Andrew. (1992). "How American Industry Stacks Up." *Fortune,* March, pp. 30–46.

Lazonick, William. (1983). "Industrial Organization and Technological Change: The Decline of the British Cotton Industry." *Business History Review* 58:195–236.

———. (1986). "Strategy, Structure, and Management Development in the United States and Britain." In Kesaji Kobayashi and Hidemasa Morikawa, eds., *Development of Managerial Enterprise.* Tokyo: University of Tokyo Press, pp. 101–46.

———. (1990). *Competitive Advantage on the Shop Floor.* Cambridge, MA: Harvard University Press.

———. (1991). *Business Organization and the Myth of the Market Economy.* Cambridge: Cambridge University Press.

———. (1992a). "Controlling the Market for Corporate Control: The Historical Significance of Managerial Capitalism." In Frederic M. Scherer and Mark Perlman, eds., *Entrepreneurship, Technological Innovation, and Economic Growth.* Ann Arbor: University of Michigan Press, pp. 153–199.

———. (1992b). *Organization and Technology in Capitalist Development.* Aldershot: Edward Elgar.

———. (1993). "Industry Clusters Versus Global Webs: Organizational Capabilities in the U.S. Economy." *Industrial and Corporate Change* 2:83–106.

———. (Forthcoming). "Cooperative Employment Relations and Japanese Economic Growth." In Stephen Marglin and Juliet Schor, eds., *Restructuring Capital–Labor Relations.*

Lewchuk, Wayne. (1987). *American Technology and the British Vehicle Industry.* Cambridge: Cambridge University Press.

Marshall, Alfred. (1920). *Industry and Trade.* 2nd ed. London: Macmillan.

Mass, William, and William Lazonick. (1990). "The British Cotton Industry and International Competitive Advantage: The State of the Debates." *Business History* 32:9–65.

McCartney, Robert J. (1992). "Wall Street and the Road Not Taken." *Washington Post,* February 5, p. D1.

McCraw, Thomas K., ed. (1986). *America Versus Japan.* Boston: Harvard Business School Press.

Michie, R. C. (1987). *The London and New York Stock Exchanges, 1850–1914.* London: Allen & Unwin.

Montgomery, David. (1987). *The Fall of the House of Labor.* Cambridge: Cambridge University Press.

Morikawa, Hidemasa. (1989). "The Increasing Power of Salaried Managers in Japan's Large Corporations. In William D. Wray, ed., *Managing Industrial Enterprises: Cases from Japan's Prewar Experience.* Cambridge, MA: Harvard University Press, pp. 27–51.

Mowery, David C., and Nathan Rosenberg. (1989). *Technology and the Pursuit of Economic Growth.* Cambridge: Cambridge University Press.

———. (1990). "The U.S. National Innovation System." Consortium on Competitiveness and Cooperation Working Paper no. 90-3.

Musson, A. E. (1965). *Enterprise in Soap and Chemicals.* Manchester: Manchester University Press.

Narin, Francis, and Dominic Olivastro. (1991). "Status Report: Linkage Between Technology and Science." *Research Policy* 20:1–13.

Navin, Thomas R., and Marian V. Sears. (1955). "The Rise of a Market for Industrial Securities, 1887–1902." *Business History Review* 29:105–38.

Nelson, Richard R. (1990). "U.S. Technological Leadership: Where Did It Come from and Where Did It Go?" *Research Policy* 19:117–32.

Noble, David. (1977). *America by Design: Science, Technology, and the Rise of Corporate Capitalism.* New York: Oxford University Press.

Nussbaum, Bruce. (1986). "The End of Corporate Loyalty?" *Business Week,* August 4, pp. 42–49.

———. (1992). "Downward Mobility: Corporate Castoffs Are Struggling Just to Stay in the Middle-Class." *Business Week,* March 23, pp. 57–63.

Odagiri, Hiroyuki, and Akira Goto. (1993). "The Japanese System of Innovation: Past, Present, and Future." In Richard R. Nelson, ed., *National Innovation Systems.* New York: Oxford University Press, pp. 76–114.

Okayama, Reiko. (1983). "Japanese Employer Policy: The Heavy Engineering Industry, 1900–1930." In Howard Gospel and Craig Littler, eds., *Managerial Strategies and Industrial Relations.* London: Heinemann, pp. 157–70.

Porter, Michael E. (1990). *The Competitive Advantage of Nations.* New York: Free Press.

Reader, William J. (1975). *Imperial Chemical Industries.* Vol. 1. Oxford: Oxford University Press.

Reich, Leonard. (1985). *The Making of American Industrial Research: Science and Business at GE and Bell, 1876–1926*. Cambridge: Cambridge University Press.

Reich, Robert B. (1991). *The Work of Nations: Preparing Ourselves for 21st-Century Capitalism*. New York: Knopf.

Robertson, Alex J. (1990). "Lancashire and the Rise of Japan, 1910–1937." *Business History* 4:87–105.

Servos, John W. (1980). "The Industrial Relations of Science: Chemical Engineering at MIT, 1900–1939." *ISIS* 71:531–49.

Smitka, Michael. (1991). *Competitive Ties: Subcontracting in the Japanese Automotive Industry*. Cambridge: Cambridge University Press.

Tyson, Laura D'Andrea, and David B. Yoffie. (1991). "Semiconductors: From Manipulated to Managed Trade." Paper presented at the World Trade and Global Competition Seminar, Harvard Business School, December 1–3.

U.S. Congress, Office of Technology Assessment. (1991). *Competing Economies: America, Europe, and the Pacific Rim*. Washington, DC: U.S. Government Printing Office.

U.S. Department of Commerce, Bureau of the Census. (1991). *Statistical Abstract of the United States 1991*. Washington, DC: U.S. Government Printing Office.

Vietor, Richard H., and David B. Yoffie. (1991). "International Trade and Competition in Global Telecommunications." Paper presented at the World Trade and Global Competition Seminar, Harvard Business School, December 1–3.

Williamson, Jeffrey G. (1991). "Productivity and American Leadership: A Review Article." *Journal of Economic Literature* 29:51–68.

Wilson, Charles. (1984). *The History of Unilever*. Vol. 1. Cambridge: Cambridge University Press.

Womack, James P., Daniel T. Jones, and Daniel Roos. (1991). *The Machine That Changed the World*. New York: Harper & Row.

Yonekawa, Shin'ichi. (1984). "University Graduates in Japanese Enterprises Before the Second World War." *Business History* 26:193–218.

III

What Lies Behind Convergence?

7

Capital Intensity and TFP Convergence by Industry in Manufacturing, 1963–1985

DAVID DOLLAR
EDWARD N. WOLFF

Recent work has demonstrated that the OECD countries have become more similar in terms of aggregate characteristics. This growing similarity is evident in the marked convergence of overall labor productivity among industrialized countries in the postwar period, as well as in the convergence of aggregate total factor productivity (TFP) and capital–labor ratios.[1] A recent study of ours (Dollar and Wolff 1988) began the investigation of how this productivity convergence has been manifested in particular industries. We addressed two issues in particular: the extent to which shifts in employment from low value–added to high value–added activities in manufacturing have contributed to aggregate labor productivity convergence, and the extent to which there has been labor productivity convergence in individual industries.

We found strong evidence of convergence toward the U.S. level in virtually every industry covered by the study. However, differences in employment mix explained almost none of the difference in labor productivity for all manufacturing, and changes in industry employment mix over time accounted for none of the productivity convergence observed in the aggregate. We concluded that the convergence of productivity within industries was the proximate cause of the convergence in aggregate labor productivity noted in many studies.[2]

Our earlier work left open the question of the source of the intercountry variation in industry labor productivity, as well as the explanation for the changes in these differentials over time. In this chapter, we consider two, not mutually exclusive, hypotheses: first, that there are differences in degree of technological sophistication, though these have narrowed among the countries and, second, that industry-level capital–labor ratios differ but have converged among industrialized countries.

We find evidence in this study of the convergence of TFP levels both in the aggregate and within industries between 1963 and 1985. This process of technological catch-up was, however, much faster before 1972 than after. Moreover, the degree of convergence varied considerably among industries and was particularly strong in the heavy industries, which had much greater dispersion in TFP levels in the early 1960s. As a result, by 1985 the cross-country disparity in TFP levels was similar among industries.

We also find convergence in capital–labor ratios in both the aggregate and by industry, though this process was also much stronger before 1972 than after. By 1985 the variation in capital intensity among countries was much greater in heavy industries than in medium or light industries, which helps explain its greater dispersion in labor productivity levels. Differences in aggregate capital intensity were explained almost totally by differences in capital intensity at the industry level (more capital-abundant countries had higher industry capital–labor ratios). Moreover, the convergence of aggregate capital–labor ratios could be attributed almost entirely to the convergence of capital intensity within industries, rather than to changes in the employment mix.

Our results indicate that there were two distinct phases. Between 1963 and 1972, TFP, capital intensity, and labor productivity all converged rapidly, though most of the catch-up in labor productivity was attributable to the catch-up in TFP. Furthermore, industries and countries that were particularly far behind the leader, the United States, demonstrated the greatest degree of TFP catch-up, a finding consistent with Gerschenkron's notion that backward countries can benefit from borrowing advanced technology pioneered by the leader. Between 1963 and 1972 it was also the case that the convergence of industry TFP was correlated with the convergence of capital–labor ratios. This result could mean that some advanced technology is embodied in machinery, so that rapid capital accumulation occasions fast TFP growth. Alternatively, it could be that rapid TFP growth brought about by acquiring disembodied technology makes an industry especially profitable and attractive to investment. It is quite plausible that causality runs in both directions, with high investment spurring TFP growth, which in turn attracts more investment. After 1972, convergence slowed in both TFP and labor productivity, and labor productivity caught up to the United States primarily through increasing capital intensity. Indeed, several countries surpassed the United States in terms of the capital intensity of production.

Finally, we find that the variation in TFP, capital intensity, and labor productivity was greater at the industry level than in aggregate manufacturing. These results indicate that the countries specialized in different industries, particularly since the mid-1970s. Countries have invested heavily in new technology in different industries, which explains the emergence of countries other than the United States as productivity leaders in some industries. Changes in international comparative advantage thus can be attributed to a combination of worldwide shifts in technology leadership and investment strategies.

The remainder of this chapter is organized into six parts. First we discuss the measurement of TFP and describe the data sources being used. Then we compare the TFP levels for total manufacturing and for individual industries within manufacturing. Next we examine changes in capital intensity in both the aggregate and individual industries. We provide a decomposition of the growth in labor productivity into an element attributable to technological change and another element attributable to rising capital intensity. Then we look at further evidence on the relation among labor productivity growth, TFP growth, and the change in capital intensity in a regression framework. Finally we offer some concluding remarks and consider several implications of our findings.

The Measurement of Total Factor Productivity and Data Sources

Because of the nature of the available data, the total factor productivity (TFP) index is measured as the ratio of a sector's value added (Y) to a weighted average of employment (L) and gross capital stock (K):

$$TFP = Y/[\alpha L + (1 - \alpha)K] \tag{7-1}$$

where α is the wage share.[3] Two different wage shares are used for each industry: (1) the individual country's averages of the ratio of wages to value added over the full period in each industry and (2) the mean over all the countries of the individual country's wage shares for each industry, called the *international average*.[4] The TFP index is normalized so that the U.S. TFP index in 1963 equals 1.0 in each industry. The proper choice between the wage share figures is debatable; hence we report results for the two choices.

We use two different databases. The first, which we call the *Dollar–Wolff database,* is assembled from a variety of sources and includes information on employment, value added, wages, and gross capital stock. The data are available for 9 countries: Belgium, Canada, France, Federal Republic of Germany (Germany, for short), Italy, Japan, the Netherlands, the United Kingdom, and the United States. Because of differences in data classification schemes from the various sources, we aggregated the data to 12 industries: ferrous and nonferrous metals (13);[5] nonmetallic minerals and products (15); chemicals (17); (finished) metal products, excluding machinery and transportation (19); machinery (21 and 23); electrical goods (25); transport equipment (28); food, beverages, and tobacco (36); textiles, clothing, footwear, and leather (42); paper and printing (47); rubber and plastic products (49); and other industries (48).

Data on output, employment, and labor compensation are taken from the United Nations' *Yearbook of Industrial Statistics* for various years. Our output measure is value added, which is reported in current prices, denominated in the domestic currency.[6] We use the GNP deflator of each country to convert output values of different years into 1983 prices and then apply the PPP index calculated by the OECD to convert all output values into 1983 U.S. dollars.[7] Our labor input measure is employment.[8] Our capital stock data for the EEC countries come from Eurostat worksheets, for Canada from Statistics Canada worksheets and Statistics Canada (1987), for Japan from the Japan Economic Planning Agency (1988), and for the United States from Musgrave (1986a, 1986b) (for details, see the Appendix to this chapter). Only gross capital stock data are available for the 9 countries.[9]

The second data source is the OECD International Sectoral Databank on Microcomputer Diskette (referred to hereafter simply as the *OECD Database*). This contains data for 14 countries, including the 9 just listed plus Australia, Denmark, Finland, Norway, and Sweden and 9 manufacturing industries: (1) food, beverages, and tobacco; (2) textiles; (3) wood and wood products; (4) paper, printing, and publishing; (5) chemicals; (6) nonmetal mineral products; (7) basic metal products; (8) machinery and equipment; and (9) other manufactured products. The dataset covers the period from 1960 to 1986, though the period of greatest data availability is from 1970 to 1985. The data consist of GDP, already calculated in 1980 U.S. dollar equivalents, total employment, number of employees, compensation of employees, and gross capital stock, already measured in 1980 U.S. dollars. Calculations of productivity were performed using both the number of employees and total employment (the sum of the number of employees and the number of self-employed). Since self-employment is relatively unimportant in manufacturing, the results from the two sets of calculations are almost identical, and we report the results only for the number of employees.

TFP Comparisons

Table 7-1 shows the TFP levels for the whole manufacturing sector for selected years between 1963 and 1985. Although the United States has maintained its lead in TFP for the manufacturing sector as a whole, there is strong evidence that other countries have been catching up. Using the Dollar–Wolff database and own country factor shares, the unweighted average of TFP levels of other countries increased from 61 percent of the U.S. level in 1963 to 76 percent in 1983. In fact, every country except Canada gained relative to the United States over this period, with the largest relative gains made by the United Kingdom and Belgium. The coefficient of variation, a measure of intercountry dispersion, declined from 0.24 in 1963 to 0.14 in 1983. The ratio of maximum to minimum TFP levels fell from 2.16 in 1963 to 1.52 over the same period.

Because of data availability, the sample of countries in the preceding calculation changed over the period. We therefore also show the same set of summary statistics for two constant sample sets of countries (Panels B and C). The pattern is similar, as are the summary statistics. We also show the same set of results for TFP measures based on international average factor shares (Panel II). Here, again, the summary statistics are almost identical.

Most of the convergence had occurred by the early 1970s. In 1973, the coefficient of variation in TFP levels was 0.15. The unweighted average of TFP levels of other countries relative to the United States was 0.73, and the ratio of maximum to minimum TFP was 1.63.

Another point of interest is that the dispersion in labor productivity was larger than that of TFP in the early 1960s but that its rate of convergence was greater than that of TFP. For the same sample of 9 countries in the Dollar–Wolff database, the coefficient of variation of labor productivity fell from 0.37 in 1963 to 0.15 in 1982; the unweighted average of labor productivity levels relative to the United States increased from 0.52 to 0.73; and the ratio of maximum to minimum labor productivity declined from 2.9 to 1.7. By 1982, the dispersion in labor productivity levels was almost identical to that of TFP.[10]

The same pattern can be seen in individual industries, as shown in Table 7-2. On the basis of the Dollar–Wolff database, convergence, as indicated by the decline in the coefficient of variation, occurred in every industry between 1967 and 1979. Moreover, the average TFP level of other countries relative to the United States increased in 9 of

Table 7-1. TFP Levels in Total Manufacturing Relative to the United States, 1963–1985 (Index Number, with U.S. = 100)

	Dollar–Wolff Database						OECD Database		
	1963	1967	1970	1973	1979	1982	1970	1979	1985
I. *TFP calculations based on country-specific wage shares*[a]									
Australia							81	79	76
Belgium	46	47	61	66	63	66	63	78	81
Canada	68	65	69	72	72	n.a.	81	77	71
Denmark							56	62	59
Finland							61	59	61
France	69	71	84	67	72	80	79	84	75
Germany	n.a.	74	90	78	78	87	84	87	81
Italy	n.a.	47	52	62	60	63	83	85	82
Japan	n.a.	74	92	80	77	88	75	79	86
Netherlands	67	69	85	87	78	69	66	69	68
Norway							77	67	63
Sweden							74	66	65
United Kingdom	56	n.a.	65	74	70	73	66	63	65
United States	100	100	100	100	100	100	100	100	100
Coeff. of variation	.24	.23	.20	.15	.14	.15	.15	.15	.15
Maximum/ minimum	2.16	2.14	1.92	1.63	1.66	1.58	1.78	1.68	1.70
Unweighted average (excluding United States)	.61	.64	.75	.73	.71	.75	.73	.74	.72
Coeff. of var. (TFPU)	.24	.21	.19	.14	.13	.15			

A. Summary statistics based on 7-country sample: Belgium, Canada, France, Germany, Japan, Netherlands, and United States

Coeff. of variation	n.a.	.20	.15	.14	.14	n.a.			
Unweighted average (excluding United States)	n.a.	.67	.80	.75	.73	n.a.			
Coeff. of var. (TFPU)	n.a.	.19	.16	.13	.12	n.a.			

B. Summary statistics based on 7-country sample: Belgium, France, Germany, Italy, Japan, Netherlands, and United States

Coeff. of variation	n.a.	.25	.20	.16	.16	.16			
Unweighted average (excluding United States)	n.a.	.63	.77	.73	.71	.76			
Coeff. of var. (TFPU)	n.a.	.22	.20	.15	.15	n.a.			

II. *TFP calculations based on international average wage shares*									
Australia							81	80	78
Belgium	49	48	62	65	60	62	64	76	78
Canada	67	64	67	70	69	n.a.	81	77	71
Denmark							57	62	59
Finland							61	61	63

Table 7-1. TFP Levels in Total Manufacturing Relative to the United States, 1963–1985 (continued)

	Dollar–Wolff Database						OECD Database		
	1963	1967	1970	1973	1979	1982	1970	1979	1985
France	69	71	83	67	71	79	79	85	79
Germany	n.a.	74	90	78	78	87	83	88	84
Italy	n.a.	49	55	65	64	68	84	87	86
Japan	n.a.	68	88	80	79	92	68	82	93
Netherlands	68	69	84	85	76	67	66	68	67
Norway							77	66	62
Sweden							72	62	61
United Kingdom	58	n.a.	65	74	69	70	68	64	64
United States	100	100	100	100	100	100	100	100	100
A. Summary statistics based on available data only									
Coeff. of variation	.23	.23	.19	.14	.15	.16	.15	.15	.16
Maximum/ minimum	2.05	2.09	1.83	1.54	1.66	1.62	1.75	1.65	1.71
Unweighted average (excluding United States)	.62	.63	.74	.73	.71	.75	.72	.74	.73

B. Summary statistics based on 7-country sample: Belgium, Canada, France, Germany, Japan, Netherlands, and United States

Coeff. of variation	n.a.	.20	.15	.15	.15	n.a.			
Unweighted average (excluding United States)	n.a.	.66	.79	.74	.72	n.a.			

C. Summary statistics based on 7-country sample: Belgium, France, Germany, Italy, Japan, Netherlands, and United States

Coeff. of variation	n.a.	.24	.19	.16	.16	.17			
Unweighted average (excluding United States)	n.a.	.63	.77	.73	.71	.76			

[a]See the Appendix for details on data availability and the years used to calculate the wage shares in each country.

Table 7-2. Indices of TFP Convergence by Manufacturing Industry, 1967–1985[a]

		Coefficient of Variation			Average TFP relative to United States[b]		
I. Dollar–Wolff Database[c]							
	NACE	1967	1972	1979	1967	1972	1979
Heavy industries[d]		.45	.38	.24	.70 (GER)	.90 (GER)	.84 (GER)
Ferrous and nonferr. metals	(13)	.29	.25	.20	.63 (USA)	.73 (GER)	.70 (USA)
Chemicals	(17)	.47	.28	.23	.45 (USA)	.60 (USA)	.63 (USA)
Nonmetallic minerals	(15)	.58	.61	.30	1.03 (FRA)	1.37 (NET)	1.20 (NET)
Medium industries[d]		.32	.30	.24	.66 (USA)	.67 (USA)	.70 (USA)
Machinery	(21/23)	.22	.21	.21	.74 (USA)	.77 (USA)	.75 (CAN)
Rubber and plastics	(49)	.51	.43	.35	.55 (USA)	.52 (USA)	.64 (USA)

		Coefficient of Variation			Average TFP relative to United States[b]		

I. Dollar–Wolff Database[c]

	NACE	1967	1972	1979	1967	1972	1979
Paper and printing	(47)	.28	.31	.18	.65 (USA)	.71 (JPN)	.73 (USA)
Transport equipment	(28)	.26	.26	.22	.71 (USA)	.69 (USA)	.67 (USA)
Light industries[d]		.33	.28	.23	.60 (USA)	.68 (USA)	.69 (USA)
Metal products	(19)	.45	.29	.28	.49 (USA)	.70 (USA)	.66 (USA)
Other industries	(48)	.32	.38	.28	.73 (NET)	.60 (USA)	.64 (USA)
Textiles	(42)	.28	.25	.23	.56 (USA)	.62 (USA)	.68 (USA)
Electrical goods	(25)	.26	.20	.14	.60 (USA)	.78 (FRA)	.77 (USA)
Food, beverages, tobacco	(36)	20	.18	.17	.74 (USA)	.74 (USA)	.70 (USA)
All manufacturing[d]		.34	.30	.27	.66 (USA)	.74 (USA)	.73 (USA)

II. OECD Database[e]

		1970	1979	1985	1970	1979	1985
Heavy industries[d]		.30	.27	.24	.71 (USA)	.77 (JPN)	.87 (JPN)
Basic metals		.42	.37	.27	.73 (NET)	.83 (JPN)	1.05 (JPN)
Chemicals		.31	.26	.20	.69 (GER)	.76 (GER)	.93 (GER)
Nonmetallic minerals		.18	.18	.24	.70 (USA)	.71 (USA)	.64 (USA)
Medium industries[d]		.22	.22	.23	.73 (USA)	.73 (USA)	.71 (USA)
Machinery and equipment		.24	.21	.20	.65 (USA)	.67 (USA)	.63 (USA)
Paper, Printing, Publ.		.17	.21	.24	.71 (USA)	.72 (USA)	.74 (ITA)
Food, beverages, tobacco		.25	.24	.25	.83 (UK)	.81 (JPN)	.75 (ITA)
Light industries[d]		.20	.23	.22	.88 (CAN)	.78 (ITA)	.72 (USA)
Textiles		.20	.21	.20	.88 (ITA)	.77 (ITA)	.71 (USA)
Wood and wood products		.20	.25	.24	.87 (CAN)	.78 (ITA)	.73 (ITA)
Other industries		.38	.28	.47	.65 (CAN)	.63 (USA)	.42 (USA)
All manufacturing[d]		.26	.24	.26	.75 (USA)	.74 (USA)	.73 (USA)

	Japanese TFP Relative to U.S. TFP		

I. Dollar–Wolff Database

	NACE	1965	1972	1982
Heavy industries				
Ferrous & nonferr. metals	13	.58	.79	1.15
Chemicals	17	.78	.88	.94
Nonmetallic minerals	15	n.a.	n.a.	1.07
Medium industries				
Machinery	21/23	.66	.90	.96
Rubber and plastics	49	n.a.	n.a.	n.a.
Paper and printing	47	.85	1.13	.90
Transport equipment	28	.64	.75	.77

Table 7-2. Indices of TFP Convergence by Manufacturing Industry, 1967–1985 *(continued)*

		Japanese TFP Relative to U.S. TFP		
I. Dollar–Wolff Database	NACE	1965	1972	1982
Light industries				
Metal products	19	.70	.94	.91
Other industries	48	n.a.	.41	.63
Textiles	42	.57	.74	.81
Electrical goods	25	.57	.91	.97
Food, beverages, tobacco	36	.68	.89	.87

	1970	1979	1985
II. OECD Database			
Heavy industries			
Basic metals	1.14	1.39	1.68
Chemicals	.99	1.05	1.20
Nonmetallic minerals	.65	.67	.61
Medium industries			
Machinery and equipment	.44	.58	.71
Paper, printing, publ.	.54	.47	.45
Food, beverages, tobacco	1.13	1.09	.85
Light industries			
Textiles	.54	.43	.48
Wood and wood products	n.a.	n.a.	n.a.
Other industries	.76	.67	.59

[a]Calculations are based on country-specific wage shares. See the Appendix for details on data availability.

[b]The country leader in each year is shown in parentheses.

[c]All countries are included in the Dollar–Wolff database except as follows:

NACE 13:	1967	All except the Netherlands and the United Kingdom.
	1972,79	All except the Netherlands.
NACE 15:	1967	All except Japan and the United Kingdom.
	1972	All except Japan.
NACE 17:	1967	All except the Netherlands and the United Kingdom.
	1972	All except the United Kingdom.
	1979	All except Netherlands.
NACE 19:	1967	All except Belgium and the United Kingdom.
	1972	All except Belgium, the Netherlands, and the United Kingdom.
	1979	All except Belgium.
NACE 21–23:	1967	All except Belgium, the Netherlands, and the United Kingdom.
	1972,79	All except Belgium and the Netherlands.
NACE 25, 28:	1967	All except Belgium and the United Kingdom.
	1972,79	All except Belgium.
NACE 36, 48:	1967	All except the United Kingdom.
NACE 42, 47:	1967,72	All except the United Kingdom.
NACE 49:	1967	All except Japan, the Netherlands, and the United Kingdom.
	1972,79	All except Japan and the Netherlands.

[d]Unweighted average of industries within group.

[e]Countries included in the OECD database for each industry are as follows:

1970–83 All except Australia and Finland.

1984–85 All except Australia, Finland, and Netherlands.

The exceptions are

Wood and wood products: 1970–85: Canada, Denmark, Germany, Italy, Norway, Sweden, United States.

All manufacturing: 1970–85: All.

the 12 industries in this classification scheme. However, the average dispersion of TFP in manufacturing industries (the unweighted average of the coefficient of variation) was still substantially greater than the degree of dispersion in the total manufacturing sector (0.34 versus 0.23 in 1967 and 0.26 versus 0.15 in 1985).

The industries have been divided into three groups—heavy, medium, and light—on the basis of the unweighted average of the capital–labor ratios among the relevant group of countries.[11] Convergence was strongest among the heavy industries, in which the (unweighted) average coefficient of variation of industries within this group fell by almost half over the 1967–79 period according to the Dollar–Wolff database and by 20 percent between 1970 and 1985 according to the OECD data. The average TFP level of the other countries exceeded that of the United States by 1979 according to the first dataset and reached 87 percent of the U.S. level by 1985 according to the second.

Among medium and light industries, the average coefficient of variation fell by about a third between 1967 and 1979 according to the first dataset, and the average productivity of the other countries pulled to about 70 percent of the U.S. level. According to the OECD data, dispersion remained unchanged among both medium and light industries between 1970 and 1985. By 1985, the dispersion of TFP levels within the three groups of industries was almost equal, whereas it was considerably higher among heavy industries in 1967. This finding is an interesting contrast with our 1988 results, which showed that convergence in labor productivity was strongest among light industries and weakest in heavy industries and that by 1982 there was considerably more dispersion among heavy industries than among medium or light ones.

The leading country in terms of TFP level is also indicated for each industry in Table 7-2. In the Dollar–Wolff database, the United States led in 10 of the 12 industries in 1967 and 10 in 1979. According to the OECD data, the United States led in 4 of the 9 OECD industries in 1970 and 5 in 1985. In our 1988 study, we found that the United States led in virtually all of the 28 manufacturing industries in our sample in 1963 in terms of labor productivity, but in only 10 of the 28 in 1982. Seven countries, besides the United States, held the lead in at least 1 industry in 1982. Part of the reason for the difference in results is that the sample of countries used in this study is different and the industry classifications are more aggregated than in our previous study. However, the major explanation, as we shall see, is that other countries have not only caught up to but have also surpassed the United States in capital intensity.

The case of Japan merits special attention. According to the Dollar–Wolff database, its TFP level converged on that of the United States in every industry between 1965 and 1982, and in two, metals (13) and nonmetallic minerals (15), its TFP surpassed that of the United States (see Table 7-2).[12] The catch-up was strongest in the heavy industries, in which the ratio of the unweighted average of the TFP levels to that of the United States was 1.05 in 1982; second strongest in the medium industries, in which the ratio was 0.88; and weakest in the light industries, with a ratio of 0.83. This is in accord with our earlier findings regarding labor productivity. However, most of the catch-up had been achieved by the early 1970s, and in both datasets, Japanese technology actually declined relative to the United States in several industries over the ensuing decade.

Productivity movements are sensitive to business cycle fluctuations. There is a sizable literature on the proper techniques to use to adjust output and input measures for business cycle changes. Because of the availability of data, we use capacity utilization indices to adjust our TFP measures. Our new measure is

$$\text{TFPU} = Y/[\alpha L + (1 - \alpha)uK] \tag{7-1'}$$

where u is the capacity utilization rate. Unfortunately, we do not have data on capacity utilization by individual industry for each of the countries, and so we must rely on the utilization index for the whole manufacturing sector to compute our adjusted TFP index. (Data on utilization rates are from OECD, *Main Economic Indicators, 1960–1979,* and Coe and Holtham 1983.) The results for the coefficient of variation of TFPU are almost identical to (unadjusted) TFP (see Table 7-1).

Capital Intensity in the Aggregate and by Industry

As we noted in our introduction, recent studies have documented a convergence in aggregate, economywide capital–labor ratios among industrialized countries over the postwar period. We next look at the extent to which the convergence in aggregate capital–labor ratios has been translated into a convergence in capital–labor ratios in individual industries. Because the summary statistics are very sensitive to the sample of countries we chose, we show the results for ony constant sample sets of countries (see Table 7-3). The choice of countries is based on the availability of data. For each industry, we selected those countries with employment and capital stock data for the maximum number of years.

Table 7-3. Measures of Convergence in Capital–Labor Ratios by Industry, 1965–1985

I. Dollar–Wolff Database[b]		Average Capital–Labor Ratio Relative to United States				Coefficient of Variation of Capital–Labor Ratios			
	NACE	1965	1972	1979	1983	1965	1972	1979	1983
Heavy industries[a]		.59	.66	.76	.68	.47	.37	.36	.36
Ferrous and nonferr. metals	13	.83	.72	.92	.72	.43	.45	.43	.37
Chemicals	17	.62	.83[e]	.83	.85	.40	.25[e]	.34	.35
Nonmetallic minerals	15	.34[d]	.43	.52	.47[g]	.57[d]	.41	.30	.35[g]
Medium industries[a]		.74	.83	.95	.99	.39	.28	.22	.25
Machinery	21/23	.47	.67[e]	.83	.70	.40	.19[e]	.13	.20
Rubber and plastics	49	.90	.97	1.05	1.25	.17	.13	.15	.21
Paper and printing	47	.83	.94[e]	1.05	1.12	.71	.59[e]	.40	.39
Transport equipment	28	.78	.75	.87	.88	.29	.21	.18	.18
Light industries[a]		.85	1.07	1.21	1.26	.35	.44	.31	.33
Metal products	19	.69	.94[e]	.98	.93	.49	.51[e]	.43	.37
Other industries	48	1.08	1.44	1.40	1.60	.29	.50	.29	.29
Textiles	42	1.15	1.42[f]	1.62	1.80	.23	.27[f]	.38	.47
Electrical goods	25	.82	.76	.89	.84	.31	.36	.27	.26
Food, beverages, tobacco	36	.82	.95	1.05	1.03	.35	.30	.26	.24
All manufacturing[a]		.75	.88	1.00	1.00	.39	.36	.29	.30

II. OECD database[c]	Average Capital–Labor Ratio Relative to United States			Coefficient of Variation of Capital–Labor Ratios		
	1970	1979	1983	1970	1979	1983
Heavy industries[a]	.88	1.04	1.02	.50	.45	.46
Basic metals	.60	.68	.56	.49	.42	.42
Chemicals	.86	1.02	.97	.21	.27	.28
Nonmetallic minerals	1.19	1.42	1.54	.82	.67	.69
Medium industries[a]	1.10	1.26	1.26	.36	.31	.29
Machinery and equipment	1.05	1.25	1.13	.33	.26	.21
Paper, printing, publ.	1.19	1.37	1.56	.53	.45	.46
Food, beverages, tobacco	1.06	1.17	1.10	.24	.22	.22
Light industries[a]	1.44	1.64	1.79	.29	.32	.31
Textiles	1.37	1.73	1.72	.25	.35	.26
Wood and wood products	1.52	1.55	1.86	.35	.30	.38
Other industries	1.12	1.23	1.24	.56	.50	.59
All manufacturing[a]	1.11	1.27	1.30	.41	.38	.39

[a]Unweighted average of industries within group.

[b]Countries included in the Dollar–Wolff database are as follows:

NACE 13: All except the Netherlands and Italy.

NACE 15: All except Canada and Japan.

NACE 17: All except the Netherlands and Italy.

NACE 19: All except Belgium and Italy.

NACE 21–23: Canada, France, Germany, Japan, United Kingdom, United States.

NACE 25: All except Belgium and Italy.

NACE 28: All except Belgium and Italy.

NACE 36: All except Italy.

NACE 42: All except Italy.

NACE 47: All except Italy.

NACE 49: Belgium, Canada, France, Germany, United Kingdom, United States.

NACE 48: All except Italy.

Total manufacturing: All except Italy.

[c]Countries included in the OECD database for each industry are as follows:

1970–83 All except Australia and Finland.

1984–85 All except Australia, Finland, and Netherlands.

The exceptions are

Wood and wood products: 1970–85: Canada, Denmark, Germany, Italy, Norway, United States.

All manufacturing: 1970–85: All.

[d]1967.

[e]1973.

[f]1974.

[g]1982.

There is strong evidence of convergence in capital intensity among the group of 9 countries in the Dollar–Wolff database. The coefficient of variation fell from 0.36 to 0.20, and the ratio of maximum to minimum capital–labor ratio fell from 3.4 to 1.8. For the whole manufacturing sector, the (unweighted) average capital–labor ratio among countries other than the United States increased from three-fourths of the U.S. level in 1965 to almost perfect equality by 1983. The catch-up in capital intensity was much stronger than in TFP (in 1985, the average TFP of other countries was only 72 percent that of the United States). Every country gained on the United States in capital intensity between 1963 and 1983, and those countries with lower initial capital endowments gained more (the correlation coefficient between the 1965 capital–labor ratio and the annual rate of growth of the capital–labor ratio over the 1965–83 period was 0.85 among the 9 countries). The aggregate capital–labor ratio of Japan, in particular, increased from 40 percent of the U.S. level in 1965 to 83 percent in 1983.[13] Aggregate capital stock data indicate that Canada was first in 1963 and the United States second.[14] In 1983 Canada still ranked first, the Netherlands was second, Italy was third, and the United States was fourth, with Belgium a close fifth.

As in the case of TFP, most of the convergence had been achieved by the mid-1970s. In 1974, the coefficient of variation for total manufacturing (based on the aggregate data) was 0.23, and the unweighted average capital–labor ratio among other countries had climbed to 91 percent of the United States' capital intensity. The OECD data confirm this result. The dispersion of capital–labor ratios among the 14 countries in this sample reached a minimum in 1975 and then remained relatively unchanged over the next 10 years. In 1985, the leading country in terms of capital intensity was the Netherlands, followed by Canada, Sweden, Belgium, and Norway. The United States ranked eighth out of 14.

The same pattern is also seen for individual industries. Between 1965 and 1983, the (unweighted) average capital–labor ratio in the 8 countries relative to the United States increased in 11 of the 12 industries according to the Dollar–Wolff data; the coefficient of variation fell in 9 of the 12 industries and remained the same in 1; and the ratio of maximum to minimum capital–labor ratio fell in 9 of the 12 and in 2 remained almost unchanged. By 1983 the other countries were, on average, considerably ahead of the United States in capital intensity in the light industries,[15] at virtual parity with the United States in the medium industries, but still rather far behind the United States in the heavy industries. The disparity in capital–labor ratios was greatest among the heavy industries and smallest among the medium industries.[16]

As with TFP, the dispersion of capital–labor ratios is more marked in individual industries than in the aggregate. This result emerges from a comparison between the unweighted average coefficient of variation among the various industries with that of the aggregate data: 0.30 versus 0.20 in 1983 according to the Dollar–Wolff data and 0.39 versus 0.20 in 1985 on the basis of the OECD data. This finding is somewhat surprising. In a comparison between a developed and a developing country, one generally finds capital–labor ratios more similar in industries than in the aggregate. A recent study of South Korea and West Germany, for instance, found that differences in capital–labor ratios were modest at the industry level, though Germany had a far higher aggregate ratio (Dollar 1991). The reason for this is that compared with South Korea, Germany's employment mix is shifted toward capital-intensive industries. This pattern is predicted by the Heckscher–Ohlin model of international trade. Given the capital abundance of the United States in the early postwar period, we expected to find a similar relationship between the United States at that time and the other OECD countries: greater dispersion of capital–labor ratios in the aggregate than within industries. However, this was not the case.[17]

We can address this issue more formally. Define:

s_i^h Country h's employment in Industry i as a proportion of Country h's total employment;

κ_i^h ratio of Country h's capital–labor ratio to the U.S. capital–labor ratio in Industry i;

where we have standardized the industry capital–labor ratios in each country by expressing them as ratios to the U.S. levels. Then,

$$\kappa^h = \Sigma_i s_i^h \kappa_i^h, \tag{7-2}$$

where κ^h is Country h's capital–labor ratio in all manufacturing. The international average employment shares by industry and the international average capital intensity of an industry are calculated as weighted averages:

$$\bar{s}_i = \Sigma_h L_i^h / [\Sigma_h \Sigma_i L_i^h] \tag{7-3}$$

and

$$\bar{\kappa}_i = \Sigma_h r_i^h \kappa_i^h, \tag{7-4}$$

where $r_i^h = L_i^h / \Sigma_i L_i^h$. In both cases, we defined the international average aggregate capital–labor ratio as

$$\bar{k} = \Sigma_i \bar{s}_i \bar{\kappa}_i. \tag{7-5}$$

Then the deviation of a country's aggregate capital–labor ratio from the international average capital–labor ratio is given by

$$\text{DEV}(\kappa^h) = \kappa^h - \bar{k} = \Sigma_i s_i^h \, \text{DEV}(\kappa_i^h) + \Sigma_i \bar{\kappa}_i \, \text{DEV}(s_i^h), \tag{7-6}$$

where $\text{DEV}(\kappa_i^h) = \kappa_i^h - \bar{\kappa}_i$ and indicates the deviation of Industry i's capital–labor ratio in Country h from the international average for Industry i, and

$$\text{DEV}(s_i^h) = s_i^h - \bar{s}_i$$

and indicates the difference between Industry i's employment share in Country h from the international average for Industry i. The first term on the right-hand side of Equation 7-6 reflects the relative capital intensities of the industries within a country. The second term reflects the allocation of labor among industries of different capital intensities.

The results of these calculations, shown in Panel A of Table 7-4, indicate that differences in capital intensity by industry explain almost all of the differences in aggregate capital–labor ratios. This held true for every country except Italy and Japan and for each of the 3 years: 1972, 1979, and 1985. Countries with high aggregate capital–labor ratios tend to have higher-than-average capital–labor ratios in most industries, and conversely.[18]

Another interesting issue is the extent to which convergence in the overall capital–labor ratio among countries has resulted from the convergence of the industry-

employment mix. We can address this issue in a fashion similar to the preceding calculation. According to Equation 7-2,

$$\Delta\kappa^h = \Sigma_i s_i^h(\Delta\kappa_i^h) + \Sigma_i(\Delta s_i^h)\kappa_i^h, \tag{7-7}$$

where a Δ indicates change over time (e.g., $\Delta\kappa^h = \kappa_t^h - \kappa_{t-1}^h$). From Panel B of Table
7-4, we see that almost all the change in the aggregate country capital–labor ratios
between 1972 and 1985 can be attributed to the change in industry capital–labor ratios
rather than to changes in employment mixes among industries. This was the case for
each country, with the exception of Canada, and for each of the time periods considered, 1972–79 and 1979–85.[19] In fact, the results from Panel C indicate that there was
virtually no greater similarity among countries in their employment mixes in 1985
than in 1972.

Finally, we should note that in the 1980s, the dispersion of capital–labor ratios in
all manufacturing, as measured by the coefficient of variation, was greater than that of
TFP levels. This was also true for each of the three industry groups and for the great
majority of individual industries. This suggests that technology transfer is relatively
easy among industrialized countries and, as a result, the state of technology is becoming very similar among these nations but that national investment rates, as well as
investment rates in particular industries, still display relatively great differences among
countries.

Table 7-4. Decomposition of Country Capital–Labor Ratios into Industry-Level Employment
and Capital–Labor Effects[a]

A. *Decomposition of the deviation of country's capital–labor ratio from the international average*[b]

	1972			1979			1985		
	$DEV(\kappa^h)$	$DEV(\kappa_i^h)$	$DEV(s_i^h)$	$DEV(\kappa^h)$	$DEV(\kappa_i^h)$	$DEV(s_i^h)$	$DEV(\kappa^h)$	$DEV(\kappa_i^h)$	$DEV(s_i^h)$
Belgium	5.2	5.4	−0.3	21.6	24.4	−2.8	28.5	32.4	−3.9
Canada	50.3	61.2	−10.9	40.2	37.3	2.8	44.4	42.0	2.4
Denmark	−1.8	−5.7	3.9	9.2	6.7	2.5	−7.1	−9.5	2.4
France	9.9	12.5	−2.6	17.3	20.4	−3.1	23.8	28.4	−4.6
Germany	−8.9	−8.1	−0.8	−11.1	−10.5	−0.6	−15.7	−13.8	−1.8
Italy	20.0	13.4	6.6	9.4	4.4	5.0	8.7	2.1	6.6
Japan	−20.7	−16.6	−4.1	−5.1	−1.8	−3.4	−1.0	2.5	−3.4
Netherlands	35.3	36.9	−1.6	50.4	53.9	−3.5	44.5	49.0	−4.5
Norway	7.0	4.7	2.3	17.4	16.1	1.3	27.7	26.6	1.1
Sweden	54.9	54.2	0.7	65.1	64.5	0.6	59.7	58.7	1.1
United Kingdom	−17.5	−14.2	−3.2	−21.0	−16.6	−4.4	−12.9	−8.4	−4.5
United States	5.6	3.1	2.5	−3.3	−5.4	2.1	−1.8	−4.9	3.1
Average[c]	11.6	12.2	−0.6	15.8	16.1	−0.3	16.6	17.1	−0.5

B. *Decomposition of the change over time in country's capital–labor ratio*[d]

	1972–79			1979–85			1972–85		
	$\Delta\kappa^h$	$\Delta\kappa_i^h$	Δs_i^h	$\Delta\kappa^h$	$\Delta\kappa_i^h$	Δs_i^h	$\Delta\kappa^h$	$\Delta\kappa_i^h$	Δs_i^h
Belgium	22.5	25.3	−2.9	5.4	5.4	0.0	28.1	30.7	−2.6
Canada	26.8	−1.2	28.0	1.9	2.7	−0.8	28.6	1.5	27.1
Denmark	18.7	19.9	−1.2	−17.8	−17.8	−0.0	0.8	2.1	−1.3

	1972–79			1979–85			1972–85		
	$\Delta\kappa^h$	$\Delta\kappa_i^h$	Δs_i^h	$\Delta\kappa^h$	$\Delta\kappa_i^h$	Δs_i^h	$\Delta\kappa^h$	$\Delta\kappa_i^h$	Δs_i^h
France	15.1	16.2	−1.2	5.3	5.1	0.3	20.5	21.3	−0.8
Germany	4.6	6.6	−2.1	−7.8	−6.0	−1.8	−3.3	0.6	−4.0
Italy	−2.2	−1.8	−0.4	−2.5	−2.1	−0.4	−4.4	−3.9	−0.4
Japan	22.8	24.5	−1.6	1.8	2.7	−0.9	23.9	27.2	−3.3
Netherlands	18.1	24.0	−5.9	−12.3	−9.5	−2.9	7.0	14.6	−7.6
Norway	19.7	19.3	0.4	8.2	8.8	−0.6	28.3	28.1	0.2
Sweden	19.4	19.1	0.3	−7.4	−6.8	−0.5	12.9	12.3	0.6
United Kingdom	3.7	5.4	−1.7	7.4	6.6	0.7	10.9	12.0	−1.1
Average[c]	15.4	14.3	1.1	−1.6	−1.0	−0.6	13.9	13.3	0.6

C. Addendum: Change in country employment distribution $[\Sigma_i \, |s_i^h - \bar{s}_i|]$

	1972	1979	1985
Belgium	.38	.35	.39
Canada	.33	.33	.30
Denmark	.35	.33	.26
France	.28	.26	.30
Germany	.19	.21	.25
Italy	.38	.36	.42
Japan	.40	.39	.40
Netherlands	.33	.40	.46
Norway	.40	.38	.39
Sweden	.29	.29	.27
United Kingdom	.12	.13	.16
United States	.15	.17	.19
Average[c]	.30	.30	.32

[a]Results are based on the OECD database. For the Netherlands, 1983 is used instead of 1985.
[b]This decomposition is based on Equation 7-6:

$$\text{DEV}(\kappa^h) \equiv \kappa^h - \bar{\kappa} = \Sigma_i s_i^h \, \text{DEV}(\kappa_i^h) + \Sigma_i \bar{\kappa}_i \, \text{DEV}(s_i^h).$$

[c]Unweighted average.
[d]This decomposition is based on Equation 7-7:

$$\Delta\kappa^h = \Sigma_i s_i^h(\Delta\kappa_i^h) + \Sigma_i(\Delta s_i^h)\kappa_i^h.$$

The United States is excluded from this panel because the value of κ_i^h is defined as unity in each year for each U.S. industry.

Decomposition of Labor Productivity Growth

We established in our 1988 study that the convergence of aggregate labor productivity among industrial countries has resulted from the convergence of labor productivity within industries. We next investigate the sources of this labor productivity convergence within individual industries. As we showed, between the early 1960s and the mid-1980s, both TFP and capital–labor ratios converged toward the U.S. level, though most of this had occurred by the early 1970s. The next issue we address is the extent to which the convergence in labor productivity within industries could be attributed to the convergence in TFP and to what extent it was a result of the catch-up in capital deepening.

We use a standard growth-accounting framework. Formally, assume that for each Industry i and Country h there is a Cobb–Douglas value-added production function:

$$\text{Ln } Y_i^h = \zeta_i^h + \alpha_i \text{ Ln } L_i^h + (1 - \alpha_i)\text{Ln } K_i^h. \qquad (7\text{-}8)$$

The parameter ζ_i^h is country specific and indicates Country h's technology level in Industry i. The output elasticity of labor in Industry i, α_i, is assumed to be the same among countries. If factors are paid their marginal products, then the output elasticity will be equal to labor's distributive share. In our study, we take the cross-country (unweighted) average of labor's share in Industry i as our estimate of α_i.

We use two measures of TFP growth. The first is crude TFP growth, defined as the time derivative of Equation 7-1. The second measure of TFP growth is the Divisia index, defined as

$$\rho_i^h = \hat{Y}_i^h - \alpha\hat{L}_i^h - (1 - \alpha)\hat{K}_i^h, \qquad (7\text{-}9)$$

where a hat (^) denotes the time derivative or relative rate of change. Consistent with this measure of TFP growth is a second method of calculating the TFP level, often referred to as the Translog Index of TFP:

$$\text{Ln TFP}_i^h = \text{Ln } Y_i^h - \alpha_i \text{ Ln } L_i^h - (1 - \alpha_i)\text{Ln } K_i^h. \qquad (7\text{-}10)$$

A comparison of Equation 7-10 with Equation 7-8 reveals that this measure of TFP is implicitly based on a Cobb–Douglas form for the production function.

We can now formally decompose the convergence of labor productivity growth into a component attributable to technology convergence and a component attributable to convergence in capital–labor ratios. Let the United States be the benchmark country, and define

   π_i^h ratio of Country h's labor productivity to U.S. labor productivity in Industry i;

   τ_i^h ratio of Country h's technology level to the U.S. technology level in Industry i;

and, as before,

   κ_i^h ratio of Country h's capital–labor ratio to the U.S. capital–labor ratio in Industry i.

Equations 7-8 and 7-10 then imply that

$$\text{Ln } \pi_i^h = \text{Ln } \tau_i^h + (1 - \alpha_i)\text{Ln } \kappa_i^h. \qquad (7\text{-}11)$$

Differentiating this with respect to time yields

$$\hat{\pi}_i^h = \hat{\tau}_i^h + (1 - \alpha)\hat{\kappa}_i^h. \qquad (7\text{-}12)$$

Hence, the convergence of Country h's labor productivity in Industry i on the U.S. level can be decomposed into the convergence of technology and the convergence of capital–labor ratios.

The results for Equation 7-12 are shown in Table 7-5 for the Translog Index of TFP.[20] Between 1963 and 1972, most of the catch-up in labor productivity can be attributed to the catch-up in technological capabilities. Although there is some variability among countries, the unweighted cross-country average indicates that about

Table 7-5. The Decomposition of Labor Productivity Convergence into a Technology and Capital–Intensity Component, 1970–1985[a] (annual rates of growth in percentages)

	1963–72			1970–85		
	LPROD $(\hat{\pi}_i^h)$	TFP $(\hat{\tau}_i^h)$	K/L $[(1-\alpha)\hat{\kappa}_i^h]$	LPROD $(\hat{\pi}_i^h)$	TFP $(\hat{\tau}_i^h)$	K/L $[(1-\alpha)\hat{\kappa}_i^h]$
A. Total manufacturing by country						
Australia				−0.03	−0.23	0.20
Belgium				2.41	1.62	0.78
Canada	0.61	0.50	0.11	−0.53	−0.55	0.02
Denmark				0.09	−0.01	0.10
Finland				0.42	0.36	0.06
France	0.51	−0.30	0.81	0.55	0.12	0.42
Germany	2.23	1.38	0.85	0.00	−0.15	0.15
Italy	0.29	1.87	−1.58	0.17	0.24	−0.06
Japan	6.82	3.20	3.62	2.74	1.77	0.97
Netherlands				1.70	0.99	0.71
Norway				−0.85	−1.32	0.46
Sweden				−0.53	−0.78	0.25
United Kingdom	2.11	1.49	0.61	−0.05	−0.61	0.55
B. Unweighted industry average across countries[b]						
All manuf.	2.09	1.36	0.74	0.47	0.11	0.35
Heavy industry	2.90	2.43	0.47	1.93	1.62	0.31
Basic metals	3.42	3.87	−0.46	2.78	2.95	−0.17
Chemicals	4.32	2.72	1.60	2.22	1.86	0.36
Minerals	4.71	1.77	2.94	0.53	−0.17	0.71
Medium industry	0.64	0.82	−0.18	0.07	−0.27	0.34
Machinery	0.86	−0.53	1.39	0.08	−0.15	0.23
Rubber, plastics	0.70	1.09	−0.39			
Paper, printing	1.62	0.81	0.82	0.88	0.32	0.56
Transport equip.	1.87	2.37	−0.49			
Food, beverages	1.70	0.27	1.43	−0.49	−0.80	0.31
Light industry	1.71	1.43	0.28	−0.40	−0.79	0.39
Metal products	3.48	2.38	1.10			
Textiles	1.34	0.28	1.06	−0.01	−0.57	0.56
Electrical goods	2.06	3.65	−1.59			
Wood products				−0.29	−0.69	0.40
Other industries	0.28	−1.26	1.53	−2.00	−2.52	0.52

[a]The decomposition is based on Equation 7-12:

$$\hat{\pi}_1^h = \hat{\tau}_1^h + (1-\alpha)\hat{\kappa}_1^h.$$

The Translog Index of TFP growth is used. Calculations for 1963–72 are based on the Dollar–Wolff database, and those for 1970–85 are based on the OECD database. International average wage shares are used. The periods are as indicated in the table, with the following exceptions:

  For Germany, 1965–72 is used instead of 1963–72.
  For Italy, 1967–72 is used instead of 1963–72.
  For Japan, 1965–72 is used instead of 1963–72.
  For the Netherlands, 1965–72 is used instead of 1963–72, and 1970–83 is used instead of 1970–85.
  For the United Kingdom, 1963–73 is used instead of 1963–72.

See the Appendix for additional details on data availability.

[b]Unweighted average among countries with available data in each industry or industry group.

two-thirds of the labor productivity convergence can be attributed to technology transfer and the remaining third to increasing capital intensity.[21] Japan's results are interesting. They indicate that a little over half of Japan's labor productivity convergence
came from increasing capital intensity. There also are differences among individual
industries, although for the aggregate heavy, medium, and light industries, the pre-
ponderance of the catch-up was achieved from convergence in technology.

In contrast, between 1970 and 1985, the labor productivity catch-up toward the
United States was achieved primarily through increasing capital intensity (three-
fourths on the basis of the unweighted cross-country average). Although there are both
country and industry differences, this result held for 8 of the 13 countries and 7 of the
9 industries. Japan is, again, an exception, since about two-thirds of its labor productivity convergence toward the United States was achieved through technology catch-
up. The heavy industries, particularly basic (ferrous and nonferrous) metals and chemicals, were another exception, for which about four-fifths of the labor productivity
convergence was attributable to technology transfer.

This analysis still begs the question of whether there is any connection between
technology catch-up and the rate of capital accumulation in a country. We now turn
to this issue using a regression analysis.

Regression Analysis

We now turn to a regression framework to test two hypotheses concerning technology
convergence. The first can be labeled the *catch-up hypothesis,* which states simply that
those industries and countries that lagged furthest behind the United States in technological sophistication in the 1960s had the most opportunities to imitate and purchase advanced technology and hence should exhibit the fastest rate of technology
convergence. Taking each industry in each country as an observation, this hypothesis
implies that the rate of growth of τ_i^h between the mid-1960s and the mid-1980s is
inversely correlated with the level of τ_i^h at the beginning of the period. Our approach
provides a large number of observations to test this hypothesis.

A second hypothesis is the *vintage hypothesis,* which states that a dollar's worth
of new capital is more productive than a (constant) dollar's worth of old capital. (This
might also be called the *embodiment effect,* since it implies that at least some technological innovation is embodied in capital.) If the capital stock data do not correct for
vintage effects, then this hypothesis suggests that the rate of growth of τ_i^h will be positively correlated with the rate of growth of κ_i^h. Again, we can treat each industry in each
country as an observation to test this hypothesis.

Both hypotheses can be tested using the following regression specification:

$$\hat{\tau}_{it}^h = b_0 + b_1 \tau_{it}^h + b_2 \hat{\kappa}_{it}^h + \Sigma_h c_h \text{ CNTYDUM}^h + \Sigma_i d_i \text{ INDDUM}_i + \epsilon_t^h, \quad (7\text{-}13)$$

where τ_{it}^h is Country h's (Translog) TFP relative to the United States at the start of each
period, CNTYDUM^h is a dummy variable for each Country h (except the United
States), INDDUM$_i$ is an industry dummy variable (excluding other industries), and ϵ
is a stochastic error term. Country and industry dummy variables are included to control for country-specific effects, such as the degree of trade openness, culture, and government policy; and industry-specific effects, such as market structure and diffusion

patterns for new technology. Both 2-year and 3-year averages are used for the growth variables to reduce random noise. The regression is performed on both the Dollar–Wolff database and the OECD database. For the former, we introduce an additional dummy variable, D6372, defined as unity on or before 1972 and zero thereafter, which interacts with κ_i^h to control for period effects. The United States was excluded from this regression equation, since the value of the dependent variable is always unity.

The results, shown in Table 7-6, confirm the catch-up hypothesis, showing a highly significant inverse relation between the rate of TFP convergence by industry and country and its initial TFP level, relative to the United States. The results for the vintage hypothesis are interesting. The term κ_i^h has a negative and significant coefficient for the regressions performed on the OECD database between 1970 and 1985. The term also has a negative coefficient in the Dollar–Wolff database, but the interactive term $\kappa_i^h \cdot D6372$ is positive and highly significant. These results suggest that the embodiment effect was probably important during the 1963–72 period, when productivity convergence was very strong among OECD countries but inoperative between the mid-1970s and the mid-1980s. Indeed, the negative sign of the coefficient suggests that adjustment costs associated with the introduction of new capital equipment may actually inhibit productivity growth once an industry has reached the technological frontier.[22]

Table 7-6. Regression of Relative Productivity Growth ($\hat{\tau}_{it}^h$) on Relative Productivity Level and Growth in Relative Capital Intensity[a]

Dependent Variable	Independent Variables				R^2	Adj. R^2	Std. Err. Of Reg.	Sample Size
	Const.	τ_{it}^h	κ_{it}^h	$\kappa_{it}^h \cdot D6372$				
A. OECD database[b]								
Two-year averages								
$\hat{\tau}_{it}^h$	0.0097	−0.057*	−0.227*		0.18	0.15	0.055	643
	(0.4)	(4.6)	(5.7)					
Three-year averages								
$\hat{\tau}_{it}^h$	0.0006	−0.042*	−0.194*		0.25	0.21	0.039	457
	(1.0)	(4.0)	(4.9)					
B. Dollar–Wolff database[c]								
Two-year averages								
$\hat{\tau}_{it}^h$	0.054*	−0.048*	−0.673*	0.490*	0.21	0.18	0.065	694
	(4.2)	(5.8)	(9.9)	(6.3)				
Three-year averages								
$\hat{\tau}_{it}^h$	0.066*	−0.061*	−0.646*	0.455*	0.30	0.26	0.047	460
	(5.6)	(7.8)	(8.4)	(6.1)				

[a]t-ratios are shown in parentheses below the coefficient estimate. Country and industry dummy variables are included in the specification, but the results are not shown. The observations are based on 2- or 3-year averages, as indicated. Key:

> τ_i^h: Ratio of Country h's technology level to U.S. technology level in Industry i at the beginning of the period.
> $\hat{\tau}_{it}^h$: Annual rate of growth of τ_i^h.
> $\hat{\kappa}_i^h$: Annual rate of change of ratio of Country h's capital–labor ratio to U.S. capital–labor ratio in Industry i.
> D6273: Dummy variable, defined as unity on or before 1972 and zero thereafter.

[b]The period covered is 1970–85.

[c]The period covered is 1963–83.

*Significant at the 1 percent level.

Concluding Remarks

The United States' aggregate labor productivity advantage in the early 1960s was rooted in superior labor productivity in virtually all industries. The United States had higher TFP than did the other OECD countries in each industry and also employed more capital per worker in each industry. It is interesting that the United States' capital abundance at that time was reflected almost totally in the use of more capital per worker in industries. It was not the case that U.S. capital abundance led to the employment of a larger share of its work force in capital-intensive industries. Indeed, there was no significant difference between the United States' employment mix and those of other developed countries in relation to their capital or labor intensity of production.

Between the early 1960s and the mid-1970s, the labor productivity levels of other OECD countries converged on the United States in every manufacturing industry. The convergence of TFP was the primary source of this development, with the convergence of capital–labor ratios playing a secondary role. In addition, there is evidence that those countries and industries that lagged particularly far behind in terms of technological capability experienced the most rapid TFP convergence. This finding is consistent with Gerschenkron's notion of the advantage of relative backwardness. The countries and industries that were particularly far behind had the most to gain from technology transfer and proceeded to grow most rapidly.

Between 1963 and 1972 there was also a positive correlation between the TFP convergence and the convergence of capital intensity. This result can be interpreted in two ways: Advanced technology is embodied in machines, and so rapid capital accumulation occasions rapid TFP growth; or high TFP growth, through the acquisition of disembodied technology, improves the profitability of an industry, thereby attracting new investment. These issues of causality are difficult to sort out, but we think it is likely that the causality runs in both directions.

In Chapter 3, Baumol distinguishes between two potential sources of aggregate productivity convergence: "common forces" or "contagion." In practice, technology transfer is likely to be the main driving force of contagion, whereas diminishing marginal returns to capital (as in the neoclassical growth model) is the common force most often cited as a potential engine of convergence. Our results support the notion that contagion is an important, though perhaps not the only, source of productivity convergence. The findings that the other OECD countries quickly converged toward the United States' TFP level in the early postwar period and that this TFP convergence was the main source of labor productivity convergence are consistent with the argument that the United States had a technology lead in virtually all industries at the end of World War II, a lead that subsequently eroded through the international diffusion of technology. Chapters 4 and 5 analyze different factors that led to the emergence and eventual dissipation of U.S. technological superiority. Our empirical results are consistent with the arguments that they present.

By the mid-1970s, the TFP levels of industrial countries were fairly similar, though the United States continued to hold a lead in most industries. There has been no further convergence of TFP since the mid-1970s. The convergence of labor productivity within industries has continued, though at a slower rate than before and, in the recent period, has resulted almost entirely from capital accumulation. By the late

1980s, differences in the capital–labor ratios among OECD countries were minor. What labor productivity lead the United States still has today results from the modest technology lead that it retains in most industries.

The nature of the international economy has changed significantly between the 1960s and today. In the earlier period, the United States had labor and total factor productivity advantages in all manufacturing industries. What appears to be the situation today is that different countries are developing modest labor and total factor productivity leads in different industries. With this kind of international specialization, the dispersion of productivity measures is greater within industries than in the aggregate. These results accord with Abramovitz's conclusion that the industrial countries today are nearly equal technological rivals.

What we are likely to see in the future is aggregate productivity levels in the OECD countries that remain close together while different countries' technological advance and investment are concentrated in different industries and subindustries. There is nothing automatic about this process, however. The sources of productivity growth for individual industries are innovation and investment. The continued U.S. TFP lead in most industries suggests that the United States is performing at least satisfactorily in regard to the former. However, the lackluster U.S. savings and investment situation, and the fact that other OECD countries have overtaken the United States in terms of capital abundance, raise some concerns about the United States' ability to maintain its position among the advanced countries.

Our results have a number of policy implications. That other countries are catching up with the United States should not necessarily be viewed as evidence of its decline. With ever-increasing economic integration among the OECD countries, it is inevitable that a large productivity gap cannot be sustained. This conclusion, however, does not mean that America should be complacent about economic growth. Although it seems unlikely to us that any one industrial country will lag far behind the others in this period, a nation may certainly lag modestly behind if its innovation and investment do not proceed at a pace comparable to those of its rivals. Furthermore, the United States continues to be the largest economy in the world, and thus its own growth is likely to have significant spillover effects on the other industrial economies (as well as on developing countries in the Third World). A strong performance in regard to the United States' innovation and investment cannot produce the kind of leadership that the country enjoyed in the 1950s, but it can ensure the continuation of America's present position as first among equals.

Notes

The authors are very grateful for the generous support of the research for this chapter to the Division of Information Science and Technology of the National Science Foundation and the C. V. Starr Center for Applied Economics. We are also indebted to Maury Gittleman for his very valuable assistance.

1. On the convergence of aggregate labor productivity, see Baumol 1986, Matthews, Feinstein, and Odling-Smee 1982, Abramovitz 1986, and Maddison 1987. Wolff (1991) found convergence in aggregate total factor productivity (TFP), defined as the ratio of output to a weighted sum of labor and capital inputs, during the postwar period among the "Group of Seven" or G-7 (Canada, France, Italy, Japan, West Germany, the United Kingdom, and the United States).

Dowrick and Nguyen (1989) similarly demonstrated a significant catch-up in TFP levels among 24 OECD countries between 1950 and 1985. In addition, Wolff (1991) found that aggregate capital–labor ratios have become more similar among the G-7 countries: The coefficient of variation in the aggregate capital–labor (gross capital to hours) ratio fell from 0.52 in 1950 to 0.23 in 1979. Bowen (1983) also showed that the U.S. position as a capital-abundant country has declined relative to other industrialized countries.

2. There were three other findings of interest in this study. The first was that the degree of catch-up varied considerably among industries—more rapid in so-called light industries, defined as those with low capital–labor ratios, than in heavy industries. A second finding was that whereas in 1963 the United States led in virtually every industry in terms of labor productivity, by 1982 8 different countries held the lead in at least 1 industry, and U.S. leadership was limited to only 10 of 28 industries. The third was that the convergence in industry labor productivity slowed down rather sharply after 1973 or so.

3. This form represents, perhaps, the most intuitive formulation of total factor productivity as the ratio of output to a weighted sum of inputs. We also used the more standard Translog definition of TFP, shown in Equation 7-10. However, this formulation depends on a particular functional form for the production function and, as a result, is less general than Equation 7-1. The actual results were very similar for the two formulations of TFP.

4. We also used the average wage share in the United States for the calculations. However, its value differs so little from the international average wage share that the results are not reported. Also see the Appendix for exceptions to these rules and for the years of data availability by industry and country.

5. NACE numbers are shown in parentheses.

6. It would be preferable to use gross output, together with a third input, materials, in the TFP measure, but the requisite data are not available.

7. The PPP indices were obtained from Ward 1985. It would be more desirable to deflate the output measures with industry-specific price deflators and then convert to a common currency with PPP exchange rates for tradable goods. However, the necessary data are not available.

8. The ideal labor input measure would be hours worked. Unfortunately, such data are not available on the industry level. However, data on average hours worked per year are available by country in Maddison 1982. Adjustment by these data does not significantly alter the results.

9. Note that countries differ in their assumptions with regard to the service life and scrapping behavior of various capital components. Canada, for example, uses longer service lives than does the United States for buildings and many types of capital equipment in its calculation of gross capital stock. Differences in assumptions may distort international comparisons of TFP. Unfortunately, there is no way of correcting for these differences without worksheet data on annual capital flows by industry.

10. The results are almost identical for the two 7-country samples shown in Panels B and C of Table 7-1. Moreover, results from the OECD database indicate that the coefficient of variation of labor productivity levels declined from 0.19 in 1970 to 0.15 in 1985 and that the average labor productivity relative to the United States increased from 0.68 to 0.73. The 1985 figures for labor productivity are almost identical to those for TFP.

11. The food, beverages, and tobacco industry does not fit easily into this three-way division because of several anomalies and, as a result, is tabulated separately.

12. Our results on Japanese TFP compare rather well with those reported by Nakamura (1989).

13. The importance of capital accumulation as a source of Japanese productivity growth has been well documented. See, for example, Bronfenbrenner 1985, Jorgenson, Kuroda, and Nishimizu 1985, Jorgenson and Nishimizu 1978, Kendrick 1984, and Norsworthy and Malmquist 1983, 1985.

14. As noted earlier, Statistics Canada uses a lower scrapping rate and longer lifetimes in computing gross capital stock, which may bias upward its estimate of the Canadian capital stock relative to that of the other countries.

15. This result actually accords quite well with our casual observation that European economies have streamlined their light industries, whereas the United States has tended to continue relying on cheap immigrant labor.

16. According to the OECD data, by 1985, other countries had far surpassed the United States in capital intensity in the light industries, were ahead of the United States in the medium industries, and had reached equality with the United States in the heavy industries. However, as with the first set of results, the dispersion in capital–labor ratios was greatest among the heavy industries and smallest among the medium industries.

17. Measurement error is another possible source of the finding that there is greater dispersion at the industry level than in the aggregate. If each industry observation is measured with some error and these errors are randomly distributed among countries, there will be greater dispersion in the industries than in the aggregate. As noted, however, there is a theoretical expectation that the intercountry dispersion of capital–labor ratios will be greater in the aggregate than in industries, which is borne out empirically in some studies. The fact that the opposite relationship was found for the OECD countries is thus interesting and not likely to be solely the result of measurement error, though the latter may exaggerate the results.

18. Actually, the first term on the right-hand side of Equation 7-6 also reflects the correlation of a country's employment mix (s_i^h) with the relative capital intensities of its industries, but this latter effect is found to be insignificant. We can rewrite Equation 7-6 as

$$\mathrm{DEV}(\kappa^h) = \kappa^h - \bar{\kappa} = \Sigma_i \bar{s}_i \, \mathrm{DEV}(\kappa_i^h) + \Sigma_i \kappa_i^h \, \mathrm{DEV}(s_i^h).$$

The results were very similar to those shown in Panel A of Table 7-4. Using the unweighted averages for $\bar{s}_i$ and $\bar{\kappa}_i$, we obtained

	$\Delta\kappa^h$	$\Delta\kappa_i^h$	Δs_i^h
1972	11.6	12.6	−1.0
1979	15.8	16.9	−1.1
1985	16.6	18.7	−2.1

19. The unweighted average for the 1979–85 period is a bit misleading, since the aggregate capital–labor ratio in 5 of the 11 countries actually declined relative to the United States. If we compare the unweighted average value of absolute changes in $\kappa^h[\Sigma_h \, |\Delta\kappa^h| \, /n]$ with the corresponding unweighted average $[\Sigma_h \, |\Sigma_i s_i^h(\Delta\kappa_i^h)| \, /n]$, we find that 95 percent of the change in aggregate capital intensity was due to changes in industry-level capital–labor ratios.

20. Although there are differences in industry classification between the Dollar–Wolff database and the OECD database, we have tried for illustrative reasons to line up the two classification schemes as closely as possible in Panel B of this table.

21. We should stress that in our framework, we do not (and cannot) distinguish between movements in the technology frontier and changes in an industry's position inside the frontier (changes in so-called X-inefficiency). In our framework, both types of movements would be reflected as changes in total factor productivity.

22. It is perhaps not coincidental that the post-1970 period is also associated with the rapid introduction of computerization among manufacturing industries. Many commentators have suggested that there are sizable adjustment costs associated with this new technology. See, for example, David 1991.

References

Abramovitz, Moses. (1986). "Catching Up, Forging Ahead, and Falling Behind." *Journal of Economic History* 46:385–406.

Baumol, William J. (1986). "Productivity Growth, Convergence, and Welfare: What the Long-Run Data Show." *American Economic Review* 76:1072–85.

Bowen, Harry P. (1983). "Changes in the International Distribution of Resources and Their Impact on U.S. Comparative Advantage." *Review of Economics and Statistics* 65:402–15.

Bronfenbrenner, Martin. (1985). "Japanese Productivity Experience." In William J. Baumol and Kenneth McLennan, eds., *Productivity*

Growth and U.S. Competitiveness. New York: Oxford University Press, pp. 70–102.

Coe, David, and Gerald Holtham. (1983). "Output Responsiveness and Inflation: An Aggregate Study." *OECD Economic Studies,* no. 1, Autumn, pp. 93–148.

David, Paul A. (1991). "Computer and Dynamo: The Modern Productivity Paradox in a Not-Too-Distant Mirror." In *Technology and Productivity: The Challenge for Economic Policy.* Paris: OECD, pp. 315–48.

Dollar, David. (1991). "Convergence of South Korean Productivity on West German Levels, 1966–78." *World Development* 19:263–73.

Dollar, David, and Edward N. Wolff. (1988). "Convergence of Industry Labor Productivity Among Advanced Economies, 1963–1982." *Review of Economics and Statistics* 70:549–58.

Dowrick, Steve, and Duc-Tho Nguyen. (1989). "OECD Comparative Economic Growth 1950–85: Catch-up and Convergence." *American Economic Review* 79:1010–30.

Japan Economic Planning Agency, Department of National Accounts, Economic Research Institute. (1988). *Gross Capital Stock of Private Enterprises, 1965–1986,* February.

Jorgenson, Dale W., Masahiro Kuroda, and Mieko Nishimizu. (1985). "Japan–U.S. Industry-level Productivity Comparison, 1960–1979." Paper presented at the U.S.–Japan Productivity Conference, Cambridge, MA, August.

Jorgenson, Dale W., and Mieko Nishimizu. (1978). "US and Japanese Economic Growth, 1952–1974: An International Comparison." *Economic Journal* 88:707–26.

Kendrick, John W., ed. (1984). *International Comparisons of Productivity and Causes of the Slowdown.* Cambridge, MA: Ballinger.

Maddison, Angus. (1982). *Phases of Capitalist Development.* Oxford: Oxford University Press.

———. (1987). "Growth and Slowdown in Advanced Capitalist Economies: Techniques of Quantitative Assessment." *Journal of Economic Literature* 25:649–706.

Matthews, R.C.O., C. H. Feinstein, and J. C. Odling-Smee. (1982). *British Economic Growth, 1856–1973.* Stanford, CA: Stanford University Press.

Musgrave, John C. (1986a). "Fixed Reproducible Tangible Wealth in the United States, 1982–1985." *Survey of Current Business* 66:36–39.

———. (1986b). "Fixed Reproducible Tangible Wealth in the United States: Revised Estimates." *Survey of Current Business* 66:51–75.

Nakamura, Shinichiro. (1989). "Productivity and Factor Prices as Sources of Differences in Production Costs Between Germany, Japan, and the U.S." *Economic Studies Quarterly* 40:701–15.

Norsworthy, J. R., and David H. Malmquist. (1983). "Input Measurement and Productivity Growth in Japanese and US Manufacturing." *American Economic Review* 73:947–67.

———. (1985). "Recent Productivity Growth in Japanese and U.S. Manufacturing." In William J. Baumol and Kenneth McLennan, eds., *Productivity Growth and U.S. Competitiveness.* New York: Oxford University Press, pp. 58–69.

OECD. (1980). *Main Economic Indicators, 1960–1979.* Paris: OECD.

Statistics Canada, Science, Technology and Capital Stock Division. (1987). *Fixed Capital Flows and Stocks,* September.

Ward, Michael. (1985). *Purchasing Power Parities and Real Expenditures in the OECD.* Paris: OECD.

Wolff, Edward N. (1991). "Capital Formation and Productivity Growth over the Long-Term." *American Economic Review* 81:565–79.

Appendix: Data Sources and Availability

I. Dollar–Wolff Database

A. *Manufacturing industry NACE codes*

    13 Ferrous and nonferrous metals.

    15 Nonmetal minerals and products.

    17 Chemicals.

    19 Finished metal products, except machinery and transportation equipment.

  21/23 Machinery.

    25 Electrical goods.

    28 Transport equipment.

    36 Food, beverages, and tobacco products.

    42 Textiles, clothing, footwear, and leather goods.

    47 Paper and printing.

    49 Rubber and plastics.

    48 Other manufacturing.

I. Dollar–Wolff Database (continued)

B. *Capital stock data availability by country and industry*
   Belgium: Industries 13, 15, 17, 36, 47, 48, 49: 1963–84; Industry 42:1963–72, 1973–84; total manufacturing: 1963–71, 1974–83.
   Canada: All industries, 1963–82 and 1984.
   France: All industries, 1963–84.
   Germany: All industries, 1963–84.
   Italy: All industries, 1963–84.
   Japan: All industries except 15 and 49: 1965–84; Industry 15: 1975–84.
   Netherlands: Industries 15, 25, 28, 36, 42, 48: 1963–83; Industry 19: 1963–71, 1973–84;
   Industry 47: 1963–76, 1978–84; All manuf. 1963–71, 1974–77, 1979–83.
   United Kingdom: Industries: 13, 15, 21–23, 25, 28, 36, 48, 49: 1963–83; Industries 17, 19, 42, 47, and All Manuf.: 1963–71, 1973–83.
   United States: All industries, 1963–84.

Sources:

Belgium: Eurostat worksheets.
Canada: For 1983 and 1984, Statistics Canada, Science, Technology and Capital Stock Division, *Fixed Capital Flows and Stocks,* September 1987; other years are from Statistics Canada worksheets.
France: Eurostat worksheets.
Germany: Eurostat worksheets.
Italy: Eurostat worksheets.
Japan: Economic Planning Agency, Department of National Accounts, Economic Research Institute, *Gross Capital Stock of Private Enterprises, 1965–86,* February 1988.
Netherlands: Eurostat worksheets.
United Kingdom: Eurostat worksheets.
United States: John C. Musgrave, "Fixed Reproducible Tangible Wealth in the United States: Revised Estimates," *Survey of Current Business,* January 1986, pp. 51–75; and John C. Musgrave, "Fixed Reproducible Tangible Wealth in the United States, 1982–1985," *Survey of Current Business,* August 1986, pp. 36–39.

C. *Employment data availability by country and industry*
   Belgium: All industries except 19, 21–23, 25, 28: 1963–84.
   Canada: All industries, 1963, 1965–84.
   France: All industries, 1963, 1965–84.
   Germany: All industries, 1965–83.
   Italy: All industries, 1967–82.
   Japan: All industries, 1963, 1965–83.
   Netherlands: All industries except 13, 17, 21–23, 49: 1963, 1965–84.
   United Kingdom: All industries, 1963, 1965–83.
   United States: All industries, 1963, 1965–83.

Source: United Nations, *Yearbook of Industrial Statistics,* various years.

D. *Value-added data availability by country and industry*
   Belgium: All industries except 19, 21–23, 25, 28: 1963, 1965–83.
   Canada: All industries, 1963, 1965–84.
   France: All industries, 1963, 1965–84.
   Germany: All industries, 1965–82.
   Italy: All industries, 1963, 1965–82.
   Japan: All industries, 1963, 1965–83.
   Netherlands: All industries except 13, 17, 21–23, 49: 1963, 1965–82.
   United Kingdom: All industries, 1963, 1968, 1970–83.
   United States: All industries, 1963, 1965–83.

Source: United Nations, *Yearbook of Industrial Statistics,* various years.

E. *Employee compensation data availability by country and industry*
   Belgium: All industries except 19, 21–23, 25, 28: 1963, 1965–82.
   Canada: All industries, 1963, 1965–84.
   France: Not available.

Appendix: Data Sources and Availability *(continued)*

I. Dollar–Wolff Database (continued)

Germany: All industries, 1965–83.
Italy: All industries, 1968–82.
Japan: All industries, 1963, 1965–83.
Netherlands: All industries except 13, 17, 21–23, 49: 1963, 1965–82.
United Kingdom: All industries, 1963, 1965–83.
United States: All industries, 1963, 1965–83.

Source: United Nations, *Yearbook of Industrial Statistics,* various years.

F. *Documentation of industry wage share calculations*
Belgium: All industries except 19, 21–23, 25, 28: 1963, 1965–82.
Canada: All industries, 1963, 1965–82.
France: Not available.
Germany: All industries, 1965–82.
Italy: All industries, 1968–82.
Japan: All industries, 1963, 1965–82.
Netherlands: All industries except 13, 17, 21–23, 49: 1963, 1965–82.
United Kingdom: All industries, 1963, 1968, 1970–82.
United States: All industries, 1963, 1965–82.

Source: United Nations, *Yearbook of Industrial Statistics,* various years.

Industry wage shares for each country were calculated as the ratio of employee compensation to value added, averaged over all the years between 1963 and 1982 for which the relevant data are available. The two exceptions are (1) for France, the international average wage share is used for each industry; and (2) for NACE 49 in Belgium, because the calculated wage share exceeded 1, the wage share for Belgian manufacturing as a whole is used.

II. OECD Database

All data are from the OECD International Sectoral Databank on microcomputer diskette.
A. *Manufacturing industry codes*
  1. Food, beverages, and tobacco.
  2. Textiles.
  3. Wood and wood products.
  4. Paper, printing, and publishing.
  5. Chemicals.
  6. Nonmetal mineral products.
  7. Basic metal products.
  8. Machinery and equipment.
  9. Other manufactured products.

B. *Capital stock data availability by country and industry*
  Australia: Total manufacturing, 1970–85.
  Belgium: All industries except Industry 3, 1970–85.
  Canada: All industries, 1970–85.
  Denmark: All industries, 1970–85.
  Finland: Total manufacturing, 1970–85.
  France: All industries except Industry 3, 1970–85.
  Germany: All industries, 1970–85.
  Italy: All industries except Industry 9, 1970–85.
  Japan: All industries except Industry 3, 1970–85.
  Netherlands: All industries except Industry 3, 1970–83; total manufacturing, 1984–85.
  Norway: All industries, 1970–85.

Sweden: All industries, 1970–85.
United Kingdom: All industries except Industry 3, 1970–85.
United States: All industries, 1970–85.

C. *Employment data availability by country and industry*
Australia: Total manufacturing, 1970–85.
Belgium: All industries except Industry 3, 1970–85.
Canada: All industries, 1970–85.
Denmark: All industries, 1970–85.
Finland: All industries, 1970–85.
France: All industries except Industry 3, 1970–85.
Germany: All industries, 1970–85.
Italy: All industries, 1970–85.
Japan: All industries except Industry 3, 1970–85.
Netherlands: All industries, 1970–85.
Norway: All industries, 1970–85.
Sweden: All industries, 1970–85.
United Kingdom: All industries except Industry 3, 1970–85.
United States: All industries, 1970–85.

D. *GDP data availability by country and industry*
Australia: Total manufacturing, 1970–85.
Belgium: All industries except Industry 3, 1970–85.
Canada: All industries, 1970–85.
Denmark: All industries, 1970–85.
Finland: All industries, 1970–85.
France: All industries except Industry 3, 1970–85.
Germany: All industries, 1970–85.
Italy: All industries, 1970–85.
Japan: All industries except Industry 3, 1970–85.
Netherlands: All industries except Industry 3, 1970–85.
Norway: All industries, 1970–85.
Sweden: All industries, 1970–85.
United Kingdom: All industries except Industry 3, 1970–85.
United States: All industries, 1970–85.

E. *Employee compensation data availability by country and industry*
Australia: Total manufacturing, 1970–85.
Belgium: All industries except Industry 3, 1970–85.
Canada: All industries, 1970–85.
Denmark: All industries, 1970–85.
Finland: All industries, 1970–85.
France: All industries except Industry 3, 1970–85.
Germany: All industries, 1970–85.
Italy: All industries, 1970–85.
Japan: All industries except Industry 3, 1970–85.
Netherlands: All industries except Industry 3, 1970–85.
Norway: All industries, 1970–85.
Sweden: All industries, 1970–85.
United Kingdom: All industries except Industry 3, 1970–85.
United States: All industries, 1970–85.

F. *Documentation of industry wage share calculations*
Australia: Total manufacturing, 1970–85.
Belgium: All industries except Industry 3, 1970–85.

Appendix: Data Sources and Availability *(continued)*

II. OECD Database (continued)

Canada: All industries, 1970–85.
Denmark: All industries, 1970–85.
Finland: All industries, 1970–85.
France: All industries except Industry 3, 1970–85.
Germany: All industries, 1970–85.
Italy: All industries, 1970–85.
Japan: All industries except Industry 3, 1970–85.
Netherlands: All industries except Industry 3, 1970–85.
Norway: All industries, 1970–85.
Sweden: All industries, 1970–85.
United Kingdom: All industries except Industry 3, 1970–85.
United States: All industries, 1970–85.

Country-specific average wage shares were calculated for each industry on the basis of the longest time span for which data on employee compensation and GDP were available. Exceptions are (1) For industry 8 in the Netherlands, because the calculated wage share exceeded 1, the wage share for the Netherlands' manufacturing sector as a whole is used; and (2) for Industry 9 in Sweden, because the calculated wage share exceeded 1, the wage share for Sweden's manufacturing sector as a whole is used.

The international average wage share was computed for each industry as an unweighted average of country-specific industry average wage shares, except as follows:

1. Food, beverages, and tobacco: All countries except Australia.
2. Textiles: All countries except Australia.
3. Wood and wood products. All except Australia, Belgium, France, Japan and the United Kingdom.
4. Paper, printing, and publishing: All countries except Australia.
5. Chemicals: All countries except Australia.
6. Nonmetal mineral products: All countries except Australia.
7. Basic metal products: All countries except Australia.
8. Machinery and equipment: All countries except Australia and the Netherlands.
9. Other manufactured products: All except Australia and Sweden.

8

Have International Differences in Educational Attainment Levels Narrowed?

FRANK R. LICHTENBERG

Simple models of aggregate production imply that productivity (output per worker or per unit of total input) depends on the "quality" of labor input in general and the distribution of the work force by educational attainment in particular. International variation in (the level and growth rate of) educational attainment should result in variation in (the level and growth rate of) productivity. The purpose of this chapter is to analyze longitudinal, country-level data on educational attainment (and its determinants, enrollment rates) and to consider the "effect" of education differences on international productivity differences.

Data

We have not been able to find data for a large sample of countries on either average educational attainment or the total stock of human capital, although such data exist for the United States and perhaps a few other countries.[1] But both direct and indirect time-series data on the fraction of the adult population in various education groups are available for reasonably large samples of countries.

UNESCO publishes data on the distribution of the adult population by the highest level of schooling completed. These data are derived from population censuses. There are six categories: (1) no schooling, (2) first level (primary)—incomplete; (3) first level (primary)—complete; (4) second level (secondary)—first stage; (5) second level (secondary)—second stage; and (6) third level (tertiary).[2] In two important respects, however, the coverage of the educational attainment data is not uniform. First, for many countries, several categories are aggregated. In particular, (2) and (3) are often combined, as are (4) and (5). The classification scheme that appears to make best use of the data is the following: (1') no schooling, (2') attended primary school—(2) + (3), (3') attended secondary school—(4) + (5), and

(4′) attended tertiary school.[3] Second, not all the attainment distributions of different countries are observed in the same year, and these distributions have changed significantly over time.

In addition to the attainment data, UNESCO publishes data on primary, secondary, and tertiary *enrollment* rates, that is, the fraction of the relevant age group enrolled in school (e.g., the number of children enrolled in primary school divided by the population aged 6 to 11). These data permit us to pursue an alternative approach to measuring educational attainment by country. This approach is less direct, but the enrollment data are in several respects superior to the attainment distributions: They are available for more countries, in identical years, and there are fewer missing data.

The Relationship Between Attainment Rates and Enrollment Rates

Let PRI, SEC, and TER denote a country's primary, secondary, and tertiary enrollment rates, respectively. Let l_1, l_2, l_3, and l_4 denote the fraction of the adult work force whose highest level of educational attainment is no school, primary school, secondary school, and tertiary school, respectively. The l_i are distributed lag functions of the enrollment rates. For simplicity, assume that the age distribution of the population is uniform, that is, that the number of people in each age group is the same. Suppose that if people attend school, they do so k_0 years before entering, and k_1 years before retiring from, the labor force (people work for $k_1 - k_0 + 1$ years). Then the probability that a member of today's labor force has no schooling is the simple average of the probability of children not attending primary school k_0 to k_1 years ago.

$$l_{1t} = (k_1 - k_0 + 1)^{-1} \sum_{k=k_0}^{k_1} (1 - \text{PRI}_{t-k}).$$

Similarly, the fraction of today's labor force that has less than secondary education is

$$l_{1t} + l_{2t} = (k_1 - k_0 + 1)^{-1} \sum_{k=k_0}^{k_1} (1 - \text{SEC}_{t-k}).$$

Hence

$$l_{2t} = (k_1 - k_0 + 1)^{-1} \sum_{k=k_0}^{k_1} (\text{PRI}_{t-k} - \text{SEC}_{t-k}).$$

Moreover,

$$l_{3t} = (k_1 - k_0 + 1)^{-1} \sum_{k=k_0}^{k_1} (\text{SEC}_{t-k} - \text{TER}_{t-k})$$

$$l_{4t} = (k_1 - k_0 + 1)^{-1} \sum_{k=k_0}^{k_1} \text{TER}_{t-k}.$$

The educational-attainment distribution of today's labor force depends on enrollment rates k_0 to k_1 years ago. If people enroll at age 10, enter the labor force at 18, and retire at 65, then today's stock of human capital per worker depends on enrollment rates 8 to 55 years ago.[4]

In the steady state, the attainment rate equals the enrollment rate, for example, l_4 = TER. But the attainment rate adjusts slowly to changes in the enrollment rate. Suppose that the primary school enrollment rate had remained at 60 percent for many years and increased in 1992 to 70 percent, remaining permanently at that level. The fraction of the work force with no schooling, l_1, would remain at 40 percent until the year 2000, when it would gradually begin to decline by about 0.2 percentage points per year. Thus l_1 would not reach its new steady-state value of 30 percent until the year 2047.

Trends in Educational Attainment and Enrollment, 1960–1985

Aggregate Data

We begin by examining time-series data on enrollment rates for aggregates of countries: the world, developed countries, and developing countries (as defined by UNESCO). A comparison of the series for developed and developing countries provides some evidence on the extent of convergence in human capital investment. Later, we will analyze both enrollment and attainment data for individual countries.

Table 8-1 presents data on enrollment rates by level of education for the world, developed countries, and developing countries, quinquenially for 1960 to 1985. These aggregate rates are population-weighted averages of country-specific rates. Worldwide enrollment rates, particularly primary and secondary rates, increased substantially during the quarter-century between 1960 and 1985: The primary rate increased from

Table 8-1. Gross Enrollment Rates by Level of Education

Area	Year	Gross Enrollment Rates (%)		
		Primary	Secondary	Tertiary
World total	1960	80.7	27.5	5.2
	1965	85.0	32.1	7.4
	1970	83.8	35.2	8.8
	1975	94.7	43.1	10.3
	1980	94.4	45.1	11.2
	1985	98.8	46.3	11.8
Developed countries	1960	101.5	62.1	13.3
	1965	100.3	74.7	19.2
	1970	100.1	78.6	23.2
	1975	100.7	83.5	28.1
	1980	101.8	83.9	29.9
	1985	102.3	87.9	33.1
Developing countries	1960	72.8	15.1	2.0
	1965	79.8	17.5	2.7
	1970	78.6	22.4	3.1
	1975	93.1	31.4	4.3
	1980	92.7	35.8	5.4
	1985	97.8	37.7	6.4

Source: 1987 UNESCO Statistical Yearbook, Table 2.10.

Table 8-2. Public Expenditure on Education as
Percentage of GNP

Area	1970	1975	1980	1985
World total	5.2	5.6	5.6	5.8
Developed countries	5.7	6.1	6.1	6.2
Developing countries	2.9	3.5	3.8	4.1

Source: 1987 UNESCO Statistical Yearbook, Table 2.12.

81 to 99 percent; the secondary rate from 28 to 46 percent; and the tertiary rate from 5 to 12 percent. All three enrollment rates were higher for developed countries in 1960 than they were for developing countries. Moreover, the *growth rate* (*percentage* rate of change) of the enrollment rates between 1960 and 1985 was higher for developing countries than it was for developed countries. In other words, the *ratio* of developing-country to developed-country rates increased in all three cases. In this sense, enrollment rates (which are the "leading indicators" of attainment rates) "reverted toward the mean." Mean reversion is a necessary, but not a sufficient condition, for convergence. In the case of secondary and tertiary enrollment, however, the difference between the developing- and developed-country growth rates was not sufficiently high to prevent the *absolute* difference in enrollment rates from increasing.[5] For example, the tertiary enrollment rate for developed countries increased by 19.8 percentage points, from 13.3 to 33.1 percent, whereas the rate for developing countries increased by only 4.4 percentage points, from 2.0 to 6.4 percent. The *percentage* difference between developed-country and developing-country rates declined for all three levels of education, but the *absolute* difference fell only in the case of primary enrollment. (Primary enrollment scarcely increased in the developed countries, since there was already virtually universal enrollment there in 1960.)

Data on public expenditure on education as a percent of GNP (PUB.EDU/Y), presented in Table 8-2, confirm that there has been a worldwide increase in the human-capital investment rate and that the increase has been greater in developing countries. The ratio of developing- to developed-country investment rates increased from about 1:2 in 1970 to 2:3 in 1985. These investment rates are determined in part by primary enrollment rates. But these figures must be interpreted with caution, since slow relative productivity growth in the education sector of the economy has caused the real cost of education—as measured, for example, by the cost per pupil day—to rise continuously almost everywhere. Thus the share of calculated educational investment as a percentage of GDP would have risen even if enrollment rates had remained constant.

Country-Level Data

Three different kinds of statistics can be used to examine changes in the distribution of education among countries: attainment rates by year, attainment rates by cohort, and enrollment rates by year. Attainment rates by year are the most direct indicator of changes in the distribution of human capital per worker. Unfortunately, data for two or more years are available for only 55 countries. Moreover, the attainment rates are measured in different years for different countries. For each of these countries, we refer to the earliest and latest available attainment rates as the "initial" and "final" attainment rates, respectively. The average year for the "initial" observations is 1958, and the average year for the "final" observations is 1979.

Attainment rates by cohort are available for a larger sample of (about 70 to 80) countries. We analyze and compare the attainment rates of two cohorts: young (in the mid-1960s) adults (people who were 25 to 34 years old then) and older adults (people who were 55 to 64 years old then). Because these cohorts are about 30 years apart, the "time window" provided by cohort differences in educational attainment is about 50 percent longer than the time window provided by initial-versus-final year differences.

We also examine data on enrollment rates for the 1960s and 1980s. As we discussed earlier, attainment rates are weighted averages of lagged enrollment rates. If the enrollment rate is increasing, one would expect the attainment rate to be both below the enrollment rate and increasing. One might hypothesize an adjustment equation of the form $(a_{t+k} - a_t) = \Theta(e_t - a_t)$, where a_t and e_t are, respectively, the attainment and enrollment rates at time t and $\Theta > 0$. The difference between today's enrollment and attainment rates helps predict the future increase in attainment rates.

Table 8-3 presents summary statistics for all three indicators of education. The top panel displays data on educational attainment in initial and final years. These figures refer to the fraction of the adult population with at least the indicated amount of education. For example, in the initial year the mean share of the population with at least primary education was 53 percent, and the share with at least secondary education was 9 percent. We may infer that 47 percent (= 100% − 53%) had less than primary education and that 44 percent (= 53% − 9%) had completed primary, but not secondary, education.

Mean educational attainment increased substantially during the 1960s and 1970s. The mean percentage of adults who had completed at least primary, secondary, and tertiary (higher) education increased from 53, 9, and 2 percent in the initial year to 69, 23, and 5 percent, respectively, in the final year. Because there were substantial increases in mean attainment, in order to judge whether educational attainment tended to converge (attainment became less unequally distributed), we should "adjust" for mean differences by using the coefficient of variation (cv) and/or the standard deviation of the logarithm (sd-log) of the attainment rate. To test formally the null hypothesis of no convergence, we compute the statistic—(sd-log (initial)))/(sd-log (final)))^2—which is distributed $F_{n-1,n-1}$.

For all three education levels, both cv and sd-log were lower in the final year than in the initial year. But only in the case of primary attainment can we reject the null hypothesis of no convergence at the 5 percent level of significance. The secondary initial-to-final attainment ratio is only marginally significantly greater than one (prob. value = .08), and the tertiary ratio is completely insignificant. Apparently the upper tail of the attainment distribution has converged much more slowly than the rest of the distribution.

The impression produced by the data on educational attainment by cohort in Panel B of the table is remarkably similar. The means and standard deviations for the 55- to 64-year-olds in the mid-1960s are close to the corresponding figures for the entire adult population in the late 1950s (the "initial" numbers in Panel A), and the statistics for mid-1960s 25-to 34-year-olds are similar to the ("final") figures for the

Table 8-3. Summary Statistics: Country-level Educational Attainment and Enrollment Rates

	Mean	S.D.	C.V.	S.D. (ln)	F-stat. (prob.)
A. Attainment rates by year					
Primary (N = 55)					
initial[a]	.53	.27	.51	.82	2.69
final[b]	.69	.25	.36	.50	(.0004)
Secondary (N = 55)					
initial	.09	.09	.95	.93	1.61
final	.23	.17	.73	.73	(.0842)
Tertiary (N = 55)					
initial	.02	.02	1.26	1.21	1.11
final	.05	.06	1.19	1.15	(.6938)
B. Attainment rates by cohort					
Primary (N ≈ 70)					
old[c]	.45	.31	.70	1.16	2.17
young[d]	.63	.31	.49	.79	(.0016)
Secondary (N ≈ 82)					
old	.10	.11	1.08	1.34	1.53
young	.21	.20	.94	1.08	(.0568)
Tertiary (N ≈ 76)					
old	.02	.02	1.28	1.47	1.19
young	.04	.04	1.13	1.35	(.4597)
C. Enrollment rates by year					
Primary (N ≈ 118)					
1960	.72	.35	.49	.75	5.31
1985	.92	.25	.27	.32	(.0000)
Secondary (N = 117)					
1960	.20	.21	1.05	1.47	2.82
1985	.48	.30	.62	.88	(.0000)
Tertiary (N ≈ 100)					
1965	.05	.07	1.26	2.82	2.82
1988	.15	.14	.95	1.68	(.0000)

[a]The average year for the "initial" observations is 1958.

[b]The average year for the "final" observations is 1979.

[c]"Old" refers to people 55 to 64 years old in about 1960.

[d]"Young" refers to people 25 to 34 years old in about 1960.

Sources: Attainment data: UNESCO publications. Enrollment data: Barro and Wolf database (primary, secondary), *World Development Indicators* (tertiary).

entire population in the late 1970s. Again, the convergence test statistic is highly significant for primary attainment, marginally significant for secondary attainment, and insignificant for tertiary attainment.

Enrollment statistics are reported in Panel C. A comparison of the means in Panel A with those in Panel C reveals that there is a long mean lag between enrollment and attainment rates. The 1960 or 1965 enrollment rates are substantially above the initial attainment rates and are approximately equal to the final attainment rates; it takes a couple of decades for attainment rates to catch up to enrollment rates.

The secondary and tertiary, as well as the primary, enrollment rates exhibit a marked tendency towards convergence.

Comparison with Investment in Physical Capital

The rate of investment in *physical* capital also increased in the postwar period, but not as rapidly as did the rate of human capital investment.[6] The (GDP-weighted) average ratio of fixed investment to GDP (I/Y) for the entire world was as follows:

Year	I/Y
1950	17.9%
1955	18.7
1960	19.4
1965	20.3
1970	21.8
1975	21.4
1980	22.5
1985	22.3

Between 1970 and 1985, the PUB.EDU/Y increased five times as fast as I/Y, 11.5 as opposed to 2.3 percent.[7]

To determine whether the rate of investment in physical capital converged, we calculated the following statistics on I/Y in 1960 and 1985:

Year	N	Mean	S.D.	C.V.	S.D. (ln)
1960	119	.168	.105	.625	.817
1985	138	.183	.090	.492	.651

The F-statistic (the squared ratio of the standard deviations of the log of I/Y) is 1.57, which is significant at the .01 level. Thus we can reject the null hypothesis that the rate of investment in physical capital did not converge during the postwar period.

The Effect of Educational Attainment on Productivity

There are two different ways in which human capital can be incorporated in the production function.[8] The first is to specify the production function as follows:

$$Y = K^{\alpha}H^{\beta}L^{(1-\alpha-\beta)} \tag{8-1}$$

where

Y = output
K = stock of physical capital
H = stock of human capital
L = quantity of "raw labor."

This approach is discussed by Uzawa, Lucas, Romer, and others. In practice, L can be thought of as the number of workers (or hours worked), and H as the total number of person years of education embodied in those workers. Then the logarithm of output per worker is

$$ln\ y = \alpha\ ln\ k + \beta\ ln\ h \qquad (8\text{-}2)$$

where $y \equiv Y/L$, $k \equiv K/L$, and $h \equiv H/L$. The average number of years of schooling of the work force might serve as a proxy for h, the human capital per worker.

Under the second approach, the production function is specified as follows:

$$Y = K^{\Theta}E^{1-\Theta} \qquad (8\text{-}3)$$
$$= K^{\Theta}[L_1^{(1-\mu)}L_2^{\mu}]^{1-\Theta}$$

where $E \equiv L_1^{(1-\mu)}L_2^{\mu} =$ "effective labor input"
$L_1 =$ number of workers with "low" (or no) schooling
$L_2 \equiv L - L_1 =$ number of workers with "high" schooling.[9]

We may define the average "quality," Z, of the work force as the quantity of effective labor input per worker:

$$Z \equiv E/L$$
$$= [L_1^{(1-\mu)}L_2^{\mu}]/[L^{(1-\mu)}L^{\mu}] \qquad (8\text{-}4)$$
$$= (1 - l_2)^{(1-\mu)}l_2^{\mu}$$

where $l_2 \equiv L_2/L =$ the employment share of workers with high schooling.

Let MP_i and w_i denote the marginal product and wage rate, respectively, of labor of type i ($i = 1, 2$), and let $w \equiv l_1 w_1 + l_2 w_2$ denote the (weighted) average wage rate of all workers. The hypothesis that $MP_2 > MP_1$ implies that $\mu > l_2$: The elasticity of E with respect to L_2 exceeds the employment share of workers with high schooling. If workers are paid their marginal products, that is, if the private and social returns to education are equal, then $\mu = l_2 \cdot (w_2/w)$: The output elasticity equals the employment share times the wage rate relative to the average wage. Equality of private and social returns also implies that $\mu/(1 - \mu) = (l_2/(1 - l_2)) \cdot (w_2/w_1)$: The ratio of output elasticities equals the ratio of employment shares times the relative wage. If there are positive externalities from education—if the social returns exceed the private returns—then $\mu > l_2 \cdot (w_2/w)$ and $\mu/(1 - \mu) > (l_2/(1 - l_2)) \cdot (w_2/w_1)$.

In this model, the logarithm of output per worker is

$$ln\ y = \Theta\ ln\ k + (1 - \Theta)[(1 - \mu)\ ln\ (1 - l_2) + \mu\ ln\ l_2]. \qquad (8\text{-}5)$$

The percentage response of per-capita output to a unit increase (from 0 to 100 percent) in l_2 is

$$(d\ ln\ y)/(d\ l_2) = (1 - \Theta)[(\mu/l_2) - ((1 - \mu)/(1 - l_2))] \qquad (8\text{-}6)$$

which is positive as long as $\mu > l_2$. If $MP_i = w_i$ for both i, then

$$(d\ ln\ y/(dl_2) = (1 - \Theta)[(w_2 - w_1)/w].$$

Both models (8-1) and (8-3) imply that there is a positive relationship between per-capita income and educational attainment, but the functional form of this relationship differs among models: In Equation 8-2, y is a function of *average* educational attainment, whereas in Equation 8-5, y is a function of the employment shares of the education groups.[10] Either model can be used to determine the effects of changes in the distribution across countries of physical and human capital on the international distribution of productivity. Equation 8-2, for example, implies that

$$\frac{\text{var}(ln\ y_0)}{\text{var}(ln\ y_1)} = \frac{\alpha^2\ \text{var}(ln\ k_0) + \beta^2\ \text{var}(ln\ h_0) + 2\alpha\beta\ \text{cov}(ln\ k_0, ln\ h_0)}{\alpha^2\ \text{var}(ln\ k_1) + \beta^2\ \text{var}(ln\ h_1) + 2\alpha\beta\ \text{cov}(ln\ k_1, ln\ h_1)} \quad (8\text{-}7)$$

where var( ) denotes the variance across countries and the subscripts 0 and 1 refer to two different years. An analogous expression can be derived from Equation 8-5. Equation 8-7 reveals that in order to determine the effect of physical and human capital accumulation on international income inequality, we require estimates of production–function parameters, as well as time-series data on the joint distribution of physical and human capital.

Human-capital parameters such as β or μ can be estimated in two alternative ways: (1) by using data on income shares or wage rates by education category (provided we are willing to assume that workers are paid their marginal products) and (2) by econometric estimation of the production function.

Wage Rates by Education

Unfortunately, there appear to exist only fragmentary international data on earnings by education category; UNESCO does not publish earnings data. Psacharopoulos (1984, p. 342) reported estimates for four countries of the "returns to primary school": the ratio of the mean earnings of private-sector employees with primary educational qualifications to the mean earnings of private-sector employees with less than primary educational qualifications. The estimates are Portugal—1.12, Brazil—1.92, Colombia—1.48, and Malaysia—1.13; the mean of these estimates is 1.41.

More complete data exist for the United States and some other industrialized countries. The U.S. Bureau of the Census reports the following mean total money annual earnings in 1975 of persons by highest level of educational attainment:

Elementary:	total	$5964
	<8 years	5419
	8 years	6510
High school:	total	7462
	1–3 years	6380
	4 years	7843
College:	total	11,174

Since the Census Bureau does not report the mean earnings of persons with no schooling, we can define just three categories—primary, secondary, and tertiary—and use $5,419 as the wage rate of the primary school category, $7,462 as that of the secondary school category, and $11,174 as that of the tertirary school category. The secondary/primary wage ratio is 7,462/5,419 = 1.38, and the tertiary/primary ratio is 11,174/5,419 = 2.06.

Katz and Revenga (1989) reported time-series data on the earnings of college relative to high school in both the United States and Japan. They found that in the United States this ratio fell from about 1.35 in 1970 to 1.16 in 1978 and rose to 1.5 in 1985. In Japan, it declined from 1.2 in 1967 to about 1.1 in 1984.[11] Thus wage differentials (and perhaps income shares) vary substantially across countries and over time.

Estimates of Production Functions Incorporating Human Capital

Mankiw, Romer, and Weil (1990) estimated the parameters of Equation 8-1 even though they lacked data on the total or per-capita stock of human capital (H or h).[12] Instead, they used an indicator of the rate of (gross) investment in human capital (I^H); H is related to I^H via the accumulation equation $H_t = (1 - \delta_H) H_{t-1} + I_t^H$. The indicator is the number of people enrolled in secondary school divided by the working-age population. Mankiw, Romer, and Weil show that under certain assumptions, a country's steady-state value of y is determined by the shares of output devoted to physical and human capital investment and by its rate of population growth. They estimated an equation in which both α and β, in principle, are identified (indeed, overidentified).[13]

Mankiw, Romer, and Weil (1990) argue that their model is consistent with the finding that among all countries, productivity (output per capita) levels have not converged, that is, with the finding that the coefficient β_{d0} in the regression

$$y_1 - y_0 = \beta_{d0} y_0 + u \qquad (8\text{-}8)$$

is insignificant, where $y_1 \equiv$ log (productivity in 1985) and $y_0 \equiv$ log (productivity in 1960).[14] (We use d to represent the dependent variable $y_1 - y_0$, and we suppress the intercept for simplicity.)[15] However, Mankiw, Romer, and Weil implicitly assume that the determinants of steady-state income are stable over time, in particular, that these determinants are not converging. But this assumption appears to be inconsistent with the data, since we saw earlier that national rates of investment in both human and physical capital appear to have converged.[16]

The Mankiw, Romer, and Weil model suggests that convergence in enrollment rates should contribute to convergence in per-capita income. Their reduced-form equation for steady-state income per capita is

$$ln\,[Y(t)/L(t)] = ln\,A(0) + gt - [(\alpha + \beta)/(1 - \alpha - \beta)]\,ln\,(n + g + d)$$
$$+ [\alpha/(1 - \alpha - \beta)]\,ln\,(s_k) + [\beta/(1 - \alpha - \beta)]\,ln\,(s_h)$$

where $A(0)$ is the initial level of productivity, g is the exogenous rate of labor-augmenting productivity growth, n is the population growth rate, d is the rate of depreciation of physical capital, s_k is the physical capital saving rate, and s_h is the human capital saving rate. Their proxy for s_h is roughly proportional to the secondary school enrollment rate, SEC. We want to consider the effect of ceteris paribus variation in s_h, so suppose that s_h is the only variable on the right-hand side that varies across countries. Then

$$\text{s.d.}\{ln\,[Y(t)/L(t)]\} \approx [\beta/(1 - \alpha - \beta)]\,\text{s.d.}\{ln\,(\text{SEC})\}.$$

Substituting Mankiw, Romer, and Weil's estimates $\alpha = \beta = \frac{1}{3}$, we obtain

$$\text{s.d. } \{ln\,[Y(t)/L(t)]\} \approx \text{s.d. } \{ln\,(\text{SEC})\}.$$

This implies that the 40 percent reduction in s.d. $\{ln\,(\text{SEC})\}$ between 1960 and 1985 should result in a similar decline in s.d. $\{ln\,[Y/L]\}$.

The Effect of Enrollment Convergence on Income Convergence

In this section we pursue an alternative approach to determining whether convergence in enrollment rates should contribute to future convergence in per-capita income, and if so, how much. To do this, we will estimate (some of) the parameters of the following production function:

$$Y = K^{\theta}E^{1-\theta} \tag{8-9}$$
$$= K^{\theta}[L_1^{(1-\mu2-\mu3-\mu4)}\,L_2^{\mu2}L_3^{\mu3}L_4^{\mu4}]^{1-\theta},$$

where $E \equiv [L_1^{(1-\mu2-\mu3-\mu4)}L_2^{\mu2}L_3^{\mu3}L_4^{\mu4}]$ = "effective labor input"
  L_1 = the number of workers with no schooling
  L_2 = the number of workers with primary schooling
  L_3 = the number of workers with secondary schooling
  L_4 = the number of workers with tertiary schooling.

This leads to the following expression for the logarithm of output per worker:

$ln\,y$
  $= \Theta\,ln\,k + (1 - \Theta)[(1 - \mu2 - \mu3 - \mu4)\,ln\,l_1 + \mu2\,ln\,l_2 + \mu3\,ln\,l_3 + \mu4\,ln\,l_4]$

where $l_i \equiv L_i/(\Sigma_i L_i)$; $i = 1, \ldots 4$; y is defined as output per capita in 1985; and l_1 through l_4 are defined as follows:

$$l_1 = 1 - \text{PRI}$$
$$l_2 = \text{PRI} - \text{SEC}$$
$$l_3 = \text{SEC} - \text{TER}$$
$$l_4 = \text{TER}$$

where PRI and SEC are the primary and secondary enrollment rates, respectively, in 1960 and TER is the tertiary enrollment rate in 1965. We are assuming, in other words, that the fraction of the adult population with no schooling in 1985 is equal to the fraction of 6- to 11-year-old children who did not attend primary school in 1960.

Unfortunately, data on k (physical capital stock per worker in 1985) are not available for most countries, so this relevant regressor (which is likely to be correlated with the l_i's) must be excluded from the equation. We may be able to reduce the bias produced by excluding k by including the "lagged dependent variable": the logarithm of per-capita income in 1960. Countries with high incomes in 1960 were likely to have high investment rates during the subsequent quarter-century, hence high values of k in 1985. Including the value of y in 1960 as a regressor also controls for any permanent, or slowly changing, unobserved determinants of per-capita output other than k. The regression of y_{1985} on 1960 enrollment rates and y_{1960} allows us to answer the following question: Given a country's income in 1960, how much higher would its income be in 1985 if it had high enrollment rates in 1960?

It is reasonable to hypothesize that output per capita depends positively on both the quality and the quantity of schooling. One dimension of the quality of education is the number of teachers per student. We therefore augment Equation 8-9 to include the logarithms of teachers per student in both primary and secondary school.[17]

Estimates of the regression of 1985 per-capita income on 1960 enrollment rates and teacher/student ratios are reported in Table 8-4. The equation in Column 1 does not include 1960 income as a regressor. The coefficients on $ln\ l_2$, $ln\ l_3$, and $ln\ l_4$ are highly statistically significant. The coefficient on the primary teacher/student ratio is also positive and significant: Better-quality schooling in 1960 is associated with higher income in 1985. The "returns to schooling" implied by the estimates in Column 1 are extremely large, perhaps implausibly so. Recall that we can calculate the relative marginal product (RMP) of each category of worker by dividing its associated elasticity by its mean employment share. These employment shares are displayed in Column 3. These estimates imply that the marginal product of workers with no schooling is negative and that the MP of college-edcuated workers is 20 times as large as the MP of workers with a primary education. We saw earlier that in the United States, the wage rate of college-educated workers is about twice as high as that of workers with a primary education. Wage differentials may be higher in other countries, and MP differentials may be greater than wage differentials (i.e., the social returns to education may exceed the private returns), but the 20-to-1 MP ratio stretches credulity. The returns to education may be overestimated in Column 1 owing to the *simultaneous-equations*

Table 8-4. Regression of 1985 Per-Capita Income on 1960–1965 Enrollment Rates

Regressor	(1)	(2)	(3)	(2)/(3)
ln(1-PRI)	−.017	.064	.28	.23
	(0.6)	(2.4)		
ln(PRI-SEC)	.190	.331	.52	.64
	(2.2)	(4.2)		
ln(SEC-TER)	.503	.429	.15	2.86
	(5.3)	(5.3)		
ln(TER)	.243	.114	.05	2.28
	(3.7)	(1.9)		
$ln(T_p/S_p)$	.607	.338		
	(2.2)	(1.4)		
$ln(T_s/S_s)$	.085	−.039		
	(0.5)	(0.3)		
$ln(y_{1960})$		.594		
		(5.6)		

Notes: The dependent variable is y_{1985}, the per-capita income in 1985. PRI and SEC are the primary and secondary enrollment rates in 1960, and TER is the tertiary enrollment rate in 1965. T_p/S_p and T_s/S_s are the number of teachers per student in primary and secondary school, respectively, in 1960, and y_{1960} is the per-capita income in 1960. The figures in Column 3 are the mean values of the antilogs of the corresponding regressors, for example, mean(1-PRIM)= .28. t-statistics are in parentheses.

bias. In addition to education's having a positive effect on income (via the production function, as we have hypothesized), income may have a positive effect on education. The regression coefficients that we have estimated may be mixtures of output (supply) elasticities and income (demand) elasticities. The fact that we are regressing income in 1985 on enrollment rates in 1960 should reduce the importance of the ("feedback") effect of income on education but not eliminate it entirely, since there is relatively high serial correlation in per-capita income.

The second column of Table 8-4 shows estimates of the model generalized to include the lagged dependent variable, per-capita income in 1960. The education-MP profile implied by these estimates, although still quite steep, is much flatter than that implied by Column 1. The coefficients on the two lowest education groups are positive and significant. These estimates imply that the MP of a worker with primary school education is almost three times as high as the MP of a worker with no schooling and that the MP of a worker with secondary school education is about four times that of a worker with a primary school education. The MP of college-educated workers is estimated to be lower than the MP of high school–educated workers, but the difference between these estimates is not statistically significant.

Let us define PC ("predicted convergence") as the convergence in per-capita income implied by the convergence in enrollment rates documented in Table 8-3. The PC may be calculated as follows:

$$PC \equiv \{\text{s.d.} \ [a_1 \ ln \ (1 - PRI_{1960}) + a_2 \ ln \ (PRI_{1960} - SEC_{1960})$$
$$+ \ a_3 \ ln \ (SEC_{1960} - TER_{1965}) + a_4 \ ln \ (TER_{1965})]\}/\{\text{s.d.} \ [a_1 \ ln \ (1 - PRI_{1985})$$
$$+ \ a_2 \ ln \ (PRI_{1985} - SEC_{1985}) + a_3 \ ln \ (SEC_{1985} - TER_{1988}) + a_4 \ ln \ (TER_{1988})]\}$$

where the a_i ($i = 1, \ldots, 4$) are the "weights" associated with the different education groups. We will perform this calculation using two alternative sets of weights. The first set of weights consists of the estimated coefficients, $\mu 1$ through $\mu 4$ in Column 2 of Table 8-4, which, we have argued, may be interpreted as relative output elasticities. Since the social returns to education (except college education) implied by these elasticities are very large, our calculation should perhaps be viewed as an upper-bound estimate of the income convergence yielded by enrollment convergence.

The second set of weights consists of income shares that we have imputed to each of the four groups using the employment shares shown in Column 3 and the following assumed values of wage rates (relative to the wage rate of workers with a primary education): no schooling—0.71, primary school—1.00, secondary school—1.38, and tertiary school—2.06.[18] The weights based on imputed income shares are $a_1 = .181$, $a_2 = .474$, $a_3 = .189$, and $a_4 = .094$.[19] The income-share approach assigns much larger weights to the two lowest-schooling groups and smaller weights to the two highest groups—particularly secondary school—than does the output-elasticity approach. If the social returns to education exceed the private returns, the income-share approach will yield a lower-bound estimate of the income convergence yielded by enrollment convergence.

The predicted convergence statistics based on these two approaches are as follows:

$$\text{output elasticities } PC = .77/.37 \quad F = 4.44$$
$$= 2.1 \quad (\text{prob.} = .000)$$

income shares $PC = .55/.66$ $F = 1.43$
$= .83$ (prob. $= .114$).

When we use the estimated output elasticities as weights in the index of "labor quality," there is strong support for the hypothesis of convergence of labor quality: The
standard deviation of the index of 1960–65 enrollment rates is over twice as large as
the standard deviation of the index of 1985–88 enrollment rates. The null hypothesis
that changes in enrollment rates did not contribute to convergence in per-capita
income is decisively rejected.

When the index of labor quality is constructed using income shares as weights,
however, the results point in the opposite direction, albeit not as strongly. The standard deviation of the income-weighted index of 1985–88 enrollment rates is about 20
percent greater than that of the 1960–65 enrollment rates, although we are unable to
reject the null hypothesis at the 10 percent significance level.

Why do the two sets of weights yield opposite implications about the impact of
changing enrollment patterns on international income inequality? Because the magnitude, and even the sign, of changes in s.d. $-$ $log(l_i)$ varies greatly across i:

i	$[s.d. - log\,(l_{i0})]/[s.d. - log\,(l_{i1})]$
1	$3.6/3.8 = .95$
2	$0.7/0.8 = .88$
3	$1.3/0.8 = 1.63$
4	$2.7/1.8 = 1.50$

where the subscripts 0 and 1 denote 1960–65 and 1985–88 values, respectively. The
standard deviations of the logarithms (roughly similar to the coefficients of variation)
of the employment shares of the two lowest groups increased slightly, whereas those
of the two highest groups decreased sharply. The income share–weighted index of
labor quality implied mild divergence of income because it gives substantial weight to
the first two groups, whereas the output elasticity–weighted index implied strong convergence because it gives substantial weight to the last two groups.

The apparent ambiguity of these results may reflect a more fundamental problem
of applying the concept of, and tests for, convergence to proportions. Suppose the population was divided into just two groups, for example, literate and illiterate. Suppose
too that between 1960 and 1985, the mean literacy rate increased from .25 to .75 and
the standard deviation remained constant at .25. Then the coefficient of variation of
the literacy rate fell from 1 to ⅓, and so we would conclude that the literacy rate had
converged. But if we looked instead at the illiteracy rate, we would draw exactly the
opposite conclusion, that the coefficient of variation had increased from ⅓ to 1.[20] It is
possible, of course, to construct examples in which the CVs of both the literacy and
the illiteracy rates decrease. Suppose that the mean literacy rate remained constant at
.5, and the standard deviation declined from .25 to .20.[21]

We showed in Table 8-3 that primary, secondary, and tertiary enrollment rates
have converged over time. However, all the complements of these enrollment rates (1
$-$ PRI, 1 $-$ SEC, 1 $-$ TER) have diverged. It is therefore not clear whether education
distributions have been converging.

Summary and Conclusions

All of the data that we examined suggested that both attainment rates and enrollment rates have converged. The convergence has been stronger and more significant for enrollment rates than for attainment rates, and at lower levels of education than at higher levels of education. Convergence in the rate of human capital investment appears to have been accompanied by convergence in the rate of physical capital investment.

We have tried to determine the effect of enrollment convergence on income convergence using estimates of both (1) a production function with human capital, physical capital, and raw labor, and (2) a production function with labor disaggregated into four education categories. The first production function implied that convergence in the secondary school enrollment rate (the proxy for the rate of saving in human capital) should result in a similar degree of convergence in per-capital income. The second production function implied even more rapid income convergence when econometrically estimated output elasticities of different education groups were used. The social returns to primary and secondary schooling implied by these output elasticities were extremely large, however. When we replace these estimated elasticities by income shares derived from (fairly crude) relative wage data, the model predicts that changes in enrollment should result in *divergence* in per-capita income, since the fraction of the population in the two lowest schooling groups has diverged.

Enrollment rates and (to a lesser extent) attainment rates have converged, but the consequences of this for international income inequality depend on the form of the aggregate production function and on the returns to investment in education in many countries. We still have much to learn about these issues.

Notes

1. Time-series data for the United States are presented in Jorgenson and Fraumeni 1989.
2. For some countries, finer classifications—even by single years of schooling completed—are available.
3. Generally, children attend primary school from age 6 to age 11 and secondary school from age 12 to age 17.
4. In practice, the age distribution of the population is not uniform—there are more young people than old people—so the l_{it} are *weighted* averages of past enrollment rates, and recent enrollment rates receive greater weight.
5. The ratio of developing- to developed-country growth rates was smaller than the reciprocal of the ratio of their respective initial (1960) sizes.
6. This is at least partly a result of the tendency (already noted) of the relative cost of investment in human capital to rise in real terms, a tendency not matched by the cost of physical capital.
7. PUB.EDU/Y undoubtedly substantially understates the true share of GNP devoted to human capital investment I^H/Y, since much of the cost of this investment is in the form of forgone earnings of students rather than government outlays. But if the ratio of forgone earnings to government outlays is constant over time, PUB.EDU/Y and I^H/Y will grow at the same rate.
8. For simplicity, we assume in both cases that there are constant returns to scale.
9. This approach can be generalized to $k > 2$ schooling categories.

10. There are, of course, clear links between these two models. The first model attempts to divide total labor income into two components:

$$Y_L = w_1 L_1 + w_2 L_2$$
$$= w_1(L_1 + L_2) + \quad (w_2 - w_1)L_2$$
$$= \text{raw labor income} + \text{return to human capital}$$

This requires the assumption that L_1 workers have zero human capital. If factor markets are competitive, then

$$\beta/(1 - \alpha - \beta) = l_2[(w_2/w_1) - 1].$$

Also, as Mankiw, Romer, and Weil (1990) observe,

$$w_1/w = \text{(raw labor income)/(total labor income)}.$$

The parameters of the second model are related to the same underlying variables (relative employment and wage rates), as follows:

$$\mu/(1 - \mu) = (l_2/(1 - l_2)) \cdot (w_2/w_1).$$

11. They also reported for both countries the following percentages of males with college degrees:

Year	U.S.	Japan
1973	16.1	16.9
1979	20.7	19.5
1987	24.9	24.8

12. In an earlier study, Jamison and Lau (1982) (cited in Psacharopoulos 1984, p. 341) studied the effect of primary education on agricultural productivity. They found that productivity increases by 8.7 percent as a result of a farmer's completing 4 years of primary education.

13. Mankiw, Romer, and Weil (1990) estimated that both α and β are approximately equal to ⅓.

14. As demonstrated in Lichtenberg (1991), $\beta < 0$ is a necessary (but not sufficient) condition for convergence, that is, for var $(y_0) > $ var (y_1).

15. Mankiw, Romer, and Weil (1990) argue that this equation is misspecified, that the reduced-form equation implied by the Solow model is

$$y_1 - y_0 = \beta_{d0 \cdot}(y_0 - y^*) \tag{8-8a}$$
$$= \beta_{d0 \cdot} y_0 - \beta_{d0 \cdot} y^*$$

The Solow model implies that $\beta_{d \cdot 0} < 0$, that a country's growth rate is inversely proportional to its initial deviation from its steady state. OLS (Ordinary Least Squares) estimation of Equation 8-8 yields a consistent estimate of $\beta_{d0 \cdot}$ if, and only if, y^* is uncorrelated with y_0 (e.g., if y^* is invariant across countries):

$$\text{plim } \beta_{d0} = \beta_{d0 \cdot}(1 - \beta_{\cdot 0}),$$

where $\beta_{\cdot 0}$ is the slope from the auxiliary regression of y^* on y_0. Even if $\beta_{d0 \cdot} < 0$ (which Mankiw, Romer, and Weil refer to as "conditional convergence"), one would expect to find "unconditional convergence" ($\beta_{d0} < 0$) only if $\beta_{\cdot 0} < 1$. If $\beta_{\cdot 0} = 1$, then plim $\beta_{d0} = 0$; Mankiw and his colleagues are unable to reject the hypothesis that $\beta_{d0} = 0$. They also estimate an equation based on Equation 8-8a. Instead of including y^* as a regressor, they include the determinants of y^* according to the Solow model: the rates of investment in physical and human capital and the population growth rate. When these regressors are added, the coefficient of y_0 (which may be interpreted as $\beta_{d0 \cdot}$) becomes negative and significant.

Mankiw and his colleagues argue that rejection of the unconditional convergence hypothesis is neither surprising nor inconsistent with the Solow model. That is because the true model of output growth is Equation 8-8a rather than Equation 8-8 and because $\beta_{\cdot 0} = 1$: The difference

$(y_0 - y^*)$ is uncorrelated with y_0. They do not explain why one would expect $(y_0 - y^*)$ to be uncorrelated with y_0.

16. A third determinant of y^*, the rate of population growth, n, does not appear to have converged. We calculated for each of 115 countries the average annual rates of population growth between 1960 and 1970 and 1970 and 1985; we denote these by n_0 and n_1, respectively. Summary statistics are as follows:

	n_0	n_1
mean	.022	.021
std. dev.	.011	.011
c.v.	.514	.519

The coefficient of variation was essentially unchanged, which implies that the population growth rates did not converge.

17. Note that an increase in the teacher/student ratio in primary school, for example, is likely to improve the quality (marginal productivity) of workers in groups l_3 and l_4 as well as the quality of l_2 workers.

18. The first number is based on Psacharapoulos' estimates cited earlier; the latter two on the U.S. Census Bureau data.

19. These weights are normalized to have the same sum as the output elasticities. Inferences about convergence depend only on the relative weights, not on their sum.

20. This is because for a random variable x, s.d.$(1 - x)$ = s.d.(x), and mean $(1 - x)$ = 1 $-$ mean(x).

21. Instead of calculating the s.d. of log(x) or of log$(1 - x)$, where x denotes the literacy rate, one could calculate the s.d. of log$[x/(1 - x)]$, the log ratio of literate to illiterate population. This turns out to be equal to the sum of the s.d. of log(x) and of log$(1 - x)$.

References

Baumol, William. (1986). "Productivity Growth, Convergence, and Welfare: What the Long-Run Data Show." *American Economic Review* 76:1072–85.

Baumol, William, and Edward Wolff. (1988). "Productivity Growth, Convergence, and Welfare: Reply." *American Economic Review* 78:1155–59.

De Long, J. Bradford. (1988). "Productivity Growth, Convergence, and Welfare: Reply." *American Economic Review* 78:1138–54.

Dowrick, Steve, and Duc-Tho Nguyen. (1989). "OECD Comparative Economic Growth 1950–85: Catch-up and Convergence." *American Economic Review* 79:1010–30.

Griliches, Zvi. (1970). "Notes on the Role of Education in Production Functions and Growth Accounting." In W. Lee Hansen, ed., *Education, Income, and Human Capital.* New York: Columbia University Press, for the National Bureau of Economic Research, pp. 71–115.

Jamison, D., and L. Lau. (1982). *Farmer Education and Farm Efficiency.* Baltimore: Johns Hopkins University Press.

Jorgenson, Dale, and Barbara Fraumeni. (1989). "The Accumulation of Human and Nonhuman Capital, 1948–84." In Robert Lipsey and Helen Tice, eds., *The Measurement of Saving, Investment, and Wealth.* Chicago: University of Chicago Press, pp. 227–82.

Katz, Lawrence F., and Ana L. Revenga (1989). "Changes in the Structure of Wages: The United States vs Japan." *Journal of the Japanese and International Economies* 3:522–53.

Kendrick, John, ed. (1984). *International Comparisons of Productivity and Causes of the Slowdown.* Cambridge, MA: American Enterprise Institute/Ballinger.

Lichtenberg, Frank. (forthcoming). "On Testing the Convergence Hypothesis." *Review of Economics and Statistics.*

Lipsey, Robert, and Helen Tice, eds. (1989). *The Measurement of Saving, Investment, and Wealth.* Chicago: University of Chicago Press.

Mankiw, N. Gregory, David Romer, and David Weil. (1990). "A Contribution to the Empirics of Economic Growth." *Quarterly Journal of Economics* 107:407–37.

Pencavel, John. (1990). "Higher Education, Productivity, and Earnings: A Review." Paper, Stanford University, July.

Psacharopoulos, George. (1984). "The Contribution of Education to Economic Growth: International Comparisons." In John Kendrick, ed., *International Comparisons of Productivity and Causes of the Slowdown.* Cambridge, MA: American Enterprise Institute/Ballinger, pp. 335–55.

9

What Explains the Growth of Developing Countries?

MAGNUS BLOMSTRÖM, ROBERT E. LIPSEY, AND MARIO
ZEJAN

The growing literature on income and productivity convergence among countries
seems to suggest that the developing countries have benefited to a relatively small
degree from being backward (see, e.g., Baumol 1986, Baumol, Blackman, and Wolff
1989, and Zind 1991). Over the last 40 years, only a few developing countries have
joined the "convergence club." The majority have gained on the highest-income countries, the United States and Canada, but have lost ground relative to the industrialized
countries as a group.

The failure of many poor countries to gain on the rich ones has recently received
a lot of attention from economists. Some have turned to endogenous growth models,
which are characterized by nondecreasing returns to the reproducible factors of production (see, e.g., Lucas 1988, and Romer 1986). In such models, a country's per-
capita growth rate is uncorrelated with its initial level of income per person. Others,
using standard neoclassical growth models with diminishing returns, still expect an
inverse relation between a country's per-capita income (or productivity) level and its
rate of per-capita income (productivity) growth, but if the country has reached a
threshold level of infrastructural development (see, e.g., Helliwell and Chung 1992,
Mankiw, Romer, and Weil 1992, and Wolff 1991). However, the empirical basis for
both these views is still weak.

One reason for the flurry of recent studies covering many countries is the appearance of the series of articles by Alan Heston and Robert Summers (of which Summers
and Heston 1991 is the latest) in which they extrapolated the results of successive
rounds of the United Nations International Comparison Program (ICP) to the years
between the ICP surveys and before the ICP began, to countries never in the ICP, and,
for countries participating in some years but not in others, to the years of nonpartici-
pation. The extrapolations now cover almost all the countries in the world for the
period since 1950 and are even available on diskettes. That service seems to relieve the

users of the necessity of following the arduous path of earlier writers such as Kuznets, Abramovitz, and Maddison in piecing together fragments of ill-matching national income estimates made by different authors using different techniques and different income concepts.

The new data, convenient as they are, still contain hidden dangers for the users, because they are mostly extrapolations. A third of the developing countries did not participate in even one round of the International Comparison Program. For those countries, every real-income figure is estimated from much weaker sources by relationships found in the participating countries. Even if the extrapolation method is the best possible, the analyst of the data is in danger of extracting the extrapolation formula rather than any independent knowledge.

Even for the countries that did participate in one or more of the ICP rounds, the estimates for other years are extrapolations. They are dependent for their reliability on the quality of their countries' national income accounts and the degree to which their weighting schemes diverge from that of the ICP. Since only 18 developing countries participated in Phase III of the ICP for 1975, and only 7 developing countries participated in Phase II for 1970 and 1973, all the developing countries' income-level data for the 1950s and 1960s and almost all for the 1970s consist of extrapolations. Thus, any defects in a country's estimates of real national income produce errors in the estimates of income levels: An overestimated rate of growth underestimates early-period income levels, and an underestimated growth rate overestimates early income levels. Convergence could be built into the estimating procedure.

Aside from these extrapolation problems that affect most estimates of the effect of initial income levels on growth rates, what we call the *catch-up variable,* we focus on three other aspects of these studies that we thought deserved closer examination. One is the strong influence of the developed countries on most cross-country results to date. For example, Lipsey and Kravis (1987, p. 13) found a strong catch-up relationship among industrial countries from 1950 to 1984, especially when Japan was included, but none for the whole set of 115 developed and developing countries in the Summers and Heston data available at that time. Here, we wish to examine the catch-up and the influences on growth for developing countries separately, although they cover a wide range of income levels and rates of growth, and some are among the great success stories of the last 30 years. The exclusion or inclusion of developed countries is one aspect of the larger issue of sampling, since the results of earlier studies seem to depend considerably on which set of countries is included.

A second issue we study is the influence of changes in the price structure on income changes. Some cross-country studies of growth and convergence have measured the initial distance from the United States in 1980 or 1985 prices, even though the prices in the initial period were vastly different. That is, a high 1960 income measured in 1985 prices does not mean that the country was rich in 1960. This problem has been noted in relation to the oil producers, and most studies have dealt with it by excluding major oil exporters from their regressions (see, e.g., Barro 1991). We were not satisfied with that approach, for two reasons. One is that the list of countries excluded was rather arbitrary; it varied from study to study because there are many oil producers of varying degrees of dependence on that product. The second reason is that since 1960 there have been major price changes in goods other than oil. To incorporate the effects of price changes, including those of oil, on real-income changes, we experimented with two variables. One was the ratio of oil output, measured in physical terms, to real GDP, in the year 1985/86. The second was the ratio of 1960 real GDP per capita relative to the United States in 1985 prices to that at 1960 prices. This was a measure of the effect of changes in the structure of prices in general on the level of real income. The price structure measure performed somewhat better in the equations and is the one reported in the text tables that follow, although it omits much of the effect of price changes, because the ICP price measures are based on expenditure weights rather than value added or production weights.

Finally, we examine the influence on growth of certain interchanges with foreign countries. With respect to one of these, trade, there has been a wide range of views among economists over the last two centuries. These range from the optimistic assessments of Adam Smith and John Stuart Mill to the pessimism of Nurkse and many development theorists after the experience of the 1930s, at least with respect to the situation in the twentieth century. An appraisal by Kravis (1970) took a favorable view of the effects of trade, mixed with skepticism about the importance of trade in any era.

Interchanges among countries can take many forms, including trade, tourism, licensing of technology, foreign direct investment, and exchanges of students. In this chapter we examine two of these, the inflow of direct investment capital from abroad, as a possible measure of the inflow of disembodied technology, and imports of machinery and transport equipment, a possible measure of the inflow of technology embodied in new machinery. Neither measure is more than a rough proxy for the underlying concept, but each seemed to us the best approximation that was almost universally available. The investment flow is a purely financial measure and may not reflect actual operations in a host country of the sort likely to lead to the absorption of technology. This is most obvious for investments in finance subsidiaries, which may not operate at all in the host country but use it only to avoid or reduce taxes. The import measure, although it is confined to machinery and transport equipment, includes many consumer goods (automobiles, home appliances, TV) that do not contribute in any direct way to the technology level of production in the importing country.

We have used per-capita income as our dependent (growth) variable rather than national labor productivity, as some authors have done. These national labor productivity measures, if they cover many countries and all industries, are derived from income measures. The difference between the growth of income per capita and the growth of labor productivity is that the former must be divided by the growth of labor input per capita to calculate the latter. We have chosen to enter an approximation to the growth in labor input per capita as an independent variable, referred to as the *participation rate*. Thus the other independent variables measure the various contributions to growth in income per capita, taking account of changes in labor input per capita.

This chapter is organized as follows. First we examine the effects on growth of several variables not typically studied. These are changes in the world price structure and our two international variables, the inflow of foreign direct investment and imports of machinery and transport equipment. Second we discuss the effects of sample choice on estimates of the relation of various factors to growth. In particular, we ask whether our results differ from those of earlier studies because we are concentrating on developing countries rather than on countries at all stages of development. We also ask whether there is any evidence for the idea of a "convergence club" or, more prop-

erly, a "catch-up club," of higher-income developing countries more responsive or dif-
ferentially responsive to the forces promoting growth. Third we investigate the possibility that biases arising from the method by which the data provided by Summers and
Heston (1991) were calculated could account for the apparent catch-up phenomenon.
Finally, we summarize and draw conclusions from the chapter.

Determinants of Economic Growth

Domestic Variables

The empirical analysis focuses on growth in real income per capita (RGDPCG) for 78
developing countries.[1] Using data from Summers and Heston (1991), supplemented
with data from various other sources (see Appendix Table 9A-1), we first compare the
results for these countries and these variables with those of other studies.

If we relate the catch-up variable (1960 income per capita relative to that of the
United States, labeled GDUS) by itself to growth in per-capita income from 1960 to
1985, no effect is visible. As Table 9-1 shows, there is no pure or "gross" catch-up,
either for the developing countries as a group or for the whole set of countries including
also 23 developed countries.

To test for "conditional" or "net" catch-up among developing countries, Equation 9-1 relates the growth of real per-capita income from 1960 to 1985 in all developing countries in our data set to the initial income level and a collection of other
influences. Two of the independent variables in Equation 9-1, PRICE and PART, refer
to changes between the beginning and the end of the period. Two others (SCND and
INV) are average levels for the whole period, and one (GDUS) is an initial condition.
The use of the averages for the whole period raises the problems of the direction of
causation and possible mutual causation between dependent and independent variables. Using only initial levels of these variables would have avoided that difficulty, but
at the expense of ignoring most of the period's investment in fixed capital formation
and education, a trade-off we thought was unfavorable. The problem, and one possible
solution, were discussed briefly in Lipsey and Kravis (1987), but an adequate solution,
tracing all the possible feedbacks between income growth and the variables treated
here as independent, does not seem to have appeared in the literature so far.

Among the variables for which the coefficients are expected to be positive are the
following:

1. The average (1960–85) ratio of the number of students enrolled in secondary
education to the numbers in the population in the"appropriate" age groups (SCND).
Ratios above 100 percent in some cases suggest that some students are attending this
school level at ages outside the standard range.[2]

2. The ratio of 1960 income in 1985 prices to 1960 income in 1960 prices
(PRICE). This variable measures income changes that are due to changes in the price
structure and is used as an alternative to excluding oil-producing countries.[3]

3. The average (1960–85) ratio of fixed capital formation to GDP, measured in
current purchasing power parities (INV).

4. The change (1960–85) in the labor force participation rate, the ratio of labor
force to total population (PART). This is different from the usual participation rate,

Table 9-1. "Gross" Catch-Up Coefficients for All
Countries and Developing Countries

	Coefficient for Catch-Up Variable	t-Statistic	$\bar{r}^2$	No. of Obs.
All countries	.381	.97	.00	101
Developing countries	4.54	.54	.00	78

Source: Appendix Table 9A-1.

which relates labor force to population of working age. It is intended to catch the effects of demographic changes, particularly birthrates, on the ratio of dependent population to working population.

A negative relation to subsequent growth rates was expected for the variable measuring 1960 real per-capita income relative to that of the United States (GDUS), if low income provided more scope to the gain from the transfer of technology, already developed by the advanced countries.

$$\text{RGDPCG} = \underset{(2.22)}{-6.98} + \underset{(3.70)}{.024} \text{ SCND} + \underset{(2.68)}{.356} \text{ PRICE} + \underset{(2.49)}{.029} \text{ INV}$$

$$+ \underset{(2.23)}{6.9} \text{ PART} - \underset{(3.81)}{3.42} \text{ GDUS} \quad \bar{R}^2 = .40$$

$$\text{(t-statistics in parentheses)} \tag{9.1}$$

All of our expectations regarding the signs of the coefficients were met, with statistically significant coefficients. Two variables were of particular interest to us: PRICE and GDUS. PRICE had a positive coefficient that was statistically significant at the 1 percent level in a two-tailed test. The coefficient of the catch-up variable was also significant despite the lack of association when the other variables were excluded. The initial real-income level relative to the United States (GDUS) carried a significant negative coefficient, suggesting a "conditional" catch-up.

To compare our results with those of other investigators who studied the whole range of countries, we ran the same equations for the combination of our 78 developing countries and 23 developed countries. The differences between those equations and the equations for all developing countries were small (see Table 9-2): There were

Table 9-2. Equations for Growth in Real GDP per Capita
in Developing Countries and in All Countries, 1960–1985

	Developing Countries		All Countries	
	Coefficient	t-Statistic	Coefficient	t-Statistic
Constant	−6.98	2.22	−5.82	2.39
SCND	.024	3.70	.021	4.57
PRICE	.356	2.68	.271	2.51
INV	.029	2.49	.029	2.97
PART	6.90	2.23	5.98	2.48
GDUS	−3.42	3.81	−2.50	5.34

Source: Appendix Table 9A-1.

lower coefficients for catch-up, price structure, and participation in the all-country equation, but all the same variables were again significant.

These results differed from some reported by others for the combination of developed and developing countries. For instance, Wolff (1991, Table 2.4), using a sample of 94 developed and developing countries, got positive coefficients that were strongly significant not only for the investment rate but also for primary education (where we found either weak or no significant coefficients).[4] Similar results were also reported by Mankiw, Romer, and Weil (1992), using a sample of 98 countries.

International Variables

One might suppose that the rate of economic growth of a backward country would depend on the extent of technology transfers from the leading countries and the efficiency with which they are absorbed and diffused. Technology may be transferred to developing countries (and other countries as well) through a variety of channels. In what follows, we add to our equations two of these, the flow of foreign direct investment, as a measure of the flow of disembodied technology, and imports of machinery and transport equipment, as a measure of the inflow of technology embodied in new machinery.

Foreign direct investment by multinational corporations (MNCs) is often suggested as a vehicle for the international diffusion of technology. MNCs have undertaken a major part of the world's research and development (R&D) efforts, and today they control most of the world's advanced technologies. The developing countries, with limited indigenous resources for R&D, are particularly dependent on foreign multinationals for access to modern technology.

Foreign direct investment may influence productivity in the host countries in various ways (see Blomström 1991). Simply by setting up operations abroad that are beyond the technological capabilities of the host country's firms, foreign investors may increase productivity in the recipient countries. Furthermore, if the foreign affiliates' technology leaks out to local firms, foreign direct investment may also result in indirect productivity gains for host countries ("spillovers").

To analyze the influence of foreign direct investment (FDI) on growth in our sample of countries, we are forced to use a crude measure of FDI based on flow data provided by the International Monetary Fund (IMF). Our FDI variable measures the ratio of inflow of foreign direct investment to GDP, measured in current dollars, averaged over the 1960–85 period. For a few countries we have the average for only a shorter period (generally 1975 to 1985), because of the lack of data for earlier periods. It would have been preferable to have measures of real FDI activity in a host country, such as employment, plant and equipment assets or expenditures, or production. Financial flows can take place with little actual production or employment resulting, and production by affiliates of MNCs can take place without substantial financial flows. It would also have been preferable to have some industry breakdown of the FDI so that differences in technological content among investing industries could be taken into account.

Our import variable is the average (1960–85) ratio of imports of machinery and transport equipment (SITC 7) to GDP. This variable, denoted IMP, is intended to reflect the importation of foreign technology in embodied form.

Adding IMP and FDI to the variables used in Equation 9-1, we get the results in Table 9-3. These regressions suggest that inflows of foreign direct investment encourage more rapid economic growth. Adding FDI to the other variables in Equation 9-1 tends to lower quite substantially the influence of the coefficient for the fixed investment ratio, particularly in the developing countries (see Appendix Table 9A-1).

We found no evidence for an effect of our other possible channel of technology imports, the importation of machinery and transport equipment. The IMP variable never had any significant influence on our dependent variable. Thus we concluded that of our two international variables, it is mainly foreign investment that has a significant positive impact on income growth.

One possible objection to this conclusion is that the opposite causal relationship may be present, that is, that foreign investment is not causing higher growth but that higher growth is attracting multinationals. This cannot be tested by means of cross-section analysis, but as an alternative to the long-period analysis, we examined changes over successive 5-year periods in order to determine lines of influence and their timing. We found that growth rates of GDP per capita over 5-year periods were associated with direct investment flow ratios only in preceding and current 5-year periods, but not with direct investment in the following periods. This suggests that the causation runs from foreign direct investment to growth rather than the other way around. A similar test for the ratio of fixed investment to GDP found a stronger association between the income growth in a particular period and the investment rate of the following period than between the income growth and the investment ratios for the preceding or contemporary periods.

Another possibility that we explored was that there were interactions among the independent variables, particularly between the education investment (SCND) and the physical investment ratio (INV) and between education and the foreign interchange variables (IMP and FDI). None of these showed any significant relation to rates of economic growth, and they have not been included here.

Table 9-3. Coefficients for Imports of Machinery and Inflow of Foreign Direct Investment in Growth Equations for All Countries and Developing Countries

	IMP	FDI	$\overline{R}^2$
All countries	−.015	.278	.46
	(.67)	(2.42)	
Developing countries	−.001	.321	.45
	(.05)	(2.43)	
	t-statistics in parentheses		

Source: Appendix Table 9A-1.

Is There a "Convergence Club"?

The belief or suspicion is often expressed that the developing countries are not homogeneous in the factors that influence their growth. The idea is that there is a "convergence club" of better-off developing countries that are in a good position to catch up to the leaders, but other developing countries are so far behind that they are not able to gain from their backwardness by absorbing technology from the leaders. Furthermore, the lagging countries may gain relatively little from educational or physical investment or from contacts with foreign firms because there is so little local infrastructure for absorbing foreign influences.

The proposition is difficult to test because it is not clear what characteristics of a country would place it inside or outside the club. We have defined higher- and lower-income developing countries simply by dividing the group in half on the basis of initial per-capita income. The question we then asked is whether the two groups differ with respect to the relationship between their growth rates and the independent variables discussed earlier.

With respect to the gross catch-up, the results for the two groups essentially agree. As Table 9-4 shows, the coefficient is negative for both groups, but not statistically significant, and the variable explains almost none of the cross-country variation in income growth. If we run Equation 9-1 for the two income groups separately, we find that the coefficient for "conditional" catch-up is significant only in the poorer half (see Table 9-5). This contradicts the idea that there is a "convergence club" of higher-income developing countries close enough to the developed countries to absorb their technology and thus grow rapidly but that the poorest countries are too far behind the advanced countries to gain from their backwardness. Given their levels of education, investment, and so on, the poorer countries have still benefited, in terms of growth rate, from being backward.

The equations for the two groups of developing countries differ sharply in other respects.[5] Secondary education and price structure were of no importance for the higher-income group, whereas the investment rate was important only to the higher-income countries.

The effects of the foreign contact variables could also differ between the income groups. For example, the effects of foreign investment on productivity may differ among host countries depending on their level of development. The "least developed countries" may learn little from the multinationals, because local firms are too far

Table 9-4. "Gross Catch-Up" in Higher- and Lower-Income Developing Countries

	Coefficient for Catch-Up Variable	t-Statistic	$\overline{R}^2$	No. of Obs.
Higher income	−1.20	1.16	.01	39
Lower income	−.49	.09	.00	39

Source: Appendix Table 9A-1.

Table 9-5. Growth Equations Based on Domestic Variables for Developing Countries with High and Low Initial Income per Capita

	Lower Income		Higher Income	
	Coefficient	t-Statistic	Coefficient	t-Statistic
Constant	−8.54	1.95	−6.93	1.65
SCND	.049	6.97	.002	.18
PRICE	.208	1.42	.034	.16
INV	.008	.60	.054	2.87
PART	9.22	2.12	7.81	1.93
GDUS	−6.72	2.24	−.988	.69
$\overline{R}^2$	.73		.18	
No. of obs.	39		39	

Source: Appendix Table 9A-1.

behind in their technological levels to be either imitators or suppliers to the multinationals. Any foreign operations are likely to be enclaves detached from most of the host country's economy. Moreover, the multinationals invest little in such countries if they do not have important natural resources.

The higher-income developing countries are the major recipients of FDI in the developing world, and they are also the likeliest candidates for spillovers. They have local firms that are advanced enough to learn from the foreigners. Thus we expect the growth effects of foreign investment to be more important in the higher-income countries than in the lower-income countries. The results for these variables from the two halves of the distribution are shown in Table 9-6.

The coefficient for FDI is positive and significant only in the equation for higher-income countries, as predicted. Thus from this comparison, one might conclude that there is a threshold level of income below which foreign investment has no significant effect.

The story told by the other coefficients is not very different from that in the equations without the international variables. All the effects of low initial income, of secondary education levels, and of participation rates are much stronger among the lower-income countries, whereas the effect of inflows of foreign direct investment is important only among the higher-income countries (see Appendix Table 9A-1).

Table 9-6. Coefficients for Imports of Machinery and Inflow of Foreign Direct Investment in Growth Equations for Higher- and Lower-Income Developing Countries

	IMP		FDI			
	Coeff.	t-Stat.	Coeff.	t-Stat.	$\overline{R}^2$	No. of Obs.
Higher income	.031	1.09	.437	2.69	.44	39
Lower income	.034	.76	.100	.52	.73	39

Source: Appendix Table 9A-1.

The Quality of Data

Given the large extent to which the underlying data we and others use depend on extrapolation, as discussed earlier, we were concerned that some of the results might be artifacts built in by the construction of the data. The variable most subject to this danger is the catch-up measure, the initial distance behind the United States, because as mentioned earlier, any error in the dependent variable would have a corresponding reflection in this independent variable.

Ideally, the quality grading of the data should reflect the coverage and character of each country's national income and product accounts, but a judgment on these is beyond our competence. What we did do was to grade a country's data quality by whether it had participated in any phase of the ICP, on the ground that the income-level estimate for a country that had never participated rested on a flimsier foundation than did that of a country that had participated at least once. Summers and Heston included a quality measure in their article but used a different criterion. As we did, they gave a country their lowest-quality rating, D, if it had never participated in the UN International Comparison Program, but they also gave a country a low rating if it initially had been a low-income country.

As before, we first relate the catch-up variable (GDUS) by itself to growth in income per capita for the high-quality and low-quality subsamples of countries. This is a test for "gross" convergence, but as Appendix Table 9A-1 shows, no such effect is visible. This lack of relationship is reassuring in one sense because it suggests that the previously discussed bias in the initial income measures may not be as strong as seems possible from the extrapolation method used.

A comparison of the corresponding equations used in these sections for the two subgroups of developing countries with different data qualities is shown in Table 9-7. A Chow test showed no significant difference in the equations between "low"- and "high"-quality data countries. The most important, and reassuring, result was that the catch-up effect was not associated with low-quality data. In fact, it was stronger in the equation for countries with higher-quality data. Both equations showed a positive effect of secondary education on growth rates and included negative coefficients for

Table 9-7. Growth Equations for Developing Countries with Lower- and Higher-Quality Data

	Lower Quality		Higher Quality	
	Coefficient	t-Statistic	Coefficient	t-Statistic
Constant	−2.75	.47	−10.3	2.58
SCND	.031	2.53	.020	2.42
PRICE	.366	1.98	.465	1.45
INV	.013	.65	.013	.76
PART	2.18	.38	10.0	2.61
IMP	−.021	.55	.047	1.45
FDI	.510	2.41	.080	.43
GDUS	−2.13	1.56	−4.10	3.32
R^2	.52		.38	
No. of obs.	29		49	

Source: Appendix Table 9A-1.

levels of initial (1960) income, but only the one in the equation for countries with higher-quality data was statistically significant. That equation also had a significant positive effect for the participation rate, but no such effect was seen in the countries with lower-quality data. Neither equation gave much weight to imports of machinery and transport equipment, but fixed investment was significant in the equation for countries with lower-quality data.

In sum, the worry that the Summers and Heston extrapolations might be responsible for some of the reported catch-up results is not confirmed here. Although the coefficient for initial income was negative in the equations for both groups of countries, it was significantly different from zero only in the equation for the countries whose data were of a higher quality.

Conclusions and Directions for Further Research

Most of the research on growth and convergence has concentrated on developed countries or on some mixture of developed and developing countries. On the theory that the factors determining growth rates might be different for the developed and the developing countries, we have focused on the latter group.

We have attempted to answer several questions. The first was whether the factors found to be important in studies covering all types of countries played the same role when only developing countries were studied. Our main interest, however, was to introduce several variables that had not typically been studied. Two of them were to measure the acquisition of technology through international contacts. One of these was the inflow of direct investment capital, and the other was the import of machinery and transport equipment. A third new variable was a measure of the gains (or losses) from changes in the structure of prices. It was intended to obviate the need to eliminate arbitrarily some countries from the analysis because they were to some extent oil producers and to find a more general indicator of gains from price changes that was not confined to oil.

Finally, we began our study with the worry that some of the findings of convergence or catch-up may have reflected the fact that very few of the initial relative percapita income levels used to represent a country's distance from the leaders had been measured directly. Virtually all that had any direct comparison of income levels as part of the calculation were extrapolations over time from the periods when direct measures were made. The rest were extrapolations over space, extended to other years by extrapolations over time. If individual countries' national income and product accounts were used in these extrapolations and if they were biased in their trends over time relative to those that would result from frequent and univeral income-level measurements, bias in the income growth rates would produce opposite biases in estimated initial income levels and, therefore, spurious catch-up coefficients. We examined this possibility by investigating whether the convergence results arose mainly from the countries with poorer-quality data or whether these countries showed particularly strong convergence tendencies.

Our results supported earlier findings that backwardness by itself is not associated with rapid growth; there was no pure or "gross" catch-up. On the other hand, we confirmed the existence of what has been called "conditional" or "net" catch-up. When other factors are taken into account, we found that the lower the initial (1960) per-capita income was, relative to that of the United States, the faster the subsequent growth in per capita income would be. The "net" catch-up was particularly strong among the poorest half of the developing countries, contradicting the idea that there has been a "catch-up club" confined to relatively well-off countries. This provides some basis for optimism with respect to the poorer countries in the world, in the sense that even they are not so far from the frontier that they cannot gain from the avail-ability of technology and other knowledge developed by others. Finally, we did not find that apparent evidence of a conditional or net catch-up reflected only the effects of extrapolation; in fact, the conditional catch-up was stronger for the countries in which the quality of the data was relatively good.

Of the two variables intended as measures of the potential for technology transfer, the imports of machinery and transport equipment did not seem to have any impact. However, the inflow of foreign direct investment had a significant positive influence on income growth rates. The influence seemed to be confined to higher-income devel-oping countries. It was not evident among the poorer countries. These results may therefore imply that inward FDI is a source of more rapid growth only for a country already at a relatively high level of development. We suggest that a certain threshold level of development is needed if the host countries are to absorb new technology from investment by foreign firms.

Changes in the price structure were a significant influence on growth rates for the developing countries as a whole, although their significance faded when the countries were divided into higher-income and lower-income groups. That is, countries for which the 1985 price structure was much more favorable than the 1960 price struc-ture—as shown by a high ratio of 1960 income in 1985 prices to 1960 income in 1960 prices—tended to have faster real-income growth. Although this price structure mea-sure is correlated with a measure of the importance of oil production to a country ($r = .63$), it probably omits some of the effects of price gains because the real income in the ICP is built up from consumption and investment rather than from the production side of the account.

Among the other variables, the extent of enrollment in secondary education and the participation rate generally showed the expected positive relation to income growth and were mostly significant.

One surprise was the small influence of the variable for the fixed-investment ratio, particularly once the inflow of foreign direct investment was included in the equation. Even without the FDI variable, the fixed-investment ratio was, at best, marginally sig-nificant.[6] Ambiguity about the role of fixed investment runs through much of the recent development literature, but even critics of the earlier "capital fundamental-ism," which attributed all growth to physical capital investment (see the discussion in, e.g., Sen 1983, and Yotopoulos and Nugent 1976) would probably expect a stronger relationship than we found.

An unresolved question in all studies, including our own, relating income or pro-ductivity change over long periods to average fixed investment, imports, education, capital flows, or other variables, is the uncertainty about directions of causation. This question is raised particularly with respect to the fixed-investment ratio by Lipsey and Kravis (1987), who suggest that there is as much or more evidence that the investment ratio in a period depends on earlier-period output growth rates as there is that the growth rate depends on earlier or contemporaneous fixed investment. We confirmed this finding with some further experiments, using the present set of developing countries, but we did not find the same ambiguity for the FDI variable. Although the idea that growth spurts may precede increases in investment ratios is not common in the development literature, examples of such timing were cited by Kuznets (1973) and were a basic feature of many studies of capital investment in developed economies, such as Eisner's (1978). In that case, for example, "capital expenditures are taken as a freely estimated distributed lag function of past changes in sales, profits, and depreciation charges" (Eisner 1978, p. 69). We believe that some effort is needed to model the sequence of developments and the two-way interactions between growth and the many independent variables that have been included in the long-period studies.

Notes

The research reported here is part of the NBER program in International Studies. We are indebted to Martin N. Baily, David Dollar, and Ed Wolff for comments on earlier drafts. Blomström's and Zejan's work on the study was supported by the Swedish Council of Research in the Humanities and Social Science.

1. A list of countries included in the study is provided in the Appendix.

2. A variable for primary education was also tried, but since it never had any impact (probably because of too little variance) it is not shown.

3. We also tried a continuous "oil variable," based on the average 1985/86 oil production (from *Energy Statistics Yearbook*) divided by the average real GDP for the same period, but this did not change the result, except that the explanatory power of the regressions was lowered somewhat.

4. Wolff's import variable, defined as the ratio of total merchandise imports to GDP, was strongly significant in his regression, whereas our more narrowly defined import variable, as discussed here, was not.

5. The Chow test rejected the hypothesis that the equations for the two groups of developing countries were identical.

6. Eichengreen and Uzan (1992), studying a period different from ours, also found only a marginal growth effect of fixed investment.

References

Barro, Robert. (1991). "Economic Growth in a Cross Section of Countries." *Quarterly Journal of Economics,* May, pp. 407–43.

Baumol, William. (1986). "Productivity Growth, Convergence, and Welfare: What the Long Run Data Show." *American Economic Review,* December, pp. 1072–85.

Baumol, William, Sue Anne Batey Blackman, and Edward Wolff. (1989). *Productivity and American Leadership: The Long View.* Cambridge, MA: MIT Press.

Blomström, Magnus. (1991). "Host Country Benefits of Foreign Investment." In D. G. McFetridge, ed., *Foreign Investment, Technol-*

ogy and Economic Growth. Calgary: University of Calgary Press, pp. 93–108.

Eichengreen, Barry, and Marc Uzan. (1992). "The Marshall Plan: Economic Effects and Implications for Eastern Europe and the Former USSR." *Economic Policy,* April, pp. 13–75.

Eisner, Robert. (1978). *Factors in Business Investment.* Cambridge, MA: Ballinger, for the National Bureau of Economic Research.

Helliwell, John, and Alan Chung. (1992). "Convergence and Growth Linkages Between North and South." National Bureau of Economic Research Working Paper no. 3948, January.

Kravis, Irving B. (1970). "Trade as a Hand-maiden of Growth: Similarities Between the Nineteenth and Twentieth Centuries." *Economic Journal,* December, pp. 850–72.

Kuznets, Simon. (1973). *Population, Capital, and Growth: Selected Essays.* New York: Norton.

Lipsey, Robert, and Irving Kravis. (1987). *Savings and Economic Growth: Is the United States Really Falling Behind?* New York: The Conference Board.

Lucas, Robert (1988), "On the Mechanics of Economic Development."*Journal of Monetary Economics,* January, pp. 3–42.

Mankiw, Gregory, David Romer, and David Weil. (1992). "A Contribution to the Empirics of Economic Growth." *Quarterly Journal of Economics,* May, pp. 407–37.

Romer, Paul. (1986). "Increasing Returns and Long Run Growth." *Journal of Political Economy,* October, pp. 1002–37.

Sen, Amartya. (1983). "Development: Which Way Now?" *Economic Journal,* December, pp. 745–62.

Summers, Robert, and Alan Heston. (1991). "The Penn World Table (Mark 5): An Extended Set of International Comparisons, 1950–1988." *Quarterly Journal of Economics,* May, pp. 327–68.

UNCTC. (1988). *Transnational Corporations in World Development.* New York: United Nations.

Wolff, Edward. (1991). "Productivity Convergence at the Aggregate Level: A Survey." Paper, New York University, January.

Yotopoulos, Pan, and Jeffrey Nugent. (1976). *Economics of Development: Empirical Investigations.* New York: Harper & Row.

Zind, Richard. (1991). "Income Convergence and Divergence Within and Between LDC Groups." *World Development* 19:719–27.

Appendix Table 9A-1. Regressions of Growth in Real GDP per Capita (RGDPCG), 1960–1985, on Initial Real per-Capita Income and Other Factors

Const.	GDUS	SCND	PRICE	INV	PART	IMP	FDI	$\bar{R}^2$	Obs.
All countries									
1.73	.381							.00	101
(13.5)[a]	(.97)								
−5.82	−2.50	.021	.271	.029	5.98			.43	101
(2.39)	(5.34)	(4.57)	(2.51)	(2.97)	(2.48)				
−6.05	−2.43	.020	.299	.024	6.13	−.015	.278	.46	101
(2.37)	(5.25)	(4.46)	(2.81)	(2.33)	(2.41)	(.67)	(2.42)		
All developing countries									
1.64	4.54							.00	78
(9.81)	(.54)								
−6.98	−3.42	.024	.356	.029	6.90			.40	78
(2.22)	(3.81)	(3.70)	(2.68)	(2.49)	(2.23)				
−7.56	−3.28	.021	.391	.018	7.38	−.001	.321	.45	78
(2.39)	(3.81)	(3.29)	(3.05)	(1.52)	(2.35)	(.05)	(2.43)		
Higher-income developing countries									
2.22	−1.20							.01	39
(7.95)	(1.16)								
−6.93	−.988	−.002	.034	.054	7.81			.18	39
(1.65)	(.69)	(.18)	(.16)	(2.87)	(1.93)				
−2.98	−1.68	−.003	.255	.017	3.45	.031	.437	.44	39
(.77)	(1.40)	(.28)	(1.27)	(.97)	(.93)	(1.09)	(2.69)		

Const.	GDUS	SCND	PRICE	INV	PART	IMP	FDI	$\bar{R}^2$	Obs.
Lower-income developing countries									
1.54	−.492							.00	39
(3.33)	(.09)								
−8.54	−6.72	.049	.208	.008	9.22			.73	39
(1.95)	(2.24)	(6.97)	(1.42)	(.60)	(2.12)				
−10.70	−8.01	.050	.165	−.004	11.57	.034	.100	.73	39
(2.20)	(2.49)	(6.40)	(1.08)	(.22)	(2.34)	(.76)	(.52)		
Developing countries with higher-quality data									
1.68	.298							.00	49
(8.2)	(.27)								
−10.9	−4.36	.021	.504	.020	10.70			.38	49
(2.74)	(3.55)	(2.66)	(1.58)	(1.21)	(2.83)				
−10.31	−4.10	.020	.465	.013	10.00	.047	.080	.38	49
(2.58)	(3.32)	(2.42)	(1.45)	(.76)	(2.61)	(1.45)	(.43)		
Developing countries with lower-quality data									
1.60	.587							.00	29
(5.21)	(.43)								
−.219	−2.16	.037	.260	.030	−1.55			.42	29
(.04)	(1.43)	(2.83)	(1.30)	(1.50)	(.03)				
−2.75	−2.13	.031	.366	.013	2.18	−.021	.510	.52	29
(.47)	(1.56)	(2.53)	(1.98)	(.65)	(.38)	(.55)	(2.41)		

[a]t-ratios in parentheses.

Key:

RGDPCG: Growth in real income per capita, 1960–85. *Data Source:* Summers and Heston 1991.

GDUS: The 1960 real income per capita in 1960 prices relative to that of the United States. *Data Source:* Summers and Heston 1991.

SCND: The average (1960–85) ratio of secondary education to the number in the "appropriate" age group. *Data Source: UNESCO Yearbook,* various issues.

PRICE: Ratio of 1960 income in 1985 prices to 1960 income in 1960 prices. *Data Source:* Summers and Heston 1991.

INV: Ratio of fixed-capital formation to GDP, measured in current purchasing power parities and averaged over the 1960–85 period. *Data Source:* Summers and Heston 1991.

PART: The change (1960–85) in the labor force participation rate, the ratio of labor force to total population. *Data Sources:* ILO, *Labor Statistics Yearbook,* and Summers and Heston 1991.

IMP: The average (1960–85) ratio of imports of machinery and transport equipment (SITC 7) to GDP. *Data Sources:* United Nations, *Yearbook of International Trade Statistics,* various issues; and Summers and Heston 1991.

FDI: Ratio of inflow of foreign direct investment to GDP, measured in current dollars and averaged over the 1960–85 period (for some countries, lack of data forced us to use shorter periods). *Data Sources:* IMF Balance of Payments tape and UNCTC 1988.

Appendix: List of Countries Included and Characterization by Type of Country and Quality of Data

	Developed Country	Developing Country Income		Developing Country Data Quality	
		Higher	Lower	Higher	Lower
1 Algeria		X			X
2 Argentina		X		X	
3 Australia	X				
4 Austria	X				
5 Bangladesh			X	X	
6 Barbados		X		X	
7 Belgium	X				
8 Benin			X	X	
9 Brazil		X		X	
10 Cameroon			X	X	
11 Canada	X				
12 Central African Republic			X		X
13 Chad			X		X
14 Chile		X		X	
15 Colombia		X		X	
16 Congo			X	X	
17 Costa Rica		X		X	
18 Cyprus		X			X
19 Denmark	X				
20 Dominican Republic		X		X	
21 Ecuador		X		X	
22 Egypt			X	X	
23 El Salvador		X		X	
24 Ethiopia			X	X	
25 Fiji		X			X
26 Finland	X				
27 France	X				
28 Gabon		X			X
29 Gambia			X		X
30 Germany	X				
31 Ghana			X		X
32 Greece	X				
33 Guatemala		X		X	
34 Guyana		X			X
35 Haiti			X		X
36 Honduras			X	X	
37 Hong Kong		X		X	
38 Iceland	X				
39 India			X	X	
40 Iran		X		X	
41 Iraq		X			X
42 Ireland	X				
43 Israel		X		X	
44 Italy	X				
45 Ivory Coast			X	X	
46 Jamaica		X		X	
47 Japan	X				
48 Jordan		X			X
49 Kenya			X	X	

	Developed Country	Developing Country			
		Income		Data Quality	
		Higher	Lower	Higher	Lower
50 Korea, South			X	X	
51 Liberia			X		X
52 Madagascar			X	X	
53 Malawi			X	X	
54 Malaysia		X		X	
55 Mali			X	X	
56 Malta		X			X
57 Mauritania			X		X
58 Mauritius		X		X	
59 Mexico		X		X	
60 Morocco			X	X	
61 Netherlands	X				
62 New Zealand	X				
63 Nicaragua		X			X
64 Niger			X		X
65 Nigeria			X	X	
66 Norway	X				
67 Pakistan			X	X	
68 Panama		X		X	
69 Papua New Guinea			X		X
70 Paraguay		X		X	
71 Peru		X		X	
72 Philippines		X		X	
73 Portugal	X				
74 Rwanda			X	X	
75 Saudi Arabia		X			X
76 Senegal			X	X	
77 Sierra Leone			X	X	
78 Singapore		X			X
79 Somalia			X		X
80 South Africa			X		X
81 Spain	X				
82 Sri Lanka		X		X	
83 Sudan			X		X
84 Suriname		X			X
85 Sweden	X				
86 Switzerland	X				
87 Taiwan			X		X
88 Tanzania			X	X	
89 Thailand			X	X	
90 Togo			X		X
91 Trinidad and Tobago		X			X
92 Tunisia			X	X	
93 Turkey	X				
94 Uganda			X		X
95 United Kingdom	X				
96 United States	X				
97 Uruguay		X		X	
98 Venezuela		X		X	
99 Zaire			X		X
100 Zambia			X	X	
101 Zimbabwe			X	X	

IV

The NICs and the LDCs

10

Multinational Corporations and Productivity Convergence in Mexico

MAGNUS BLOMSTRÖM
EDWARD N. WOLFF

During the last 30 years, the developing countries have witnessed very different experiences regarding income and productivity growth and the extent to which they have converged on developed countries. Some, like the Asian newly industrialized countries (NICs), clearly are in a process of rapid convergence, whereas others, like most countries in Africa, show no sign of convergence. This indicates that the realization of the potentiality for productivity catch-up simply because of backwardness depends strongly on another set of causes, some of which are internal and others external to the countries themselves (see Abramovitz 1986).

Among the external factors that may influence a country's productivity, the multinational corporation (MNC) deserves special attention. In recent times, the MNC has become an important agent in the production of technology. Such firms now produce, own, and control most of the world's advanced technologies. They also play a central role in the international diffusion of new technology (see Blomström 1991). Over four-fifths of the stock of foreign direct investment originates from only a half-dozen countries—the United States, the United Kingdom, Japan, Germany, Switzerland, and the Netherlands—where most of the new technology is produced and from where it is spread to the rest of the world. However, despite the enormous amount of controversy over the transfer of technology by multinationals, in both their home and host countries, there are no studies dealing with the role of these firms in productivity convergence among countries.

In this chapter we examine the impact of the operations of foreign-owned multinational firms on the productivity of growth of Mexican manufacturing industries. We investigate both the extent to which the penetration of a sector by foreign-owned firms affects the productivity of local firms in that sector and whether there is any evidence of convergence between this industry's productivity level and that of the United

States. Thus we concentrate on intraindustry influences and primarily on the external effects or "spillovers" of foreign direct investment.

Earlier studies of such technology spillovers—focusing on Australia (Caves 1974), Canada (Globerman 1979), Mexico (Blomström 1989, and Kokko 1992), Morocco (Haddad and Harrison 1991), and Venezuela (Aitken and Harrison 1991)—generally found some support for the spillover benefit hypothesis, although it was weaker for the cases of Morocco and Venezuela. Because of great methodological difficulties in investigating these effects and a relative paucity of data, none of these studies was able to analyze in any depth the nature of spillover efficiency. Furthermore, none of them tried to evaluate the importance of such spillovers for productivity growth in the host country.

This chapter has two major sections: The first looks at the productivity spillovers between domestic and foreign firms in Mexico, and the second, on Mexico's international catch-up. There is also a brief summary section at the end.

Convergence Between Foreign and Local Firms in Mexico

Multinationals, Technology Transfer, and Convergence

The convergence hypothesis asserts that when the productivity level of one (or several) country(ies) is substantially superior to that of a number of other economies, largely as a result of differences in their productive techniques, those laggard countries that are not too far behind the leaders will be in a position to embark on a catch-up process. This catch-up process will continue as long as the economies that are approaching the leader's performance continue to be able to learn from the leader. But as the distance between the two groups narrows, the stock of knowledge unabsorbed by the laggards will grow smaller and approach exhaustion. The catch-up process then usually terminates unless some supplementary and unrelated influence fortuitously comes into play. Meanwhile, those countries that are so far behind the leaders that it is impractical for them to profit substantially from the leaders' knowledge will generally not be able to participate in the convergence process at all, and so many such economies will find themselves falling even further behind.

The most important influence underlying this hypothesis is the transfer of technology that constantly takes place among economies. Technology may be transferred from one place to another through a variety of channels, but in the postwar period, the multinational corporations have become a powerful institution for the spread of new technology. Multinational firms not only establish subsidiaries abroad, but they also transfer technology through a number of other arrangements, including licensing, franchising, management contracts, marketing contracts, and technical service contracts.

Subsidiary production, or what we might call foreign direct investment, is still the dominant mode in which multinational firms exploit their intangible assets in foreign markets, and there are several ways in which such investment may facilitate the diffusion of technology from advanced to developing countries. One is simply that the multinationals set up operations in developing countries that are beyond the technological capabilities of the host country's firms. Even if there were no leakage of the technology to local firms, there would still be a geographical diffusion of technology, but without any change in its ownership.

Technology transfer through foreign direct investment can also result in indirect productivity gains for the host developing countries, through the realization of external economies. Generally these benefits are referred to as *spillovers,* which indicates the importance of the way in which the influence is transmitted. There are several ways in which these spillovers may occur. Presumably the most important channel is via competition (see Blomström 1986). Existing inefficient local firms may be forced by the competition of foreigners to make themselves more productive by investing in physical or human capital or importing new technology.

Another source of gain to the host economy is the training of labor and management provided by the multinationals, which may then become available to the economy in general. Since such resources are in a short supply in developing countries, this type of spillover efficiency is expected to be more important there.

A third potential source of spillover efficiency benefits is through the impact made by the foreign subsidiaries in the host economy on their local suppliers, by insisting that they meet standards of quality control, delivery dates, prices, and the like. This aspect should be particularly important to countries like Mexico, where legislation requires domestic content.

Although all these influences would cause positive long-run effects on the host country's productivity, there are, to be sure, also several offsetting forces at work. First, technology transfer within multinationals is far from free (see Teece 1976). It involves a substantial commitment of real resources and a sequence of overlapping stages of activities. This slows down the technology transfer process and makes multinationals unwilling to share information. Second, the technology that is used by the MNCs may be unsuitable for local firms in developing countries. Kokko (1992) shows, for instance, that there may be no spillovers if the technological gap between foreign and local firms is too large. Both of these positions suggest little technology spillover between the MNCs and the local firms in the country. Third, Lall (1980) argues that imports of technology through foreign investment may work as an important first injection to local technological development but that too much reliance on foreign technology may retard the basic design and development activity in the host country, causing negative long-run effects on productivity.

To determine whether the presence of MNCs acts as a catalyst or a hindrance to the productivity growth in Mexico, we begin by investigating productivity convergence among foreign and local firms in Mexican manufacturing industries. For this purpose we use unpublished data from the Mexican Census of Manufactures 1970 and 1975 (see Appendix). These are the only two years for which data by ownership are available. Though the period is unfortunately short, the results are nonetheless quite strong. We first investigate trends within 20 broad manufacturing industries and then perform a regression analysis.[1]

Aggregate Trends

It is clear from Table 10-1 that in 1970, foreign firms displayed higher labor productivity than did Mexican firms (also see Appendix Table 10A-1 for data on the extent

Table 10-1. Comparison of Labor Productivity Levels Between Foreign and Domestic Firms in Mexico, 1970[a]

	Productivity Level by Segment as a Fraction of the Overall Productivity Level of the Industry							
	Value Added per Employee				Gross Output per Employee			
		Locally Owned		Total		Locally Owned		Total
Industry[b]	MNC	State	Private	Domestic[c]	MNC	State	Private	Domestic[c]
20—Food	2.19	0.78	0.85	0.84	2.12	0.79	0.86	0.85
21—Tobacco	1.17	—	0.16	0.16	1.16	—	0.19	0.19
22—Textile mill	1.43	0.62	0.96	0.94	1.38	0.60	0.97	0.95
23—Apparel	2.48	1.75	0.95	0.96	2.31	1.92	0.95	0.96
24—Lumber and wood	2.41	1.42	0.92	0.95	2.58	1.13	0.93	0.94
25—Furniture	1.41	1.85	0.94	0.97	1.10	1.93	0.95	0.99
26—Paper	1.33	1.51	0.87	0.91	1.52	1.22	0.83	0.86
27—Printing and publishing	2.00	0.99	0.95	0.95	1.72	0.86	0.97	0.97
28—Chemicals	1.28	0.94	0.75	0.77	1.17	1.20	0.82	0.86
29—Petroleum and coal	2.04	1.63	0.54	0.74	1.87	1.60	0.60	0.78
30—Rubber and plastics	2.50	—	0.65	0.65	2.36	—	0.68	0.68
31—Leather	1.87	1.36	0.98	0.98	1.70	3.36	0.98	0.98
32—Stone, clay, and glass	1.74	0.88	0.90	0.90	1.84	0.81	0.89	0.88
33—Primary metals	1.13	1.13	0.79	0.92	1.16	1.11	0.78	0.91
34—Fabricated metals	1.51	3.70	0.87	0.89	1.42	4.22	0.89	0.91
35—Nonelec. equip.	1.47	1.54	0.75	0.76	1.59	2.21	0.68	0.69
36—Electric equip.	1.49	—	0.74	0.74	1.47	—	0.75	0.75
37—Transport equip.	1.37	1.07	0.62	0.75	1.53	1.06	0.47	0.65
38—Instruments	1.54	—	0.75	0.75	1.68	—	0.69	0.69
39—Miscel. manuf.	1.45	—	0.90	0.90	1.25	—	0.95	0.95
Total manufacturing	1.88	1.33	0.75	0.79	1.85	1.53	0.75	0.80

[a]Basic data are from worksheets provided by la Dirreción de estadística de la secretaria de industria y commercio in Mexico. See the Appendix for details.

[b]Industries are classified by the U.S. SIC code and include all 4-digit SICs in each industry. See the Appendix for detailed Mexican industry codes included in each U.S. SIC code.

[c]The total domestic sector is defined as the sum of state-owned and privately owned firms, a separation that is available only for 1970.

of multinational activity by industry). The productivity of foreign firms, measured both by value-added and gross output, was, on average, more than twice that of local firms. The labor productivity level of MNCs exceeded that of locally owned firms in every industry. Among Mexican firms, labor productivity was significantly higher in state-owned than in privately owned firms, although the state companies were not as efficient as the affiliates of the multinationals.

To a large extent, the differences in labor productivity are related to differences in the firms' capital intensity. This can be seen in Table 10-2, which shows the firms' capital–labor ratio as a fraction of the overall capital–labor ratio of the industry. The capital intensity was 2.5 times higher in foreign firms than in the privately owned Mex-

Table 10-2. Comparison of Capital-Intensity Levels Between Foreign and Domestic Firms in Mexico, 1970[a]

| | *Capital–Labor Ratio by Segment as a Fraction of the Overall Capital–Labor Ratio of the Industry* | | | |
| | | *Locally Owned* | | *Total* |
Industry[b]	*MNC*	*State*	*Private*	*Domestic*[c]
20—Food	2.06	2.32	0.75	0.86
21—Tobacco	1.13	—	0.37	0.37
22—Textile mill	1.48	0.58	0.95	0.94
23—Apparel	2.48	1.62	0.95	0.96
24—Lumber and wood	4.67	1.24	0.84	0.87
25—Furniture	1.14	1.50	0.97	0.99
26—Paper	1.61	2.95	0.69	0.83
27—Printing and publishing	2.33	1.44	0.92	0.94
28—Chemicals	1.28	1.33	0.70	0.76
29—Petroleum and coal	1.01	1.36	0.92	1.00
30—Rubber and plastics	1.95	—	0.78	0.78
31—Leather	2.45	1.59	0.96	0.96
32—Stone, clay, and glass	1.75	0.65	0.90	0.89
33—Primary metals	1.10	0.92	0.96	0.94
34—Fabricated metals	1.66	3.52	0.84	0.86
35—Nonelec. equipment	1.65	3.69	0.63	0.66
36—Electric equipment	1.43	—	0.77	0.77
37—Transport equipment	1.31	1.25	0.60	0.79
38—Instruments	2.25	—	0.43	0.43
39—Miscel. manufacturing	1.62	—	0.87	0.87
Total manufacturing	1.85	1.85	0.73	0.80

[a]Basic data are from worksheets provided by la Dirección de estadística de la secretaria de industria y commercio in Mexico. See the Appendix for details. The 1970 capital stock figures are based on *capital invertido*.

[b]Industries are classified by the U.S. SIC code and include all 4-digit SICs in each industry. See the Appendix for detailed Mexican industry codes included in each U.S. SIC code.

[c]The total domestic sector is defined as the sum of state-owned and privately owned firms, a separation that is available only for 1970.

ican firms but, interestingly, about the same as in the state-owned firms. The greater efficiency of multinationals relative to both state-owned and privately owned firms in Mexico still holds for total factor productivity (TFP), defined as a ratio of output to a weighted sum of labor and capital inputs (see note a in Table 10-3 for the definition).[2] As Table 10-3 indicates, the foreign firms' TFP measured by gross output was 34 percent higher than that of local firms on average, with the difference being highest in tobacco (150 percent higher), petroleum (138 percent), rubber (89 percent), and transport equipment (78 percent). In lumber and wood products, chemicals, and miscellaneous manufacturing, the local firms' TFP exceeded that of the multinationals.

The data in Table 10-4 indicate that Mexican firms caught up with the multinationals over time. Between 1970 and 1975, the multinationals' productivity lead in terms of labor productivity diminished in the manufacturing sector as a whole, as well as in three-fourths of the individual manufacturing industries. There was also a ten-

Table 10-3. Comparison of TFP Levels Between Foreign and Domestic Firms in Mexico, 1970[a]

	Ratio of TFP Level by Segment to Overall Industry TFP							
	Value-Added Index				Gross Output Index			
		Locally Owned		Total		Locally Owned		Total
Industry[b]	MNC	State	Private	Domestic[c]	MNC	State	Private	Domestic[c]
20—Food	1.29	0.42	1.02	0.93	1.25	0.42	1.03	0.94
21—Tobacco	1.05	—	0.35	0.35	1.05	—	0.42	0.42
22—Textile mill	1.14	0.80	0.98	0.98	1.10	0.77	0.99	0.98
23—Apparel	1.37	1.31	0.97	0.98	1.28	1.43	0.98	0.98
24—Lumber and wood	0.82	1.26	1.00	1.02	0.87	1.00	1.01	1.01
25—Furniture	1.31	1.45	0.95	0.98	1.03	1.52	0.97	1.00
26—Paper	0.98	0.71	1.06	1.01	1.12	0.57	1.02	0.95
27—Printing and publishing	1.20	0.81	0.99	0.98	1.04	0.70	1.01	1.00
28—Chemicals	1.08	0.77	0.93	0.90	0.99	0.99	1.01	1.01
29—Petroleum and coal	2.03	1.28	0.58	0.74	1.86	1.25	0.64	0.78
30—Rubber and plastics	1.57	—	0.75	0.75	1.49	—	0.79	0.79
31—Leather	1.10	1.05	1.00	1.00	1.00	2.61	1.00	1.00
32—Stone, clay, and glass	1.22	1.09	0.95	0.95	1.29	1.01	0.94	0.94
33—Primary metals	1.07	1.20	0.81	0.96	1.09	1.17	0.80	0.94
34—Fabricated metals	1.11	1.56	0.95	0.97	1.04	1.78	0.97	0.99
35—Nonelec. equip.	1.07	0.61	0.95	0.94	1.16	0.87	0.86	0.86
36—Electric equip.	1.20	—	0.85	0.85	1.18	—	0.86	0.86
37—Transport equip.	1.16	0.93	0.81	0.85	1.30	0.92	0.61	0.73
38—Instruments	0.92	—	1.09	1.09	1.00	—	0.99	0.99
39—Miscel. manuf.	1.11	—	0.97	0.97	0.96	—	1.01	1.01
Total manufacturing	1.24	0.87	0.90	0.90	1.22	1.01	0.90	0.91

[a]Data are from worksheets provided by la Dirección de estadística de la secretaria de industria y commercio in Mexico. The 1970 capital stock figures are based on *capital invertido.* The TFP is measured as a ratio of industry output Y to a weighted average of employment (L) and capital stock (K):

$$TFP = Y/[\alpha L + (1 - \alpha)K]$$

where α is the industry's wage share.

[b]Industries are classified by U.S. SIC code and include all 4-digit SICs in each industry. See the Appendix for detailed Mexican industry codes included in each U.S. SIC code.

[c]The total domestic sector is defined as the sum of state-owned and privately owned firms, a separation that is available only for 1970.

dency toward convergence in total factor productivity over the same period, but these figures should be interpreted with great caution, since the capital stock figures for 1970 and 1975 are not directly comparable (see Appendix).[3]

In sum, we find that there are rather large productivity differences between foreign and local firms in Mexico but that the foreign firm's lead has been diminishing. To examine whether this productivity catch-up is related to the presence of multinationals and the existence of spillovers between foreign and local firms, we next relate the latter's productivity growth to the presence of foreign firms in various industries.

Table 10-4. Productivity Convergence Between Foreign and Domestic Firms in Mexico, 1970–1975[a]

	Ratio of Productivity Levels Between Domestic and Foreign Firms						
	All 4-Digit Industries					4-Digit Ind. with MNCs	
	Value Added per Employee	Gross Output per Employee		TFP		Gross Output per Employee	
Industry[b]	1970	1970	1975	1970	1975	1970	1975
20—Food	0.39	0.40	0.50	0.75	0.54	0.48	0.59
21—Tobacco	0.14	0.16	—	0.40	—	0.16	—
22—Textile mill	0.66	0.69	0.65	0.89	0.87	0.79	0.64
23—Apparel	0.39	0.42	0.71	0.77	1.36	0.42	0.72
24—Lumber and wood	0.39	0.37	0.44	1.16	1.19	0.36	0.44
25—Furniture	0.69	0.90	0.53	0.97	0.71	0.91	0.53
26—Paper	0.68	0.56	1.02	0.85	0.79	0.56	1.02
27—Printing and publishing	0.48	0.56	0.76	0.96	0.86	0.56	0.76
28—Chemicals	0.60	0.73	0.69	1.02	0.84	0.75	0.70
29—Petroleum and coal	0.36	0.42	0.59	0.42	0.69	0.53	0.64
30—Rubber and plastics	0.26	0.29	0.46	0.53	0.93	0.29	0.46
31—Leather	0.52	0.58	0.72	1.00	1.16	0.59	0.73
32—Stone, clay, and glass	0.52	0.48	0.57	0.72	0.84	0.52	0.62
33—Primary metals	0.81	0.78	0.79	0.87	0.75	0.78	0.79
34—Fabricated metals	0.59	0.64	0.68	0.95	1.00	0.64	0.68
35—Nonelec. equipment	0.52	0.44	1.04	0.74	1.09	0.44	1.06
36—Electric equipment	0.49	0.51	1.13	0.73	1.23	0.51	1.13
37—Transport equipment	0.55	0.42	0.36	0.57	0.45	0.43	0.36
38—Instruments	0.49	0.41	0.54	0.99	1.36	0.49	0.57
39—Miscel manufacturing	0.62	0.76	0.66	1.06	1.01	0.76	0.68
Total manufacturing	0.42	0.43	0.61	0.75	0.79	0.47	0.64

[a]Data are from worksheets provided by la Dirección de estadística de la secretaria de industria y commercio in Mexico. The TFP figures are based on gross output in each year, but for 1970 the capital stock figures are based on *capital invertido,* and for 1975, they are based on *activos fijos brutos.* Since the two concepts differ, comparisons based on the TFP figures in Columns 4 and 5 of the table should be interpreted with caution. See the Appendix for details.

[b]Industries are classified by U.S. SIC code. The results in the first five columns are based on all 4-digit SICs in each industry. The results in the last two columns are based on only the 4-digit SICs in which MNCs are present in either 1970 or 1975. See the Appendix for the detailed Mexican industry codes included in each U.S. SIC code.

Regression Analysis

We use two regression forms. In the first, the dependent variable is the rate of labor productivity growth of local firms within an industry, and in the second, it is the rate of convergence in labor productivity levels between local and foreign firms within a sector. These variables are related to the degree of foreign ownership of the industry and the gap in labor productivity between local and foreign-owned firms in 1970, as well as two other explanatory variables.

As Table 10-5 shows, the results are consistent in the two regression forms. Both labor productivity growth in local firms and productivity convergence between local and foreign firms are faster in industries with a greater share of employment accounted for by multinationals.[4] The Mexican firms' productivity growth and the rate of catch-up to the MNCs are also higher in sectors where the initial disparity in productivity levels between local and foreign firms is greater, a result that accords well with the advantages-of-backwardness thesis. Furthermore, in sectors with higher capital–labor ratios, the productivity growth of locally owned firms and the rate of catch-up are lower. This suggests that spillover gains from the new technology of multinationals are easier to incorporate when the investment requirements are small. Finally, convergence seems to be faster in industries with slower output growth, but output growth does not affect the rate of local firms' productivity growth. This indicates that the competitive pressures from the presence of multinationals in an industry may be greater in relatively stagnant industries. In rapidly growing sectors, inefficient local firms can continue to survive without improving their productivity, but in slow-growing industries, the inefficient local firms can be driven out by the multinationals.[5]

Table 10-5. Regression Analysis of Productivity Catch-Up Between Foreign and Locally Owned Firms in Mexico[a]

Independent Variables	Dependent Variable			
	LPGLOC	LPGLOC	LPGLOC	CONVLF
Constant	−0.048	0.147*	0.172**	0.219**
	(1.52)	(2.94)	(3.47)	(3.06)
FORSHARE	0.351**	0.245**	0.372**	0.734**
	(3.59)	(3.34)	(4.06)	(5.53)
LFLPGAP70		−0.318**	−0.313**	−0.446**
		(4.35)	(4.24)	(4.18)
OUTPGRTH			−0.188	−0.166**
			(0.89)	(5.41)
KL1970			−0.482*	−0.709*
			(2.15)	(2.18)
R^2	0.42	0.72	0.79	0.80
$\bar{R}^2$	0.38	0.69	0.73	0.75
Standard error σ	0.078	0.055	0.051	0.074
Sample size[b]	20	20	20	20

[a]Estimated coefficients are shown together with the absolute value of the t-statistic in parentheses.
Key:

LPGLOC: Annual rate of growth of gross output per employee in locally owned firms, 1970 to 1975.
FORSHARE: Share of employment in foreign-owned firms in total industry employment, averaged between 1970 and 1975.
LFLPGAP70: Ratio of gross output per employee in local firms to gross output per employee in foreign firms, 1970.
OUTPGRTH: Average annual rate of growth of industry output, 1970 to 1975.
KL1970:   Industry capital–labor ratio in 1970.
CONVLF: Ratio of LFLPGAP75 to LFLPGAP70.

[b]Basic data are from worksheets provided by la Dirección de estadística de la secretaria de industria y commercio in Mexico. Industries are classified by the 2-digit U.S. SIC code and include all 4-digit SICs in each industry. See the Appendix for details.

*Significant at the .05 level (two-tailed test).

**Significant at the .01 level (two-tailed test).

The results so far suggest that there exist technology spillovers from foreign direct investment, with a resulting convergence in productivity between foreign and local firms in Mexico, but are these spillover benefits large enough to generate an international catch-up? We now turn to this question by looking at the extent to which the labor productivity levels of Mexico and the United States have converged.

International Catch-up?

Aggregate Trends

We begin by comparing the productivity levels of foreign and domestic firms in Mexico with those of the United States in 1970.[6] As Table 10-6 shows, foreign firms were very close to the United States in terms of both labor productivity and TFP, whereas local firms in Mexico were far behind. The MNCs' labor productivity and TFP both

Table 10-6. Mexican Productivity Level by Segment and Industry as a Proportion of U.S. Productivity Level by Industry, 1970[a]

Industry[b]	Value Added per Employee			TFP		
	MNC	Domestic	Total	MNC	Domestic	Total
20—Food	0.94	0.36	0.43	1.05	0.64	0.71
21—Tobacco	0.45	0.06	0.39	0.46	0.15	0.43
22—Textile mill	1.09	0.72	0.76	1.17	0.95	0.98
23—Apparel	1.65	0.64	0.67	0.65	0.51	0.51
24—Lumber and wood	0.69	0.27	0.29	0.50	0.43	0.43
25—Furniture	1.03	0.71	0.73	0.82	0.62	0.63
26—Paper	0.84	0.57	0.63	0.92	0.85	0.87
27—Printing and publishing	0.82	0.39	0.41	0.64	0.48	0.49
28—Chemicals	0.85	0.51	0.66	1.15	0.87	1.01
29—Petroleum and coal	0.48	0.17	0.24	1.15	0.42	0.57
30—Rubber and plastics	1.66	0.43	0.67	1.76	0.71	1.00
31—Leather	0.97	0.51	0.52	0.50	0.47	0.47
32—Stone, clay, and glass	0.79	0.41	0.46	0.85	0.59	0.63
33—Primary metals	0.76	0.62	0.67	1.07	0.94	0.99
34—Fabricated metals	0.55	0.33	0.37	0.58	0.46	0.48
35—Nonelec. equipment	0.66	0.34	0.45	0.57	0.47	0.52
36—Electric equipment	1.10	0.54	0.73	0.96	0.66	0.79
37—Transport equipment	0.73	0.40	0.53	0.78	0.55	0.65
38—Instruments	0.87	0.42	0.56	0.42	0.56	0.48
39—Miscel. manufacturing	0.51	0.32	0.35	0.51	0.42	0.44
Total manufacturing	0.93	0.39	0.49	0.93	0.60	0.69

[a]Basic data are from worksheets provided by la Dirección de estadística de la secretaria de industria y commercio in Mexico. The U.S. data for the GDP by industry in current dollars and full-time and part-time employees are from NIPA tables. The 1970 Mexican value added was converted to 1975 pesos on the basis of the Mexican GDP deflator and then to 1975 U.S. dollars on the basis of the 1975 exchange rate. The 1970 U.S. value added was converted from 1982 dollars to 1975 dollars using the U.S. GDP deflator. The TFP index is based on value added. The Mexican 1970 capital stock figures are based on *capital invertido;* the U.S. capital stock figures are from Musgrave (1986) and are based on current dollar values (the nearest equivalent). Since the two concepts differ, the last three columns should be interpreted with caution. The productivity ratios are relative to the productivity levels of the whole U.S. industry.

[b]Industries are classified by U.S. SIC code and include all 4-digit SICs in each industry. See the Appendix for the detailed Mexican industry codes included in each U.S. SIC code.

averaged 93 percent of that of the United States, and in several industries they even exceeded the U.S. levels. Labor productivity in Mexican firms, on the other hand, averaged only 39 percent of that of the U.S. firms. The technology gap, as measured by TFP, was smaller, at 60 percent, which reflects the considerably higher capital intensity of U.S. production. The productivity levels for foreign and local firms taken together correspond rather well to those reported in Maddison and van Ark (1989).[7]

The finding that the foreign affiliates were so close to the United States in terms of productivity while local firms were lagging behind certainly suggests that multinational firms have contributed to a geographcal diffusion of technology and acted as a bridge between advanced and less advanced countries. But is this international diffusion of technology enough for an international catch-up? Table 10-7 presents the convergence in productivity between Mexico and the United States between 1970 and 1975. Overall, there seems to be no catch-up during the 5-year period, but this varies among industries. In 7 industries the U.S. productivity lead diminished, whereas it increased in 13 industries. The results for convergence are similar for the 2-digit indus-

Table 10-7. Convergence in Productivity Between Mexico and the United States: Ratio of Mexican to U.S. Value Added per Employee, 1970 and 1975[a]

Industries[b]	All 4-Digit Mexican Industries Included			Only 4-Digit Mexican Industries with MNCs Included		
	1970	1975	Ratio	1970	1975	Ratio
20—Food	0.43	0.44	1.01	0.52	0.52	0.99
21—Tobacco	0.39	0.45	1.15	0.39	0.45	1.15
22—Textile mill	0.76	0.79	1.04	0.85	0.87	1.02
23—Apparel	0.67	0.51	0.76	0.68	0.52	0.76
24—Lumber and wood	0.29	0.27	0.94	0.29	0.27	0.94
25—Furniture	0.73	0.59	0.81	0.73	0.59	0.81
26—Paper	0.63	0.57	0.90	0.63	0.57	0.90
27—Printing and publishing	0.41	0.44	1.06	0.41	0.44	1.06
28—Chemicals	0.66	0.60	0.90	0.68	0.61	0.89
29—Petroleum and coal	0.24	0.21	0.87	0.29	0.22	0.75
30—Rubber and plastics	0.67	0.64	0.96	0.67	0.64	0.96
31—Leather	0.52	0.43	0.82	0.53	0.43	0.82
32—Stone, clay, and glass	0.46	0.50	1.10	0.49	0.54	1.10
33—Primary metals	0.67	0.66	0.98	0.67	0.66	0.98
34—Fabricated metals	0.37	0.46	1.24	0.37	0.46	1.24
35—Nonelec. equipment	0.45	0.51	1.14	0.45	0.52	1.15
36—Electric equipment	0.73	0.55	0.75	0.73	0.55	0.75
37—Transport equipment	0.53	0.38	0.72	0.53	0.38	0.72
38—Instruments	0.56	0.46	0.81	0.64	0.48	0.75
39—Miscel. manufacturing	0.35	0.35	0.99	0.36	0.36	1.00
Total manufacturing	0.49	0.48	0.98	0.53	0.51	0.96

[a]Basic data are from worksheets provided by la Dirección de estadística de la secretaria de industria y commercio in Mexico. The U.S. data for the GDP by industry in current dollars and full-time and part-time employees are from NIPA tables. The 1970 Mexican value added was converted to 1975 pesos on the basis of the Mexican GDP deflator; the 1975 pesos were then converted to 1975 U.S. dollars on the basis of the 1975 exchange rate. The 1970 U.S. value added was converted from 1982 dollars to 1975 dollars using the U.S. GDP deflator.

[b]Industries are classified by U.S. SIC code. The results in the first set of columns are based on all 4-digit SICs in each industry. The results in the last columns are based on only the 4-digit SICS in which MNCs are present in either 1970 or 1975. See the Appendix for the detailed Mexican industry codes included in each U.S. SIC code.

try sample, which includes only 4-digit Mexican industries with MNCs present, though as expected, the Mexican productivity figures are higher. Since foreign participation varies among industries, it may very well be that foreign investment is related to international catch-up in one way or another. We will return to this question later in our regression analysis.[8]

With data from the United Nations we were able to examine the convergence of labor productivity between Mexico and the United States between 1965 and 1984 (Table 10-8).[9] During this longer period there was a clear convergence of productivity levels in all industries for which data are available. The biggest catch-up took place during the second half of the 1960s but slowed down thereafter. Between 1970 and 1975 there was very little convergence, just as the census data in Table 10-7 show.

Table 10-8. Convergence of Labor Productivity Between Mexico and the United States: Ratio of Mexico to U.S. Value Added per Employee, 1965–1985[a]

Industry	1965	1967	1970	1975	1977	1979	1982	1984
20—Food	0.42	0.50	0.51	0.52	0.62	0.56	0.47	0.51
21—Tobacco	0.35	0.54	0.55	0.92	1.00	1.04	0.87	0.75
22—Textile mill	NA	NA	0.54	0.55	0.51	0.61	0.60	0.66
23—Apparel	NA	NA	NA	NA	NA	NA	NA	NA
24—Lumber and wood	0.47	0.54	0.55	0.51	0.64	0.91	1.10	1.11
25—Furniture	NA	NA	NA	NA	NA	NA	NA	NA
26—Paper	NA	0.56	0.67	0.68	0.60	0.61	0.61	0.68
27—Printing and publishing	NA	NA	NA	NA	NA	NA	NA	NA
28—Chemicals	0.43	0.55	0.69	0.52	0.51	0.51	0.50	0.60
29—Petroleum and coal	0.22	0.51	0.25	0.34	0.25	0.26	0.15	0.37
30—Rubber and plastics	1.10	1.40	1.71	1.34	1.14	1.32	1.32	1.85
31—Leather	NA	NA	NA	NA	NA	NA	NA	NA
32—Stone, clay, and glass	0.56	0.64	0.68	0.78	0.73	0.75	0.91	0.79
33—Primary metals	0.55	0.58	0.68	0.64	0.58	0.62	0.64	0.83
34—Fabricated metals	NA	NA	0.51	0.45	0.45	0.51	0.53	0.61
35—Machinery, excl. electrical	NA	0.38	0.69	0.69	0.72	0.88	0.86	0.84
36—Electric equip.	NA	NA	0.70	0.63	0.63	0.74	0.66	0.83
37—Transport equip.	NA	NA	NA	0.53	0.43	0.61	0.59	0.57
38—Instruments	NA	NA	NA	NA	NA	NA	NA	NA
39—Miscel. manuf.	NA	NA	NA	NA	NA	NA	NA	NA

[a]Data for Mexican value added and average number of employees are from United Nations, *Industrial Statistics Yearbook,* various years. The U.S. data for the GDP by industry in current dollars and full-time and part-time employees are from NIPA tables. Before 1977, Mexico value added is net of nonindustrial services purchased from others. For Mexico, current pesos were first converted into 1975 pesos using the Mexican GDP deflator and then were converted to 1975 dollars using the actual 1975 exchange rate. For the United States, the GDP in current dollars was converted into 1975 dollars using the U.S. GDP deflator. Because of a discontinuity in the Mexican value-added series between 1976 and 1976, Mexican value added after 1977 was adjusted as

$$VA^*_t = VA_t(VA_{76} \cdot (GO_{77}/GO_{76})/VA_{77})$$

where VA is value added and GO is gross output. See the Appendix for the Mexican industries included in each U.S. SIC Code.

Regression Analysis

Since the main purpose of this chapter is to analyze the role of MNCs in productivity convergence among countries, we will, finally, by means of regression analysis, try to go deeper into that question by relating a sector's productivity catch-up to the degree of foreign ownership. As mentioned earlier, there are both direct and indirect effects on the total industry productivity of foreign direct investment. The direct effect is that an increase in the share of multinationals in an industry increases the productivity level of the whole industry, simply because MNCs have higher productivity than local firms do. The indirect effect, on the other hand, is the technological spillover between the multinationals and the local firms. Because of the availability of data for the pre-1970 and the post-1975 period, these two effects cannot be separated in the regression.

As before, we use two regression forms. In the first, the dependent variable is the rate of labor productivity growth of Mexican industries (local plus foreign firms), and in the second, it is the rate of convergence in labor productivity levels between Mexican and U.S. industries. These variables are related to the degree of foreign ownership of an industry in Mexico and the initial Mexican–U.S. productivity gap. Both foreign ownership and the initial productivity gap are significantly related to productivity growth within the Mexican industry and its speed of catch-up to the corresponding U.S. productivity level (see Table 10-9). This holds for both the longer 1965–77 and 1965–84 periods and the shorter 1970–75 period.[10] The capital–labor ratio is again significant and negative for productivity growth in Mexico, suggesting that catch-up with the United States is faster when the investment requirements are lower. Finally, output growth here is statistically insignificant.

Conclusion

Four principal findings emerge from this study. First, both labor productivity levels and TFP levels of locally owned firms in Mexico have converged on those of foreign-owned firms. Second, both the rate of local firms' labor productivity growth and their rate of catch-up to the multinationals are positively related to the industry's degree of foreign ownership. Third, the gap in labor productivity between Mexican and U.S. manufacturing diminished between the mid-1960s and the mid-1980s. Fourth, the rate of labor productivity growth of Mexican industries and its rate of convergence to the United States are higher in industries with a greater presence of multinationals. The results support the advantages-of-backwardness thesis in two senses: first, between more advanced and more backward countries and, second, between more modern and more backward segments of an industry.

The results also suggest that local firms in Mexico have gained productivity "spillovers" from the presence of multinational firms in the Mexican economy. But there is also another possibility, namely, that competitive pressure from multinationals forces out the inefficient local firms. This is consistent with the finding that convergence between local and foreign firms is faster when output growth is lower, though this finding might also be due to the greater efficiency gains of local firms during periods of slack demand. With the data at hand, we cannot distinguish between these two possibilities.

Table 10-9. Regression Analysis of Productivity Catch-Up Between Mexican and U.S. Industries[a]

Independent Variables	Dependent Variables				
	LPG7075	*LPG6577*	*LPG6584*	*CONV6577*	*CONV6584*
Constant	−0.069**	0.030*	0.257*	0.104**	0.106**
	(3.49)	(2.38)	(3.04)	(13.4)	(15.8)
FORSHARE	0.081*	0.078**	0.047**	0.039**	0.024*
	(2.22)	(4.21)	(3.79)	(3.43)	(2.44)
$MEXUSGAP_0$	−0.083*	−0.070**	−0.036*	−0.042**	−0.028*
	(2.65)	(3.49)	(2.42)	(3.14)	(2.38)
OUTPGRTH	−0.125				
	(1.48)				
KL1970	−0.234*				
	(2.46)				
R^2	0.46	0.72	0.62	0.64	0.49
$\bar{R}^2$	0.31	0.66	0.56	0.58	0.40
Standard error σ	0.022	0.013	0.009	0.008	0.007
Sample size[b]	20	20	20	20	20

[a]Estimated coefficients are shown together with the absolute value of the t-statistic in parentheses. Key:

LPG7075:   Annual rate of growth of value added per employee in Mexican industry, 1970 to 1975.
FORSHARE: Share of employment in foreign-owned firms in total industry employment, averaged between 1970 and 1975.
$MEXUSGAP_0$: Ratio of value added per employee in Mexican industry to value added per employee in corresponding U.S. industry at the beginning of the period.
OUTPGRTH: Average annual rate of growth of industry output, 1970 to 1975.
KL1970:   Industry capital–labor ratio in 1970.
CONV6577:   Ratio of $MEXUSGAP_1$ to $MEXUSGAP_0$, where subscript 1 designates the end of the period.

[b]The variables LPG6577, LPG6584, CONV6577, and CONV6584 are computed from data in United Nations, *Industrial Statistics Yearbook,* various years. All other Mexican data are from worksheets provided by la Dirección de estadística de la secretaria de industria y commercio in Mexico. Industries are classified by the 2-digit U.S. SIC code and include all 4-digit SICs in each industry. The U.S. data are from NIPA tables. See the Appendix for details.

*Significant at the .05 level (two-tailed test).

**Significant at the .01 level (two-tailed test).

There is strong evidence that the presence of multinational firms acts as a catalyst to the productivity growth in Mexico and that foreign direct investment speeds up the convergence process between Mexico and the United States. However, the available data do not allow us to say whether this is due to productivity spillovers or simply to the fact that MNCs are more productive than Mexican firms. Although we could not reject the spillover benefit hypothesis, the productivity convergence between Mexico and the United States might also be due, wholly or in part, to the direct effect of foreign investment. This possibility is strengthened by the finding that the productivity levels of the foreign affiliates in Mexico were very close to those of corresponding industries in the United States and that the Mexican firms were lagging far behind. Thus an increase in the share of multinationals within an industry increases the level of productivity within the total Mexican industry, without any productivity growth among local firms. Furthermore, the importance of this direct effect is strengthened by the fact that the largest catch-up effect was registered between 1965 and 1970, a time when Mexico received a large injection of foreign investment.[11]

Although we conclude that multinational firms have played an important role in Mexico's international catch-up, it may not be possible to generalize these results to all other countries. If the host country is too far behind, in the sense that it lacks the technical skills needed to respond to the foreign challenge, there may be no spillovers (for evidence, see Cantwell 1989, and Kokko 1992).[12] This is probably the case in most of the least developed countries today. One might also ask whether there are any specific circumstances in Mexico that make Mexican firms benefit more from MNC technology than do firms in other countries. For instance, there are extensive movements of labor and capital between Mexico and the United States that faciliate technology diffusion, and moreover, the dominance of the United States as a trade partner might be important.

Notes

Thanks are due to Gregory Ingram, Richard Nelson, and Jagdish Bhagwati for comments on an earlier draft of this chapter. We also gratefully acknowledge the financial support of the C. V. Starr Center for Applied Economics, New York University, and the Swedish Council for Research in the Humanities and Social Sciences (HSFR). Excellent research assistance was provided by Maury Gittleman.

1. Data on the proportion of output and employment accounted for by foreign firms in Mexican manufacturing industries are provided in Blomström 1989.

2. Unfortunately, data on capacity utilization are not available to allow for an adjustment for utilized capital input.

3. One would expect that productivity development would differ among industries depending on whether the sector produces nontradables, exportables, or import substitutes. However, because Mexico during the 1970s was strongly inward oriented, this is not a serious problem here (see Blomström 1989). Most Mexican industries were highly protected from foreign competition at that time, which excluded them from the world market.

4. Results are almost identical for the share of industry output accounted for by MNCs, as well as the share of industry capital stock owned by MNCs. Indeed, the correlation among the employment share, output share, and capital share each exceeds 0.95 (see Appendix Table 10A-1). It is also important to note that we have not included a measure of the extent of foreign-licensing agreements by industry (such data are not available). Since this variable may be correlated with the share of industry output accounted for by MNCs, there may be an omitted variable bias in the results.

5. This "excise effect" will be explored more fully in a later paper. Regressions were also performed on the 4-digit industry level, with 219 observations. The coefficient estimates of the FORSHARE variable were consistently positive but generally less significant (typically at the 10 percent level). The coefficient estimates of the other variables were quite similar to the 2-digit estimates, but again, the significance levels were generally lower. There are two possible reasons for the less robust results on the 4-digit level. First, the data are much "noisier" at the more disaggregated level, since the number of firms in each industry group is substantially smaller. Second, there were major changes in 4-digit industry codes between 1970 and 1975, thus making the alignment of the 1970 and 1975 data at this level quite problematic.

6. As indicated in note a of Table 10-6, the exchange rate was used to convert Mexican pesos to U.S. dollars. See Maddison and van Ark 1989 for a discussion.

7. Comparative results are shown in Appendix Table 10A-2. Their approach relies mainly on the industrial censuses of each country, adjusted to a national accounts basis, using both national accounts and input–output data. The main advantage of this approach is the computation of industry-specific (their so-called industry of origin) price indices, which allow direct output comparisons between two countries on the industry level. As detailed in Maddison and van Ark 1989, these price indices are derived from production censuses by dividing the gross

value of output by the corresponding quantities. Their approach is particularly advantageous, since it does not rely on general PPP conversion indices, which are based on expenditure data rather than production data. Our ratio of Mexican to U.S. value added per employee in 1975 is about 25 percent higher than that of Maddison and van Ark—0.48 compared with 0.39. For most industries, the two sets of estimates are quite close. The exceptions are textiles and apparel and, particularly, rubber and plastic products, for which our estimated ratios are substantially higher than those of Maddison and van Ark.

8. Note that this period is atypical, since 1975 was a recession year in Mexico but not in the United States.

9. Compared with the data used earlier, the UN data are based on samples of firms. Most likely, large firms are overrepresented in the sample data, since they show higher labor productivity than do the census data (compare the figures in Tables 10-7 and 10-8). An interesting question for future research is, therefore, whether only some parts of the Mexican industry (the "modern" part) is converging, whereas others (the "traditional" sector) are not. Such a pattern was suggested in Blomström 1986 and will be examined further.

10. The fact that the results are slightly weaker for the 1965–84 period than for the 1965–77 period is likely due to the effects of the debt crisis on Mexico's productivity performance after 1982.

11. We know that the United States dominates the foreign investment activities in Mexico. For instance, the U.S. Department of Commerce reports that in 1977, U.S. multinationals employed 302,000 people in Mexican manufacturing industries. The closest year for which Mexican data are available is 1975, and then all foreign firms in manufacturing employed 312,549 people. Between 1966 and 1977, the employment in U.S. majority–owned affiliates in Mexico increased from 102,000 to 171,000 (there are no data on minority-owned affiliates for 1966).

12. This is presumably the reason for the weak support for the spillover benefit hypothesis in Haddad and Harrison's 1991 study of Morocco and in Aitken and Harrison's 1991 study of Venezuela. For example, in the Venezuelan study, they found spillovers only in "low-tech" industries, such as food products, textiles, and basic metals. These are industries in which we expect local firms' technologies to be relatively close to those of foreign affiliates.

References

Abramovitz, Moses (1986). "Catching Up, Forging Ahead, and Falling Behind," *Journal of Economic History* 46:385–406.

Aitken, Brian, and Ann Harrison. (1991). "Are There Spillovers from Foreign Direct Investment? Evidence from Panel Data for Venezuela." World Bank, unpublished paper.

Blomström, Magnus. (1986). "Foreign Investment and Productive Efficiency: The Case of Mexico," *Journal of Industrial Economics* 55:97–110.

———. (1989). *Foreign Investment and Spillovers: A Study of Technology Transfer to Mexico.* London: Routledge S. Kegan Paul.

———. (1991). "Host Country Benefits of Foreign Investment." In D. G. McFetridge, ed., *Foreign Investment, Technology and Economic Growth.* Calgary: University of Calgary Press, pp. 93–108.

Caves, Richard. (1974). "Multinational Firms, Competition, and Productivity in Host Country Markets." *Economica* 41:176–83.

Cantwell, John. (1989). *Technological Innovation and Multinational Corporations.* Oxford: Basil Blackwell.

Globerman, Steven. (1979). "Foreign Direct Investment and 'Spillover' Efficiency Benefits in Canadian Manufacturing Industries." *Canadian Journal of Economics* 12:42–56.

Haddad, Mona, and Ann Harrison. (1991). "Are There Positive Spillovers from Direct Foreign Investment? Evidence from Panel Data for Morocco." World Bank, unpublished paper.

Kokko, Ari. (1992). "Foreign Direct Investment, Host Country Characteristics and Spillovers." Ph.D. diss., Stockholm School of Economics.

Lall, Sanjaya. (1980). "Developing Countries as Exporters of Industrial Technology." *Research Policy* 9:24–52.

Maddison, Angus, and Bart van Ark. (1989). "International Comparisons of Purchasing Power, Real Output, and Labour Productivity: A Case Study of Brazilian, Mexican, and U.S. Manufacturing." *Review of Income and Wealth* 35:1–30.

Musgrave, John C. (1986). "Fixed Reproducible Tangible Wealth in the United States: Revised Estimates." *Survey of Current Business* 66:51–75.

Teece, David. (1976). *The Multinational Corporation and Resource Cost of International Technology Transfer.* Cambridge, MA: Ballinger.

Appendix: Data Sources and Methods

I. *Documentation for Mexican data on multinationals and domestic firms*

A. *Sources:* The data on foreign and Mexican firms were provided by la Dirección de estadística de la secretaria de industria y commercio in Mexico and are from the Mexican Census of Manufactures, 1970 and 1975. The data are gathered at the plant level and cover the entire manufacturing industry, which is divided into 230, 4-digit manufacturing industries. Because some information was missing, 15 industries had to be discarded. In the regression analysis of productivity growth, on the 4-digit level, another 70 industries had to be discarded because of a change in the classification system between 1970 and 1975. In particular, all 4-digit industries in 1970 that were divided into two or more industry classes in 1975 were excluded.

In the 1970 data, ownership is divided into three categories: foreign, state owned, and privately owned. In 1975, it is divided into two categories: foreign and Mexican. Companies whose share are at least 15 percent foreign owned are classified as foreign. If the Mexican state owns more than 49 percent of a plant, it is defined as state owned, even if foreigners own 15 percent or more of its outstanding shares.

There are no capital stock figures that are comparable between 1970 and 1975. For 1970, we use *capital invertido,* which is the book value of net property, plant, and equipment plus intangible capital. For 1975, we use *activos fijos brutos,* which is the gross value of property, plant, and equipment. Mexican deflators for GDP and gross fixed-capital formation were derived from tables in United Nations, *National Accounts Statistics: Main Aggregates and Detailed Tables,* 1983.

B. *Concordance scheme between U.S. 2-digit SIC codes and Mexican 4-digit SIC codes*

1970 Mexican 4-Digit Codes

2-Digit U.S. SIC Code	All Industries	Industries with MNCs	2-Digit U.S. SIC Code	All Industries	Industries with MNCs
20—Food and kindred products				2051	2058
	2011	2011		2052	2059
	2012	2012		2053	2061
	2021	2021		2054	2062
	2022	2022		2055	2071
	2023	2023		2056	2073
	2024	2024		2057	2081
	2025	2025		2058	2082
	2031	2032		2059	2083
	2032	2034		2061	2084
	2033	2041		2062	2085
	2034	2051		2071	2091
	2041	2055		2072	2093

2-Digit U.S. SIC Code	All Industries	Industries with MNCs
	2073	2094
	2081	2095
	2082	2096
	2083	2097
	2084	2098
	2085	2099
	2091	2111
	2092	2113
	2093	2121
	2094	2131
	2095	2132
	2096	2141
	2097	
	2098	
	2099	
	2111	
	2112	
	2113	
	2121	
	2123	
	2131	
	2132	
	2141	
21—Tobacco manufacturers		
	2211	2211
	2212	2212
	2213	2213
22—Textile mill products		
	2311	2311
	2312	2312
	2313	2313
	2315	2315
	2316	2316
	2319	2319
	2321	2321
	2322	2322
	2323	2323
	2331	2334
	2333	2341
	2334	2343
	2341	2344
	2342	2346
	2343	
	2344	
	2345	
	2346	
23—Apparel and other textiles		
	2421	2421
	2422	2422
	2423	2424
	2424	2434
	2425	

2-Digit U.S. SIC Code	All Industries	Industries with MNCs
	2426	
	2427	
	2431	
	2432	
	2433	
	2434	
	2439	
24—Lumber and wood products		
	2511	2511
	2512	2512
	2521	2521
	2522	2533
	2531	2534
	2533	
	2534	
25—Furniture and fixtures		
	2612	2621
	2621	3521
	3521	
26—Paper and allied products		
	2711	2711
	2712	2712
	2721	2721
	2722	2722
	2723	2723
27—Printing and publishing		
	2811	2811
	2812	2812
	2813	2813
	2814	2814
28—Chemicals and allied products		
	3111	3111
	3112	3112
	3113	3113
	3121	3121
	3122	3122
	3131	3131
	3132	3132
	3141	3141
	3151	3151
	3161	3161
	3162	3162
	3171	3171
	3172	3191
	3191	3194
	3192	3195
	3193	3196
	3194	3199
	3195	
	3196	
	3199	

2-Digit U.S. SIC Code	All Industries	Industries with MNCs
29—Petroleum and coal products		
	3213	3213
	3221	3221
	3222	
30—Rubber and miscellaneous plastics products		
	3011	3011
	3012	3012
	3013	3013
	3181	3181
31—Leather and leather products		
	2411	2411
	2412	2413
	2413	2911
	2911	2912
	2912	
32—Stone, clay, and glass products		
	3311	3311
	3312	3312
	3321	3321
	3322	3323
	3323	3324
	3324	3329
	3329	3341
	3341	3342
	3342	3351
	3343	3352
	3351	3354
	3352	
	3353	
	3354	
33—Primary metal industries		
	3411	3411
	3412	3412
	3413	3413
	3421	3421
	3422	3422
	3423	3423
	3424	3424
34—Fabricated metal products		
	3511	3511
	3512	3512
	3513	3513
	3514	3514
	3517	3517
	3531	3531
	3541	3541
	3542	3542
	3543	3543
	3544	3544
	3545	3545
	3546	3546
	3547	3547
	3549	3549
	3987	3987

2-Digit U.S. SIC Code	All Industries	Industries with MNCs
35—Machinery, except electrical		
	3611	3611
	3621	3621
	3631	3632
	3632	3641
	3641	3651
	3651	3652
	3652	3653
	3653	3654
	3654	3655
	3655	3656
	3656	3659
	3659	
36—Electric and Electronic Equipment		
	3711	3711
	3721	3721
	3722	3722
	3723	3723
	3724	3724
	3731	3731
	3741	3741
	3742	3742
	3743	3743
	3749	3749
37—Transportation equipment		
	3811	3811
	3821	3821
	3831	3831
	3832	3832
	3834	3834
	3841	3841
	3842	3842
	3843	
38—Instruments and related products		
	3911	3911
	3912	3912
	3921	3921
	3922	3922
	3931	3931
	3984	
39—Miscellaneous manufacturing industries		
	3941	3942
	3942	3951
	3951	3961
	3961	3971
	3971	3981
	3981	3982
	3982	3983
	3983	3986
	3985	3988
	3986	
	3988	

II. Documentation for Mexican industries included in UN data

ISIC	Industry Name	Beginning of Series
311/2	Preparation and preservation of meat	1965
	Condensed and evaporated milk and milk powder	1965
	Canned fruits and vegetables	1965
	Canned fish and shellfish	1965
	Wheat mills	1965
	Corn flour	1969?
	Tea and instant coffee	1969?
	Chewing gum	1965
	Biscuits and pastries	1965
	Yeast, baking powder, starch, and similar products	1965
	Vegetable oils and margarine	1965
	Prepared foods for animals and fowl	1965
313	Malt	1969?
	Beer	1965
	Soft drinks	1975
	Carbonated water	1975
314	Cigarettes	1965
321	Spinning, weaving, and finishing of cotton, artificial fibers, and henequen	1967?
	Manufacture of yarns	1969?
	Manufacture of cashmere textiles, shawls, and similar products	1969?
	Manufacture of wool	1973?
331	Manufacture of plywood, veneer, and lamina	1965
341	Manufacture of pulp from fiber, paper, and paperboard	1965
	Manufacture of articles of paperboard, including oil-impregnated board	1965
351	Manufacture of cellulosic fibers and other artificial fibers	1965?
	Manufacture of fertilizers	1965?
352	Manufacture of matches and candles	1965?
	Soap, detergents, and other cleaning compounds	1967
	Paints, varnishes, and lacquers	1965
	Drugs and medicines	1975?
354	Manufacture of coke and other coal products	1965
	Regeneration of lubricating oils, including additives	1973
355	Manufacture of tires and tubes	1965
362	Manufacture of sheet glass, glass fibers, safety glass, and glass containers	1965?
369	Manufacture of hydraulic cement, brick, fireproof partitions, and refractory mortar	1965?
	Manufacture of asbestos products	1973
371	Manufacture of iron and steel tubes and rods	1967
	Founding, casting, and rolling of iron and steel	1965
372	Founding, refining, casting, extruding, and drawing of copper and its alloys	1967
	Casting, extruding, and drawing of aluminum and manufacture of aluminum solders	1965?
381	Manufacture of furniture and fixtures primarily of metal	1967?
	Manufacture of crown caps and other cast and enameled metal products	1967?
	Manufacture of containers and other products from tinplate	1973
382	Manufacture and assembly of agricultural machinery and equipment	1965
	Manufacture and assembly of typing, computing, and accounting machinery	1973
383	Manufacture of record players and receiving sets of radio and television	1969
	Manufacture of condensers and batteries	1967

ISIC	Industry Name	Beginning of Series
	Manufacture and assembly of electrical apparatus and parts	1967
	Manufacture of other electronic equipment and apparatus	1975
384	Manufacture and assembly of motor vehicles, including tractors for trailers	1965
	Manufacture of bodies for motor vehicles	1965
	Manufacture of railroad equipment	1975

? indicates that the exact year of inclusion cannot be determined from UN Yearbook. From 1975 to 1984, only 58 out of the 225, 4-digit Mexican manufacturing industries are included in the UN tabulations.

Concordance scheme between U.S. 2-digit SIC codes and UN 3-digit ISIC codes

U.S. SIC	UN ISIC
20—Food and kindred products	311/2—Food products
	313—Beverages
21—Tobacco manufactures	314—Tobacco
22—Textile mill products	321—Textiles
23—Apparel and other textiles	322—Wearing apparel
24—Lumber and wood products	331—Wood products
25—Furniture and fixtures	332—Furniture and fixtures
26—Paper and allied products	341—Paper and products
27—Printing and publishing	342—Printing and publishing
28—Chemicals and allied products	351—Industrial chemicals
	352—Other chemical products
29—Petroleum and coal products	353—Petroleum refineries
	354—Petroleum, coal products
30—Rubber and miscellaneous plastics products	355—Rubber products
	356—Plastic products, n.e.c.
31—Leather and leather products	323—Leather and leather products
	324—Footwear
32—Stone, clay, and glass products	361—Pottery, china, etc.
	362—Glass and products
	369—Nonmetal products n.e.c.
33—Primary metal industries	371—Iron and steel
	372—Nonferrous metals
34—Fabricated metal products	381—Metal products
35—Machinery, except electrical	382—Machinery, n.e.c.
36—Electric and electronic equipment	383—Electrical machinery
37—Transportation equipment	384—Transport equipment
38—Instruments and related products	385—Professional goods
39—Miscellaneous manufacturing	390—Other industries

III. *U.S. data*

U.S. data are as follows: (1) GDP is from the GDP by industry in constant dollars, Table 6.02 of the National Income and Product Accounts; (2) employment is from full-time and part-time employees, Table 6.06 of the National Income and Product Accounts; (3) capital stock figures are from John C. Musgrave, "Fixed Reproducible Tangible Wealth in the United States: Revised Estimates," *Survey of Current Business,* January 1986, pp. 51–75; and (4) U.S. deflators for GDP and gross fixed-capital formation were derived from tables in *National Accounts, Main Aggregates,* Vol. I, 1960–84, OECD, Department of Economics and Statistics.

Appendix Table 10A-1. Activity of MNCs as a Proportion of Total Industry Activity, 1970 and 1975[a]

		1970			1975		
	Plants	Employ-ment	Capital Stock	Gross Output	Employ-ment	Capital Stock	Gross Output
20—Food and kindred prod.	0.2	11.6	23.9	24.6	6.8	7.6	12.8
21—Tobacco manufactures	49.2	83.2	93.8	96.8	3.2	0.3	0.3
22—Textile mill products	1.9	11.6	17.2	16.0	6.9	10.9	10.3
23—Apparel and other textiles	0.1	2.9	7.1	6.6	0.9	2.5	1.3
24—Lumber and wood products	0.2	3.4	15.8	8.8	5.3	20.0	11.3
25—Furniture and fixtures	0.5	5.9	6.8	6.5	2.0	3.2	3.8
26—Paper and allied products	4.4	21.7	34.9	32.9	16.0	10.7	15.7
27—Printing and publishing	0.4	4.6	10.6	7.9	7.9	9.7	10.1
28—Chemicals and allied products	11.9	45.5	58.4	53.2	43.0	50.8	52.2
29—Petroleum and coal products	8.6	20.1	20.3	37.6	28.1	32.4	39.9
30—Rubber and plastics products	0.8	19.0	37.0	44.9	16.3	36.0	29.9
31—Leather and leather products	0.2	2.6	6.5	4.5	2.4	5.4	3.4
32—Stone, clay, and glass products	0.9	12.3	21.5	22.6	20.1	32.1	30.5
33—Primary metal industries	11.6	36.8	40.4	42.6	19.1	17.9	23.1
34—Fabricated metal products	0.9	17.6	29.4	25.0	16.9	27.9	22.9
35—Machinery, excl. electrical	3.1	34.2	56.3	54.4	13.5	14.5	13.1
36—Electric and electronic equipment	9.0	34.9	49.8	51.1	60.7	64.1	57.7
37—Transportation equipment	6.4	40.0	52.3	61.2	28.2	36.4	52.2
38—Instruments and related products	3.0	31.5	70.9	52.9	25.0	63.5	38.1
39—Miscel. manufacturing	0.8	17.6	28.6	22.1	24.5	41.8	33.0
Total Manufacturing	0.9	19.2	35.4	35.4	18.3	25.5	27.1

[a]Data are from worksheets provided by la Dirección de estadística de la secretaria de industria y commercio in Mexico. For 1970, the capital stock figures are based on *capital invertido,* and for 1975, they are based on *activos fijos brutos.*

Appendix Table 10A-2. Comparison of Maddison–van Ark and Our Estimates: Ratio of Mexican to U.S. Value Added per Employee, 1975

	Blomström– Wolff[a]	Maddison– van Ark[b]
Food and food products (incl. beverages)	0.44	0.44
Tobacco manufactures	0.45	0.43
Textiles and apparel	0.65	0.37
Lumber and wood products	0.27	0.22
Chemical products	0.47	0.47
Rubber and plastics products	0.64	0.24
Leather and leather products	0.43	0.44
Stone, clay, and glass products	0.50	0.40
Metal products	0.52	0.44
Machinery and transport equipment	0.45	0.36
Electric and electronic equipment	0.55	0.46
Other manufacturing	0.35	0.34
Total manufacturing	0.48	0.39

[a] *Source:* Table 10A-1.

[b] *Source:* Maddison and van Ark 1989, Table 12 (geometric averages).

11

Staying Behind, Stumbling Back, Sneaking Up, Soaring Ahead: Late Industrialization in Historical Perspective

TAKASHI HIKINO
ALICE H. AMSDEN

Infusing or Innovating Technology

A small number of "late"-industrializing countries have experienced dramatic economic growth since World War II, thereby pushing the phenomenon of economic convergence beyond Western nations. As Table 11-1 indicates, Japan, South Korea, Taiwan, Brazil, and Mexico have significantly increased their share of world production in the twentieth century. They have succeeded in industrializing even though their leading enterprises have not enjoyed the competitive asset of pioneering technology. This characteristic marks a critical departure from the past experiences of the leading enterprises of Britain, and then of the United States and Germany, which conquered world markets by successfully generating new manufacturing technology.

By contrast, the late-industrializing countries, principally those after World War II, have evolved as "learners." They have had to industrialize by borrowing and improving technology already developed by experienced firms from more advanced economies. Although innovators in the first and second Industrial Revolutions certainly borrowed and learned from one another, even the most prominent enterprises in the late-industrializing countries have had to grow without the competitive asset of new products or processes, which is the meaning we attribute to "lateness." The imperative to industrialize exclusively on the basis of learning is responsible for many shared general properties in a subset of developing countries that are otherwise diverse in resource endowment, history, and culture, such as South Korea, Taiwan, Brazil, Mexico, India, Turkey, and Japan (although Japan is suigeneris in many respects) (see Amsden 1989).

Table 11-1. Distribution of World Gross Domestic Product, 1900–1992[a]

	Year					
	1900	*1913*	*1950*	*1973*	*1987*	*1992E*
Country	*(percent of 32-country total)*					
North America and Western Europe[b]	54.0	57.5	61.7	53.5	47.0	45.4
United Kingdom	10.4	9.1	7.1	4.8	3.8	3.5
United States	21.5	25.7	34.6	26.9	24.3	23.5
Germany	5.1	5.4	4.2	5.4	4.4	4.6
Japan	2.9	2.9	3.2	8.3	8.8	9.6
South Korea[c] and Taiwan	0.6	0.5	0.5	1.1	2.0	2.5
Brazil and Mexico	1.6	1.7	3.0	4.4	5.1	4.7
India	8.6	7.0	4.4	3.4	3.8	4.4

Source: Data for 1900–87 were computed from Angus Maddison, *The World Economy in the 20th Century* (Paris: OECD, Development Centre, 1989), p. 113. Data for 1992 are estimates based on Maddison's methodology and were prepared by Claes Brundenius, "Global Restructuring," in Claes Brundenius and Bo Goransson, eds., *New Technologies and Global Restructuring* (Lund: Research Policy Institute, 1993).

[a] 1980 prices, adjusted to exclude impact of boundary changes.

[b] Austria, Belgium, Canada, Denmark, Finland, France, Germany, Italy, Netherlands, Norway, Sweden, Switzerland, United Kingdom, and United States.

[c] Rough estimate for 1900.

E = estimate.

the second Industrial Revolution. As a result of variations across countries in the timing and pattern of growth, by the 1970s one could observe a "hat-shaped" relationship between the level of relative backwardness and the rate of economic growth, as indicated in Figure 11-2. Using these two figures as a general guide, we will try to demonstrate the properties of late industrialization by comparing major successful cases in Group V (especially Japan, South Korea, and Taiwan) with three other sets of countries: (1) The innovators of the second Industrial Revolution (Group I), in particular the United States; (2) countries that also started from behind but caught up in a different historical context (Group II) (we focus on the Nordic countries, in particular, Sweden), which had the lowest GDP per capita among members of the so-called convergence club in the second half of the nineteenth century; they, too, had to catch up; and (3) countries that despite roughly similar opportunities to industrialize as Group V countries either "stumbled back" (Group VI, including Argentina and the Philippines) or "stayed behind" (Group IV, say Pakistan and Bangladesh). Table 11-2 provides the underlying data illustrating the historical "divergence" among the late industrializers.

We argue that the technology acquisition process—differentiated according to innovating or borrowing—distinctively shapes three major aspects of industrial development: first, the developmental role of government; second, the competitive focus of enterprises; and third, the strategy, structure, and operation of leading firms.[1] These are the three areas around which our chapter is organized.

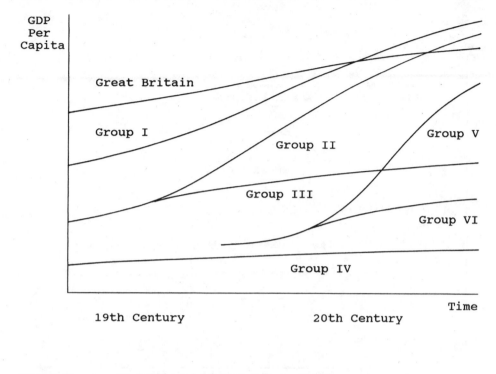

Group I:	Innovators (Convergence Club)
Group II:	19th century followers (Convergence Club)
Group III:	19th century cases of stumbling back
Group IV:	Underdeveloped or staying behind
Group V:	Learners or 20th century followers
Group VI:	20th century cases of stumbling back

Figure 11-1. Overview of historical growth paths. *Source:* Groups I–III are based on Table 11-3 and Angus Maddison, *Dynamic Forces in Capitalist Development: A Long-Run Comparative View* (Oxford: Oxford University Press, 1991), pp. 6–7, 24–25. Groups IV–VI are based on Table 11-2.

The Learning Paradigm: Three Pillars

History suggests that the larger its bundle of competitive assets is, the easier it will be for a country to industrialize, when assets are defined to consist of anything that adds to the international competitiveness of raw labor power—say, raw materials, physical capital, "social capabilities" in the form of labor skills and managerial expertise, and, of course, proprietary technology in the form of new products and processes. The more assets a country has, the higher its value added per worker will be (Lary 1968).

Low wages have been instrumental in all industrializations—witness the importance of female and child labor in the first Industrial Revolution and thereafter. Yet for all practical purposes, the only asset with which most late industrializers have had

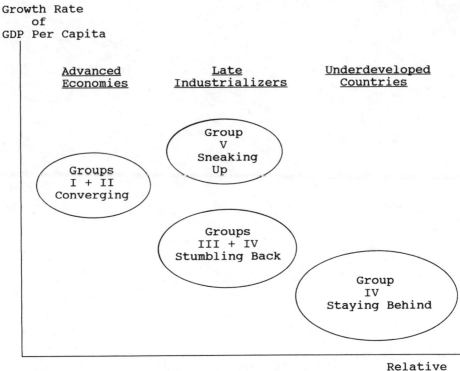

Figure 11-2. Cross-sectional spectrum of the relationships between relative backwardness and rate of growth. *Source:* See Figure 11-1.

to compete in manufacturing is low wages.[2] Nevertheless, although low wages may be a necessary condition for industrialization and may be used as a "cash cow" to generate income and foreign exchange for reinvestment in other manufacturing branches, they cannot serve as the dynamic engine of modern economic growth in the long term. As wages tend to rise in the course of industrialization, labor-intensive industries lose their competitiveness to still lower-wage countries.

Perhaps more important, even labor-intensive industries may not serve as cash cows because low wages alone may be an inadequate competitive weapon against the higher productivity levels of more advanced countries. The basic Heckscher–Ohlin trade model assumes identical production functions in the same industry in all countries, but in reality the more advanced economies may be more cost effective even in industries with high labor content, because of their superior infrastructure in their operating setting, their better management and work force skills, as well as their cache of tacit, nontransferable productivity and quality improvements. At least in the short run, the standard form of technology transfer—of designs, blueprints, and production equipment—or even a turnkey transfer, is usually not sufficient to overcome the productivity gap.[3] Under these conditions, relatively low wages do not translate into relatively low unit-labor costs and do not serve as an entrée into world markets.

Table 11-2. Growth Paths of Late-industrializing Countries, 1913–1987
(GDP per capita at 1980 international dollars and rank)

	Year					
	1913		1950		1987	
Country	$	Rank	$	Rank	$	Rank
Argentina	1,770	1	2,324	2	3,302	5
Chile	1,255	2	2,350	1	3,393	3
Philippines	985	3	898	7	1,519	11
Mexico	822	4	1,169	5	2,667	7
Peru	819	5	1,349	4	2,380	8
Colombia	801	6	1,395	3	3,027	6
Thailand	652	7	653	8	2,294	9
South Korea	610	8	564	9	4,143	2
Indonesia	529	9	484	11	1,200	12
Brazil	521	10	1,073	6	3,417	4
Taiwan	453	11	526	10	4,744	1
Pakistan	438	12	390	12	885	13
China	415	13	338	14	1,748	10
India	399	14	359	13	662	14
Bangladesh	371	15	331	15	375	15

Source: Adopted and calculated from Angus Maddison, *The World Economy in the 20th Century* (Paris: OECD, 1989), p. 19.

Exchange-rate devaluations may lower real wage costs in international markets. But currency depreciations are usually constrained by political and social conditions, workers' physiological intake requirements, and the need to import production inputs, including wage goods. Even after the real-currency devaluations in the 1960s in South Korea and Taiwan, low wages were found to be an insufficient competitive advantage against Japanese competition, notwithstanding the labor intensity of a leading sector like cotton textiles (see, e.g., Amsden 1989, Clark 1987). Latin America in the 1980s demonstrated that it was impossible to lower real wages without triggering a wage response that led to serious price instability and general macroeconomic disorder, in the form of volatile nominal and real interest rates, unpredictable foreign-exchange rates, variable and large fiscal deficits, and stop–go growth (Taylor 1988).

In contrast with conventional arguments favoring specialization in labor-intensive industries, the doyen of institutional theories of late industrialization, Alexander Gerschenkron, regards catching up as a process of "revolutionary," "eruptive" spurts, with backward countries promoting "those branches of industrial activities in which recent technological progress has been particularly rapid" (1962, pp. 9–10). Leading American and German enterprises could and did leapfrog ahead of Britain in the most dynamic sectors such as chemicals and steel because British firms could not establish impenetrable international entry barriers in the nineteenth century.

By the twentieth century this strategy had become impractical, for two reasons. First, as Table 11-3 indicates, over time the gap between the most and the least advanced countries (or even the average developed and undeveloped countries) had grown far greater. The distance to the world economic frontier, measured as the ratio

Table 11-3. Relative Backwardness of Groups of Countries, 1800–1970
(GDP per capita in 1960 U.S. dollars)

	Year				
	1800	*1860*	*1913*	*1950*	*1970*
Developed countries					
(A) Average	$198	$324	$ 662	$1,054	$2,229
(B) Most developed	240	580	1,350	2,420	3,600
Underdeveloped regions					
(C) Average	188	174	192	203	308
(D) Less developed	130	130	130	135	140
Relative backwardness					
B/A	1.2	1.8	2.0	2.3	1.6
A/C	1.1	1.9	3.4	5.2	7.2

Historical cases	Distance to World Frontier[a]
Backward Europe, late 19th century	
(example: Nordic countries)	1.8 to 3.3
Underdeveloped world, late 19th and early 20th centuries	
(example: Japan)	3.3 to 7.0
Postwar developers, average	11.9
Least developed, 1970s	25.7

Source: Adopted and calculated from Paul Bairoch, "The Main Trends in National Economic Disparities Since the Industrial Revolution," in Paul Bairoch and Maurice Levy-Leboyer, eds., *Disparities in Economic Development Since the Industrial Revolution* (New York: St. Martin's Press, 1981), p. 8.

[a]Distance is measured as the ratio of GDP per capita of the most developed economies to that of the appropriate comparison.

of GDP per capita of the most developed countries to the appropriate comparison, ranged from only 1:8 to 3:3 for the average backward European country at the end of the nineteenth century, compared with 11:9 for the average underdeveloped country after World War II and 25:7 for the typical least developed country in the 1970s.

Second, with the rise of global enterprises possessing "organizational capabilities" based on a core technology (Chandler 1990), Gerschenkron's idea of leaping to the world technological frontier could no longer work. The institutionalization of R&D in such enterprises allowed them to erect entry barriers around their proprietary technology family, which kept newcomers out. The only economy in the twentieth century to attempt to leapfrog to the world technological frontier ended in failure—namely, Russia—which was Gerschrenkron's primary analytical concern.

Gerschenkron conceived of domestic enterprises in Europe as the agents of industrialization, but increasingly after World War II, the multinational firm came to be viewed in certain development theories as the agent capable of transferring technology to backward countries. By raising productivity there, the multinational supposedly precluded the need for government intervention.[4] Whether in the role of exporter of labor-intensive manufactures (as in Taiwan and Puerto Rico), or developer of import-substitution industries (as in Mexico and Brazil), the multinational firm was credited with nudging backward countries closer to world productivity standards (see Chapter 10 for the Mexican case).

Nevertheless, casting the multinational firm at the core of the development drama has proved to be problematic in practice. Few developing countries after World War II have managed individually to attract significant amounts of foreign investment. Even in those Asian countries that the multinationals have patronized, investments from abroad have been found to amount to only a small fraction of aggregate capital requirements (Amsden 1992). Foreign capital typically *lags* rather than *leads* industrial development and tends to flow to backward countries where industrialization has already started and only then accelerates it (Herman 1991). Moreover, simply because a foreign investor is a multinational firm no longer necessarily implies that it operates at the world frontier. The production and design problems that afflict the firm at home may merely be transferred abroad, as in the case of the South American operations of some North American automobile companies (Shapiro 1993). Thus the multinational firm cannot be counted on automatically to overcome the diseconomies of backwardness mentioned earlier.

In sum, conventional development theory recommends that latecomers industrialize by "getting the prices right" (allowing supply and demand to determine prices) and typically by using low wages to gain a comparative advantage in labor-intensive industries. But in fact, successful late industrialization has been a process of using subsidies to lower production costs, such as capital, to get the prices "wrong" (preventing market forces from determining prices, such as interest rates) in order to overcome the handicap of an absence of proprietary technology, the inability to leapfrog over more advanced countries, and the inadequacy of a low wage advantage (Amsden 1989, 1992). Therefore, one necessary condition for industrializing in the twentieth century is systematic and well-coordinated government intervention to promote manufacturing investment. As we will suggest later, what seems to distinguish underdeveloped countries that are "sneaking up" from those that are "stumbling back" or "staying behind" is not less state intervention but, rather, a different set of principles governing subsidy allocation.

Export targets have been among the most important performance standards imposed by East Asian governments on business. Moreover, the long-term success of industrialization depends on achieving international manufacturing efficiency, usually first by competing against imports and then by capturing export markets (see Rodrik, forthcoming). We will stress the latter given the relatively small domestic market from which most twentieth-century countries began to industrialize and given the scale diseconomies and rigidities of certain imported technologies with respect to downsizing.

With the nondynamic bottom end of the market vulnerable to lower-wage competitors and the top end impenetrable due to technology entry barriers, successful late-industrializing countries in the twentieth century have deliberately targeted as their long-run dynamic industrializing core the postadolescent or mid-tech industries, for which technology, although expensive, is available from international suppliers and for which global demand is growing (in some cases, such as steel, simply because the world population is growing). Major examples, in historical sequence, are electrical machinery, basic chemicals, automobiles, consumer electronics, and commodity semiconductors.

Nevertheless, even if investments in mid-tech industries are the correct allocative choice, they are no guarantee of attaining international standards of productive efficiency. In order to compete against the postadolescent products from more advanced economies that enjoy higher productivity and lower cost, late industrializers in the twentieth century must sharpen their own managerial and organizational skills, shorten their learning period, and, above all, make incremental improvements in the cost, quality, and performance of their process and product. The shop floor becomes their strategic battleground. It is initially here where they must make borrowed technology work, even if it comes in the form of a "turnkey" transfer, because no technology, however mature, is fully documented, completely understood, and therefore perfectly transferable (Nelson 1987, Rosenberg 1976, chap. 9). It is on the shop floor where they must adapt borrowed technology to suit their targeted market size and other idiosyncratic conditions. It is also here where they subject borrowed technology to continuous incremental upgrading.[5]

Going one step further, even if a firm successfully identifies a mid-tech industry as the proper one to enter and even if it invests successfully in incremental product and process improvements, it faces grave uncertainties about the success of its product in international markets. These uncertainties arise because global oligopolies may come up with a revolutionary product that may render a mid-tech product—however seasoned on the shop floor—obsolete overnight (as in the case of, say, the process innovation of petrochemicals replacing coal chemicals, or the product innovation of personal computers making typewriters outmoded). Insofar as the late-industrializing firm is unable to protect itself by innovating further around a core technology family, it protects itself by routinizing a strategy of wide diversification into many technologically unrelated mature product markets, as in the case of Japanese *zaibatsu,* Korean *chaebol,* and Latin American groups (Leff 1978; Amsden and Hikino 1994). The firm structure that results from this strategy is thus a network or collection of technologically isolated firms. Because a detailed and systematic knowledge of products and processes is not embodied in the top of this type of group firm, top management tends to confine itself to the functions of resource allocation and monitoring.

We now examine in more detail how the imperative to industrialize by borrowing technology generates each of the three characteristics just noted: government intervention, shop-floor focus, and group firm structure.

Government Intervention

Even in the classic economic liberalism of the first Industrial Revolution in England, the government played a positive and significant role (Coats 1971, Taylor 1972). Starting in the late eighteenth century, governments were actively involved in developing transportation, communications, and all sorts of education as well as stable banking systems and legal and administrative frameworks generally. Over time, more direct microeconomic intervention that affected price competition increased everywhere to the extent that tariff protection to infant and other industries became widespread, for a host of reasons related not just to industrial development but also to revenue and politics (Nye 1991). Ideology aside, laissez-faire simply never existed (Goodrich 1967, Hughes 1991, Lively 1955). As Karl Polanyi observed: "The road to the free market was opened and kept open by an enormous increase in continuous, centrally organized and controlled interventionism" (1944, p. 140).

Nevertheless, given a lack of competitive assets, late-industrializing states in the twentieth century did all this and much more, examples being Brazil, Turkey, India, South Korea, Taiwan, and Japan, but because Japan was relatively less underdeveloped, its state could do less than later industrializers could.[6] A case in point is the financial markets, for which state intervention went much further than even Alexander Gerschenkron envisioned. In the absence of highly developed banking institutions, Gerschenkron recognized the need for governments to arrange financing for manufacturing investments. But late-industrializing governments have not only made finance available, they have also targeted capital to specific firms and selected industries on highly concessionary terms.

In Taiwan, for example, a market-determined interest rate could be said to have been approximated in the 1960s, 1970s, and 1980s by the "curb market" interest rate. The curb rate was not determined in perfect competition because there were large, wholesale lenders, but it was still quite competitively established. Below the equilibrium curb market rate was the rate set by the government-owned commercial banks. These banks were habitually getting the interest rate "wrong," as evidenced by the fact that the commercial bank rate was consistently below the curb rate, often for the same borrower. Moreover, the nominal interest rate paid by the big firms that received commercial bank credit was higher than their effective interest rate because they then lent to smaller firms at higher prices (Biggs 1988).

After South Korea's financial "liberalization" in the 1980s, the "right" price of capital may be said to have been approximated by the interest rate in the secondary short-term government bond market. The misnomer of "liberalization" is indicated by the fact that whereas in May 1989 the interest rate in this market was 18.9 percent, the loan interest rate of government-controlled commercial banks was only 12.5 percent (Amsden and Euh 1993). Obviously, commercial bank credit was still being subsidized even after "liberalization." South Korea had a three-tier financial structure for the first 25 years of its development. It was characterized by a curb market interest rate, a commercial bank rate, and a rate on foreign loans. Due to inflation and the relative constancy of the exchange rate, the real interest rate on foreign loans was negative throughout most of this period (Park 1985). Not all three prices that existed side by side in Korea's capital market could have been right, and the negative real interest rate on foreign loans was fundamentally "wrong" in a capital-scarce country.[7]

Even Thailand, with its reputation for economic liberalism, had positive real interest rates for only 24 out of 52 quarters between 1970 and 1982. A World Bank study called this performance "quite respectable in comparison with most developing countries" (Hanson and Neal 1984, Annex 6, p. 3).

When a "Minimalist" State Works

The "price-distorting" subsidization of business by government has been typical of late-industrializing learners but not of earlier ones. The Nordic laggards in the "convergence club" did not experience nearly as thoroughgoing government support in their initial phase of modern industrial development (Lindbeck 1974, chap. 1, for Sweden). Government intervention tended to be "minimalist" (the term is Streeten's, 1992) because Scandinavian industry was not in dire need of assistance. Economic liberalism thus offered a "historic opportunity for economic growth through special-ization" (Hodne 1983, p. 67). From the mid-nineteenth century to World War I, the global demand for Nordic raw materials and agricultural products was high. Further-more, as shown in Table 11-3, the distance separating its industry from the world fron-tier was modest: "The Scandinavian countries were not so far behind the leading industrialized nations as to need a special boost to speed up their economic develop-ment" (Berend and Ranki 1982, p. 65).

A boost was unnecessary owing partly to the Nordic countries' accumulated engi-neering skills. Writing about "protoindustrialization" in Scandinavia, Isacson and Magnusson observed:

> The industrial revolution did not bring about any definite break with the old pre-industrial society. Mechanization was a slow process, and at least within certain important industries, production continued to rely on the physical strength and skill of the individual worker for many years. This was especially true of the engi-neering industry, which played such an important part in the industrialization of Sweden, where the craftsmanship of the individual skilled worker was indis-pensable until far into the twentieth century. (1987, p. 135)

In the case of high-end luxury products, such as furniture and specialty foods, there was a strong and direct continuity in their traditional, premass production of such products and their modern manufacture. The luxury artisanal products of Europe in general found specialized international market niches that proved to be important "cash cows" for earning foreign exchange to finance industrial develop-ment. Scandinavian craft workers transplanted to modern industries may not have been able initially to compete against the higher productivity of British industry, but it was often possible to restructure production and modernize their skills (Piore and Sabel 1984; Gustavson, 1986, chaps. 10 and 11 for detailed Swedish cases). This trans-formation process was reinforced by heavy public investment in technical and voca-tional education (see Locke 1984, for Germany). According to Lindbeck, Sweden's "impressive technological development" had something to do with the establishment, "as early as the eighteenth century, of a number of technical schools, some of which during the last three decades of the nineteenth century were developed into technical colleges" (Lindbeck 1974, p. 5).

In late-industrializing countries, by contrast, an artisan tradition typically either never developed or was totally destroyed by competitive imports, as in the case of hand-loom weaving in India and indigenous iron making in Japan (see Thomson 1991, for the Mexican case). Whatever handicraft products survived did not succeed in capturing high-price specialty niches in international markets. Nor could emerging industries use indigenous skills, if any, as modern factory labor; indeed, sometimes such skills were found to be a negative factor, as in Korea's modern shipbuilding indus-try (Amsden 1989).

In addition, although Sweden was a catch-up country—borrowing technology and struggling to make it work—it became an innovator in its own right during the second Industrial Revolution (Dahmen 1970). As Lindbeck notes,

> To a very large extent the expansion of manufacturing during the first decades of the twentieth century was based on Swedish innovations—steam turbines,

centrifugal separators, ball bearings, the adjustable spanner, the safety match, air compressors, automatic lighthouse technique, various types of precision instruments, techniques for precision measurements, and so forth. (1974, p. 5)

Given all of these competitive assets, it is little wonder that government intervention could be "minimalist."

Discipline of Business

When comparing the behavior of late industrializers that are "sneaking up" closer to the world frontier with those that are "stumbling back" or just "staying behind," an important difference between them lies in their management of the subsidy allocation process. Slow-growing late industrializers have tended to blanket businesses with subsidies without being willing or able to extract concrete performance standards in exchange. By contrast, fast-growing late industrializers have generally succeeded in disciplining subsidy recipients, by imposing on them strict and "monitorable" performance standards (Amsden 1989, 1991b, 1992). By imposing performance standards on business, the government also subjected itself to evaluation by objective criteria.

In the case of Taiwan, subsidies to exporters in the 1960s were tied to targets administered by industry associations that were overseen by government agencies. These associations acted as cartels that collected dues from members out of which bonuses to exporters were paid. Firms were allocated export targets and were penalized if they fell short of their targets (Haggard 1990, Wade 1990). Loan officers of Taiwan's state-owned banks were also held personally responsible (in terms of pay and promotion) for the credit they extended. Consequently, they were both conservative in their lending policies—lending only to relatively large firms—and careful in their monitoring of how effectively borrowers used their credit (Biggs 1988).

Although "infant industry protection," as conceived in the nineteenth century, was in theory a one-shot deal designed to enable a new enterprise to reach a minimal efficient scale of operation, subsidization in late industrialization has, in practice, been multistage. It has operated not just at start-up but also at later points in an economy's catch-up trajectory (as was also the case of postwar Sweden). For instance, the Taiwan machine tool industry received little government support in its early growth phase but was subsidized later to help it acquire financially troubled American machine tool companies and ratchet up into a higher-quality market niche (Amsden 1977, OECD 1990). Ironically, the American machine tool industry was also receiving government subsidies at the same time as the Taiwan machine tool industry was receiving them, but with no performance standards attached (Amsden 1991b). By the 1990s the Taiwan government was making the preferential treatment of business dependent on the firm's meeting conditions related to R&D spending, personnel training, and even environmental protection standards (Dahlman and Sananikone 1990).

Subsidies in the slow-growing, late-industrializing countries have thus tended to be allocated according to the principle of "giveaway," whereas in the fast-growing ones they have tended to be allocated according to the principle of reciprocity. In both cases the governments have disciplined labor. What distinguishes the East Asian countries is that the governments also have disciplined capital (Amsden 1989, 1991b, 1992).

Education and Income Equality

Designing and monitoring performance standards require an able, well-educated bureaucracy. By late-industrializing standards, fast growers such as South Korea and Taiwan did, in fact, generally invest more than slow growers did in "social capabilities," as defined by Abramovitz in Chapter 4. To equip their corporate managers and workers with the capabilities to infuse and improve technology, they invested heavily in technical education (see Nelson 1993). To enable their government officials to operate macroeconomic and industrial policies, they invested heavily in the education of their civil service.[8] In an industrialization based on learning, education is obviously key.

Imposing performance standards on business in exchange for subsidies in the early phase of industrialization also requires a critical degree of "autonomy" on the state's part. This autonomy is influenced by the political power of private economic interest groups whose strength and cohesiveness, in turn, seem to depend on: (1) the level of development of the manufacturing sector and (2) income distribution. What made it possible for the East Asian states to discipline business was the relative weakness of both manufacturing and agrarian interest groups at the outset of the postwar industrial development (Amsden 1992).

Asia's manufacturing sector, except for Japan's, was extremely underdeveloped after the war even by the standards of other backward countries. According to two indicators of manufacturing development presented in Table 11-4—the ratio of manufacturing to agricultural net product and the net value of manufacturing per capita—East Asia's manufacturing sector in 1955 was much less advanced than Latin America's (the backwardness of India's manufacturing sector is exaggerated because of India's huge agrarian population). Owing to their weakness, East Asian manufacturing enterprises became dependent on state support to achieve a growth spurt and also had fewer of their own institutions than Latin American businesses did to shield them from state interference (commercial banks in South Korea and Taiwan were state-owned).

Second, East Asian income tended to be more equally distributed than Latin American income was (see Table 11-5).[9] Assuming that unequal income distribution implies access to a disproportionate share of resources by small groups in agriculture or industry, the more concentrated economic power is, the more these groups can both bypass state sources of investment finance and buy government favors. Japan, Korea, and Taiwan all underwent a land reform in the late 1940s during which their agrarian aristocracies were expropriated. With a manufacturing sector only in its infancy and an agrarian sector devoid of powerful interest groups, the challenges to state authority remained weak. The Philippines represents the outstanding Asian exception to sustained growth, and it has "stumbled back," bearing the burden of a highly unequal income distribution.

Table 11-4. Ratio of Manufacturing to Agricultural Net Product and Net Value of Manufacturing per Capita, Latin America and Asia, 1955

Country	Ratio of Manufacturing to Agricultural Net Product	Net Value of Manufacturing per Head (U.S. $)
Latin America		
Argentina	1.32	145
Brazil	0.72	50
Mexico	1.00	60
Venezuela	1.43	95
Chile	1.35	75
Colombia	0.42	45
Peru	0.52	25
Asia		
South Korea	0.20	8
Indonesia	0.20	10
Philippines	0.32	13
Thailand	0.28	10
India	0.30	7

Source: Alfred Maizels, *Industrial Growth and World Trade* (Cambridge: Cambridge University Press, 1963), as cited in Christopher Freeman, "Catching up in World Growth and World Trade," paper, Science Policy Research Unit, Sussex University, England.

Competitive Focus

If the technologies of the first Industrial Revolution were relatively simple and inexpensive to apply (Jewkes, Sawers, and Stillerman 1969, chap. 3, Musson 1972), by the late nineteenth century the commercial application of new technologies had become much more complicated and costly. Often, therefore, individual inventors did not successfully apply or commercialize their own discoveries. In Germany and particularly the United States, entrepreneurs began to exploit new technology, devised either by themselves or by others (Hughes 1989). They did so by establishing the hierarchical organizations that could systematically use and further develop the potential of new technologies.

Therefore, the strategic focus of the leading enterprises of the second Industrial Revolution became top management organization, with its proprietary asset of technologically experienced senior managers, controlling large-scale plants and distribution networks. Once founded, these organizations could exploit new technology, increasingly in the context of R&D laboratories.[10] On the basis of these assets and "organizational capabilities," the first movers firmly established themselves as members of international oligopolies, which made it difficult for newcomers, domestic or international, to upstage them in Gerschenkronian fashion (Chandler 1990).

In response, late industrializers in the twentieth century made incremental shopfloor improvements of existing products their principal competitive weapon. Of

Table 11-5. Income Distribution
(The ratio by which the income of the top fifth of the
population exceeds that of the bottom fifth)

Country	Year	Ratio
Asia		
East Asia		
Hong Kong	1981	12.1
Japan	1979	4.0
South Korea[a]	1981	4.9
Taiwan[b]	—	4.3
Southeast Asia		
Indonesia[c]	1983	11.9
Philippines	1971	16.1
Singapore	1977–78	7.5
Thailand	1975–76	11.2
South Asia		
Bangladesh	1976–77	7.6
India	1975–76	10.1
Latin America		
South America		
Brazil	1982	27.7
Mexico[d]	1977	15.4
Central America		
Dominican Republic[d]	1976–77	12.5
El Salvador[d]	1976–77	8.6
Guatemala	1979–81	10.6

Source: All countries except Taiwan and Indonesia: National survey data
reported in United Nations, "Special Study," *National Accounts Statistics*
(New York: United Nations, 1985).

[a]Urban only (data for other countries are national).

[b]Statistic reported in Kuo-Ting Li, *The Evolution of Policy Behind Taiwan's
Development Success* (New Haven, CT: Yale University Press, 1988).

[c]Rural only, as reported in Alan Gelb and associates, *Oil Windfalls: Blessing
or Curse?* (New York: Oxford University Press, 1988).

[d]Based on available rather than total households, which tends to bias estimates of inequality downward.

course, the leading enterprises in the first and second Industrial Revolutions did not
ignore the shop floor or fail to invest in incremental change. The best of them clearly
did (see Chapter 6, Hounshell and Smith 1988 for the detailed case of Du Pont, and
Rosenberg 1982, chap. 3). But in the first and especially second Industrial Revolutions,
what happened on the shop floor was a reaction to the generation or acquisition of new
technology at the top of the organization. In the second Industrial Revolution the shop
floor followed the firm's growth strategy, whereas in late industrialization, it led it, as
indicated by an example from steel making.

Steel Making

Carnegie Steel's top management and, indeed, Andrew Carnegie himself were fanati-
cal about reducing both direct and indirect production costs, especially in the 1870s

and 1880s when the trend in the general price level worldwide was downward. As Carnegie's biographer notes: "Costs would always be Carnegie's obsession in business, and his constant concern to reduce them in every department was to a large measure the secret of his success" (Wall 1970, p. 337). What is different in the histories of early and late steel-making countries is that such cost reduction in the former was pursued in conjunction with a more fundamental quest to lower costs by means of major technological breakthroughs, not least of all the costs associated with a high-wage economy. As David Brody writes in his history of American steelworkers: "The impulse for economy shaped American steel manufacture. It inspired the inventiveness that mechanized the productive operations" (1960, p. 2).

Innovation and investments in incremental improvements operated in conjunction in the sense that Carnegie's search for ways to reduce production costs was a matter of trial and error. He learned from other steel makers, both American and foreign, but he was an innovator to the extent that he had no clear model to follow. For example,

> Carnegie's insistence upon trying out the open hearth process in the mid-1870s . . . proved to be wise. The Siemens furnaces not only enabled the company to produce a higher grade of steel for special orders, but they also proved to be a valuable laboratory for experimentation that would eventually prove the practicality of the open hearth system for the mass production of steel. Carnegie's introduction of the Siemen's process at this early date gives further evidence that he did not follow his own dictum, "Pioneering don't pay." (Wall 1970, p. 321)

The absence of a model to follow made Carnegie a pioneer, whereas subsequent steel makers had an existing model to follow and target to achieve. In the case of the Brazilian USIMINAS steel mill, for example,

> A market crisis forced USIMINAS to stretch the capacity of its original equipment in order to get a better capital output ratio. Such capacity stretching was possible thanks to the implementation of a standard cost system with an elaborate organizational infrastructure to study its existing equipment, compare it to the best world performance, and then try to reach the same or higher levels. (Dahlman and Valadares Fonseca 1987, p. 163)

As followers, the steel industries of Japan, South Korea, India, Brazil, and other late-industrializing countries had a model to follow, technology to buy, and best-practice standards to achieve, but even when the technology was acquired through foreign license rather than reverse engineering, it was not transferred in complete working order. Instead, it had to be adapted and modified in a new environment in order to work at "rated" capacity, if at all. Moreover, cost constraints forced companies like USIMINAS to employ inexperienced local talent to grope toward rated capacity and beyond, whereas a first mover like Carnegie Steel employed the best engineering talent (Alexander L. Holley, who supervised the building of Carnegie's steel works, was considered "the greatest authority on Bessemer steel mills in America, if not the world") (Wall 1970, p. 312).

South Korea's highly efficient state-owned steel company (POSCO, for short), whose survival depended on how well the technology from the Nippon Steel Corporation of Japan was absorbed and improved, first assigned its best people to work with foreign plant designers and engineers and then assigned them to work on "line" rather than "staff" functions. This set a precedent of taking production seriously that was reinforced by requiring all managers to serve a term on the shop floor as part of their recruitment training. Immediately after commencing operations, POSCO faced a situation of excess demand for steel in its fast-growing domestic market. Its objective became increasing its output volume, which it did by using some of the technical skills it had acquired in the technology transfer experience, such as know-how related to downtime minimization, the stabilization of operations, and the optimization of each piece of equipment. POSCO also invested in new capital equipment but held down engineering costs by using its own staff with experience in the first phase of technology transfer to substitute for foreign technical assistance in some types of capacity additions in the second phase (Amsden 1989).

A similar regard for nurturing a dedicated corps of production-oriented managers and workers is evident in TISCO, India's integrated iron and steel company, the largest subsidiary of the Tata business group. According to Lall,

> Over the 70-plus years of its existence it has built up a team of singularly dedicated professional managers and technologists as well as a cohesive and skilled labor force which have enabled it to continue with carefully-nurtured but ancient plant. Much of its survival in adversity can be traced to the technological capability of this large group. (1987, p. 93).

Thus, the company's very survival depended on plant- or lower-level management. Lall then goes on to discuss the "innumerable process improvements" made over time by this group and by the R&D department "which has also worked on process developments" (pp. 96–97).

With respect to the research and development of Carnegie Steel's successor, the United States Steel Corporation, it was undertaken very belatedly and then only half-heartedly. U.S. Steel also did not invest aggressively in foreign markets (Chandler 1990, pp. 138–39). Therefore, when late-industrializing competitors emerged on the scene beginning in the 1960s, U.S. Steel could not fight them using either of these competitive weapons or superior shop-floor capability. The American steel industry's incipient turnaround in the early 1990s owed much to its recent technological and marketing tie-ins with Japanese and Korean steel makers (Hicks 1992).

The shop-floor orientation of late-industrializing countries did not preclude their investing in R&D (finance permitting). In absolute value, R&D investments in the steel industry in Japan exceeded those in the United States by the early 1970s (UNIDO 1988). In the case of South Korea, POSCO began producing steel in 1973, almost exactly 100 years after Carnegie Steel started production, but whereas over 50 years elapsed from the time of Carnegie's start-up to the time when U.S. Steel opened an R&D laboratory, POSCO made a large investment in R&D only 5 years after its foundation. Nevertheless, POSCO's R&D, like that of TISCO, was related principally to solving production problems or supporting process engineering.

Writing in 1974, Terutomo Ozawa observed that most R&D in a wide range of industries in Japan was also principally production related. Ozawa cites a survey by the Ministry of International Trade and Industry (MITI) of Japanese product development in 1962, which found that large Japanese manufacturers spent only ¥37.7 million for R&D but over ¥301.6 million for plant layout and production engineering. The survey also reported that ¥12.8 million for R&D and ¥175.0 million for production engineering went to "adaptive activity" related to imported technology (Ozawa 1974, p. 69). Moreover, even as Japan's competitive focus began to shift by the 1980s from the shop floor to the design office and R&D laboratory, its historical shop-floor orientation colored the way that design and R&D were undertaken. This orientation was evident in a tighter integration of R&D and shop-floor activities than in the United States (Clark and Fujimoto 1991, Dertouzos et al. 1989, chap. 5). The Japanese case exemplifies the sustained shop-floor orientation of the late industrializers.

Conglomerate Strategy and Group Structure

The leading enterprises of late industrialization ultimately target their strategic growth core to mid-tech industries. Entry barriers into these industries tend to be substantial, in terms of risk and the financial resources required to invest in foreign technical licenses, physical facilities, engineers, and managers. Thus, many mid-tech industries in late-industrializing countries are characterized by oligopolistic competition among large firms which, through technical licensing, often reflect a similar pattern of world oligopoly, as we will discuss in detail later. As is shown in Table 11-6, even Taiwan, which is usually cited as a prominent example of small enterprise-oriented industrialization, shows a pattern of large firms located in mid-tech and increasingly high-tech industries.[11]

When a country cannot develop large industrial enterprises for geoeconomic or possibly political reasons, it has to develop large financial and trading firms as organizers and coordinators of small-scale manufacturing firms. Hong Kong and Singapore are apparently the prime examples of this route to successful late industrialization, as is suggested in Table 11-7. This table also shows that all prominent late-industrializing countries exhibit both big financial intermediaries and large distribution organizations, except for Taiwan, whose efforts to boost Japanese-type trading companies failed in the 1970s.

Although many of the large industrial enterprises in late-industrializing countries have grown to be comparable in size to those from industrialized economies, their development paths have been significantly different. Without a proprietary technology family to protect it and to provide it with seeds to grow, the late-industrializing firm is squeezed from below by lower-wage countries and from above by international product innovators. It is also threatened by other firms in its domestic market that pursue a similar strategy of incrementally improving production techniques. In order to reduce the risks associated with a single product line and to overcome the absence of a core technology for purposes of related diversification, firms in late-industrializing countries have entered widely unrelated industries from an early phase of their development.

Table 11-6. Distribution of the 200 Largest Industrial Enterprises in Late-industrializing Countries, by Country and Industry Group, 1985

| Country | Industry groups[a] | | | | |
	High-tech[b]	Mid-tech	Low-tech	Petroleum	Total
Asia	23	40	36	19	118
South Korea	11	13	11	0	35
India	7	15	10	7	39
Taiwan	5	7	5	1	18
Malaysia	0	2	3	1	6
Philippines	0	0	3	3	6
Others	0	3	4	7	14
Latin America	4	15	20	12	51
Brazil	3	5	7	3	18
Argentina	0	4	6	2	12
Mexico	0	2	3	1	6
Venezuela	1	1	3	1	6
Chile	0	3	1	1	5
Others	0	0	0	4	4
Middle East	2	3	2	6	13
Turkey	1	2	2	1	6
Others	1	1	0	5	7
Africa	0	2	10	6	18
Total	29	60	68	43	200

Source: Compiled and reclassified from "South 600," *South,* August 1987, pp. 14–24, and checked against other available sources such as *Moody's International.*

[a]Enterprises included are those owned and controlled by Third World nationals or governments, and they are ranked by sales. Given the usually poor quality of data, the industry classification is sometimes arbitrary. Enterprises are operating units.

[b]High-tech: chemicals, pharmaceuticals, computers, electrical and electronic products, aircraft and aerospace, and professional and scientific equipment.
Mid-tech: rubber products; stone, clay, and glass; primary and fabricated metals; general machinery; and automobile and transportation equipment.
Low-tech: food, textiles and apparel, lumber and paper, and miscellaneous manufactures.

Diversification and Business Groups

Business groups that are widely diversified have acted as major agents of late industrialization not only in Japan (whose prewar *zaibatsu* and postwar *keiretsu* became well known) but also in Brazil, Mexico, Argentina, Peru, Turkey, India, Japan, South Korea, Taiwan, Malaysia, the Philippines, Thailand, South Africa, and elsewhere.

Historically, diversification per se has been a common strategy of large industrial enterprises in all types of modern economies. In the case of technologically advanced multidivisional firms, however, the basis of diversification is their core technology, which they exploit in related industries (Chandler 1977, 1990). For instance, I. G. Farben, a diversified chemical giant in interwar Germany, as shown in Figure 11-3, extensively used its core expertise, organic chemical technology, in its diversification into pharmaceuticals, fertilizers, photographic supplies, fibers, and explosives (Hayes 1987). Thus, diversification becomes an offensive weapon whose industry sphere is somewhat focused.

Leading firms in countries catching up in the nineteenth century followed a sim-

Table 11-7. Distribution of the 50 Largest Financial and Marketing Enterprises in Late-industrializing Countries, 1985[a]

Country	Banks	Nonbank Financial Institutions[b]	Trading and Marketing Companies
Asia	23	43	22
South Korea	7	15	10
Hong Kong	2	10	5
Malaysia	2	8	2
Singapore	1	5	2
Taiwan	6	1	0
Thailand	1	4	0
India	2	0	1
Others	2	0	2
Latin America	8	7	23
Brazil	4	5	12
Mexico	3	2	5
Others	1	0	6
Middle East	16	0	1
Africa	3	0	4
Total	50	50	50

Source: Compiled from "South 600," *South,* August 1987, pp. 14–28, and September 1987, p. 42.

[a]See Table 11-6.

[b]Nonbank financial institutions include insurance firms, investment companies, and other financial service companies.

ilar basic pattern. The biggest manufacturers in Sweden today, for example, originated in proprietary technological breakthroughs during the second Industrial Revolution: The basis of L. M. Ericsson (founded in 1876) was the telephone; that of Alfa Laval (1879), the separator; that of ASEA (1890), electrical equipment; and that of SKF (1907), bearings. Despite their sheer size, these companies' product lines are still quite focused, and their growth strategy and corporate structure have been closer to those of multidivisional enterprises than to those of diversified business groups.

By contrast, firms without a core and related technological capability have diversified into technologically unrelated or remotely related areas. Diversification constitutes a necessary but defensive tactic for growth. The Nissan *zaibatsu,* illustrated in Figure 11-4, is a good case of unrelated diversification in Japan. The enterprise group emerged in the 1930s under the strong leadership of Gisuke Aikawa and played a major role in the chemicals and heavy-industry fields. Yet as the figure shows, the group as a whole did not possess a coherent technology core around which subsidiaries and operating units could organize. The group, therefore, simply collapsed after World War II, although some individual firms within the group that nurtured a core technology within themselves survived to become prominent global players in their industries. Nissan Automobile and Hitachi Manufacturing are the best-known examples.

One of the largest industrial enterprises of the late-industrializing nations, Samsung of South Korea, shows a similar diversification strategy and group structure, which again resulted from the absence of a core technology (see Figure 11-5). Origi-

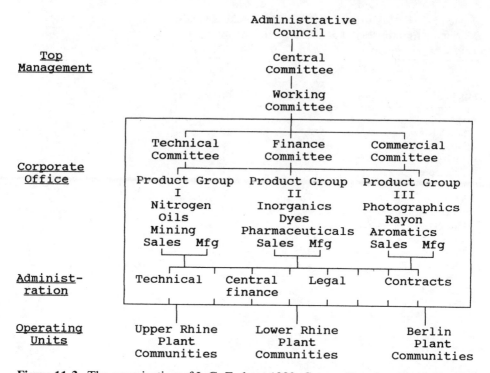

Figure 11-3. The organization of I. G. Farben, 1930. *Source:* Translated and simplified from Helmuth Tammen, *Die IG Farbenindustries Aktien-Gesellschaft, 1925–1933: Ein Chemiekonzern in der Weimarer Republik* (Berlin: H. Tammen, 1978).

nally a trading company, Samsung developed in the 1950s as one of the earliest *chaebol* groups, by expanding into sugar manufacturing, woolen textiles, and life insurance. The group in the 1970s expanded into mid-tech and later into high-tech fields such as shipbuilding, electrical manufacturing, petrochemicals, electronics, and telecommunications. Consequently, the group today, which is still family controlled despite its huge size, resembles the organization of the former Nissan *zaibatsu* rather than that of I. G. Farben.

Business groups in other late-industrializing countries also provide typical examples of unrelated diversification (see Leff 1978). In the 1970s the CYDSA group in Mexico produced as many as 80 products, including organic chemicals, textiles, cement, and services (Concheiro and Fragoso 1979). In Thailand in the 1980s the industries covered by the Saha Union Group ranged from polyester textiles, to machinery and spare parts, to construction services, to limousine services, to canned seafoods (Suehiro 1985). (For other countries, see Amsden and Hikino 1994.)

The trend toward diversification is further intensified by "bandwagon effects" in oligopolistic rivalry: If one business group diversifies into a "new" industry (for the country in question), others will feel compelled to follow suit in order to maintain parity in overall size and strength.[12] Because the "new" technology is usually available from several international firms that constitute world technological oligopolies, domestic firms also import variations of the same technological family and start com-

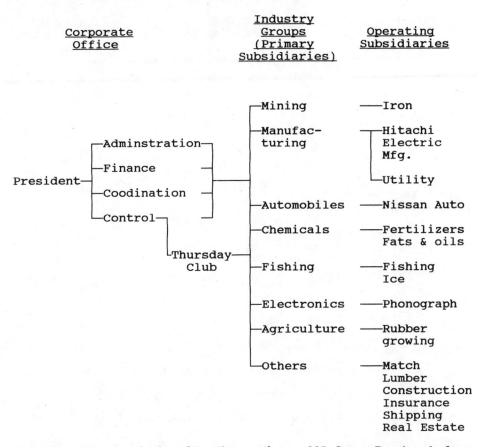

Figure 11-4. The organization of the Nissan *zaibatsu,* 1937. *Source:* Based on the figures and descriptions of Masaru Udagawa, *Shinko zaibatsu* (Tokyo: Nihon keizai shimbunsha, 1984), pp. 52–59.

peting against one another by improving them. Not only technology but also oligopolistic structures are transferred worldwide.

A classic case of this type of oligopolistic game can be found in Japan's heavy electrical machinery sector. Two domestic pioneers in the industry, both affiliated with the Mitsui *zaibatsu,* imported their technology from General Electric of the United States (the two merged to form Toshiba in 1939). Then in 1923 Mitsubishi established a heavy electrical business with technological ties to Westinghouse, and Furukawa, the copper mining and refining giant, founded Fuji Electric Manufacturing as a joint venture with Siemens (Uchida 1980, Watanabe 1984). In still later industrializers, the government provision of subsidies to develop a new industry (new to the late industrializer in question but most likely mid-tech by international standards) was also an incentive for oligopolistic bandwagon rivalry, as in the rush of the big three South Korean business groups to enter the automobile, shipbuilding, and heavy-machinery industries.

In reality, late-industrializing enterprises have pursued strategies of vertical integration and unrelated diversification simultaneously, in unsystematic and opportu-

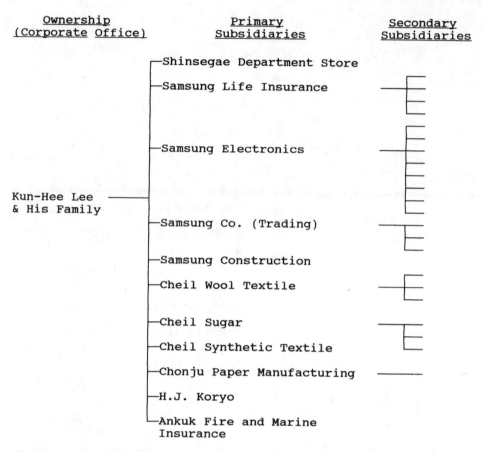

Figure 11-5. The Samsung Group of Korea. *Source:* Company information.

nistic ways. An illuminating example of this can be found in the remarks of the chairman of the Lucky-Goldstar group of South Korea:

> My father and I started a cosmetic cream factory in the 1940s. At the time, no company could supply us with plastic caps of adequate quality for cream jars, so we had to start a plastic business. Plastic caps alone were not sufficient to run the plastic-molding plant, so we added combs, toothbrushes, and soap boxes. This plastics business also led us to manufacture electrical and electronic products and telecommunications equipment. The plastics business also took us into oil refining which needed a tanker-shipping company. The oil-refining company alone was paying an insurance premium amounting to more than half the total revenue of the then largest insurance company in Korea. Thus, an insurance company was started. This natural step-by-step evolution through related businesses resulted in the Lucky-Goldstar group as we see it today. (Harvard Business School, 1985)

Lucky-Goldstar's product linkages are not always obvious, but in its chairman's view, they reflect a rational strategy.

Operational Characteristics: When Diversification Works

Top management behaves differently in the group structure just described, compared with the managerial enterprises described by Chandler (1991). The top management of technology-focused multidivisional enterprises, based on technical as well as administrative capabilities, strategically controlled all divisional units (Goold and Campbell 1987). It was concerned not only with the allocation of resources among the units but also with their manufacturing efficiency.[13]

In the successful case of the group structure of late industrialization, on the other hand, the function of top management is more or less confined to allocating resources among the units (product divisions or subsidiaries) and monitoring their performance. Each business unit is responsible for productive efficiency (see the examples of the Nissan *zaibatsu* in Figure 11-4 and the Samsung *chaebol* in Figure 11-5). This functional separation between top and operational management resulted from two factors. First, as long as the competitive weapon of late industrialization was incremental improvements on the shop floor, top management, by definition, could not contribute directly. Second, given the nature and the speed of diversification, top management could not acquire and exercise systematic technical knowledge of the firm's widely diversified products.

Foreign Operations

If late-industrializing firms adopted a strategy of diversification relatively early in their corporate histories, compared with American or European modern industrial enterprises, they were also relatively late in multinationalizing their manufacturing operations.

A major strategy of industrial enterprises of advanced economies has been jumping overseas in the form of a manufacturing investment to exploit a technological or organizational competitive asset. Tariffs overseas played only a secondary role as the motive of direct investment (Hymer 1979, Kindleberger 1969). Thus, Singer Manufacturing Company, one of the earliest multinational enterprises, established its first overseas factory in Glasgow, Scotland, in 1867, only 16 years after Isaac Singer founded the company for commercializing his patented sewing machine, and in 1874 the company sold more than half of its products overseas (Carstensen 1984, p. 75, Hounshell 1984, pp. 82–84, 93, Wilkins 1970, p. 43).

On the other hand, because individual late-industrializing firms do not possess a technological edge, they typically rely on exports to serve foreign markets and delay manufacturing overseas directly (at least in the markets intended to consume their outputs rather than supply their inputs). This is especially the case in foreign markets in which technologically advanced domestic firms occupy the dominant position. Moreover, the competitive asset of late-industrializing enterprises, incremental process and product improvements, is often too intangible to be transferred overseas easily, so only significant trade barriers can provoke them to start overseas operations as a defensive measure.

A telling example of this is the Nissan Motor Company. This Japanese automobile maker, originally established in 1933 within the Nissan *zaibatsu* (see Figure 11-

4), had various ties to foreign manufacturers, notably Austin Motors of Great Britain. Nissan started its overseas marketing activities early in its history, and by 1969 its aggregate exports topped 1 million units. The company started its overseas manufacturing in Mexico in 1961, but for the production of its most significant export market, the United States, Nissan waited to invest until 1983, a 50-year lag after its founding, when trade restrictions became too heavy to bear. Nissan's competitor, Toyota Motor, an affiliate of the Mitsui group, followed a similar pattern. It began exporting cars to the United States in 1957 but began operating in the United States (in a joint venture with General Motors) only in 1984 (Toyota Motor 1988, Udagawa 1985). By contrast, the Ford Motor Company, originally incorporated in 1903, began overseas manufacturing first in Canada in 1904 and then in Britain in 1911. By 1914 the company's Model T had become the best-selling automobile in the British market (Wilkins 1970, p. 97, Wilkins and Hill 1964, pp. 16–18, 46–48, 51).

The preference of late industrializers to serve foreign markets through exports rather than manufacturing investments resulted in the establishment of a unique organization—the general trading company. Because the late-industrializing firm's products were scattered across many industries and because overseas trade (particularly exports) occupied a critical position in the firm's profitability, late-industrializing firms formed subsidiaries to handle the trading activities of their entire group. For instance, the most prominent of the prewar Japanese *zaibatsu,* Mitsui, founded a general trading company, Mitsui & Co., in 1876 as the group's import and export activities expanded after the Meiji Restoration. Within a few years it established overseas branches in Shanghai, Hong Kong, New York, London, and Paris, handling a wide variety of agricultural, mining, and manufacturing products. By the early twentieth century, the trading company handled one-fifth of Japan's total trade (Mitsui & Co. 1977, pp. 23–54). Although Japan's trading companies became famous because of their size and scope of activities, general trading companies were also established in Malaysia, Thailand, the Philippines, Taiwan, South Korea, Turkey, and Brazil (Cho 1987, Junid 1980).

Finally, another distinctive motive behind foreign investments by late-industrializing countries is the acquisition of technology. Whereas the multinationals of advanced countries have gone overseas to exploit their own technologies, late-industrializing enterprises have gone overseas to acquire more advanced technology than they are capable of developing at home. For instance, in the late 1980s, Samsung Electronics Company opened R&D laboratories in New Jersey and Osaka, Japan, where world leaders in electronics are located. As noted earlier, the Taiwan government began to help local machine tool builders buy financially ailing American machine tool companies as a way of skirting trade barriers and acquiring advanced technology.

Convergence or Divergence?

Our major purpose has been to develop a paradigm of late industrialization at the core of which is borrowing technology that has already been developed by firms in more advanced countries. Whereas a driving force behind the first and second Industrial Revolutions was the innovation of radically new products and processes, no major technological breakthrough has been associated with late-industrializing economies. The imperative to learn from others and then to realize lower costs, higher productivity, and better quality in mid-tech industries by means of incremental improvements has given otherwise diverse twentieth-century industrializers a common set of properties. Because the leading enterprises of these countries initially had no proprietary technology and could not compete in mid-tech industries against more experienced firms from advanced economies on the basis of low wages alone, their governments had to be more interventionist and developmental. In the most successful cases, these governments' discipline of business was much greater than in the historical experiences of other countries. Because process improvements constituted their major competitive strategy, manufacturing capabilities on the shop floor became their critical focus. Because individual enterprises did not possess any core proprietary technology, they grew by integrating and diversifying into unrelated industries, and their firm structure featured business groups with technologically unrelated divisional units.

But from the viewpoint of a particular country, this industrialization process contains a paradox. The quicker a country learns and the closer it approaches the world technological frontier, the sooner it will exhaust the opportunities to grow further by borrowing. In the "learning" paradigm, the precise reason for success creates the very condition for the disfunction of this particular growth mechanism, whereas in the "innovating" paradigm, the growth mechanism can, in theory, be sustained indefinitely.

One can only speculate about how the learning paradigm will play itself out in the long run, as individual learners get closer and closer to the world technological frontier. Will they become innovators, and if so, will they become like other innovators or remain distinct? Clearly, as a country's economy matures, the effects of its early history on its behavior weaken, and new influences, both internal and external, begin to take hold. Nevertheless, to the extent that "history matters," we may expect some early influences on a country's behavior to persist, for better or worse.

Two congenital characteristics of twentieth-century late industrialization are a greater degree of state intervention than in earlier industrializations and a greater propensity to regard incremental improvements in product and process as a competitive weapon. Japan provides the only source of evidence for the proposition that early technology history matters, because it, alone among late industrializers, is already emerging as an innovator. Despite Japan's new status, its government continues to intervene more in promoting high-tech (say, high-density television and new generations of computers) and in monitoring firms than do governments in other economically advanced countries, particularly the United States. Japanese industry still continues to import new technology, as evidenced by its soaring technology exports but consistently negative balance-of-technology trade. Japanese firms also still emphasize incremental process improvements, as suggested by their large and persistent trade surplus in mid-tech industries.

It is too soon to tell whether the late-industrializing paradigm will continue to pull ahead of its rivals. But it has certainly transformed the nature of global competition in the last quarter of the twentieth century and can no longer be regarded as part of the same seamless web of economic development that began with the burst of technological inventions of the first Industrial Revolution. A new paradigm has been born.

Notes

We are thankful for helpful suggestions from Moses Abramovitz, William Baumol, Jagdish Bhagwati, Edward Buffie, Alfred Chandler, David Dollar, Christopher Freeman, Leslie Hannah, Richard Nelson, Terutomo Ozawa, Sidney Pollard, Charles Sabel, and Edward Wolff.

1. This paper takes as its analytical starting point the work of Amsden and Hikino 1993.

2. In the course of economic development, those economies with abundant raw materials and natural resources can enjoy absolute and comparative advantages, compared with countries with an abundant supply of cheap labor only. As a means of achieving sustained modern economic growth, however, natural resources become instrumental only when they are used for domestic industrial development, through either the establishment of downstream raw material–processing industries or the use of foreign-exchange earnings to finance unrelated industrial development (see Wright 1990).

3. Technology transfer basically takes one of two forms, "reverse engineering" (copying) or "apprenticeship" (learning from another enterprise by buying technical assistance) (see Kim 1980). There is eventually convergence in these two methods insofar as reverse engineering usually dead-ends without the infusion of technical assistance, and technical assistance requires adaptation (reverse engineering of a sort) if world standards and certainly incremental improvements are to be realized. It is noteworthy that technology transfer was no guarantee of narrowing a productivity gap even in the nineteenth century. As Pollard (1981) noted: "Right up to 1850 and 1860, continental centres frequently failed to achieve British productivity and economy even when using apparently similar equipment" (p. 182).

4. Many of these theories took as their analytical starting point the "product cycle" trade theory proposed by Vernon (1966) and a related "flying geese" model originally presented by Kaname Akamatsu in 1938. Shinohara (1972, chaps. 1 and 5) formalized and integrated the two.

5. When we refer to process "improvements" made by imported technology, they represent incremental alterations given fixed factor proportions. We do not mean changes that result in biased technical change, induced by different factor proportions in the countries importing and exporting technology. In the early phases of U.S. industrialization, transplanted British technology was altered toward the capital-using, resource-using, and labor-saving end of the production possibility frontier. These capital-intensive technologies, in turn, "have routinely offered extensive opportunities for improvements in productivity which seem to have had no equivalent at the labor-intensive end of the spectrum (Rosenberg 1977, p. 25). By contrast, successful late-industrializing economies seem also to have used this dynamism of capital-intensive technology. Fundamentally, they did not directly substitute labor for capital. Except for the possible and prominent case of textiles, late industrializers have largely kept the original factor proportions of the technologies they bought from outside (see Hikino, forthcoming).

6. Japan's superiority over Britain's textile industry in the 1930s derived from its more modern and integrated production facilities (theoretically, capital-rich Britain's competitive advantage), its cartelized bulk-purchase of raw cotton, its better distribution channels, and superior management (Hubbard 1938). Precisely these advantages overwhelmed the lower wages of South Korea and Taiwan in the 1960s.

7. The World Bank and many American-trained economists interpreted South Korea's "big push" into heavy industry as proof of the failure of government intervention, but the evidence is contentious. According to a study of the reputable Korea Development Institute: "Increases in Korean exports in the 1980s were most visible in such products as various kinds of consumer electronics, semiconductors, other computer related products, telecommunications equipment, and passenger cars. These were mainly the products of 'heavy' industries that were greatly favored under the industrial policy of the 1970s" (Yoo Jung-ho 1990, pp. 106–7). See also World Bank (1993) and Amsden (1994).

8. Tokyo National University, Seoul National University, and Taiwan National University (the last two in emulation of the first) all were founded with the purpose of supplying educated government officials, all of whom had to pass a "high" civil service exam.

9. Part of the differences in income distribution in Table 11-5 may be attributable to statistical error and part to the "Kuznets effect": Income distribution tends to become more unequal

after the initial phase of industrialization. It is a fact, however, that in the postwar period, when government intervention to stimulate industrial development was rising throughout the developing world, income distribution in Asia, particularly East Asia, generally tended to be more equal than income distribution was in Latin America.

The voluminous literature on the relationship between development and income distribution is overwhelmingly concerned with the issue of how income distribution changes in the course of development, rather than how, at any given time, it influences development behavior (see Adelman and Robinson 1989). Yet for a subsample of late industrializers, a simple regression equation found a strong correlation (R-squared = 0.43) between equality in income distribution and manufacturing productivity growth between 1970 and 1986 (see Amsden 1992).

10. Probably the best-documented individual case is that of Du Pont, one of the most successful firms in one of the most innovative industries. All three founders of the modern Du Pont company in 1902–4 were engineers educated at MIT. The tiny family-controlled powder enterprise established the product development department in its original organization, and its subsidiary initiated a research laboratory headed by a Ph.D. chemist in 1902 (Chandler and Salsbury 1971, Hounshell and Smith 1988).

11. Actually, in the early 1970s the share of total employment accounted for by firms employing 500 or more workers was unusually high in Taiwan among a sample of developing countries. Thereafter, Taiwanese business groups became common, although they were not as large as those in South Korea. Taiwan's public enterprises substituted for Korea's big private businesses (Amsden 1991a).

12. This phenomenon of oligopolistic behavior was first examined by Yoshikazu Miyazaki as the "one set-ism" or "complete set principle" of the industry entry behavior of postwar Japanese enterprises (Miyazaki 1980).

13. Whereas diversification in the United States since the 1960s generally failed to increase profitability or productivity, it was more successful in the late-industrializing countries, owing to the nature of top management and organizational assets (see Amsden and Hikino 1994).

When many multidivisional American industrial enterprises tried to grow by acquiring numerous firms in a short amount of time and/or diversifying into unrelated product lines—while keeping their strategic control styles—their top managers suffered from excessive decision-making burdens. Strategic communication between top and middle management, which is the key to productive efficiency, inadvertently became strained (Chandler 1990, pp. 621–28). The costs of adjustment required by the speed and nature of corporate diversification exceeded the optimal level allowed by the administrative capacity of top management. This "Penrosian dynamic constraint" worked against the performance of diversifying firms in the United States (Penrose 1959).

References

Abramovitz, M. (1986). "Catching Up, Forging Ahead, and Falling Behind."*Journal of Economic History* 46:385–406.

Adelman, I., and S. Robinson. (1989). "Income Distribution and Development." In H. Chenery and T. Srinivasan, Eds., *Handbook of Development Economics.* Amsterdam: North Holland, pp. 949–1003.

Amsden, Alice H. (1977). "The Division of Labor Is Limited by the "Type" of Market: The Taiwanese Machine Tool Industry." *World Development* 5:217–34.

———. (1989). *Asia's Next Giant: South Korea and Late Industrialization.* New York: Oxford University Press.

———. (1991a). "Big Business and Urban Congestion in Taiwan: The Origins of Small Enterprise and Regionally Decentralized Industry (Respectively)." *World Development* 19:1121–35.

———. (1991b). "The Diffusion of Development: The Late-Industrializing Model and Greater East Asia." *American Economic Review* 81:282–86.

———. (1992). "A Theory of Government Intervention in Late Industrialization." In Louis Putterman and Dietrich Rueschemeyer, eds., *The State and the Market in Development: Synergy or Rivalry?* Boulder, CO: Lynne Rienner, pp. 53–84.

Amsden, Alice H. (1994). "Why Isn't the Whole World Experimenting With the East Asian Model to Develop?: Review of the World Bank's *East Asian Miracle: Economic Growth and Public Policy.*" *World Development* 22.

Amsden, Alice H., and Yoon-Dae Euh. (1993). "South Korea's 1980s Financial Reform: Good-bye Financial Repression (Maybe), Hello New Institutional Restraints." *World Development* 21:379–90.

Amsden, Alice H., and Takashi Hikino. (1993) "Innovating or Borrowing Technology: Explorations of the Paths Towards Industrial Development." In Ross Thomson, ed., *Learning and Technological Change.* Basingstoke: Macmillan, pp. 243–66.

———. (1994). "Project Execution Capability, Organizational Know-How, and Conglomerate Corporate Growth in Late Industrialization." *Industrial and Corporate Change* 3.

Baumol, W. J. (1986). "Productivity Growth, Convergence, and Welfare."*American Economic Review* 76:1072–85.

Baumol, W. J., and Edward N. Wolff. (1988). "Productivity Growth, Convergence, and Welfare: Reply." *American Economic Review* 78:1155–59.

Berend, Ivan T., and Gyorgy Ranki. (1982). *The European Periphery and Industrialization, 1780–1914.* Cambridge: Cambridge University Press.

Biggs, Tyler S. (1988). "Financing the Emergence of Small and Medium Enterprise in Taiwan: Heterogeneous Firm Size and Efficient Intermediation." Washington, DC: U.S. Agency for International Development, Employment and Enterprise Policy Analysis Discussion Paper No. 16.

Brody, David. (1960). *Steelworkers in America: The Nonunion Era.* Cambridge, MA: Harvard University Press.

Carstensen, F. W. (1984). *American Enterprise in Foreign Markets: Studies of Singer and International Harvester in Imperial Russia.* Chapel Hill: University of North Carolina Press.

Chandler, Alfred Dupont, Jr. (1977). *The Visible Hand: The Managerial Revolution in American Business.* Cambridge, MA: Harvard University Press.

———. (1990). *Scale and Scope: The Dynamics of Industrial Capitalism.* Cambridge, MA: Harvard University Pressi.

———. (1991). "The Functions of the HQ Unit in the Multibusiness Firm." *Strategic Management Journal* (special issue) 12:31–50.

Chandler, Alfred D., Jr., and Stephen Salsbury. (1971). *Pierre S. Du Pont and the Making of the Modern Corporation.* New York: Harper & Row.

Cho, Dong Sung. (1987). *The General Trading Company: Concept and Strategy.* Lexington, MA: Lexington Books.

Clark, Gregory. (1987). "Why Isn't the Whole World Developed? Lessons from the Cotton Mills." *Journal of Economic History* 47:141–73.

Clark, Kim B., and Takahiro Fujimoto. (1991). *Product Development Performance.* Boston: Harvard Business School Press.

Coats, A. W., ed. (1971). *The Classical Economists and Economic Policy.* London: Methuen.

Conchieiro, Elvira, and Juan Manuel Fragoso. (1979). *El Gran Poder de la burgesia.* Mexico City: Ediciones de cultura popular.

Dahlman, Carl J., and Fernando Valadares Fonseca. (1987). "From Technological Dependence to Technological Development: The Case of Usiminas Steelplant in Brazil." In Jorge M. Katz, ed., *Technology Generation in Latin American Manufacturing Industries.* London: Macmillan.

Dahlman, Carl J., and Ousa Sananikone. (1990). "Technology Strategy in Taiwan: Exploiting Foreign Linkages and Investing in Local Capability." Paper, World Bank, Washington, DC.

Dahmen, Erik. (1970). *Entrepreneurial Activity and the Development of Swedish Industry, 1919–1939.* Homewood IL: Irwin, for the American Economic Association.

Dertouzos, Michael L., Richard K. Lester, Robert M. Solow, and the MIT Commission on Industrial Productivity. (1989). *Made in America: Regaining the Productive Edge.* Cambridge: MIT Press.

Gerschenkron, A. (1962). *Economic Backwardness in Historical Perspective.* Cambridge, MA: Harvard University Press.

Goodrich, Carter, ed. (1967). *The Government and the Economy: 1783–1861.* Indianapolis: Bobbs-Merrill.

Goold, Michael, and Andrew Campbell. (1987). *Strategies and Styles: The Role of the Centre in Managing Diversified Corporations.* Oxford: Basil Blackwell.

Gustavson, Carl G. (1986). *The Small Giant: Sweden Enters the Industrial Era.* Athens: Ohio University Press.

Haggard, Stephan. (1990). *Pathways from the Periphery: The Politics of Growth in Newly Industrializing Countries.* Ithaca, NY: Cornell University Press.

Hanson, J., and C. Neal. (1984). "A Review of Interest Rate Policies in Selected Developing Countries." Paper, World Bank, Financial Unit, Industrial Department, September.

Harvard Business School. (1985). "Goldstar Co., Ltd.," Case Study 9-385-264. Boston: Harvard Business School Case Services.

Hayes, Peter. (1987). *Industry and Ideology: IG Farben in the Nazi Era.* Cambridge: Cambridge University Press.

Herman, B. (1991). "International Finance of Developing Asia and the Pacific in the 1990s."

Paper, Department of International Economic and Social Affairs, United Nations, New York.

Hicks, Jonathan P. (1992). "An Industrial Comeback Story: U.S. Is Competing Again in Steel." *New York Times,* March 31, p. D1.

Hikino, Takashi. (forthcoming). "Transferred Technology and Biased Technical Change: A Puzzling Issue in Late Industrialization." Paper, Harvard Business School.

Hodne, Fritz. (1983). *The Norwegian Economy, 1920–1980.* London: Croom Helm.

Hounshell, David A. (1984). *From the American System to Mass Production, 1800–1932.* Baltimore: Johns Hopkins University Press.

Hounshell, David A., and John Kenly Smith. (1988). *Science and Corporate Strategy: DuPont R&D, 1902–1980.* Cambridge: Cambridge University Press.

Hubbard, G. E. (1938). *Eastern Industrialization and Its Effects on the West.* Oxford: Oxford University Press for the Royal Institute of International Affairs.

Hughes, Jonathan R. T. (1991). *The Governmental Habit Redux: Economic Controls from Colonial Times to the Present.* Princeton, NJ: Princeton University Press.

Hughes, Thomas P. (1989). *American Genesis: A Century of Invention and Technological Enthusiasm, 1870–1970.* New York: Viking.

Hymer, Stephen Herbert. (1979). *The Multinational Corporation: A Radical Approach.* Cambridge: Cambridge University Press.

Isacson, Maths, and Lars Magnusson. (1987). *Proto-industrialisation in Scandinavia: Craft Skills in the Industrial Revolution.* Leamington Spa: Berg.

Jewkes, John, David Sawers, and Richard Stillerman. (1969). *The Sources of Invention,* 2nd ed. New York: North.

Junid, Saham. (1980). *British Industrial Investment in Malaysia, 1963–1971.* Kuala Lumpur: Oxford University Press.

Kim, Linsu. (1980). "Stages of Development of Industrial Technology in a Developing Country: A Model." *Research Policy* 9:254–77.

Kindleberger, Charles P. (1969). *American Business Abroad: Six Lectures on Direct Investment.* New Haven, CT: Yale University Press.

Lall, Sanjaya. (1987). *Learning to Industrialize: The Acquisition of Technological Capability by India.* Basingstoke: Macmillan.

Landes, David S. (1969). *The Unbound Prometheus, Technological Change and Industrial Development in Western Europe from 1750 to the Present.* Cambridge: Cambridge University Press.

Lary, Hal B. (1968). *Imports of Manufactures from Less Developed Countries.* New York: National Bureau of Economic Research.

Lazonick, William. (1990). *Competitive Advantage on the Shop Floor.* Cambridge, MA: Harvard University Press.

Leff, Nathaniel H. (1978). "Industrial Organization and Entrepreneurship in the Developing Countries: The Economic Groups." *Economic Development and Cultural Change* 26:661–75.

Lindbeck, Assar. (1974). *Swedish Economic Policy.* Berkeley and Los Angeles: University of California Press.

Lively, Robert. (1955). "The American System: A Review Article." *Business History Review* 29:81–97.

Locke, Robert R. (1984). *The End of the Practical Man: Entrepreneurship and Higher Education in Germany, France, and Great Britain, 1880–1940.* Greenwich, CT: JAI Press.

Maddison, A. (1982). *Phases of Capitalist Development.* Oxford: Oxford University Press.

———. (1987). "Growth and Slowdown in Advanced Capitalist Economies: Techniques of Quantitative Assessment." *Journal of Economic Literature* 25:649–706.

———. (1989). *The World Economy in the 20th Century.* Paris: Development Centre Studies, OECD.

———. (1991). *Dynamic Forces in Capitalist Development: A Long-Run Comparative View.* New York: Oxford University Press.

Markham, Jesse W. (1952). *Competition in the Rayon Industry.* Cambridge, MA: Harvard University Press.

Minami, Ryoshin. (1986). *The Economic Development of Japan: A Quantitative Study.* New York: St. Martin's Press.

Mitsui & Co. (1977). *The 100 Year History of Mitsui & Co., Ltd.: 1876–1976.* Tokyo: Mitsui & Co., 1977.

Miyazaki, Yoshikazu. (1980). "Excessive Competition and the Formation of *Keiretsu.*" In Kazuo Sato, ed., *Industry and Business in Japan.* White Plains, NY: M. E. Sharpe, pp. 53–73. (The article was originally published in 1965.)

Morikawa, Hidemasa. (1976). "Management Structure and Control Devices for Diversified Zaibatsu Business." In Keiichiro Nakagawa, ed., *Strategy and Structure of Big Business.* Tokyo: University of Tokyo Press.

Musson, A. E., ed. (1972). *Science, Technology, and Economic Growth in the Eighteenth Century.* London: Methuen.

Nelson, Richard R. (1987). "Innovation and Economic Development: Theoretical Retrospect and Prospect." In Jorge M. Katz, ed., *Technology Generation in Latin American Manufacturing Industries.* Basingstoke: Macmillan, pp. 78–903.

———, ed. (1993). *National Innovation Systems: A Comparative Analysis.* New York: Oxford University Press.

Nye, John V. (1991). "The Myth of Free Trade Britain and Fortress France: Tariffs and Trade in the Nineteenth Century." *Journal of Economic History* 51:23–46.

OECD (Organization for Economic Co-operation and Development). (1990). *Industrial Policy in OECD Countries: Annual Review, 1990.* Paris: OECD.

Okochi, Akio, and Shigeaki Yasuoka, eds. (1984). *Family Business in the Era of Industrial Growth.* Proceedings of the Fuji Conference, International Conference on Business History. Vol. 10. Tokyo: University of Tokyo Press.

Ozawa, Terutomo. (1974). *Japan's Technological Challenge to the West, 1950–1974: Motivation and Accomplishment.* Cambridge, MA: MIT Press.

Park, Yung Chul. (1985). "Korea's Experience with Debt Management." In G. Smith and J. Cuddington, eds., *International Debt and the Developing Countries.* Baltimore: Johns Hopkins University Press, pp. 289–328.

Peck, Merton J., with Shuji Tamura. (1976). "Technology." In Hugh Patrick and Henry Rosovsky, eds., *Asia's New Giant: How the Japanese Economy Works.* Washington, DC: Brookings Institution, pp. 525–86.

Penrose, Edith. (1959). *The Theory of the Growth of the Firm.* Oxford: Basil Blackwell.

Piore, Michael J., and Charles F. Sabel. (1984). *The Second Industrial Divide.* New York: Basic Books.

Polanyi, Karl. (1944). *The Great Transformation: The Political and Economic Origins of Our Time.* Boston: Beacon Press.

Pollard, S. (1981). *Peaceful Conquest: The Industrialization of Europe, 1760–1970.* Oxford: Oxford University Press.

Rodrik, Dani. (forthcoming). "Trade and Industrial Policy Reform in Developing Countries: A Review of Recent Theory and Evidence." In J. Behrman and T. N. Srinivaasan, eds., *Handbook of Development Economics.* Vol. 3. Amsterdam: North Holland.

Rosenberg, Nathan. (1976). *Perspectives on Technology.* Cambridge: Cambridge University Press.

———. (1977). "American Technology: Imported or Indigenous?" *American Economic Review* 67:21–26.

———. (1982). *Inside the Black Box: Technology and Economics.* Cambridge: Cambridge University Press.

Sandberg, Lars G. (1982). "Ignorance, Poverty and Economic Backwardness in the Early Stages of European Industrialization: Variations on Alexander Gerschenkron's Grand Theme." *Journal of European Economic History* 11:675–97.

Sato, Ryuzo. (1986). "Japan's Challenge to Technological Competition and Its Limitations." In Thomas A. Pugel and Robert G. Hawkins,

eds., *Fragile Interdependence: Economic Issues in U.S.–Japanese Trade and Investment.* Lexington, MA: Lexington Books, pp. 237–54.

Scherer, F. M. (1986). *Innovation and Growth.* Cambridge, MA: MIT Press.

Shapiro, Helen. (1993). "Automobiles: From Import Substitution to Export Promotion in Brazil and Mexico." In David B. Yoffie, ed., *Beyond Free Trade: Firms, Governments and Global Competition.* Boston: Harvard Business School Press.

Shinohara, M. (1972). *Growth and Cycles in the Japanese Economy.* Tokyo: Institute of Economic Research, Hitotsubashi University.

Streeten, Paul. (1992). "Against Minimalism." In L. Putterman and D. Rueschemeyer, eds., *State and Market in Development: Synergy or Rivalry?* Boulder CO: Lynne Rienner, pp. 15–38.

Suehiro, Akira. (1985). *Capital Accumulation and Development in Thailand.* Bangkok: Chulalongkorn University Social Research Institute.

Sylla, Richard, and Gianni Toniolo, eds. (1991). *Patterns of European Industrialization: The Nineteenth Century.* London: Routledge & Kegan Paul.

Taylor, A. J. (1972). *Laissez-faire and State Intervention in Britain.* London: Macmillan, for the Economic History Society.

Taylor, Lance. (1988). *Varieties of Stabilization Experience.* Oxford: Clarendon Press.

Thomson, Guy P. C. (1991). "Continuity and Change in Mexican Manufacturing, 1800–1870." In Jean Batou, ed., *Between Development and Underdevelopment: The Precocious Attempts at Industrialization in the Periphery, 1800–1870.* Geneva: Librairie Droz, pp. 255–302.

Toyota Motor Company. (1988). *Toyota: A History of the First 50 Years.* Toyota City: Toyota Motor Corporation.

Uchida, Hoshimi. (1980). "Western Big Business and the Adoption of New Technology in Japan: The Electrical Equipment and Chemical Industries, 1890–1920." In Akio Okochi and Hoshimi Uchida, eds., *Development and Diffusion of Technology.* Tokyo: University of Tokyo Press, chapter 2.

Udagawa, Masaru. (1985). "The Prewar Japanese Automobile Industry and American Manufacturers." *Japanese Yearbook on Business History: 1985.* Vol. 2. Tokyo: Japan Business History Institute.

UNIDO (United Nations Industrial Development Review). 1988. *Industry and Development, Global Report.* New York: United Nations.

Vernon, R. (1966). "International Investment and International Trade in the Product Cycle." *Quarterly Journal of Economics* 80:190–207.

Wade, Robert. (1990). *Governing the Market: Economic Theory and the Role of Government in East Asian Industrialization.* Princeton, NJ: Princeton University Press.

Wall, Joseph Frazier. (1970). *Andrew Carnegie.* New York: Oxford University Press.

Watanabe, Hisashi. (1984). "A History of the Process Leading to the Formation of Fuji Electric." *Japanese Yearbook on Business History: 1984.* Vol. 1. Tokyo: Japan Business History Institute.

Wilkins, Mira. (1970). *The Emergence of Multinational Enterprise: American Business Abroad from the Colonial Era to 1914.* Cambridge, MA: Harvard University Press.

Wilkins, Mira, and Frank E. Hill. (1964). *American Business Abroad: Ford on Six Continents.* Detroit: Wayne State University Press.

Winslow, John F. (1973). *Conglomerates Unlimited: The Failure of Regulation.* Bloomington: Indiana University Press.

World Bank. (1993). *The East Asian Miracle: Economic Growth and Public Policy.* New York: Oxford University Press for the World Bank.

Wright, Gavin. (1990). "The Origins of American Industrial Success." *American Economic Review* 80:651–68.

Yoo, Jung-ho. (1990). "The Industrial Policy of the 1970s and the Evolution of the Manufacturing Sector in Korea." Seoul: Korea Development Institute, Working Paper no. 9017, October.

12

Social Indicators and Productivity Convergence in Developing Countries

GREGORY K. INGRAM

Much of the analysis of productivity convergence has addressed some aspect of it in industrialized countries. The approach here is broader in two respects. First, although some information is presented on productivity measures, much of the data analyzed here deals with other measures of performance that will be referred to collectively as *social indicators.* These indicators are not narrowly economic but include indices of outcomes, such as life expectancy; indices of the availability of inputs, such as doctors per capita; indices that could be labeled as inputs or outcomes, such as per-capita caloric intake of food; and measures of government expenditure patterns. Second, the sample of countries examined is large and includes 21 high-income countries and up to 88 developing countries, depending on the availability of data for the particular variables and time periods. The years covered for each variable fall within the period 1960 to 1985, with a few variables covering virtually the whole interval and some others available for only a few years within this period.

To summarize the results of the analysis, the evidence does not indicate that there is convergence in productivity levels across the whole sample of 109 countries analyzed. Differences in absolute levels of productivity are increasing, an indication of divergence. This is true within the group of developing countries and between developing and high-income countries. Statistical measures of the variation in productivity levels indicate neither convergence nor divergence for the whole sample, for all developing countries, or for low-income developing countries. Such measures do indicate covergence for high-income and middle-income developing countries. There is no convergence in average productivity growth rates across all countries, and disaggregation by income group and region reveals a divergence in growth rates among developing country groups and between these groups and high-income countries.

The evidence does indicate that there is strong convergence across the sample for several social indicators that are good measures of human welfare. Some other social indicators, however, show little evidence of convergence, and their levels increase linearly (or more than linearly) with GDP per capita measures. And still other indicators show moderate degrees of convergence.

One basic conclusion from this analysis is that a given increase in per-capita GDP in very low income developing countries is generally associated with greater improvements in the social indicators that measure human welfare than a similar increase in per-capita GDP in middle-income developing countries. To the extent that improving welfare is the objective of development efforts, it is most efficient to focus such efforts on low-income developing countries.

Productivity Measures

The analysis of productivity convergence provides a basis for comparing the convergence of social indicators, and so we examine productivity convergence first. There are many possible measures of economic performance, and a good survey is provided by Usher (Usher 1980). Because it has been widely used in similar studies and elsewhere in this volume, the measure of productivity that I shall use here is the Summers–Heston (1991) purchasing power parity per-capita GDP measured in constant 1985 prices. The data are taken from the World Bank Economic and Social Database and are available since 1960 for 21 high-income countries and 88 developing countries. To facilitate the analysis, the 21 high-income countries have been placed in one group (H), and the 88 developing countries have been grouped by income level, with 53 middle income (M) and 35 low income (L). At times the developing countries are also disaggregated by five regions of location: Mediterranean and Middle East (ME), South Asia (SA), East Asia (EA), Latin America (LA), and Sub-Saharan Africa (SS). This produces 1 high-income and 8 developing country groups because there are no middle-income South Asia countries and only 1 low-income country in the Middle East region. The income and regional country groupings are displayed in Annex Table 12A-1, which shows the GDP per capita in 1985 dollars for various years for each country. The income and regional groupings are those used by the World Bank and are described in the 1991 *World Development Report* (World Bank 1991b) and the *World Tables* (World Bank 1991c). The region and income group are invariant for each country.

Two measures of convergence are used in this section, and both are members of classes of convergence measures described in Chapter 1. The first measure is simply the difference in the average values of an indicator between countries or groups of countries over time. A reduction in the difference between country groups indicates that one group is "catching up" with another by closing the gap. The difference can be measured in absolute or proportional terms. The second measure is based on the trend over time of the coefficient of variation of an indicator. The coefficient of variation is the standard deviation of an indicator divided by its mean and is a measure of variance reduction or homogenization. Convergence is indicated when the coefficient of variation declines over time for a country group.

Figure 12-1 shows the average level of GDP per capita for the nine groups by year from 1960 to 1987. The disparity between the highest- and lowest-income group averages in 1987 is approximately twentyfold ($600 to $12,000), a doubling of the tenfold ($600 to $6000) disparity observed in 1960. This doubling in range occurs because the per-capita GDP of the poorest developing-country groups have remained roughly con-

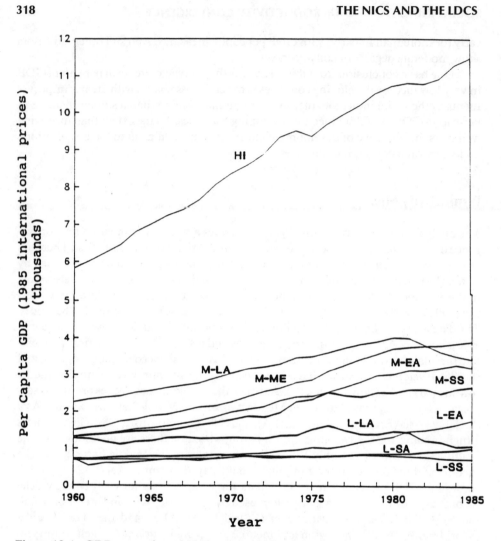

Figure 12-1. GDP per capita, 1960–85 (thousands of 1985 Summers–Heston dollars).

stant while the per capita GDP of high-income countries has doubled over this period. All of the middle-income developing-country groups have grown during the period, although not continuously, and the best performances were displayed by the Middle East, South Asia, and East Asia regions. Among low-income groups, East Asia is the fastest-growing region; South Asia has the lowest levels; and Sub-Saharan Africa has stagnated. In absolute terms, Figure 12-1 suggests there has been divergence rather than convergence in per-capita GDP across these groups over time. For the developing countries, the range of GDP per capita widens within both the medium- and the low-income groupings as well as between them. These results are similar to those shown in Chapter 2, although based here on many more developing countries and a shorter time period.

Table 12-1 shows the average level and coefficient of variation of GDP per capita

Table 12-1. GDP per Capita for Country Groups, Various Years

| | | Country Grouping | | |
| | | Developing Countries | | |
Year	All	All	Low Income	Middle Income	High Income
		Mean value, GDP per capita			
1960	2260	1350	730	1770	5830
1970	3090	1800	820	2470	8370
1980	4070	2490	890	3540	10730
1985	4150	2400	870	3420	11500
		Coefficient of Variation, GDP per capita			
1960	95.	68.	45.	54.	32.
1970	97.	72.	44.	51.	24.
1980	93.	78.	43.	52.	20.
1985	97.	72.	45.	45.	21.

for various years and country groupings. The coefficients of variation in Table 12-1 indicate that per-capita GDP levels have neither converged nor diverged over time for all 109 countries taken together. When income groupings are used, convergence over time is evident for high-income countries and for middle-income developing countries, but not for low-income developing countries. The coefficient of variation of GDP per capita for all developing countries taken together does not show a strong trend. The average values of GDP per capita in Table 12-1 indicate that both high-income and middle-income countries doubled their average GDP per capita from 1960 to 1985, whereas low-income countries increased their average by only a fifth. In absolute terms, the gaps between these three income groups widened. In relative terms, the middle-income countries nearly kept pace with the high-income countries, but the low-income countries did not. Figure 12-1 and Table 12-1 taken together support the hypothesis that developing countries are separating into two groups: one that is growing and maintaining or increasing its involvement with the world's economy, and a second that is stagnating and becoming progressively marginalized. The heterogeneity of developing countries appears to be increasing over the period shown.

The data on per-capita GDP growth rates, as opposed to levels, reinforce this hypothesis. Table 12-2 shows for each regional and income-level grouping the average growth rates for per-capita GDP over the 1960–85 period and for each decade. On a decadal basis, in the high-income countries, economic growth slowed from the 1960s to the 1980s. For the developing countries, the picture is more varied. The low-income countries grew more slowly than did the middle-income countries. Except for Latin America, the middle-income developing-country groups grew faster in the 1970s than in the 1960s or the 1980s, and the 1980s were particularly bad for Latin America and low-income Sub-Saharan Africa. The 1980s were not, however, a "lost decade" for the low-income East and South Asia country groups, which experienced their highest decadal growth then. There is some regional homogeneity, in terms of both bad performance (Sub-Saharan Africa, Latin America) and good performance (East Asia).

Table 12-2. Average Annual Growth Rate, GDP per Capita

Country Grouping (income/region)	Time Period			
	1960–69	1970–79	1980–85	1960–85
High income	3.9	2.5	1.3	2.9
All middle income	3.4	3.7	−0.6	3.2
M/East Asia	4.2	4.3	1.0	4.0
M/Latin America	2.9	2.7	−2.8	2.2
M/Medit. & Mid. East	4.4	5.2	1.3	4.3
M/Sub-Saharan Africa	2.5	3.6	1.0	3.2
All low income	1.3	0.9	−0.8	0.9
L/East Asia	−2.7	3.3	7.5	3.7
L/Latin America	0.4	1.6	−6.3	0.3
L/South Asia	1.6	1.0	2.7	1.0
L/Sub-Saharan Africa	1.3	0.7	−1.6	0.8

These patterns are similar to those presented for an overlapping but earlier period, which are based on different economic performance measures (Morawetz 1977). Regressions of decadal growth rates on decade-starting GDP per capita (not reported here) yielded no relation between the two. Growth was not random, however, and economic policy variables were strongly related to growth rates (Ingram 1990).

Table 12-3, which shows the coefficient of variation of growth rates, reveals no tendency for growth rates to converge for high-income or developing countries over time. Within each income group, the variation in country group growth rates increased over time. For each period shown, the coefficient of variation fell from low-income to high-income groups, indicating an increase in the homogeneity of growth rates across income groups.

The average growth rate from 1961 to 1985 of per-capita GDP for all developing countries taken together is 2.2 percent, compared with 2.9 percent for high-income countries. Both of these growth rates are quite respectable when compared with the long-term historical growth rates experienced by the currently high-income countries. For example, Kuznets estimated that per-capita GDP grew in the United States at 1.6 percent per annum from 1839 to 1961 (Kuznets 1966). There is little comfort in this

Table 12-3. Coefficient of Variation, Growth Rates of GDP per Capita

Period	Country Grouping				
	All	Developing Countries			High Income
		All	Low Income	Middle Income	
1960–69	80.	91.	188.	53.	41.
1970–79	107.	118.	302.	73.	43.
1980–85	1320.	556.	551.	544.	80.
1960–85	78.	89.	170.	56.	31.

comparison, however, for the low-income developing countries whose group average growth rate was 0.9 percent from 1961 to 1985.

The data used here show little evidence of convergence of per-capita GDP growth and levels among developing countries or between developing and developed countries. The convergence of GDP levels seems to be occurring mainly within high-income and middle-income country groups; across all countries there is neither convergence nor divergence of GDP levels by some measures. Growth rates have been diverging over time for all income groups. The more extensive analysis of growth in developing countries reported in Chapter 9 of this volume finds little evidence of gross convergence of GDP growth.

Social Indicators

GDP per capita is not the only performance measure available for a country. Numerous social indicators have been developed also to measure welfare outcomes across countries. Analysts are beginning to use social indicators to supplement economic measures when analyzing the impact of policy measures (e.g., Behrman and Deolalikar 1991), and we examine the convergence of several of these indicators here.

The hypothesis that GDP growth and levels should converge is based on common access to technology and knowledge in a world in which international trade and information flows are pervasive. This argument has been put forward by many authors (e.g., see Grossman and Helpman 1991). This same logic of convergence can be applied to many other measures of a country's performance, such as health outcomes or educational attainment. For those performance measures that are mainly the product of knowledge combined with nontraded inputs, the convergence of outcomes can occur at fairly low GDP levels. For example, health outcomes can be improved by techniques, such as oral rehydration therapy, that require training but little else. For performance measures that are based heavily on tradable inputs, the convergence of outcomes is more likely to be closely associated with convergence of GDP levels.

We analyze and report in this section on 16 social indicators drawn from the World Bank Economic and Social database and described in *Social Indicators of Development* (World Bank 1991a), ranging from those that involve few tradables (but probably much technological information) to those that are essentially per-capita measures of tradables. The main issue we address is the extent to which these indicators exhibit convergence in the sample of countries for which data are available. The comparators for the social indicators are the convergence patterns of GDP levels and growth rates presented in the previous section.

We add a cross-sectional measure of bounded convergence to the two time-based measures used in the previous section. This measure is based on the relation between the social indicator and per-capita GDP across countries in a particular year. If the social indicator approaches an asymptote as the GDP per capita increases, it is a converging indicator. Data are often available for several years in the 1960–88 period, such as years of census enumeration, and the elasticity of the social indicator with respect to per-capita GDP is obtained by regressing the logarithm of the social indicator on the logarithm of per-capita GDP across all countries in the sample in a given year. If the elasticity exceeds one, the indicator is growing faster than per-capita GDP and is diverging, but if the elasticity is less than one, the indicator is growing slower and is converging. An elasticity of zero indicates no variation of the indicator with per-capita GDP and can imply strong convergence or no relation. Negative elasticities also generally indicate convergence. Elasticity estimates are presented in the tables in the following sections, and regression results are summarized in Annex Table 12A-2.

Demographic Indicators

We look at four demographic indicators in this section: life expectancy, crude birthrate per thousand, age-dependency ratio (0:15 and 65+ vs. 15:65), and the female/male ratio. The summary statistics are shown in Table 12-4. Convergence is quite marked for life expectancy. The low elasticity indicates bounded convergence, and the coefficient of variation declines over time for most years. Moreover, both the absolute and the relative gap in life expectancy has decreased across low-, middle-, and high-income groups, an indicator that is improving for all income groups over time, particularly for developing countries.

Birthrates and the age-dependency ratio show patterns similar to each other and are not nearly as convergent as life expectancy is. Both are inelastic, indicating bounded convergence, and both show a reduction in the absolute gap between middle- and high-income country groups. But for both, the coefficient of variation increases

Table 12-4. Demographic Indicators

Year	No. of Obs.	Elast'y	Mean			Coeff. of Var.		
			Low	Middle	High	Low	Middle	High
			Life expectancy					
1960	103	0.21	41.3	54.1	69.4	15.	17.	2.
1970	107	0.18	45.7	58.6	72.0	14.	14.	2.
1980	108	0.16	49.5	62.7	74.4	13.	12.	2.
1985	108	0.15	51.6	64.5	75.5	13.	16.	2.
			Birthrate per thousand					
1970	106	−0.38	45.8	36.8	17.0	13.	29.	16.
1980	107	−0.41	44.5	33.1	13.9	17.	31.	21.
1985	107	−0.44	43.8	31.3	12.9	19.	34.	17.
			Age-dependency ratio					
1960	90	−0.14	0.86	0.85	0.59	9.	16.	14.
1970	100	−0.16	0.89	0.87	0.59	9.	19.	11.
1980	101	−0.19	0.89	0.79	0.54	13.	21.	10.
1985	108	−0.21	0.89	0.77	0.51	14.	22.	11.
			Female/male ratio					
1960	102	−0.00	1.02	1.01	1.03	5.	6.	4.
1970	105	0.00	1.02	1.01	1.03	4.	5.	4.
1980	106	0.01	1.02	1.01	1.04	4.	4.	3.
1985	106	0.01	1.01	1.01	1.04	4.	4.	4.

over time, and there is no relative gap reduction. There is essentially no association between the female/male ratio and per-capita GDP, which is surprising given the longer life expectancy of females in high-income economies. The only indication of convergence is the slight reduction in the coefficient of variation over time. Several low-income countries have high ratios of females to males, probably due to the effects of selective migration.

The sharp convergence in life expectancy observed in Table 12-4 largely results from a sharp reduction in infant and child mortality thought to be caused by a combination of medical and infrastructure factors such as inoculation, oral rehydration therapy, and the provision of potable water and rudimentary waste disposal facilities. That is, the improvement results from a combination of internationally available information and the use of nontradable inputs.

Health Indicators

The health indicators are the average daily caloric intake of food per capita, the number of hospitals per capita, and the number of doctors per capita; summary statistics are shown in Table 12-5. The daily caloric intake is inelastic with respect to per-capita GDP and exhibits bounded convergence. The coefficient of variation falls slightly over time except for the low-income group. The absolute gap is constant between low- and high-income groups and decreases between middle- and high-income groups. The relative gaps decrease. Improved nutrition may well have played a supporting role in increasing life expectancy, particularly in the low-income developing countries.

The number of hospital beds and doctors per capita exhibit similar patterns in Table 12-5. Both increase in proportion or more rapidly with per-capita GDP and are not bounded. The coefficient of variation decreases over time only for the high- and low-income groups, and there is little evidence for either that absolute gaps decline.

Table 12-5. Health Indicators

Year	No. of Obs.	Elast'y	Mean			Coeff. of Var.		
			Low	Middle	High	Low	Middle	High
			Daily caloric intake					
1961	98	0.18	2000	2250	3130	11.	15.	8.
1970	101	0.16	2120	2430	3220	8.	16.	7.
1980	102	0.16	2160	2610	3320	9.	15.	7.
1986	102	0.16	2190	2670	3330	11.	15.	6.
			Number of hospital beds per capita					
1960	95	0.93	.001	.003	.010	97.	59.	24.
1970	99	0.92	.001	.004	.011	79.	69.	22.
1980	49	0.91	–	–	–	–	–	–
			Number of doctors per capita					
1960	97	1.42	.0001	.0004	.0012	106.	86.	22.
1970	102	1.35	.0001	.0005	.0014	88.	92.	18.
1980	49	1.27	–	–	–	–	–	–

The relative gap narrows for both indicators between the middle- and high-income groups. These relations, when compared with life expectancy, suggest that additional doctors and hospital beds per capita have contributed little to the observed increase in life expectancy.

Education and Literacy Indicators

The major education indicator is the primary school enrollment ratio, which is the proportion of children of elementary school age who are actually enrolled. Other measures that included attendance would be preferable but are available for very few countries. Direct measures of literacy also are available for relatively few countries, and so a distant proxy—daily newspaper circulation per capita— is used instead. The summary statistics for these two indicators are shown in Table 12-6.

It is obvious from Table 12-6 that there is a strong convergence of primary school enrollment ratios as the per-capita GDP rises. Moreover, the reduction in elasticities over time indicates that the degree of convergence has been increasing strongly over the years shown. The coefficient of variation has fallen over time for all income groups, and both absolute and relative gaps have decreased.

The results for daily newspaper circulation per capita suggest that this indicator bears little relation to literacy but probably is a better measure of the availability of information. Over the years shown, this indicator grew faster than did per-capita GDP and is not bounded. The coefficient of variation drops over time only for the low-income group. There is no reduction in the absolute gap across income groups, but the relative gap shrinks.

Urbanization Indicator

Urbanization is often characterized as the handmaiden of development, and the summary statistics shown in Table 12-7 support this. The percentage of the population

Table 12-6. Education and Literacy Indicators

Year	No. of Obs.	Elast'y	Mean Low	Mean Middle	Mean High	Coeff. of Var. Low	Coeff. of Var. Middle	Coeff. of Var. High
			\multicolumn{6}{c}{Primary school enrollment rate}					
1960	97	0.50	40.	81.	110.	68.	30.	12.
1970	95	0.39	54.	90.	104.	52.	24.	10.
1980	101	0.22	72.	98.	102.	44.	18.	5.
			\multicolumn{6}{c}{Newspaper circulation per capita}					
1960	72	1.96	.010	.058	.331	149.	76.	33.
1970	66	1.74	.014	.069	.333	132.	84.	35.
1979	80	1.51	.013	.069	.357	112.	85.	35.
1985	84	1.61	.016	.074	.347	111.	81.	41.

Table 12-7. Urbanization Indicator

Year	No. of Obs.	Elast'y	Mean			Coeff. of Var.		
			Low	Middle	High	Low	Middle	High
			Percentage of urban population					
1960	101	0.84	12.7	35.3	66.7	59.	48.	22.
1970	106	0.70	16.6	40.9	72.6	52.	41.	17.
1980	108	0.56	21.2	47.2	76.0	46.	36.	15.
1985	108	0.50	24.2	50.3	77.0	45.	33.	15.

living in urban areas has become more inelastic with GDP over time, and the coefficient of variation has fallen for all income groups over time. Moreover, both the absolute and relative gaps have narrowed. It is difficult to give a direct welfare interpretation to urbanization, but we know that it has many positive indirect effects. For example, children in urban areas are more likely to attend school than are children in rural areas, and health care is more readily available in urban than in rural areas.

Labor Force Indicator

Table 12-8 shows the summary statistics for labor force participation rates. There is essentially no relation to GDP and no convergence. There is no tendency for the coefficient of variation to decrease over time, although it is markedly smaller for high-income countries than for developing countries. The means show rates falling for low-income countries while they are rising for middle- and high-income countries. This pattern reflects the age-dependency ratios (Table 12-4) that are rising in low-income countries and falling in middle- and high-income countries.

An examination of labor force participation data indicates that there may be measurement inconsistencies with respect to agricultural workers in countries with low incomes. In some countries it appears that household members working on family plots are recorded as members of the labor force, whereas in other countries they are not. This measurement problem may interact with cultural factors. In Muslim countries, for example, women working in agriculture on family-owned plots may not be recorded as being in the labor force.

Table 12-8. Labor Force Indicators

Year	No. of Obs.	Elast'y	Mean			Coeff. of Var.		
			Low	Middle	High	Low	Middle	High
			Labor force participation rate					
1960	101	−0.06	46.4	36.1	42.3	18.	21.	9.
1970	104	−0.04	44.5	35.4	42.6	19.	21.	10.
1980	105	−0.00	42.9	36.5	45.3	18.	20.	11.
1985	105	0.02	42.0	39.0	46.5	18.	19.	11.

Table 12-9. Consumption Indicators

Year	No. of Obs.	Elast'y	Mean			Coeff. of Var.		
			Low	Middle	High	Low	Middle	High
			Energy consumption per capita					
1961	95	1.74	58.	511.	2430.	132.	176.	55.
1970	100	1.68	110.	761.	3880.	134.	130.	46.
1980	103	1.54	129.	976.	4490.	127.	105.	46.
1985	103	1.54	116.	983.	4620.	118.	95.	46.
			Number of telephones per capita					
1975	83	1.82	.005	.050	.398	126.	90.	36.
1980	76	1.77	.004	.074	.509	66.	90.	30.
1985	61	1.74	.008	.109	.629	116.	93.	25.
			Number of cars per capita					
1960	96	1.69	.003	.013	.107	131.	110.	75.
1970	102	1.70	.004	.024	.221	116.	108.	37.
1980	91	1.74	.004	.048	.331	76.	92.	24.
1985	58	1.90	–	–	–	–	–	–

Consumption Indicators

Three measures of consumption—energy use per capita, number of telephones per capita, and number of cars per capita—are shown in Table 12-9. Each of them rises much more than linearly with per-capita GDP. In the case of cars, the relation is becoming more income elastic or divergent over time. The high elasticity of these three items is not surprising because each is a tradable good whose price does not vary much with per-capita GDP.

The coefficient of variation drops over time for energy use and cars per capita, but not for telephones per capita except in high-income countries. The absolute gap between income groups does not shrink for any of the three items, but the relative gap between the middle- and high-income groups becomes smaller for telephones and cars.

Central Government Expenditure Indicators

Table 12-10 shows summary statistics for two categories of central government expenditures, defense and social services. The latter includes expenditures on social security and welfare. For each, the expenditures are measured as a percentage of GNP. The lack of a relation between defense expenditure share and per-capita GDP is typical of many other categories of central government expenditure. Social expenditures are the major exception to this pattern and tend to increase more than proportionally with the GDP per capita. The growth of social expenditures with per-capita GDP is strong enough to create an upward trend in the relation between all government expenditures and per-capita GDP. Defense expenditures show no convergence by any measure in Table 12-10. For social expenditures, the coefficient of variation decreases over time

Table 12-10. Central Government Expenditure Indicators

Year	No. of Obs.	Elast'y	Mean			Coeff. of Var.		
			Low	Middle	High	Low	Middle	High
			Defense expenditures/GNP					
1975	67	0.02	.025	.030	.025	68.	100.	49.
1980	66	0.00	.024	.033	.026	60.	97.	44.
1985	70	0.05	.025	.033	.026	72.	99.	52.
			Social expenditure/GNP					
1980	65	1.25	.008	.037	.133	147.	94.	40.
1985	65	1.23	.011	.043	.139	113.	101.	34.

for low- and high-income groups, and the relative gap also shrinks between these two income groups.

Conclusion

Table 12-11 summarizes the three measures of convergence used for the 16 social indicators and compares them with similar measures for GDP level and growth. In the past three decades, absolute and relative differences in GDP per capita across low-, middle-, and high-income countries increased or stayed the same, and the developing countries' range of GDP per capita growth rates widened by all measures. All four social indicators—life expectancy, caloric intake, primary enrollment ratios, and urbanization—showed evidence of convergence or no change. The first three of these are fairly direct measures of human welfare. Two social indicators—labor force participation rates and defense expenditures as a proportion of GNP—show evidence of divergence for every measure. The remaining ten social indicators show some evidence of convergence, with social expenditures as a percentage of GNP and number of cars per capita being the next most convergent of the remaining indicators.

The "convergence club" of high-income countries established in the productivity area clearly extends to social indicators. The convergence counts at the bottom of Table 12-11 show that the coefficient of variation declines more frequently for the high-income groups than for the other two income groups, although its extent of convergence is followed closely by that for the low-income group. The middle-income group is, however, more likely to close the gap—absolute or relative—with high-income countries than is the low-income group. The high- and low-income groups are becoming more homogeneous over time in terms of their social indicator levels, and the middle-income group is becoming more like the high-income group. Needless to say, this type of convergence—increased homogeneity but at low social indicator levels—is not a benign result for low-income developing countries.

Some of the convergence in social indicators may be related to the convergence of productivity levels. This linkage may hold for high-income countries, but it cannot explain the social indicator convergence for the low-income countries because their productivity levels are not converging. Although the social indicator levels are often

Table 12-11. Summary of Convergence Measures

Indicator	Bounded vs. GDP? (inelastic)	Coeff. of Var Falls for Group?			GapFalls? Absolute		GapFalls? Relative	
		L	M	H	L-H	M-H	L-H	M-H
Productivity								
GDP level	...	−	+	+	−	−	−	=
GDP growth	−	−	−	−	−	−	−	−
Social indicators								
Life expectancy	+	+	+	+	+	−	+	+
Birthrate	+	−	−	−	−	+	−	−
Age-depend. ratio	+	−	−	+	−	+	−	−
Female/male ratio	−	+	+	+	−	−	−	−
Caloric intake	+	−	+	+	=	+	+	+
PC hosp. beds	−	+	−	+	−	=	−	+
PC doctors	−	+	−	+	−	−	−	+
Primary enrollmt.	+	+	+	+	+	+	+	+
PC newspapers	−	+	−	−	−	−	+	+
Urbanization	+	+	+	+	+	+	+	+
Lab. force part.	−	−	−	−	−	−	−	−
PC energy	−	+	+	+	−	−	−	−
PC telephones	−	−	−	+	−	−	−	+
PC cars	−	+	+	+	−	−	−	+
Defense exp/GNP	−	−	−	−	−	−	−	−
Soc. exp/GNP	−	+	−	+	−	−	+	+
Social indicator convergence count	6	10	7	12	3	6	6	10

Key: + is yes; − is no or none; = is unchanged.

closely related to GDP levels (witness the regressions in Annex Table 12A-2), other factors are clearly at work here in addition to GDP levels. The transmission of knowledge, information, and new technology across national boundaries likely plays an important role in the convergence of many social indicators.

Finally, low-income developing countries clearly have ample room for improvement in terms of the convergent social indicators that reflect human welfare outcomes. Improvement in these indicators can be obtained by raising GDP levels in these countries and also by other types of interventions that directly enhance these measures. If the goal of economic development is to promote human welfare, a redoubled effort and a focus on low-income developing countries are needed.

Note

The findings, interpretations, and conclusions expressed in this chapter are entirely mine and should not be attributed in any manner to the World Bank, to its affiliated organizations, or to members of its board of directors or the countries they represent. I am indebted to Anupa

Bhaumik and Shane Rosenthal for statistical support, and I have benefited from the comments of my conference colleagues, especially Ed Wolff, on earlier drafts of this chapter.

References

Behrman, J. R., and A. B. Deolalikar. (1991). "The Poor and the Social Sectors During a Period of Macroeconomic Adjustment: Empirical Evidence for Jamaica." *World Bank Economic Review* 5:291–314.

Grossman, G. M., and E. Helpman. (1991). *Innovation and Growth in the Global Economy.* Cambridge, MA: MIT Press.

Ingram, Gregory K. (1990). "Economic Development: Its Record and Determinants." In *Proceedings of the 1989 World Management Congress.* New York: North American Management Council, pp. 47–55.

Kuznets, Simon. (1966). *Modern Economic*

Growth. New Haven, CT: Yale University Press.

Morawetz, David. (1977). *Twenty-five Years of Economic Development—1950 to 1975.* Washington, DC: World Bank.

Usher, Dan. (1980). *The Measurement of Economic Growth.* Oxford: Basil Blackwell.

World Bank. (1991a). *Social Indicators of Development 1990.* Baltimore: Johns Hopkins University Press.

————. (1991b). *World Development Report, 1991.* Oxford: Oxford University Press.

————. (1991c). *World Tables, 1991.* Baltimore: Johns Hopkins University Press.

Annex Table 12-1. GDP per Capita for Countries in the Sample (Summers–Heston data at 1985 international prices)

Economy	Type	PCGDP 1960	PCGDP 1970	PCGDP 1980	PCGDP 1985
China	L-EA	723	895	1263	1883
Indonesia	L-EA	—	803	1430	1704
Haiti	L-LA	921	833	1051	924
Guyana	L-LA	1630	1785	1939	1265
Nepal	L-SA	584	630	686	729
Sri Lanka	L-SA	1389	1438	1584	1962
India	L-SA	617	666	628	696
Pakistan	L-SA	820	1154	1141	1452
Burma	L-SA	341	461	564	659
Bangladesh	L-SA	621	642	671	700
Liberia	L-SS	967	1210	1178	943
Nigeria	L-SS	1133	1237	1555	1066
Burundi	L-SS	473	368	482	539
Mali	L-SS	541	416	511	486
Zaire	L-SS	379	473	349	358
Zambia	L-SS	1172	1311	900	762
Somalia	L-SS	891	685	850	843
Sierra Leone	L-SS	871	1352	1160	1017
Niger	L-SS	604	871	798	625
Sudan	L-SS	975	1035	1077	946
Central African Republic	L-SS	806	844	780	699
Mauritania	L-SS	930	1180	1135	926
Ghana	L-SS	1049	1130	995	852
Burkina Faso	L-SS	—	397	463	510
Kenya	L-SS	635	730	958	845
Tanzania	L-SS	272	379	507	480
Malawi	L-SS	423	536	614	575
Rwanda	L-SS	538	603	699	731

Annex Table 12-1. GDP per Capita for Countries in the Sample
(Summers–Heston data at 1985 international prices) *(continued)*

Economy	Type	PCGDP 1960	PCGDP 1970	PCGDP 1980	PCGDP 1985
Lesotho	L-SS	346	515	1271	1236
Ethiopia	L-SS	262	315	343	325
Benin	L-SS	1075	1090	1068	1103
Madagascar	L-SS	1013	1043	862	677
Gambia	L-SS	411	564	682	725
Togo	L-SS	411	672	871	665
Uganda	L-SS	371	402	230	430
Taiwan	M-EA	964	1833	3786	4524
Thailand	M-EA	985	1487	2129	2516
Papua New Guinea	M-EA	1136	2212	1844	1669
Malaysia	M-EA	1783	2441	4427	4751
Korea	M-EA	923	1722	3033	3858
Fiji	M-EA	2354	2815	4023	3517
Philippines	M-EA	1183	1488	2028	1749
Bolivia	M-LA	1142	1578	1835	1566
Honduras	M-LA	901	1122	1413	1240
Paraguay	M-LA	1200	1431	2550	2345
Chile	M-LA	3103	3915	4234	3763
Peru	M-LA	2130	2906	3187	2730
Colombia	M-LA	1874	2387	3332	3300
El Salvador	M-LA	1305	1672	1867	1766
Jamaica	M-LA	1829	2936	2468	2381
Brazil	M-LA	1404	2540	4499	3995
Dominican Republic	M-LA	1227	1623	2265	2101
Argentina	M-LA	3381	4366	4614	3982
Panama	M-LA	1533	2579	3442	3655
Guatemala	M-LA	1667	2034	2637	2200
Mexico	M-LA	2870	4061	5758	5332
Venezuela	M-LA	3899	4903	6938	5660
Costa Rica	M-LA	2160	3007	3982	3611
Uruguay	M-LA	4401	4548	5948	4521
Barbados	M-LA	3443	5761	7124	6152
Ecuador	M-LA	1461	1818	3158	2775
Nicaragua	M-LA	1756	2594	2258	1890
Trinidad and Tobago	M-LA	4754	6264	11212	7478
Yemen Arab Republic	M-ME	—	502	1297	1415
Jordan	M-ME	1328	1600	2548	2731
Cyprus	M-ME	2039	3996	5767	6905
Poland	M-ME	—	—	4238	3817
Hungary	M-ME	—	2988	4989	5170
Yugoslavia	M-ME	1690	2932	4607	4485
Egypt	M-ME	557	795	1522	1932
Algeria	M-ME	1676	1793	3015	3209
Greece	M-ME	1889	3798	5478	5712
Portugal	M-ME	1618	2919	4500	4535
Tunisia	M-ME	1394	1773	2963	3104
Malta	M-ME	1516	2628	4979	5766
Morocco	M-ME	854	1407	1967	2013
Syria	M-ME	1787	2418	5208	5016
Turkey	M-ME	1669	2293	3003	3204
Gabon	M-SS	1373	2695	3883	4210

Economy	Type	PCGDP 1960	PCGDP 1970	PCGDP 1980	PCGDP 1985
Cameroon	M-SS	736	1023	1515	1792
Mauritius	M-SS	2113	2129	3469	3756
South Africa	M-SS	2984	4233	4619	4407
Congo	M-SS	1092	1570	1948	2647
Senegal	M-SS	1136	1184	1202	1156
Seychelles	M-SS	—	—	3646	3597
Botswana	M-SS	474	863	1881	2555
Ivory Coast	M-SS	1021	1447	1806	1447
Zimbabwe	M-SS	937	1006	1403	1434
Netherlands	HI	5587	8505	10632	10937
Finland	HI	4718	7259	9970	11225
New Zealand	HI	7222	8581	9189	10138
Iceland	HI	5352	6991	11833	11900
Canada	HI	7758	10668	13768	15013
France	HI	5344	8536	11148	11376
United States	HI	9983	12923	15310	16779
Belgium	HI	5207	7859	10499	10458
Australia	HI	7204	9978	11715	12550
Sweden	HI	6483	9279	10910	12382
Switzerland	HI	9313	12688	14143	14390
Italy	HI	4375	6937	9986	10584
Germany (West)	HI	6038	8664	10993	11646
Ireland	HI	3214	4865	6183	6008
Spain	HI	2701	5208	6514	6433
Austria	HI	4476	6781	9616	10291
Luxembourg	HI	6970	8966	11265	12382
Denmark	HI	5900	8556	10322	11980
United Kingdom	HI	6370	8006	9680	10679
Norway	HI	5443	7761	11956	13495
Japan	HI	2701	6688	9615	10781

Annex Table 12-2. Regression of Log Social Indicators
Versus Log GDP per Capita

Year	No. of Countries	Elasticity	T-ratio of Elas.	Intercept	R sqr
		Life expectancy			
1960	103	0.21	13.31	2.40	0.64
1970	107	0.18	16.20	2.63	0.71
1980	108	0.16	18.62	2.82	0.77
1985	108	0.15	19.53	2.93	0.78
		Mortality rate			
1987	92	−1.01	−20.58	11.86	0.82
1988	85	−0.98	−25.89	11.67	0.89
		Birthrate per thousand			
1970	106	−0.38	−15.24	6.36	0.69
1980	107	−0.41	−15.95	6.62	0.71
1985	107	−0.44	−17.32	6.76	0.74

Annex Table 12-2. Regression of Log Social Indicators
Versus Log GDP per Capita *(continued)*

Year	No. of Countries	Elasticity	T-ratio of Elas.	Intercept	R sqr
		Age-dependency ratio			
1960	90	−0.14	−7.14	0.80	0.37
1970	100	−0.16	−8.53	0.96	0.43
1980	101	−0.19	−12.10	1.19	0.60
1985	108	−0.21	−14.25	1.37	0.66
		Female/male ratio			
1960	102	−0.001	−0.10	0.02	0.000
1970	105	0.002	0.46	0.00	0.002
1980	106	0.006	1.45	−0.03	0.020
1985	106	0.007	1.94	−0.04	0.035
		Number of hospitals per capita			
1960	95	0.93	11.93	−12.81	0.60
1970	99	0.92	13.64	−12.94	0.66
1980	49	0.91	8.74	−13.19	0.62
		Daily calorie intake			
1961	98	0.18	12.51	6.42	0.62
1970	101	0.16	13.63	6.59	0.65
1980	102	0.16	15.11	6.63	0.70
1985	102	0.16	14.86	6.64	0.69
		Number of doctors per capita			
1960	97	1.42	15.09	−18.95	0.71
1970	102	1.35	19.03	−18.64	0.78
1980	49	1.27	12.25	−17.98	0.76
		Primary school enrollment ratio			
1960	97	0.50	7.83	0.49	0.39
1970	95	0.39	7.95	1.28	0.40
1980	101	0.22	7.07	2.71	0.34
		Newspaper circulation per capita			
1960	72	1.96	12.46	−18.11	0.69
1970	66	1.74	14.53	−16.70	0.77
1979	80	1.51	14.68	−15.17	0.75
1985	84	1.61	15.26	−16.05	0.72
		Percentage of urban population			
1960	101	0.84	13.06	−2.98	0.63
1970	106	0.70	15.51	−1.88	0.70
1980	108	0.56	15.38	−0.79	0.69
1985	108	0.50	13.74	−0.20	0.64
		Labor force participation rate			
1960	101	−0.06	−2.61	4.14	0.06
1970	104	−0.04	−1.73	3.95	0.03
1980	105	−0.00	−0.06	3.69	0.00
1985	105	0.02	1.27	3.49	0.02

Year	No. of Countries	Elasticity	T-ratio of Elas.	Intercept	R sqr
		Energy consumption per capita			
1961	95	1.74	16.23	−7.54	0.74
1970	100	1.68	22.59	−6.98	0.84
1980	103	1.54	26.85	−5.93	0.88
1985	103	1.54	29.92	−5.94	0.90
		Number of telephones per capita			
1975	83	1.82	28.96	−17.78	0.92
1980	76	1.77	26.09	−17.34	0.90
1985	61	1.74	20.79	−16.79	0.88
		Number of cars per capita			
1960	96	1.69	15.23	−17.32	0.71
1970	102	1.70	24.24	−17.14	0.85
1980	91	1.74	23.71	−17.47	0.86
1985	58	1.90	19.41	−18.76	0.87
		Defense expenditures/GNP			
1975	67	0.02	0.14	−4.07	0.00
1980	66	0.00	0.03	−3.87	0.00
1985	70	0.05	0.54	−4.22	0.00
		Social expenditures/GNP			
1980	65	1.25	9.75	−13.91	0.60
1985	65	1.23	4.59	−13.13	0.25

Index